JOHN FISHER was born in 1945 and educated at King Edward VI School, Southampton and Magdalen College, Oxford. His long and distinguished career as a television producer and executive working in light entertainment for both the BBC and Thames Television has embraced shows as diverse as *Parkinson*, *The Bob Monkhouse Show*, *The Ken Dodd Show*, *Wogan*, *Joan Rivers: Can't We Talk?*, *The Best of Magic*, *This Is Your Life*, *Des O'Connor Tonight*, *The Paul Daniels Magic Show*, with which he won the Golden Rose of Montreux, and specials with names ranging from Spike Milligan, Max Wall and Bruce Forsyth to Paul Merton, David Copperfield and Tommy Cooper. His most recent work has included the critically acclaimed series *Heroes of Comedy* for Channel 4 and its sister show *Heroes of Magic*.

An authority on the history of popular entertainment, he includes amongst his published works *Funny Way To Be A Hero*, regarded as the seminal work on British variety comedians. *Jus' Like That!* – his celebration for the stage of the life of Tommy Cooper – has enjoyed recent success at London's Garrick Theatre and on tour throughout the United Kingdom.

He shares with Tommy Cooper the distinction of being a Gold Star Member of The Inner Magic Circle. A past recipient of The Magic Circle's 'Magician of the Year' award, he was also the first person to receive the Houdini Award for services to international magic on American television's prestigious 'World Magic Awards', and is one of only a handful of people to win The Magic Circle's Devant Award for his contribution to Magic.

JOHN FISHER

Tommy Cooper
Always Leave Them Laughing

for Bob
   a dear friend
and fellow enthusiast
for magic's heritage.
      All gen,
            John
         (fisher)

HARPER Magic live,
            2007

For Gwen,

For Vicky,

And for Henry & Doris Lewis,
who also had a daughter named Victoria.

HARPER

An imprint of HarperCollins*Publishers*
77–85 Fulham Palace Road,
Hammersmith, London W6 8JB

www.harpercollins.co.uk

First published by HarperCollins*Publishers* 2006
This paperback edition published 2007

4

A catalogue record for this book is
available from the British Library

ISBN-13 978-0-00-721511-9
ISBN-10 0-00-721511-8

Set in Sabon

Printed and bound in Great Britain by
Clays Ltd, St Ives plc

Contents

List of Illustrations

16. A sensation on the Ed Sullivan Show, New York, 1967. (Private Collection)
17. 'When autumn leaves start to fall . . .' (Fremantle Media)
18. 'And ven zey are caught everyone vill be shot . . .' (Fremantle Media)
19. Funny bones: with Anita Harris, promoting Tommy's Palladium show, 1971. (Private Collection)
20. A rare private moment backstage. (Hulton Getty)

Section Two

1. A modern Mad Hatter. (Fremantle Media)
2. The caricature by Bill Hall. (© Bill Hall)
3. 'Where's Jerry Lewis when I need him?': Dean Martin at the Variety Club Lunch held in his honour, with Tommy and Morecambe & Wise. (Mirrorpix)
4. Master of his terrain: playing the clubs in the Seventies. (John Curtis/Rex Features)
5. With Mary Kay during the latter years. (Private Collection)
6. 'Look into my eyes': the New London Theatre television series, 1978. (Fremantle Media)
7. A modern Punch and Judy: 'That's the way to do it!' (Fremantle Media)
8. 'On a clear day . . .' (Fremantle Media)
9. 'Look at the buffalo and speak into the tennis racquet': with his son, Thomas Henty. (Fremantle Media)
10. 'You've done some terrible, terrible things in your life!': with Frank Thornton. (Fremantle Media)
11. T. C. – Totally Convulsed. (Fremantle Media)
12. With staunch straight man, Allan Cuthbertson. (Fremantle Media)
13. 'And do have a piece of my homemade cake': with Betty Cooper and Robert Dorning. (Fremantle Media)
14. Tommy as the public seldom saw him: at rehearsals during the late Seventies. (Fremantle Media)
15. Our hero sleepwalks for his hero, Arthur Askey. (Fremantle Media)
16. With Eric Sykes, special champion and dear friend. (Fremantle Media)

List of Illustrations

Acknowledgements

This book could not have been written without the ongoing support and friendship of Gwen Cooper and her daughter, Vicky. Their lives, and those of their son and brother, Thomas, are entwined with this project. In the years after Tommy's death, their decency, modesty and complete lack of side stood proud as a major part of his legacy. The part played by Miff and Beatrice Ferrie in these pages is also recognized with affection. A large part of this story is theirs, at least fifteen per cent! Mary Kay's contribution to the life of my subject is also acknowledged in the spirit of the happy memories I retain of working with them both.

I also wish to thank all the other people who have enhanced my knowledge and illuminated my understanding of Tommy Cooper, as well as those who have helped the progress of this book in so many different ways. The roll call – extending back as it does over many years – embraces:

Russ Abbot, Ian Adair, Robert Agar-Hutton, Alan Alan, Ray Alan, Val Andrews, John Archer, John Arnatt, Brad Ashton, Tom Atkinson, Alan Ayckbourn, Larry Barnes, Kenneth Baily, Michael Bailey, Roy Baker, David Ball, Carl

Acknowledgements

Ballantine, 'Wizard' Edward Beal, Laurie Bellew, Michael
Bentine, David Berglas, Bobby Bernard, Michael Black, Peter
Black, Sonia Blandford, Arturo Brachetti, Richard Briers,
George Brightwell, Ken Brooke, Peter Brough, Max Bygraves,
Simon Callow, Roy Castle, Paul Cave, Garry Chambers, Jack
Chambers, Levent Cimkentli, Anthony Clare, Eve Colling,
Alistair Cooke, Brian Cooke, Zena Cooper, Alan Coren, Sir
Bill Cotton, David Croft, Barry Cryer, Paul Daniels, Jim
Davidson, John Howard Davies, Dabber Davis, Eddie Dawes,
Les Dennis, John Derris, Bernard Diggins, Ken Dodd, Richard
Drewett, David Drummond, Geoffrey Durham, Kenneth
Earle, David Elstein, Lee Evans, Gabe Fajuri, Norma Farnes,
Janet Farrow, Jimmy Farrow, Richard Fawkes, Colin Fay,
Norbert Ferré, Ben Fisher, Jerome Flynn, Bruce Forsyth,
Martin Freeman, Johnnie Gale, Patrick Garland, Carl Giles,
William Gillette, Billy Glason, Michael Grade, Barry Gran-
tham, Gilbert Harding, Rolf Harris, Yvonne Harris, Sir Rex
Harrison, Bob Hayden, Trish Hayes, David Hemingway,
Dickie Henderson, Lenny Henry, David Hibberd, Benny Hill,
Dick Hills, Edwin Hooper, Sir Anthony Hopkins, Roy Hudd,
Peter Hudson, Derek Humby, Clive James, Jimmy Jewel, Betty
Jones, Freddie Jones, Philip Jones, Tudor Jones, Todd Karr,
Richard Kaufman, Alan Kennauth, Joe Kerr, Dennis Kirkland,
Bobby Knoxall, John Lahr, Anthony Lane, Peter Lane, Mark
Leddy, Michael Legg, Derek Lever, Henry Lewis, Mark
Lewisohn, Bob Loomis, Frankie Lyons, Garry Lyons, Alasdair
Macmillan, John Edgar Mann, Kathleen March, Alfred
Marks, David Marsden, Billy Marsh, Jay Marshall, Sandy
Marshall, Topper Martyn, John Maxwell, Royston Mayoh,
John McCabe, Billy McComb, Cecil McGivern, William
McIlhany, John Kennedy Melling, Geoff Miles, Spike
Milligan, Iris Mitchell, Bob Monkhouse, Ron Moody, Eric
Morecambe, Frank Muir, John Muir, Tom Mullica, Murray

Acknowledgements

liffe Neale, Peter Newcombe, Denis Norden, Peter North, Pat-
rick Page, John Palfreyman, Ann Parchot, Michael Parkinson,
Johnny Paul, Gordon Peters, Jean Pike, Michael Pointon,
Channing Pollock, Paul Potassy, Bob Potter, Lynda Lee Potter,
Pete Price, Peter Prichard, J. B. Priestley, Mark Raffles, Marian
Rashleigh, Betty Rawlins, Dennis Rawlins, Ted Ray, Brian
Reade, Graham Reed, Tim Reed, Peter Reeves, Charles
Reynolds, Brian Rogers, Patrick Ryecart, Derek Salberg, John
Salisse, Ian Saville, George Savva, Terry Seabrooke, Sir Harry
Secombe, Neil Shand, Ivor Shattock, Alan Shaxon, Aldo
Silvan, Neil Simon, Anthony Slide, Tom Sloan, Nancy Banks
Smith, Neil Somerville, Mrs. K. Spacagna, Johnny Speight,
Harry Stanley, Freddie Starr, Richard Stone, Harry Stoneham,
Roy Storer, Eric Sykes, Don Taffner, Jimmy Tarbuck, Brian
Tesler, Johnny Thompson (aka the Great Tomsoni), David
Thomson, James Thurber, Barry Took, Kenneth Tynan, Tim
Vine, Dick Vosburgh, Ronnie Waldman, Orson Welles, Bill
'Hoppy' Wilson, Michael Winner, Sir Norman Wisdom, Ernie
Wise, Chris Woodward, Jack Wright, Terry Wright, Mike
Yarwood, Denis Yetman and Cy Young.

Resources and institutions that proved of major help to
research were the Family Records Centre and the General
Register Office of Great Britain; the Hampshire Records
Office, Winchester; the BBC Written Archives Centre at
Caversham Park, Reading; the British Film Institute; the Magic
Circle Reference Library; Southampton City Centre Reference
Library; the West of England Studies Library, Exeter;
Caerphilly County Borough Library; Caerphilly Twyn Visitor
Centre; and the Tommy Cooper Appreciation Society. One
wishes the latter well in its attempt to erect a statue of our
hero overlooking the castle in the town where he was born.
Invaluable in helping to amass information were the staffs of

the *Southern Daily Echo*, the *Exeter Express & Echo*, and the *South Wales Echo*. While every effort has been made to trace the owners of copyright material produced herein, the publishers would like to apologise for any omissions and will be pleased to incorporate missing acknowledgements in any future editions, provided that notification is made to them in writing.

The latter stages of this project have been made easier by the careful diligence and support of my editor, Chris Smith, and assistant editor, Jane Bennett. Thanks too to Trevor Dolby for launching the project in the first place and the rest of the enthusiastic team at HarperCollins. I shall always be indebted to my agent, Charles Armitage of Noel Gay Management, for his patience, advice and comradeship at all stages, as well as to his colleague, Di Evans, for her contribution.

Most important of all is the debt I owe to my wife, Sue, and my daughters, Genevieve and Madeleine, for allowing me leave of absence from so much domestic and family routine as my love and fascination for my childhood hero crystallized into the form that you are reading now. It is only matched by what I owe my parents, James and Margaret Fisher, for indulging their starstruck young son in his passion for all things magical and comedic in his formative years.

PREFACE

'*I Didn't Let You Down, Did I?*'

Tommy Cooper has been a part of my comic consciousness for almost as long as I can recall. Back in the Fifties I remember waiting despondently with my mother for her to be served in a greengrocer's shop in the Southampton suburb of Shirley and being briefly distracted by a giant cardboard cut-out of the fez-capped zany producing a large citrus specimen of South African origin from the folds of his mysterious cloak. The caption said it all with the conciseness that characterized a Cooper one-liner: 'Cape Fruit! Grapefruit!' It might have been the other way around. It does not matter. Even without the trademark chortle that the man himself would have added in performance, my impatience gave way to laughter. I was scarcely out of short trousers at the time.

In later years I have often thought how appropriate it was to be familiarized with this great clown in a store for fruit and vegetables. For a child of the time his outsize noddle resembled the prototype of Mr Potato Head, the craze that encouraged kids to rummage in the vegetable bin and then to create an identity from the plastic accessories provided for his ears, eyes, and other facial features. A more academic allusion might align the whole Cooper appearance with the work of the sixteenth-century Italian artist, Giuseppe Arcimboldo, skilled at creating faces out of the constituent parts of the aforesaid bin. He would surely have applauded the appearance of Cooper that we all call to mind, one with not only a spud for a head, but runner beans for legs, bunches of bananas for hands, turnip nose, dark olive eyes, crinkly endive hair, even an upturned flowerpot for headwear. Today, when gardeners and chefs appear to command more air time and celebrity than clowns and gagsters, Tommy might have appreciated the irony.

It was not always so. There was a time when a mere two-channel television service lost no opportunity to put main-stream performing talent on screen. One opening was provided by the summer season shows that were an essential part of the British seaside holiday. Every Friday during high summer the BBC Outside Broadcast vans would decamp to the coast to provide the viewer with a grainy black and white sample of what they were missing at one resort or another. This was how I first came to see Cooper in performance, televised to the nation from the end of a pier in Great Yarmouth on a bill with the singer Eve Boswell and the now forgotten stand-up comic Derek Roy sometime in the late Fifties. The fact that I can pinpoint the first time I saw this remarkable comedian, whereas the personalized debuts of others have long since become indistinct, is significant. Whereas other comedians of my then limited experience made the act of comedy a challenge with the audience, he made it a game. The hilarious abandon as he zigzagged his way from one crazy prop to another, the sheer delight he managed to communicate through the veil of his own frustration and bewilderment were things to savour. Television had never been so entertaining and I could hardly wait to see him live on stage. Another summer, another resort, and nearby Bournemouth claimed the comedy wizard. I was not disappointed, my initial response enhanced a hundred times. Like all the true Variety greats, he was always at his most effective in the welcoming environment of a real theatre, even if he worked in an era when visibility on television was essential to fill seats in the first place.

The years moved on and in my late teens I found myself attending a magicians' convention in Eastbourne. It was the morning of the 'Dealers' Dem', the event at which those who devise and sell tricks to the rabbit in the hat brigade are given the opportunity to perform their new miracles for their prospective clientele. The event was already under way. I was sitting about six rows from the back. There was an empty seat to my left. Then I became aware of a minor disturbance caused by somebody clambering past the knees of those already seated to take up the empty position. It was the gentle giant of comedy magic. Nobody clambered to funnier effect than Cooper. All eyes around him were now averted from the stage. Finding his place, he briefly acknowledged myself and his neighbour on the other side, before settling down into his chair. What then happened was a scene of unintentional comic chaos caused by the fact that throughout this Tommy was holding a cup and saucer in one hand, a glass of something stronger in the other, juggling a convention programme and a newspaper under one arm, and smoking a cigar, all at the same time. At no point did he ask the help of either of us sitting alongside him. At no point was a drop of liquid spilt. He was not consciously putting on an act. It just happened that way.

This memory achieved piquancy a few years later when, playing the fiancé in a sketch on his television show, he sits on a sofa between his prospective in-laws and attempts to juggle cup of tea, glass of whisky, plate of cake, and cigar. His handling of the situation is one of applause-worthy brilliance, not least because it came so naturally to him. More importantly, in that Eastbourne auditorium, the atmosphere seemed to brighten the moment he appeared on the scene. To meet him in such a situation was to realize that his stage persona was indistinguishable from his offstage presence. To be in his company was a pick-me-up, a tonic, a carnival with no need for fairground music or fancy dress. The sense of fun was endemic in the man. If those struggling to ply their wares on that Eastbourne stage that morning had been able to package this quality, they would have become millionaires overnight.

It was a privilege to enjoy Tommy's company on many occasions provided by the social side of the magic scene in the years to come. At the time of Eastbourne, however, in the early Sixties, I had no idea that I would one day come to work with my hero, producing several of his last television appearances. One of those turned out to be his penultimate performance in the medium prior to his death on live television in 1984. Tommy was far from a well man. He speech was slightly slurred, his stance slightly stooped, but his comedic playfulness and unerring sense of audience control were undiminished. That night he slew them. As the credits rolled the crowd cheered him as never before. Within minutes I went to his dressing room to congratulate him. Tommy was standing there in his under vest and long johns, drenched in sweat and drained, a semi-deflated Michelin Man. I instinctively flung my arms around him in gratitude and exclaimed how well he had done. I can feel the clamminess to this day and often reflect on the ludicrous image of such an incongruous hug. He didn't say a word. There was a pause. He sat down, took a sip from a glass of brandy that he should not have been drinking, took a puff from a cigar that he should not have been smoking, and only then did he speak: 'I didn't let you down, did I?'

When he died the most visible of deaths on live television

on the stage of London's Her Majesty's Theatre on 15 April 1984, I had no idea that I had not worked with Tommy for the last time. By the end of the decade an executive role with Thames Television enabled me to promote the Cooper legend through several series of programmes that repackaged his best material. Along the way he became an inevitable subject of my Channel 4 series, *Heroes of Comedy*. Indirectly this led to the idea of a stage show based on his life and repertoire. *Jus' Like That!* brought Cooper back to the West End when it was staged at the Garrick Theatre in 2003. Throughout these activities I was supported by Tommy's widow, Gwen.

My visits to the Cooper household to discuss these projects were over laden with generosity, not to mention the bountiful supply of the strongest gins and tonics in Chiswick. I never came away without a personal memento of the man I was getting to know even better in death than in life: one day the police whistle travelled by Tommy for use at the end of his 'Hats' routine, another the prototype – found on holiday in a French antique shop – of the cone and ball connected by a string with which he brilliantly managed to knock himself into a semi-dazed condition at virtually every show he performed. There were his thumb tip – the secret flesh-toned magician's gimmick that makes many a miracle possible – and false noses attached to elastic and trick billiard cues, even a tea cup with one straight side, to all intents and purposes sliced in half – with its handle still attached – for those occasions when he'd joke in company that he wanted 'just half a cup' of tea. On one occasion this magnificent lady even went to the trouble of baking for me to take away one of her husband's favourite raspberry sponges, distinguished by its triple layering to maximize the jam content. In life as in performance Tommy had little appetite for half measures.

More relevant, however, to a project like this was the gift

of scripts and papers galore. An extended literary treatment of the man whom I am convinced will remain the pre-eminent single icon of late twentieth-century British comedy was always on the cards. This gave Gwen the impetus to consult Beatrice Ferrie, the widow of Tommy's long serving manager and agent, Miff, thus granting me access to the surviving documentation on her husband's career. Miff Ferrie had died ten years after his protégé in 1994. When Beatrice died in 2000, through Gwen's prompting and the kindness of her estate, this material came into my possession. Miff had been the most punctilious of men, keeping not only records, contracts and correspondence relating to Tommy's career from the moment the two men met in 1947, but also date books and journals that recorded the bulk of the telephone calls made to his office from the early Fifties. The resultant archive is beyond the imagining of any biographer, often providing what amounts to a 'fly on the wall' look at aspects of both the personal and professional life of one's subject.

Much of the material plays like a trivia buff's dream. At random, the date of 16 February 1968 reveals a routine round of telephone enquiries: Shirley Bassey wanting Cooper jokes for a wedding speech, the *TV Times* needing to know the colour of Tommy's eyes, Anthony Newley's film company wanting to know whether Tommy can walk on stilts for a film cameo. On 22 September 1970 it befell Miff to extricate Tommy from jury service, pointing out to the authorities that the presence on any jury of the most naturally funny man in the land could prove to be an embarrassment for all concerned. Relations with the law had been put on a fairly solid grounding in January 1958 when two parking offences in Argyll Street were commuted to a couple of cautions traded in against a charity cabaret for Bow Street Police at the Savoy the following month!

A random selection of messages reported by his manager from Tommy himself gives a flavour of the man away from the public gaze, as well as providing justification for the exclamation mark as the symbol of mounting frustration:

'Does not know where rehearsal is!'

'Is on his way to Brighton. Which hotel is it? He has forgotten to take the letter!'

'What number in Garrick Street? It's No. 20 – in my letter. He hasn't opened my letter yet!'

'Is sun bathing. Could he make it next week? Okay! He then said he'd be here as agreed today.'

'Where is he working and when? Told him tomorrow at the Dorchester. All in his letter. He can't find it!!'

'Re cabaret at Southend tonight. Has he signed contract for it? YES!!!'

'Band call? Band gone!!'

'Re contract – where does he sign? I did not pencil it!!! Told him where it says ARTIST.'

'I said I'd told him yesterday the show was off through strike action! He went along today and found no one there!!!'

This could be the material for a comedy sketch. Other parts of the material, however, show Cooper in a more rounded, less favourable way than any previous appraisal of him. It was never the intention of my approach to take a sensationalistic path. But, 'Use what you like,' had been Gwen's pragmatic response to what I found. It is the stuff of fact and not conjecture and some of what it reveals will upset some. The opportunity to take full advantage of unique material has influenced parts of the book immeasurably since I first contemplated an appraisal of his performing skills bolstered by biographical detail and an exploration into the roots of his magic and comedy. However, the writer's intrinsic need for truth, backed by Gwen's reaction, has hopefully led to a fuller picture. Unlike several of his contemporaries, including Tony Hancock, Spike Milligan, and Peter Sellers, Tommy was not a complicated man – or not consciously so. But all were exceptional talents whose greatness came as part of a complete package alongside their faults and frailties. To those who complain of the approach, the question should be asked, 'Who are we to accept the one and to criticize the other?' With that lumpish physique it should come as no surprise that he possessed feet of clay. At a personal level I may be disappointed that at times he resorted to the behaviour he did, but never without forgiveness, never at any time without knowing that were the chance to occur again I would not hug that sweat-drenched body more affectionately than before. One's love and admiration for the man remain unconditional.

Throughout the archival documentation the voices of agents and producers, friends and journalists all have their moment on stage. But essentially it is a record of a professional *ménage à trois* inhabited by Tommy, Gwen and Miff. The other key person to figure in my own pages is his partner outside of marriage. She is almost entirely absent from Miff's records – such was his discretion – and her role in Tommy's life as stage manager, mistress, and handmaiden only fully came to light after his death. Within a short time, Mary Fieldhouse, professionally known in Tommy's television circles as Mary Kay (the name by which I have always known her), had sadly cashed in on her relationship with a quick tabloid memoir of their affair. Unnecessary hurt was caused to his widow, who lost no time in dismissing the association as little more than the distraction of a one night stand. However, anyone who worked with Cooper from the time of his meeting Mary in 1967 until the end of his life would have to testify to the genuineness of the feelings between them. In this context her memoir in book form assumed a passing dignity and provides an additional insight into the life of the man she loved.

My own volume never loses sight of its initial objective to chart the progress and impact of his immense comedy talent. Within these pages his fans will hopefully find happy reminders of their favourite one-liners and bits of business. I make no apology for chronicling the obvious. The box of hats, the bottle and the glass, the Nazi Kommandant and the British officer together in one costume may be played back in the minds of his devotees on an almost daily basis, and of course are available in various formats for viewing afresh today. However, it is still hard to come to terms with the fact that going on a generation and a half will not have seen him per- forming in full flow, whether live or on television. Working on the assumption that the printed page will have the last laugh over the mechanized media, I hope this volume succeeds in evoking the magic of an extraordinary entertainer whose skills and vitality might otherwise be lost to some distant future when the video tapes have all disintegrated, the DVDs become corroded. As we shall see his comedy is more timeless than that of any of his contemporaries. There is a new generation or two or three who deserve to discover his lunacy for their own sanity.

This is not to champion nostalgia for nostalgia's sake, the idealized memory of some blurred mythical past. Tommy had little truck for nostalgia anyhow. Whenever his cronies began to evoke the legend of some distant comic talent from the music halls, he would query if they remembered Fuzzy Knight.

'He was simply wonderful, he was,' asserted Cooper. 'What was that bit of business he did on the trapeze, the bit with the chimpanzee applauding with the banana?' Before long everyone would be volunteering their recollection of this absurd imaginary act. Not that Tommy didn't have his heroes, as we shall see. But truly great comedians like Max Miller, Bob Hope, and Tommy Cooper are like colours in the spectrum. Try to imagine a new one. It is impossible to do so. The modern entertainment media appear happier to opt for shallow celebrity in lieu of genuine talent and the life force of the great performer. For these reasons Tommy Cooper must never be toppled from his pedestal in the minds of all those who – as his contemporary, Alfred Marks once remarked – were already laughing at him as they queued to buy tickets at the box office. Sadly Gwen never got to see *Jus' Like That!* having died some six months before the play opened. Nor will she get to read this book. But I hope with genuine affection that I have not let her – or Tommy – down.

ONE

All in the Branding

Tommy Cooper off stage and on was his own best magic trick, a bumper fun package of tantalizing twists and turns, a cornucopia of paradox and surprise. He was the most loved of entertainers, but never, like so many in his profession, asked his audience openly for affection. He was the most original of funny men, with hardly an original gambit in his repertoire. He became the most imitated man on the planet, his audience appreciating his individuality all the more. He came to epitomize the world of bumbling ineptitude in both magic and comedy, but with precision and technique to die for. He exploited the comedy of failure and nervousness, but seemingly with utter confidence. He exuded good cheer on stage and off, but was happiest when absorbed in his own private world of sleight of hand and illusion. He was a child in the body of a giant, an amateur with the sparkle of the professional, a heavyweight with the light-footedness of Fred Astaire. His catchphrase could as easily have been 'riddle-me-ree': you never knew who was fooling whom as he plied his trade of the tricks, his penchant for practical jokes. The one certainty was his success at so doing. Paradoxically again, no one ever felt let down by the process.

1

The one aspect of the man that was above question was his physical identity. No British comedian since Charlie Chaplin has displayed a surer grasp of the need for distinctive personal branding on the road to achieving personal immortality, the process that helps to keep him in the forefront of our shared comic consciousness over twenty years after his death when other funny men and women of his era have begun to recede into oblivion. Remove the fez and smooth down the tufts of jet black hair that were trained to sprout like a pair of upturned inverted commas from beneath its brim and you might as well start packaging Coca-Cola in blue cans. On one occasion the great Eric Morecambe – incidentally Tommy's greatest fan – suggested to the author that he would be better off losing the headgear. He perceived it as a barrier between the performer and the audience. I did not have the temerity to suggest to Eric that he should replace his horn rims with contact lenses.

What he would have done in life had he not found his niche in show business is the great unanswerable question. Mary Kay concedes that he was fully aware of his physical idiosyncrasies, every detail of his gauche six feet three and a half inch, shoe-size-thirteen frame being put into the service of comedy. Of course add on the fez and the inches literally stack up. Through the years critics and fellow comics alike have been thrown into crazy competition in attempts to describe him. Clive James conjured up, 'A mutant begot by a heavyweight boxer in a car crash in Baghdad'; Barry Cryer with one-liner panache contributed 'like Mount Rushmore on legs'; Ron Moody added 'he has a profile like the coast of Scandinavia; his chin is like the north face of the Eiger; Easter Island is like a Cooper family reunion.' Alan Coren evoked fond cinematic memories of King Kong, remembering 'the time when it roamed free, this strange, shambling creation unconfined by any human limitation, magnificent in its anarchy, going through its weird,

2

hilarious routines. And none of its tricks worked, and all its half-heard mumbled patter meant nothing at all, and occasionally it would erupt in bizarre, private laughter.' Nancy Banks-Smith incorrigibly pronounced that 'he has the huge dignity and innocence of some large London statue with a pigeon sitting impudently on its head and a workman scrubbing him in impertinent places with a stiff bristled brush.' For me he has always epitomized in spirit as much as in form the abominable snowman as fathered by Santa Claus, or maybe vice versa, with a touch of Desperate Dan – without the stubble on his chin – thrown in for good measure. Whichever you opt for, they all say he was born funny, he looked funny, and he had funny bones. Moreover, perhaps he was the Wagner of comedy. Here is Dylan Thomas on the composer: 'Whatever I can say about him, he is a big man, an overpowering man, a man with a vast personality, a dominant, arrogant, gestureful man forever in passion and turmoil over the turbulent, passionate universe.' The only word that confirms he was not writing about his fellow Welsh wizard is 'arrogant'. Tommy was never that.

Once seen he would never be forgotten, but what you remember, of course, is the broad image of an ungainly hulk in a red hat. Analyse his performance and he is seen to represent a far more complex range of expression and body language than the immediate impact of his branding suggests. Facially he is as interesting as Keaton, the stone face comic of the silent screen who supposedly never smiled but in whose countenance one can read all of human emotion. The legendary guru of British comedy, Spike Milligan once described the Cooper visage to me as 'a call for help, wasn't it? "Please help me out of this. Please. Please."' His deep-set, almost mournful wide blue eyes were perfect for registering a resigned astonishment at life's ups and downs. In time the perplexed Cooper look, characterized by a glance upwards and through forty-five degrees and as such betraying his theatrical roots, would become as much a part of his comic persona as Jack Benny's stare. No one had a more beseeching glance of puzzlement as he scrutinized a prop that was new to him, observed a more manic look of desperation when a trick failed, a guiltier look of complicity – like that of a child with his hand stuck in the cookie jar – as he discovered you had caught him out while fumbling some secret manoeuvre, or a more radiant searchlight grin born out of a relentless optimism that the next task can't possibly prove as calamitous as the last. Eric Sykes, who directed Tommy on several occasions, once defined comedy as a way of looking at the world askew. He knew instinctively that no performer physically played cockeyed more effectively than Cooper: all great clowns, Eric included, might be said to have been born at forty-five degrees out of kilter to the world and that is the way they see it.

One would have expected his long gangling limbs to provide a three-ring-circus of incoordination, but the mad, flapping hands – 'See that hand there, look. Well this one's just the same!' – clasping his heart one moment, nervously flittering back to his props the next, and the outsize feet that when still seemed set in a permanent ten to two position were the lie to the general pattern. Interwoven throughout his whole performance was a surprising grace and delicacy of movement that might have been choreographed with sensitivity and skill. His movement at times was reminiscent of a matador swerving from one table of magical nonsense to the other as he eluded the advance of some invisible bull. At other times his lurching body seemed to defy gravity, like some inflatable figure being kept aloft as air rippled with amazing fluidity through his shoulders, arms, and fingers. He'd subscribe to this process as a regular device to follow the punch line of a joke. The theatre

4

critic, Gordon Craig once said of the actor, Henry Irving, 'Irving did not walk on the stage, he danced on it,' and the same might be said of Cooper as he lifted his feet and replaced them, as if threading his way through some imaginary maze with *haute école* finesse. As the American poet, E. E. Cummings commented, 'The expression of a clown is mostly in his knees.' Cooper was certainly as capable of doing double takes with his legs and feet as with those soulful eyes. A favourite pose as he went from one piece of nonsense to another involved standing in profile beside one of his tables, hand touching, head tilted back, his right leg kicked up at right angles at the knee, his face turned to the audience in a gleeful grin, as if to say it's all a game. Even tentative burlesque ballet movements were not beyond him. With arms outstretched, he would pirouette accordingly amid the magical chaos: 'I taught myself, I did. I was in Swan Lake. I was. I fell in.'

His maniacal, throaty laugh was the perfect counterpoint to the whole catalogue of gestures and the reckless abandon with which his props were cast aside, leaving the stage at the end of his performance a stagehand's nightmare. Shoulder-heaving in its intensity, the Cooper guffaw has come to be recognized as the grand sonic emblem of British comedy. Capable of warding off disapproval, excusing failure, registering delight, born – so he claimed – of nerves, it epitomized the Cooper stage persona, co-existing with that self-deprecating cough that presumably in this outrageous game of make-believe we weren't supposed to hear as he faced the reality of the gag misfired, the trick gone wrong. Laugh and cough were the interjections that saved a thousand words. Those that remained were thrown to the mercy of the most distinctive voice in comedy since that of W. C. Fields. Once described as an impressionistic blur that made Eddie Waring sound like Julie Andrews – for today, say, read Ray Winstone and Emma

Thompson – it was characterized by a slightly hoarse West Country burr bordering on a slur that at times could pass for insobriety, but only seldom was. It invested his jokes, his monologues, his shaggy dog stories with a kind of rough poetry. And then there was the matter of his catchphrase. 'Just like that!'

He always claimed this came about by accident. 'I may have done it and not thought anything of it at the time,' he once mused. Anyhow, it gathered momentum through repetition and became fodder for the generation of impressionists who hitched their imitative wagon to his star. It is a fairly innocuous expression, but today cannot be said among the British public without triggering instant amusement. Once he had given in to the concept, he was only too happy to embroider upon it with those expressive hands gesturing down in counterpoint at waist level: 'Not like that! Like that!' followed by some incomprehensible incantation of dubious foreign extraction that might have been spelled 'Zhhzhhzhhzhh', but probably wasn't. In retrospect it was the perfect verbal trademark for a comedy exponent of a demonstrative art like magic. Twenty years after his death it was voted, in one of those polls upon which unimaginative television executives seem to thrive, the second most popular catchphrase in British comedy history. Since the one that preceded it and those in close proximity soon after were all phrases of the moment, the likelihood is that his will endure, while the others will shrivel away. Reference to being the only gay in the village is hardly the stuff of everyday conversation.

The unavoidable cliché is that Cooper remains the most impersonated figure in recent British show business, the beckoning fez an instant token of fun and frivolity. The catchphrase and the hat became inseparable, as Tommy found with his wife Gwen when he returned on holiday to Egypt, where he had served in the war: 'We were in Cairo and we came across a guy selling fezzes in the market. I went up to try one on and the guy turned to me and said, "Just like that!" I said, "How do you know that? That's my catchphrase!" He said, "What's a catchphrase? I know nothing about any catchphrase. But I do know that every time an English person comes up here and tries on one of these fezzes, they turn to their friends and say 'Just like that!' And you're the first one not to say it." Marvellous, isn't it!'

The fez acted as a beacon of merriment the moment he stepped on stage. That first entrance was irresistible as he strode to the centre like a barrel of bonhomie come crashing towards the footlights. He was possessed of a crazy comic spirit from the end of the tassel to the tips of his toes. In this regard I have always considered that he was to magic and comedy what Louis Armstrong was to music, their performance modes extensions of their natural being, underpinned by an essential playfulness and a keenness to share this quality with their audience. In his early days his attack was irrepressible. Never had such a surge of idiocy been unleashed into an auditorium with such vigour. So contagious was the atmosphere he created that from that moment everything he did would be funny, however seemingly unfunny any one constituent part of his routine might have appeared in the cold light of a lesser performer's act. By the time his fame was established, it was only necessary for those expectant for his entry to hear the opening strains of his signature tune, the ever present 'Sheik of Araby', for the laughter bottled up inside them to gush forth in waves. For the next twenty, thirty, forty minutes he would grant us entry into his weird world, a crazy magical paradise where reality was turned on its head as he panicked his way to a closing ovation.

His stage tables always resembled some surreal Argos

catalogue made real. There were props for playing with, like the rose in the bottle with the secret thread attached: 'Rose, Rose, Arisen!'; props for dropping for the sole purpose of picking them up: 'See that. I'm not afraid of work!'; props for questioning: 'I don't know what that's for!'; props for his own comfort, as when he would blow up a balloon for no other purpose than to deflate it into his face: 'It's the heat that does it!'; props with which to impress, as when he threw an egg into the air only for it to shatter the plate upon which it was supposed to land intact; props he had presumably brought from home to sneak in some vestige of domestic routine, like the flower in the pot which wilts the moment he turns away from watering it, not once, not twice, but ad infinitum; and occasionally props for genuinely succeeding with, moments when the magic came right and his look of triumph was a wonder to behold. Ostensibly no object on stage served a more useful purpose than the rubbish bin slightly to the right of centre, but when he went to activate it an absurd jack-in-the box head from some distant Hammer horror movie emerged to send him into instant shock and the stage became more littered still. Working in tandem with the chaos was a stream of anarchy that was nothing if not liberating, ahead of its time in reflecting the message of modern stress therapists to rid us of the clutter of our own lives, the Christmas presents never used, the gadgets that never worked, even the jokes we wish we had never started to tell.

In mocking the conventions of magic and comedy he made fun of the performer that we might like to think exists in us all. James Thurber had a special insight into the formula. It is unlikely that the great American humorist ever saw Tommy Cooper. Even if his failing eyesight allowed him the privilege on a visit to London in the Fifties, he showed amazing prescience in the Thirties when he entitled a *New Yorker* article

'The Funniest Man You Ever Saw'. To read it today is to play an instant game in which Cooper has to be cast into the main part, not merely because he possibly *was* the funniest man you ever saw, but because here was a type, that of the compulsive gagster, that Thurber and Cooper clearly intuitively understood. 'He's funnier'n hell,' explains one character. 'He'd go out into the kitchen and come in with a biscuit and he'd say: "Look, I've either lost a biscuit box or found a cracker,"' says another. As for card tricks, there was no stopping him:

> 'And then he draws out the wrong card, or maybe he looks at your card first and then goes through the whole deck till he finds it and shows it to you or –'
> 'Sometimes he just lays the pack down and acts as if he'd never started any trick,' said Griswold.
> 'Does he do imitations?' I asked.
> 'Does he do *imitations*?' bellowed Potter. 'Wait'll I tell you –'

As the title character passes off the use of a pencil eraser as some magnificent vanishing trick, claims the invention of the hole in the peppermint wondering whether it will prove a commercial proposition, or emerges from the bathroom with a tap in his hand, 'I've either lost a bathtub or found a faucet!', one can imagine Cooper bringing the whole piece to life. But the telling line is yet to come:

> 'Laugh? I thought I'd pass away. Of course, you really ought to see him do it; the way he does it is a big part of it – solemn and all; he's always solemn, always acts solemn about it.'

For all the outward mayhem, Tommy never performed without solemnity. Seriousness and sincerity never failed to hallmark anything he did in the cause of laughter. And as for
imitations? Well, wait till I tell you! There was the one of the
swallow ('Gulp!'), the one of his milkman that no one seemed
to get, not to mention Robert Mitchum's father and Frank
Sinatra, where he donned a trilby for effect. After the laugh,
he'd drop the hat and the ground shook. It happened to be
made of cast iron. Even Louis Armstrong was conjured up
with a scrunched up handkerchief and a single toot on a child's
plastic trumpet. 'Right!' he would sheepishly admit to himself
as he faced up to the fact that it was not quite what the
audience expected.

He corresponded to the Lord of Misrule in ancient times,
licensed to make play of our expectations of life, right down
to the bare bones of language itself: 'Now before I begin my
act proper, I'd like to say this. *This*. Funny word that, isn't it?
That. Now that's funnier than this!' That he had far greater
effect than any distant forebear may be attributed to the fact
that the world in which he operated has become more complicated, more ambitious, more self-satisfied than it ever was
when the original Tom Fool would have been expected to
wear cap and bells in lieu of red felt and tassel. The mass
media of our own time have also helped to raise Cooper to
the status of an enduring national figure. Since his death his
caricature by Gerald Scarfe has been the subject of a postage
stamp in 1998; he has featured as the lead figure in the poster
campaign for the celebrations staged nationwide by the
National Film Theatre to mark the fiftieth anniversary of Independent Television in 2005; even the 2001 discovery in a
garden shed of the earliest known television footage of our
hero dating back to 1950 occasioned headlines that might
have been fitting, had the technology allowed, for a Christmas

10

Day broadcast by Queen Victoria. In the Nineties, National Power went as far as using the image of a pylon with fez, bow tie and outstretched metallic arms to tell the world that it was now generating more power from less fuel – 'Just like that!'

The catchphrase was quoted by Margaret Thatcher in one of her last party conference speeches, although it is said in such circles that her speech writer, the dramatist Ronald Millar was required to give her lessons in the correct intonation ahead of the delivery, the PM being possibly the one person in the land ignorant of the most famous three words in popular culture. Politicians of all parties still find themselves caricatured fez on head when disaster crosses their path, an error of judgement is made. It only seems yesterday that *The Times*, courtesy of cartoonist John Kent, ran an image of a be-fezzed Home Secretary waving a magic wand with the caption, 'It's Magic! "Tommy" Blunkett turns an asylum-seeker into a tax-payer.' It was almost unnecessary to add the catchphrase. It was a change in the summer of 2005 to discover by chance an article on of all things glass collecting in the investment pages of *The Business* headlined, 'Glass, bottle – Bottle, glass.' It is one thing to have one's catchphrase remembered way beyond the time it was meant to serve, quite another to have one's very speech patterns enter the subconsciousness of the nation.

The most bizarre manifestation of his fame came in 2000 when he was featured in the Body Zone at the ill-fated Millennium Dome built on the Meridian Line in Greenwich. Visitors were literally able to get inside the mind of Tommy Cooper, which found itself vying for attention with a giant model of an eyeball and an enormous, throbbing heart which beat faster whenever anyone let out a blood-curdling scream. Footsore tourists and day-trippers queued to stand behind massive teeth in sight of fez, microphone and glass of water as the distinctive voice was heard once again telling not only its familiar one-liners, but responding to the heckling of other so-called comic brains. The public complained that nothing was explained properly, which seems in keeping with the Cooper way of doing things. Tommy had become the most effective byword for incompetence and confusion since his own heroes, Laurel and Hardy. It was appropriate that he should prove to be the most popular aspect of an exhibition and building that in their own way quickly came to symbolize those qualities. All that is left is for Cooper to be granted the posthumous knighthood he deserves and for his iconic image to be discovered by some enterprising animation film company ready to transmute his sense of the ridiculous into further comic gold.

To the British public he has acquired a mythic status on a par with John Bull, Robin Hood, Mr Pickwick, even Mr Punch. It was with a degree of seriousness that in 1998 the *Daily Mirror* recommended foregoing the celebration of St George's Day, in favour of a Tommy Cooper day. The saint had been revealed as the patron saint of syphilis sufferers and as someone who never set foot in England. It proclaimed the idea of a national day in which we all wear fezzes in tribute to 'someone who sums up our unique attitude to ourselves and the world and someone who is eternally cool. Look no further than Tommy Cooper.' Classless, timeless, ludicrous, his qualifications speak for themselves. Maybe Lenny Henry should think about converting Red Nose Day into Red Fez Day.

He also tapped into that rich vein of surrealism that links the comedy of the British music hall tradition back to the century of Lear and Carroll. It was another era when the diminutive clown Little Tich danced in his elongated boots, absurdist sketch comedian Harry Tate sported a moustache that he could twirl like an aeroplane propeller, and pioneer patter comedian Dan Leno claimed to have tramped the streets so often that he had to resort to turning his legs up at the ends where the feet had been worn away. But Cooper would have been perfectly at home in the company of these early superstars. Indeed, I am convinced that had fate not destined Tommy for a role in twentieth-century show business, Lewis Carroll would have had to invent him, this manic Mad Hatter with a Cheshire cat grin and a profile as forbidding as the Queen of Hearts. That the guillotine trick was one of his favourite illusions is telling, his love of outrageous wordplay even more so. And if he had not been one of the royal family's favourite entertainers, one can imagine judgement being passed at the Palace: '"It's a pun" the King added in an angry tone, and everybody laughed. "Let the jury consider their verdict."' When donning one of those absurd half and half costumes, he might have been Tweedledum and Tweedledee in one body. His whole world was one of playing cards rising up in a rebellious swirl around him. The perpetual lateness of the White Rabbit provides its own sly grace note for those who knew him off stage.

Others have seen him in different contexts. With a meaningful twinkle in his eye, Spike Milligan once suggested to me that Cooper would have been his ideal choice for casting as Jesus Christ: 'You can almost see him now. Fishes, loaves. Loaves, fishes. Huh huh huh! And here's a little trick I'd like to show you now. As you can see there is nothing on my feet. I will now walk on this water over here. Not over there. Over here!' Barry Cryer has taken up the theme: 'I threw the money changers out of the temple the other day. Silly really, cos I wanted two fivers for a tenner. Huh huh!' Milligan also said that when God made Cooper he got it wrong and that if he were a self-made man he made a terrible job of it. They point to the same thing. Given that the world is not a perfect place, the idea that one day one might meet one's maker and discover he is wearing a red fez is a consoling one. Kenneth Tynan, while not subscribing to the Christian hypothesis or approving of the current state of the world, once nominated Ralph Richardson for the part of God, qualifying his choice, 'if we imagine him as a whimsical, enigmatic magician, capable of fearful blunders, sometimes inexplicably ferocious, at other times dazzling in his innocence and benignity.' In addition, the actor and the comedian shared that abstruse air that hints of knowledge deprived to lesser mortals, linked to an ability to make the trivial sound as if it were the secret of the Universe, as for instance in this typical Cooper pronouncement: 'They say that 20 per cent of driving accidents are caused by drunken drivers. That must mean that the other 80 per cent are caused by drivers that are stone cold sober. In other words, if all drivers got drunk, there would be far less accidents.'

Magic of course provided him with the perfect metaphor with which to comment upon the human condition. Whereas Chaplin and Keaton needed vast expanses of Hollywood real estate, not to mention in those early movie-making days lashings of sunshine to pursue their craft, Cooper's happiest arena was on a stage. Where else would a magician have plied his wares? His act was not a matter of merely standing at a microphone. Here was as well-defined a milieu for his personal comic vision as Galton and Simpson ever constructed for Tony Hancock or for Steptoe and Son. Of his British contemporaries only Frankie Howerd, Ken Dodd, and Max Wall succeeded in creating anything resembling a three-dimensional world out of their solo spoken monologues. Unintentionally, Tommy's dysfunctional approach to magic – neither totally burlesque nor obviously straight – became the most consistently successful public relations device conjuring has enjoyed in its deep and distant history. He is every one of us who has ever fumbled his or her way through a conjuring trick in a social situation.

His success becomes our success. He was clever enough to ensure that triumph occasionally sneaked up on him regardless.

Significantly for all his relevance to real life, he hardly ever made reference to topical issues, whether sport, celebrity, politics, or opinion of any kind. As a private individual cocooned in his private world of jokes and magic, he was not interested. Ken Dodd once said that to be a great comedian you need to know the price of cabbage. So sure is that vibrant performer's grasp of the lives of his public, one cannot disagree. But in Cooper's case it just didn't matter. He succeeded in attaining the widest possible audience appeal by keeping up the barricades around his own lunatic world. Only occasionally would a product reference intrude, as when he yo-yoed a can of hair cream on a length of elastic: 'Brylcreem bounce!' Or picked up a loaf of 'Nimble' sliced bread with a balloon attached: 'She flies like a bird through the sky – high – high!' As he let go, it plummeted to the floor. Funny at the time, they did not last in the act for long. Many stand-up comedians of his era would have found it difficult to work without a copy of that day's newspaper within reach. Cooper nevertheless stayed thoroughly genuine, an ordinary bloke to the last, never less than the people's comedian. And how we need him now – a funny man who knows that success in his role is not about getting awards, playing cold, cavernous, overlarge arenas, cropping up on pretentious panel shows, or signing off from the job in hand to write novels we possibly do not need.

Some might have dismissed his comedy as mad, but as Eric Sykes put it, 'He was about as big an idiot as Einstein and he got more laughs.' He was a one-off. He was not necessarily the funniest comedian, the greatest clown, the most entertaining magician of all time. He may have been all three; he may have been none of these. But he was without question Tommy

Cooper. Like Sinatra, Satchmo, Astaire, his very name will endure as a superlative all of its own. Let us now trace his beginnings.

TWO

Laughing Over Spilt Milk

He was born Thomas Frederick Cooper on 19 March 1921, although like Cole Porter and many another in the entertainment profession he cheated his death by a year when show business claimed him: 'As I popped into the world, blinking at the light and wondering what to do for an encore, someone grabbed me by the legs, held me upside down and whacked me. Already I could see life wasn't easy.' Indeed the reality was even more painful. Even Cooper's birth bore the stamp of adversity that came to characterize his stage act. In more serious moments he would ruminate on the actual conditions in which prematurely he came into this world: 'They tell me that when I was born the midwife gave me up for a weakling. Slung me to the bottom of the bed. Gave up on me. If my mother hadn't kept me alive on drops of brandy and condensed milk, I wouldn't be here now.' That midwife was Maud Shattock, although according to her son, Ivor, she was not officially recognized as such, rather the informal pillar of the community whose combined efficiency and kindliness brought upon her the responsibility of delivering babies, laying out the dead, and acting as a Mother Courage figure in the lives of those around her. The arrival of young Thomas would have been one chore among many on a typical day. Ivor says, 'My mother never went to bed before twelve and was up at four.' A few days before she had taken pity on Tommy's parents as they came searching for accommodation. His mother was seven months pregnant. She had just returned from the cinema when her waters broke. In later years he had his own version: 'I was a surprise to my parents. They found me on the doorstep. They expected a bottle of milk.'

His birthplace still stands at 19 Llwyn Onn Street, Caerphilly, a tiny terraced house, with two bedrooms upstairs and two living rooms downstairs, the white stucco of the upper storey in stark contrast to the tessellated red and slate brick of the lower level. His parents rented the front room on the lower floor. 'Llwyn Onn' translates as 'Ash Grove', thus hinting at the semi-rural environment that distinguishes it from the centre of the Welsh cheese capital dominated by the gloomy remains of its thirteenth-century castle. The wide street slopes down to fields that give way to railway sidings, the area retaining the prospect of childhood exploration and adventure that was taken from Tommy when only a few years after his birth his parents moved to Exeter. The tip a few yards away from the house where all around would dump the ashes and embers from their coal fires remains in use to this day, serving almost as a spiritual hearth for this most famous of sons.

Thomas Samuel Cooper, Tommy's father, was born on 13 October 1892. A Caerphilly man, he lost his first wife and child at childbirth before the First World War, making the near tragedy of Tommy's own birth even more poignant. The son of a coalminer, he too found himself drawn down the mines upon leaving school. Invalided out of the First World War with honourable discharge on 1 April 1917, he never went back to the Coegnant Colliery at Caerau that had sustained his early

18

adulthood. One version says that he was gassed at the Somme, another that he was gassed working in the hold of a ship unloading petrol cans. Whatever, he suffered the after-effects to the end of his days. He had been acquainted with Gertrude Catherine Wright before the hostilities, but any attraction between them had been forestalled by her earlier engagement to a clergyman. Born on 1 March 1893, she was the daughter of a farm bailiff from Stoke Canon, a few miles from Exeter. What brought Gertrude to Wales, or Thomas to Devon in the first place, before or after the war, is lost to history. Their wedding at the Register Office, Pontypridd on 16 October 1919 provided him with happy consolation at the end of a traumatic decade.

An early photograph of the couple suggests that Tommy inherited his looks from his mother. Here are the soulful eyes, the heavy nose, the straight line of mouth that he came to twist up and down from grin to frown with quicksilver flexibility. However, the consensus is that he derived his sense of fun from his father. Cooper always described his dad as 'a happy-go-lucky fellow. He loved talking to people. He'd talk to a complete stranger. Before you knew where you were he'd be sitting down talking to them. A very nice man.' In the Welsh tradition, he used to sing informally at concerts, but at heart he was a frustrated clown. Zena Cooper, Tommy's sister-in-law recalls: 'He never stopped laughing. A deep throaty laugh. Obviously a family trait! He was a natural and he was hilarious. On the beach you had these deckchairs and he'd put one up the wrong way and suddenly the people sunbathing would start to laugh and he'd make it worse. He loved the audience and would milk the crowd.' His father had been one of a family of seventeen. Having weathered the depression and the war, he was way ahead of his son in discovering the value of laughter as shield and safety valve in the front line of sanity.

His talent for comedy was also shared by his brother, Tommy's uncle, Jimmy Cooper. A photograph survives depicting a pudgy-faced individual in a stylized clown make-up crouching alongside a top-hatted straight man. He sports two outsize black circumflex accents in lieu of eyebrows, marks repeated in mirror image beneath his eyes. Unlike his brother, he obviously adopted a more than incidental approach to the business of laughter. He wears a cap one size too small and fondles an accordion, one of a string of talents that extended to magic as well as comedy. Tommy's cousin Betty Jones, daughter of Aunt Lizzie, his dad's sister, remembers his flair for tricks with eggs, a skill not to be dismissed at a time when they were scarce and precious. He achieved laughter and mystery together by supposedly swallowing a borrowed watch on a chain. There was nowhere else it could have gone. Bend down and you could hear it ticking in his tummy. Another cousin, Bernard Diggins recalls that he was originally employed down the mines, but became branded as a Communist and was subsequently banned for causing trouble in the pits. He would go the rounds of the legion halls and miners' clubs and have everywhere in an uproar as he enacted a sketch depicting a sentry on duty wanting to spend a penny. Both Betty and Bernard recall that this was considered too risqué for the children to watch and they would be shooed from the room. 'Ooh gosh! He'd go behind the box. He must go. The things he used to do!' exclaims Betty. 'But like Tommy, he was natural, see.'

Many people are surprised when they learn of Tommy's Welsh heritage, although town and country have in recent years become increasingly alert to the potential commercial value of the fact. Wales does not profess a great comic tradition. Contemporary with Cooper have been the redoubtably chirpy Stan Stennett (his billing 'Certified Insanely Funny' might have been coined for Tommy himself); the pantomime kingpin of the valleys, Wyn Calvin; and funniest of them all, Fifties radio star, Gladys Morgan with her ear-splitting laugh that could cause a leek to wilt at a distance of ten miles. Most recognizably Welsh, Harry Secombe came nearest to Tommy in fame and recognition but was puzzlingly overlooked in a recent poll of the top 100 Welsh heroes that rated Cooper at thirty-four and Aneurin Bevan in poll position. It must say something about laughter and the Welsh that Cooper is the only intentionally funny man to figure in a list that honours actors, writers, sportsmen, politicians and kings, but in which even more recent comedy recruits like Max Boyce, Rob Brydon and Paul Whitehouse fail to make the running. Even one of Tommy's personal heroes, Bob Hope was absent. Cooper would have been impressed that Hope was Welsh on his mother's side. Iris Townes hailed from Barry and used to sing in the local music halls before her marriage to Hope's father.

Tommy had no show business link on his mother's side. Gertrude was perceived as the strong-minded individual who held the family together, the business sense she had acquired from her own family paying dividends throughout the marriage. It is hard to make out what employment her husband took up after the war, although his profession is still given as 'collier' on their marriage certificate and as 'coalminer hewer' on Tommy's formal registration of birth. Essentially the family income would appear to embrace his service pension – a substantial one according to his daughter-in-law – and what she might accrue from her own training as a dressmaker and needlewoman, skills she kept into her eighties, progressing from door-to-door transactions in Caerphilly to, much later, her own shop in Southampton. From her he undoubtedly acquired his determination and sense of ambition. In contrast, Jack Wright, Tommy's cousin on his mother's side, also recalls a lady 'who would dither a lot. When she went into the kitchen, she always seemed to panic. "Oh dear! Oh dear!" A real ditherer.' In other words her presence was not completely absent from Tommy's act.

Tommy was three when the family moved to Exeter. His doctors had condemned the damp, dank polluted air of the coal mining community and Gertrude took her husband and son to find refuge among her own people. They settled in an even tinier house in a similar terrace in a much narrower street, at 3 Fords Road, at the back of Haven Banks in the district of St Thomas, a modest distance across canal and river from the city centre. Cottage industry became the order of the day as ice-cream was added to sewing to supplement the family finances. The summer months would see the minuscule kitchen turned into an unlikely hive of confection and refrigeration. Tommy would either help or hinder his parents as they sold the delicious Devon dairy product through the front sash window of the small abode. There were times subsequently when it must have all come back to him: 'I said "I'd like a cornet, please." She said, "Hundreds and thousands?" I said "No. One will do me very nicely".' In time they acquired a van and peddled the delicacy around the fairgrounds, at race meetings, and on forays into the small resort towns, like Dawlish Warren. The Coopers became quickly accepted by the fairground folk, who took a shine to this curly headed cherub. They thought nothing of leaving him in the caravan of friends who kept a tame chimpanzee and people in the family still smile over who or which might have been perceived as the brighter of the two. The consensus is that the chimp might well have ended up looking after Tommy, not the other way around. And so another joke of later years assumes a nostalgic dimension: 'The other week I had to share my dressing room with a monkey and the producer came in and said, "I'm sorry about this," and I said, "That's okay," and he said, "I wasn't talking to you."'

An early photograph of him astride his tricycle outside the house in Fords Road suggests that the clear Devon air had its desired recuperative effect. He had obviously taken the vigour of the valleys with him in his veins and we see a child destined soon to be a dead ringer for Richmal Crompton's 'Just William'. He would reminisce of the occasion around this time when his mother took him into an ironmonger's. Suddenly she noticed a crowd peering into the shop window. There seated on a toilet seat, part of the window display, was young Thomas. 'Come off that,' yelled his mum. 'I can't,' replied her son, 'I haven't finished yet!' After receiving his early education at the Comrie House Prep School a hop, skip, and a jump away in Willeys Avenue, he was sent to Mount Radford School at 56 St Leonard's Road, on the other side of the city. Established in 1827, it was advertised during Tommy's sojourn as a 'boarding and day school for boys, recognized and inspected by the Board of Education, Headmaster Theodore Ernest Vine, M.A., assisted by an efficient staff of resident and visiting masters.' Every day Tommy would cycle the couple of miles there and back. It is significant that the pupils were fee-paying.

When I asked the surviving members of his family how on earth his parents could have afforded this, cousin Betty did not demur: 'His mother was from moneyed folk, see. Very lady-like, Aunt Gertie. Posh-like and she worked very hard. She was good with money, born into a family used to handling it. My cousin and I used to do sewing too, but we never charged for it. Aunt Gertie said, "You must charge and then people will appreciate the work."' Zena Cooper saw no difficulty either: 'His father's pension was very good. Even after his death (from chronic bronchitis and emphysema in a Southampton nursing home in 1963), the army looked after his mother very well.' Further research reveals that it might not have been so expensive. Upon its foundation one of the objects of the school was stated as 'to reduce the tuition fees to as low a scale as would defray the expenses of the establishment and afford a fair remuneration to competent masters.' The school closed in 1967. The solid two-storey building with its imposing portico and white Georgian façade still stands in compact splendour in its leafy suburb today. It is now office accommodation.

Mother wasted no time in instilling a sense of thrift in her son, a trait that would have lasting, even paranoiac effects on his character in due course. Bernard Diggins recalls how when he was being despatched on an errand or sent to visit his Welsh grandparents by train, his mother insisted that any money on his person be distributed through his various pockets, so that if some went missing from one, he would still have some left in the others. Betty has even witnessed the money being sewn into his clothes. At the end of the decade, on 10 June 1930, David John would be born, a brother for Tommy. This time the birth certificate lists the father's profession as army pensioner. The ice-cream was still profitable, but there were other pressures on the family finances in addition to the new mouth to feed. His mother's financial skills were needed more than ever as his father's chronic gambling habits left them without a roof over their heads. According to his niece, Betty, the trait was always perceived by the family as the forgivable backlash to the tragedy of his first wife and child. Now he had literally gambled the house away.

Tommy's daughter, Vicky recalls her grandmother describing the unhappiest day of her life when with baby David in her arms, Tommy and her husband at her side, and a single suitcase holding their worldly possessions they had to walk away from the house in Fords Road. The Depression notwithstanding, the scene suggests some persecuted eastern European country rather than the balmy south coast of England in 1933. They relocated to the village of Langley, a scraggly rural backwater on the edge of the refinery town of Fawley on the east of the New Forest in Hampshire, with Southampton seven miles away on the indefatigable Hythe Ferry. One of the earliest memories of Tommy in those days comes from Kathleen March, his fellow pupil at Fawley Junior School. She recalls Cooper Senior working at the nearby RAF camp at Calshot, and cites this employment as the reason for their moving to the area, a fact that has not been verified. More vividly she remembers Tommy's mum as a rather strait-laced lady who would cycle the couple of miles of gravelly roads to meet Tommy from school with his younger brother perched in a child's seat on the bicycle. A mischievous child, he was constantly reprimanded by their teacher, Miss Nightingale, 'Stop pulling that girl's hair.'

Within a couple of years their resources had improved to the extent that they were able to build a modest bungalow of their own. Scarcely half a mile from their temporary home in Home Farm Lane, 'Devonia' was tucked away at the distant end of the little developed Lea Road. His father was now allocated a strict allowance of pocket money – 'a couple of shillings to bet on the horses' – and any scheme he might devise to raise extra cash was not discouraged. A vast acreage to the side of the abode that doesn't appear to have belonged to anybody in particular fortuitously provided him with the opportunity of raising turkeys and chickens. In time his son would joke about the family diet: 'We had chicken every day. We always looked forward to Christmas for the vegetables!' There is no doubt that poultry exerted a nostalgic fascination for Tommy to the end of his days: for one of his last television appearances he made an unforgettable entrance wearing chicken legs. But Zena Cooper recalls it wasn't an easy trade:

'Make a lot of noise and the turkeys all die.' Whatever the hazards, the poultry business did not last long. Besides, her mother-in-law hated the things.

An old school chum of Tommy's brother, Roy Storer, recalls helping their father with his work sheets when he was employed as a truck driver engaged in demolition work making way for the construction of the new Fawley oil refinery after the war. He remembers a man with thick, wavy, grey hair, a pronounced tan and a facial appearance like Sid James; in contrast, his wife always struck Roy as 'tall, dark, and mysterious'. One morning he told Storer quite excitedly that he had just received some photos of Tommy from Egypt. He proudly shared them with his young colleague, but said he couldn't understand why Tommy was wearing a silly hat with a tassel. For Roy, the funny hat with magical connotations was not necessarily out of keeping with the boy his family remembered. The defining moment of Tommy's childhood had come one Christmas in Exeter when at the age of seven or eight he was given a box of tricks by his Aunt Lucy, on his mother's side. Lucy Westcott lived not too far away on the Exeter to Sidmouth road near Aylesbeare, where she used to breed Samoyed dogs. The gift instantly captivated him and remains, alongside his West Country burr, the great legacy of his Devon years. When Commercial Television reached Wales and the West Country in January 1958 he paid his bright and breezy tribute to her when interviewed by radio comedy stalwart, Jack Train for the opening transmission, *The Stars Rise in the West*: 'Auntie, if you're watching, thank you very much for that magic set, but I still can't do the tricks.'

In the late Twenties the likelihood is that the gift came from one of the Ernest Sewell range of conjuring sets. Sewell was a private 'society' entertainer who came to have almost a monopoly in this specialized area of the toy trade. His credentials were proclaimed from the lids of these enticing cabinets: 'whose entertainments have been presented at Windsor Castle before members of the Royal Family.' If anyone had told Cooper then that within twenty-five years he would have been performing his own stylized form of hocus pocus at the same venue he may have run scared from conjuring for the rest of his life. Tucked away in the neat cardboard recesses of the interior would have been the playing card that mysteriously changed into a matchbox, the coin that disappeared when dropped into a glass of water under cover of a handkerchief, and the perennial nail through the finger 'mystery'. Here were intriguing devices for conjuring a borrowed coin into the centre of a ball of wool, for plucking a never-ending stream of cigarettes from the air, and for secretly divining the age of compliant audience members.

If Tommy had been lucky enough to secure the set at the top of the range he might well have encountered for the first time elementary versions of those classics of magic that became shorthand references to his own act in the years to come: the linking rings, the egg and bag, and the 'Passe Passe' bottle and glass. In time it became a mark of a successful commercial magician to endorse his own box of tricks. In Cooper's career there were no fewer than four attempts made by prominent toy companies to package similar compendiums under his name. He always claimed to be unhappy with the poor quality of the proposed contents – 'I didn't want children to be disappointed, you see' – but in at least two instances a failure to secure favourable business terms was the answer. The simple props in cardboard, metal and string that had appealed in his childhood had moved into the plastic age. But Tommy overlooked the fact that it was never about the quality of the materials, always about the dream offered by the colour, the glow, the expectation, when the lid was raised.

For the young Cooper that Christmas Day was also Annunciation Day. Tommy said, 'I took to magic straightaway. All my spending money went on new tricks and all the time I could spare went on practising them.' According to his school friend, Peter North, he eagerly awaited the next issue of boy's comics like *Rover* and *Wizard*, but not for the sharp-shooting, goal-scoring heroes of its inside pages. His attention was drawn immediately to the back page, which was dominated by an advertisement for Ellisdons, the High Holborn firm that proclaimed itself to be 'the largest mail order house in the world for jokes, magic and novelties'. In the manner of many a young conjuror before and since he would commandeer his mother's dressing table with its all-seeing mirror as a practice zone; squeeze every last magical function out of every potential scrap of spare tissue, ribbon, cardboard he could find; and, when elementary manipulation skills failed him, despair constantly of dropped balls, eggs, and playing cards until his bed was called into play as a safety net.

No one has more intimate memories of the young Tommy from his Langley days than Peter North. They reveal a complex child, on the one hand reclusive and lonely with few friends, himself the butt of people's jokes, who would rather run from than face up to a situation – 'A lot of people would shun him, not want anything to do with him.' – on the other obsessed with fun for himself and, so he hoped, for others with a liking for the centre of attention this provided. Eventually when Peter first saw him on television he couldn't believe that he appeared 'so forward. He'd always been the outsider. Never one of the gang, you see. Never went out with the lads. We could never fathom what he did with his spare time.' Such is the consuming power of a hobby as fascinating as magic. Who needed the fleapit up the road in Hythe with its three changes of film a week?

His solitude would have been intensified by having no brothers and sisters of a playable age and, according to Zena Cooper, a mother who found it difficult to express love to her children: 'In fact she was as hard as nails. She was not an outwardly loving woman and had shown him little affection as a child. There were no cuddles and grandpa was just a laugh. That's why Tommy had to have the applause. And that need extended throughout his life. He had to be loved and was always afraid that one day his audience wouldn't love him.' Vicky, his daughter recalls her grandmother as a very stern person with a brisk business manner who 'talked in a strange way – she had a kind of speech impediment as if she were talking with pursed lips like through a drinking straw.' This may have been due to her deafness. The specifics aside, it is a not unfamiliar background to the psychology of the enter- tainer, the difference being that in Tommy's case his solitar- iness provided the crucible in which his future métier would be fashioned so early. The nearest he ever came to voicing parental rejection was when he recalled performing his tricks on his parents: 'I'd do it and then I'd say, "Did you see how it was done?" And they used to say, "Yes." Then I used to cry.'

Aspects of his childhood would mirror themselves in the years of his greatest success. 'Loner' was the first word to come to Barry Cryer's mind in a discussion of his nature offstage: 'In real life he looked so singular and strange, he always seemed alone, even in the middle of the crowd.' But the need for an audience was always there. 'He could sit and sulk a bit if he sensed the attention that he felt justified to himself was not forthcoming. This usually meant he had a trick he wanted to show you while everyone else was deep in conversation about sport or politics or whatever. Then once he got his opportunity and had enchanted you with this piece of magic or convulsed you with that gag, all was right with the world.'

Many is the discussion of the economy or of Manchester United's chances in Europe that has ground to a halt because Tommy had a pack of cards in his pocket, the latest joke shop novelty up his sleeve: 'Look, this is funny!'

Especially engaging about Cooper the performer on stage was the child that stayed locked within him, coupled with the child he brought out in every one of us. It is a cliché among magicians to state that children are the hardest audience to fool. There is a complementary side to that view that is seldom ever voiced, namely that the child magician thinks his own audience is the easiest to deceive. Anyone who owned a magic set or placed an order with Ellisdons can recall the pride and wonder with which we set out to mystify our senior family members, buoyed along as we were by their willingness to applaud our elementary efforts. Common sense tells us now that there was little to perplex an adult mind among those most basic of tricks, but still they applauded and possibly, unlike Tommy's mum and dad, feigned amazement. And at one level that is what happened when audiences watched Cooper. Surely nobody was really fooled as the spoon on the end of the thread jiggled about in the jar or the unsophisticated little black bag was turned inside out to show the egg had vanished? But everyone entered the fantasy.

One of the most telling moments in his entire repertoire occurred when having failed to produce the promised bouquet from the empty vase on the plinth, he surreptitiously activated the secret switch on the top of the pedestal with an expression that dared the audience not to see a thing. It is as if he literally expected us to edit from our visual experience anything he did not wish us to see, corresponding to every occasion a child magician ever fleetingly turned his back to the audience to make the crucial move that, if spotted, will give the trick away. In the process to the very end of his days he thus summed up the wonder and optimism of every child who ever woke up to discover that box of tricks at the foot of his bed on Christmas morning.

In an interview with Ken Dodd, the psychiatrist Anthony Clare professed: 'There is about a lot of comedy a regression. It is a negative word, a return to childhood. In fact it's the endorsement of childhood values, of fun, of anarchy, of colour in a grey and dull world.' The comment pinpoints the spirit of play that characterizes Dodd's humour; it applies equally to Cooper. The world he came to create on stage can be seen as a metaphor for what his childhood became with its desperate frustration to get his magic right, and when he could not engage an audience by baffling them, at least to leave them laughing. Roy Storer's adopted sister, Joan, recalls how the kids would gather in a circle around Tommy in the school playground to witness an impromptu magic show. As his confidence increased he staged more formal displays for a halfpenny admission in the shed in the garden of 'Devonia'. Even then, according to Joan, he took the practice of his magic seriously. He certainly had picked up on his mother's philosophy that a service, a commodity became more important if you had to pay for it. More importantly he discovered that magic provided his ticket to a form of social acceptance: he admitted in later life that it was only when he started to do conjuring tricks that he found the other kids took any notice of him.

The days when parcels arrived from Holborn were red letter ones, although Peter North recalls, 'he'd always rush to perform the tricks before he had mastered them, like the one with the egg cup with a lid and the ball inside. People would laugh at him then. But he never seemed to mind. He just laughed it off.' Peter intimates that the teenage Tommy might not have been bright enough to appreciate what was really happening here. Like the scarecrow on the road to Oz, he was a non-starter academically: 'He used to sit next to me in class and copy my answers in maths. I had no idea he was looking over my shoulder. But in addition to the answers you had to show the stages that brought you to your conclusion. Tommy always had the bottom line correct, but merely inked in the intermediate figures at random. He just gave himself away! And, of course, whenever I was wrong, Tommy was wrong. The teacher only had to see the exercise books side by side.' The same teacher used to give his hair a disciplinary tweak a hundred times more than anybody else. Maybe unwittingly she set the style for the protruding tufts that later on added definition to the fez.

By way of compensation for his intellectual shortcomings he went out of his way to promote himself as the high panjandrum of practical jokes, all the while endorsing the old Will Rogers adage, 'Everything is funny, as long as it's happening to somebody else.' Some were jokes you could order through the mail, like the giant spring snakes that jumped out of jam jars (a mainstay of his act for years to come); the noisy metal plates that sounded like a window shattering whenever they were dropped (Tommy was never without these in his back trousers pocket); the sneezing powder that made everyone in the class sneeze but you (if you blew it in the right direction); and the mysterious imitation ink blot left on desk or window-sill for someone to report to teacher ('Who's upset the inkwell? It must be Cooper!'). Other gags needed more careful stage-managing. He would prevail upon Mrs Knight, the owner of the local sweetshop to give him any spare imitation chocolate bars used for window display purposes. To one of these he would attach a long length of invisible thread – magician's parlance for a fine, black filament scarcely visible to the naked eye – and place it in a prominent position in the school play-ground. Keeping hold of the other end he would hide behind the toilet building and patiently wait for the first person to discover the chocolate, at which point he would jerk the thread away to leave his school colleague as perplexed as Tantalus. By now Tommy would be running away, laughing his head off, just as the other kids would guffaw at him whenever he set off down the road on his bicycle, his big pelican feet spread out like flippers. He could never ride in a straight line, since his knees were constantly clashing against the handlebars.

His surreal sense of humour extended out of the school arena into the surrounding environs. Roy Storer can clearly recall Tommy riding his bike down nearby Hampton Lane holding a newspaper in both hands and appearing to read it at the same time. This appeared to be quite a feat given the rough surface of the road and the fact that not surprisingly the saddle was adjusted to its highest point. Roy recalls his disappointment when he learned that he managed the feat by virtue of two holes cut in the newspaper to give him an approximate view of where he was travelling. Roy's mother kept the grocery shop in the Lane, half a mile from where Tommy lived. She has known him to enter with a huge suitcase wearing a turban and long silk dressing gown, blacked up like a renegade from a minstrel show: 'He kept repeating "Veree cheep, veree cheep" until my mother had to insist, "I don't want anything today Tommy," and he would go on his way.'

So much of it came down to his size. When Spike Milligan made the comment that when God made Cooper he got it wrong, he was not far from the truth. Size and shape have long been accepted as key components in a comedian's armoury and Tommy was no exception, his individual body parts contributing to the living cartoon his outward appearance presented from an early age. In later life he would joke that he could palm an ostrich. The outsize hands made his misplaced dexterity all the funnier, the feet his walking – not to mention his cycling – all the more peculiar. He once admitted to his daughter, Vicky, an amazingly easy tendency to blush when he was a boy, recalling how when still at school his mother would take him into a shoe shop and ask for a size thirteen. All the shop girls would snigger at the thought of someone so young endowed with feet so enormous. That he was still in short trousers at the time didn't help matters. In later life he could still feel the heat suffusing his cheeks. When Vicky asked how he dealt with the situation, he replied that he developed a tendency to turn away from it either facially or, if possible, with his whole body, a form of psychological ducking and diving. To this day Vicky wonders whether this motor response survived in some degree in her father's constant motion on stage, first this way, then that, as he went from table to table surveying which prop to display next in his comedy of indecision.

In January 1935 Tommy moved from Fawley Junior to the new Hardley Secondary School two miles away. He completed his education only a couple of months later, leaving school at fourteen to take up an apprenticeship at the British Power Boat Company in nearby Hythe, the principal employer in the area, where for a short while his father undertook menial work in the saw mill. According to Peter North, who was close behind in entering the company, Tommy was among the ten per cent of the new intake whose parents subsidized the arrangement by paying a premium for their son to be taken on, a practice common among moneyed families who wanted their boys to have a trade: 'An awful lot of premium apprentices had double-barrelled names.' Presumably his mother's financial acumen and family resources secured for him the privilege. His mum and dad would certainly have perceived it as the best they could do for Tommy amid the limited work opportunities in the area. Not that the small town was anything but prosperous. In 1936, of the approximate working population of 1,800 in Hythe and Fawley combined, only sixty-four were unemployed. When compared with the average northern industrial town that had up to seventy per cent of its workforce idle at this time, the figure was impressive.

The agreement would have been for seven years and according to Derek Humby, who joined as an apprentice at the same time as Tommy, the starting pay was a staggering two and a half pence an hour in old money, or ten shillings for a forty-eight hour week, rising by two shillings per week for the term of the apprenticeship. Fully qualified men were earning half-a-crown or two shillings and sixpence as the hourly rate. The firm specialized in producing torpedo boats and similar vessels and its motto – 'Tradition, Enterprise, Craftsmanship' – was known for miles around. At about the time Tommy joined, a new scheme was brought in based on the so-called 'Three Principles' of good time-keeping, good discipline, and progress in craftsmanship. According to Bill 'Hoppy' Wilson, who set up the scheme, apprentices were awarded ten points on attaining each principle: 'For ten points they were given a voucher to purchase a tool for their trade free of charge. Higher points were given a voucher of greater value. These were granted every three months and by the end of the apprenticeship they had a complete tool box.' Initially three months at a time were spent in each department, the chromium plating division, the carpentry shed, the coppersmith's shop, the electrics area, and so on. There is no record that Tommy acquired even a single screwdriver!

Tommy and Derek saved up their pennies to enable them to take the ferry into Southampton every Saturday. They would invariably target Canal Walk – notoriously known as 'The Ditches' – in the rough part of the old town where 'Tommy White's' served the best faggots and peas around. They then made their way to Chiari's café and ice-cream parlour across the street. In addition Chiari was a landscape painter who incorporated a gallery into his establishment, as well as an amateur magician. He fascinated Tommy with the tricks he knew and taught him several, including the one where you wrap a marked matchstick inside a handkerchief, ask someone to break it through the cloth, and then produce it whole again. When they couldn't afford the price of a cup of tea, Tommy would be allowed to perform for the patrons in lieu of payment. On one occasion Chiari promised Cooper he would teach him the secret of the Indian Rope Trick. The tuition never materialized, but its promise ensured Tommy's constant return. On those Saturdays when Derek was unable to accompany him, he would head straight for Chiari's. The following Monday he would always confront his friend with a cheery, 'I've got a good one to show you today.'

On the work front Tommy's concentration did not hold up for long. Every new trick in his pocket was an excuse to disrupt work in the boatyard as his mates gathered around to be amused and amazed. The constant downing of tools intimated that he must even then have had a quality that held the attention of observers, even if his bosses were less than tolerant. Humby recalls the occasion he caused an official stoppage of work. He and Tommy were officially designated tea boys with responsibility for readying the tea for the workmen during their dinner breaks, a task for which they received an additional three old pence a week. One day the formidable canteen lady, Mrs Youren, was pouring the tea for them when Tommy took three of her cups and proceeded to show Derek his version of the centuries-old trick with the cups and the balls. She was not amused and threatened to stop pouring if he didn't stop messing around. It all sounds like a storm in one of her teacups, but Tommy persisted, the men veered from cheering to jeering, and it was hard to know who was on whose side. In the end the foreman had to be called to reprimand him before the normal day's work could proceed.

It was in that very canteen – little more than a wooden shack – where one of the most widely reported incidents of his career took place, marking as it did a shift of allegiance from performing serious magic to burlesque conjuring. It was Christmas and the management had insisted Cooper should rise to the occasion by performing in a more organized way. Tommy described the occurrence many times over the years. Stage fright had turned his body to jelly, his throat to sandpaper. His props and his table went flying in all directions. The egg that should have disappeared was left dangling on elastic from his sleeve. The big trick where the milk was supposed to stay suspended in its upturned bottle failed to work. As he remembered it, 'The stage was swimming with milk. I dropped my wand. I did everything wrong. But the audience loved it. The more I panicked and made a mess of everything, the more they laughed. I came off and cried, but five minutes later I could still hear the sound of the laughter in my ears and was thinking maybe there's a living to be made here. When I joined the forces I began to do some shows in the NAAFI and started to do tricks that all went wrong.'

Tommy never lost his passion for straight magic and once established as a star relished those moments when he could turn the tables on his audience by sneaking in an example of genuine skill and, to his apparent surprise, a miracle would result. We can never be sure how black and white things appeared to him that day back in the British Power Boat canteen, but the escapade can certainly be pinpointed as the occasion when he first entertained the idea of an act based on incompetence, even if at that stage he could have had little inkling of where he would get to perform it. From that point on his ineptitude was deliberate. His friend and fellow magician, Val Andrews, has commented, 'From the very start of his performing career Tommy worked extremely hard to ensure that everything he touched would break, fall over, refuse to work, or by arranged accident reveal its secret. Years of hard work and experience went into honing the perfect comic article.' At other times, as the mood of the interview took him, Tommy would shift the scene of the Hythe catastrophe to a service concert in Egypt or a postwar audition in a London nightclub. However, there can be little doubt that his comic agenda was set that Christmas lunchtime. Derek Humby had been there to witness the fiasco. Nor was he the first comedian to be switched on to his trade in this way. As Eric Sykes has observed: 'What people fail to realize is that you don't decide to be a comic; the audience decides that you *are* a comic.' Juggler W. C. Fields, fiddler Jack Benny, aspirant thespian Frankie Howerd, frustrated pianist Les Dawson all accidentally discovered a talent for laughter when their original talents failed to make the grade.

The variety theatres of Southampton provided Tommy with his first appreciation of magic as performed before a proper audience on a large stage. The great illusionists of the day passed through the stage doors of the Hippodrome, the Palace, and the Grand. Horace Goldin, Chris Charlton, The Great Carmo, and Murray the Escapologist were all major names who in the late Thirties visited the town that proudly billed itself as 'The Gateway to the Empire'. One particular performer attracted Tommy's attention, as he later confided to 'Wizard' Edward Beal, a kindly small-time local entertainer who found time to run a bookshop next door to the business Tommy's family ran in Southampton in the late Forties. In his book *Particular Pleasures*, which contains an appreciation of Cooper, J. B. Priestley queried, 'I wonder if he is old enough to have seen, even as a young boy, the wildly original act of the American, Frank Van Hoven.' Van Hoven, billed as 'The American Dippy Mad Magician' and one of the first of the true burlesque conjuring acts, died in 1929. While Tommy did not see the original, he did see the man who copied his act, namely Artemus. The week of 20 March 1939 saw the Southampton Palace Theatre featuring a bill headed by 'Artemus and his Gang – Juggling with Water, Eggs, and Ice.'

Van Hoven's other billing had been 'The Man Who Made Ice Famous', placing due emphasis on his main prop, namely a huge block of ice, the slippery peregrinations of which kept audiences in uproar as it slithered across the boards, causing freezing havoc among the three stooges enlisted to hold it and to keep it in a state of perpetual motion with the table and the goldfish bowl slopping full of water that they were supposed to hang on to at the same time. A borrowed handkerchief also came into it somewhere: only when the block of ice was in fragments, the bowl emptied of its contents, the table smashed to smithereens and the audience reduced to hysteria did Van Hoven get a chance to explain that he had been trying to pass it into the ice. Those who saw both considered Artemus mediocre in comparison with the original, but those who came to him fresh would rave enthusiastically. He did vary the routine, substituting the production of real eggs from a hat in lieu of the handkerchief business. The accidental omelette that materialized as eggs smashed on the wet and icy stage made the surface even more hilariously hazardous. In later years, as we shall discover, Tommy made great play of a burlesque magician sketch in which someone else played the wizard and he played a stooge from the audience. Eggs were the operative prop on this occasion. Tommy was too practical to have to bother about ice and goldfish bowls. But, as he reminisced to Ted Beal about the act, there was no doubt that Artemus had impressed him. Assuming he saw him in March 1939 and not before, the experience postdates the Hythe canteen episode, but must have further heightened his perception of the burlesque conjuror in entertainment terms. Ted also confided in Tommy his special philosophy: 'The trouble with so many magicians is that they are purveyors of puzzles without the humour'; but by the late Forties, Tommy had already come to that conclusion for himself.

Meanwhile he was getting nowhere fast at the Power Boat Company. He was totally unsuitable for the task – 'I can't even knock a nail in straight!' – but they couldn't give him the sack because the premium had been paid: 'The course I was on was one you had to pay for, so I got off with a warning and being sent home.' Afraid to tell his parents, he spent his time cycling to nearby towns and villages looking for odd jobs. It is hard to think that the situation could have continued for seven years, but world events intervened. As war clouds darkened and Chamberlain's umbrella looked insufficient protection against the storm, a combination of patriotism and self-esteem found Cooper volunteering for the services. There is no way the Company could stand in his way and besides his height made him a natural for the Guards. His mother had the shock of her life when one day he arrived on the doorstep of 'Devonia' in uniform. That the Company could in fact tolerate his antics no longer was bypassed in the elation of the moment. And as Peter North says, 'He wouldn't have lasted there during the war. You had to tow the line. The work was classified as a restricted occupation and there was no mucking about then.' In the circumstances, it is amazing that he did manage to accept the discipline of the army as he did.

When war was declared, Southampton became one of the major targets of the Blitz. His parents made frequent visits back to Devon and Caerphilly to stay out of harm's way with family and friends. When peace arrived they appear to have lost their appetite for the semi-rural community. They moved from 'Devonia' around the beginning of 1948, ploughing all their resources into a shop at 124 Shirley Road, a major thoroughfare out of the centre of Southampton to the North West in the Romsey direction. Today the premises accommodate 'Johnny's Fish and Chips' emporium. The nearby Rotrax café and cycle store are no more, while the tattoo parlour a few doors down has survived all trends. It has been said that Tommy set his parents up in the shop, but this is not the case, since they were up and running with at first a fresh fish business long before he achieved lasting success. The fish business did not prosper. Zena Cooper recalls how on a Saturday her father-in-law would sell the fish left over at the end of the week for next to nothing. In the end the neighbourhood got wise and bought nothing earlier in the week. Gertrude had to put her foot down and any fish not sold at full price by the end of Saturday she buried in their little postage stamp of a garden. Obviously a lady of amazing industry, she once again kept the family buoyant financially by harking back to her dressmaking skills. Within a short time she converted the shop into a haberdashery to act as a front for them, with alterations and repairs a profitable sideline.

In these final years of their lives the surviving memories of those who knew them give us further insight into the characters and eccentricities of his parents. Members of Gertrude's family recall that to deter shoplifters she used to tie all the stock together with some of her son's invisible thread, so that if someone sneaked something away when she wasn't looking, all the rest would come with it. Mrs Spacagna, who had a hairdressing business in the vicinity, remembers her as a very private person, but a brisk business woman, always distinctive on her own shopping round from the long black cloak she wore. I have a memory too. As a child brought up in

Southampton's Shirley district in the Fifties, no sooner had I heard that the mother of my television hero had a shop less than a mile from where I lived than nothing could hold me back from making the pilgrimage to seek her out for myself. I could not summon the courage to enter, but remember peering through the window past the displays of knitting needles, zip fasteners, ribbon, braid, and buttons galore to spy sitting behind the counter what could have been a smaller version of Tommy Cooper in drag. It all looked dusty and higgledy-piggledy. I could have been peering into a pantomime set. I was later told she was only too happy for people to go in to talk to her about her son, of whom she was rightly proud. Photographs of his career festooned the walls, and albums would be brought from the back room at the merest beckoning. I regret missing the opportunity.

Michael Legg, who worked nearby, was called into the shop one day and told by Mrs Cooper that 'Dad' wanted to speak to him. He was shown into the living quarters at the back and Mr Cooper asked if he would call in each day on his lunch break to take a betting slip down to the betting shop in nearby Park Road: 'I always remember he had wads of notes in his waistcoat, trousers and shirt, as he did not believe in banks.' Their nephew, Bernard Diggins remembers a narrow passage shut off from the road running down the side of the shop: 'He grew his own tobacco and had strung up a line on the wall on which he was hanging the large tobacco leaves to dry.' Thomas died on 2 December 1963, his death certificate listing his occupation as 'night watchman (retired)'. This reminded his daughter-in-law that he did spend a spell at the nearby Atherley cinema, and may even have been a projectionist there. It would help to explain the notes sprouting out of his pockets, while the tobacco leaves provided their own poignant footnote to his death, which, as we have seen, was due to bronchial troubles.

Tommy's mother survived her husband by over twenty years. By the early Seventies the dressmaking had become too much for her and she shifted the emphasis of her stock to costume jewellery, although to anyone looking inside it was still the same ramshackle repository it had always been. According to neighbour Marian Rashleigh, necklaces and brooches were now hung in the windows 'like net curtains, but I don't remember them ever being cleaned or changed for more modern pieces. I can't remember when the shop was vacated, but by then cobwebs adorned the necklaces.' In fact it was vacated twice. When Gertrude became seriously ill in her mid-eighties Zena began to clear the stock. Both Tommy and David had offered their mother a home, but she valued her independence and they found themselves putting it all back to give her something to do! As her niece, Betty says, 'She was still in the shop at 88 years. It was time she closed up. But she was an obstinate old woman.' She died of a heart attack in the Royal South Hants Hospital on 13 February 1984 two weeks before reaching her ninety-first birthday and just two months before her elder son.

According to his daughter, Tommy's relationship with his parents was fragile. His father complained that he never visited his Mum as much as he should, and when he *did* go there always seemed to be a blazing row because they'd argue about why he didn't go more often. Their worlds had not unnaturally drifted apart. They had no proper grasp of the erratic working hours and travelling that show business entailed. However, while the Shirley haberdashery was an unlikely environment in which to picture Tommy, another local resident, Sonia Blandford has an affectionate memory of him there:

One day I was sent after school to collect a present that had been ordered as a gift for my Auntie. I was surprised to see

'Closed' on the door. I knew I was expected and found the nerve to bang on the door. It was opened by Tommy himself. You can imagine how overwhelmed I felt. While his mum found the item Tommy entertained me by producing lengths of material from my sleeve and eggs from my ear! Although he was a TV favourite of mine, I was terrified of him. He was a giant of a man and his overwhelming personality was too much for a small child such as myself to feel able to cope with comfortably. I think he sensed this and chatted to me about the animals I kept as pets and what I was doing at school until his mum rescued us both from the discomfort of the other. My memories of them both are very fond. He was very kind and although not comfortable with a small girl to entertain who was clearly scared of him found something to talk about that would reassure.

Tommy may well have been embarrassed himself, but whatever decisions he had made about his professional approach to magic in the works canteen, it is encouraging to know that twenty years later he could still empathize with the sense of wonder that magic pure and simple could arouse in a child. Indeed, throughout his life he stayed a kid at heart.

THREE

'Let Me See Your Dots'

The idea of Trooper Cooper resplendent in the plume and pomp of The Royal Horse Guards astride a charger with sword held to attention is a sublime comic image. But in later years he was always keen to downplay the impression: 'I've done sentry duty in Whitehall many times. Khaki uniform though – nothing fancy.' His basic training at Pirbright was interrupted by the outbreak of war and Tommy found himself learning to ride a horse sooner than he expected. Riding army fashion – that is riding one horse, while leading two others – in Rotten Row at 6.30 in the morning became another established part of his early routine. With his fast gained reputation as 'The life and soul of the NAAFI', it is hard not to imagine him trotting down the Mall, boots burnished and spurs glinting, without his mind wandering to the latest gags and gimmicks to be shopped from the magic supply depots, the practical joke with which he could bring uproar to the barracks that evening.

Tommy's height made him a natural for the Blues. He joined as a private and took seven years to achieve the rank of sergeant, by which time the fighting was over. He always said that what he liked best about the early years was the boxing.

There were 100 guards in his unit and he stood out among them. He claimed never to have won any championship, contrary to reports that he did win a heavyweight title, sufficient to be offered a contract to turn professional at a later date. However, the sport did teach him how to look after himself, giving the lie to his later claim that he spent so much time on canvas that he was going to change his name to Rembrandt. His nose *was* broken, but not in the ring, rather when he slipped alongside an army swimming pool. In later years his son, Thomas, reminisced about his dad's prowess in this area: 'Everyone thought of him as a big softie who would not hurt a fly. In fact he was capable of laying you out with one punch and would not hesitate to do so if he thought someone had asked for it. He hated trouble, but I remember one time in a pub in Golders Green when three yobbos were giving the landlord a bad time. One broke a bottle over the counter and went to stick it in the landlord's face. And dad, who had been standing at the bar minding his own business, just turned round and flattened the yobbo with a right-hander on the chin. The other two looked on in amazement and scarpered.'

A less valuable legacy in civilian life was his proficiency on horseback, although he always retained a love for horses. Zena Cooper recalls that when Tommy returned from the war he would go riding with his brother, David, in the New Forest and show off by emulating feats better associated with the Cossack riders, passing under the belly of the mount and up again the other side while at a gallop, even riding backwards. Not that he would have won any regimental trophies in this area. He made a veritable party piece out of the detail of one catastrophe: 'I remember one Christmas, at a full-dress ceremonial parade, there were one hundred of us neatly lined up by the sides of our horses. Now, as a recruit I didn't know this, but when you get on a horse, when you put the girth around the horse, the horse blows himself out because he doesn't want to be tight. So you've got to wait. Well, I didn't know this, and he looks at you. He's a little bit suspicious, you know what I mean? Then all of a sudden you have to go quick and he goes "Ooh!" But I didn't know this, so as a recruit I just went like that with the girth and he went out with his stomach and I thought I was tight. So the order came, "Prepare to mount" and I put my foot in the stirrup and they said "Mount" and the saddle went underneath. Ninety-nine of us rose as one man and I'm in a heap on the ground.' The look of dismay on his big, baffled face as he gathered himself up from the floor would have been worth the price of admission.

His regimental misadventures could fill a book or certainly an episode of one of those forces comedies that, in the Fifties, Phil Silvers as Sergeant Bilko brought to a comic zenith worthy of Cooper himself. In the British theatre of service comedy it is easy to picture William Hartnell as the sadistic sergeant going the rounds to prod Cooper and his cohorts out of their slumbers for roll-call at four o'clock in the morning. As Tommy remembered it, ' "Good morning." "Good morning." "Good morning." And he had a bayonet in his hand!' Outside it was pitch black and the corporal used to emerge with a huge hurricane lamp. 'Good morning, men,' he'd shout. 'Good morning, lamp,' Cooper would answer back. It was a fair response. They were too blinded by it to see him. Michael Medwin or Harry Fowler would have been spot-on casting for the barrack room lawyer who led the protest when the sergeant insisted on a rifle inspection no less than ten minutes after they had come back from a route march and flopped exhausted onto their beds. His departure was the cue for said barrack room lawyer to lay down their rights: 'I'm not going to clean mine at all. The King's rules and regulations say we're entitled to half an hour's rest. It says so – under section twenty-nine, subsection six.' 'I listened to him, I did,' said Tommy, 'I believed him. Then the sergeant came in. He said, "Right, get your rifles ready."' Cooper stepped forward and stood up to him through clenched teeth, 'We're not cleaning them.' The sergeant was taken aback. 'We're not cleaning them, are we fellows? Are we fellows?' As his voice became more questioning, the realization dawned that the rest of the troop behind him were working away like the clappers. It is unlikely that any member of the British comedy acting establishment could have done justice to the crestfallen vulnerability of our hero at a moment like this.

One incident in Cooper's military career has practically assumed the status of an urban myth, although on separate occasions Tommy assured both Barry Cryer and myself that it did take place and that it happened to him. He was lucky not to be court-martialled. One morning in the early hours he was on sentry duty and dozed off standing up by the side of the sentry box. Within seconds the sergeant came round the corner with the orderly officer: 'And all of a sudden I open my eyes just a little bit and I can see them standing there. So I've got to think of something now or otherwise I'm going to end up inside. So I wait for a second and I'm standing there and I open my eyes fully and I say, "Amen!"' Assuming they noticed at all, it did the trick and nothing was said. Many years later the episode became the basis of a regular routine in his stage act, Tommy playing his dozy self and the fierce sergeant major in mimed counterpoint amid a flurry of 'not like that's' and 'like that's'. But there was no denying the potential seriousness of the situation: 'I fell asleep. I did. That's a crime, isn't it? You could go to the Tower for that.'

The comic capital he made out of the incident perhaps compensated for the downside of a life spent constantly standing to attention and stamping on parade. He put many of his later health problems – varicose veins, phlebitis, thrombosis in the leg, ulcers too – down to his guardsman's duties. In fact, he could have had treatment for the veins while he was in the services. He told his friend, Bobby Bernard of the occasion he went into the surgery to see the medical officer about the problem. Another soldier was standing there in his shorts. He turned to Tommy and said, 'Look at mine. They're getting better.' According to Tommy, 'His veins were worse than mine.' 'If that's better, I'm going,' shouted the cowardly conjuror.

In an article in the *Lancashire Evening Post* in May 1974, his fellow trooper Ben Fisher provided a vivid recollection of Cooper the serviceman. No sooner had Ben joined the Blues in 1943 than he found himself sharing a tent with Tommy. Come morning, it quickly became apparent that his colleague enjoyed special privileges: 'While all around echoed to the whacking of the duty Corporal of Horse's cane on tent walls, we were left in peace, for this, as I was soon to learn, was "Cooper's Tent" and as such apparently beyond the pale of military discipline.' As their friendship grew, Fisher discovered that Tommy had developed a disarming flair for avoiding the more onerous military duties. Indeed, he can never actually recall Tommy being 'on duty', but there was no question that the most familiar name in the camp was 'Cooper': 'It was usually shouted at the top of his voice by our Corporal Major. On hearing the call Tommy would emerge from some nook or cranny with the air of a man interrupted during some urgent assignment, and wanting nothing more than to get back to it.' Fisher stressed that he never emerged empty-handed. There was always a bucket, a brush or some utensil or other dangling from his hand as proof of his unstinted industry.

In off-duty hours he would give impromptu concerts in front of the tent, not only performing his crazy conjuring, but also comedy sketches: 'Our favourites were "The Death of Robin Hood" and one about the Home Guard.' In the latter, with possible echoes of his Uncle Jimmy, he improvised a one-man *Dad's Army*. A rifle and tin hat with the lining removed so that it fell around his ears were the only props he required to pantomime his way through a series of disastrous drill movements. For the Robin Hood scene he would make a dramatic entrance from the woods around the camp, pretending to be mortally wounded with an arrow clutched to his chest. Staggering to the front of his tent, he would summon Little John to help him find a suitable burial place. Tommy would then switch to the other character. It is hard now to imagine him playing Little John as camp as he then did, a prissy individual, 'fussy about keeping the camp tidy, making all sorts of excuses about why this or that spot wouldn't do'. After much pleading from the folk hero, the routine ended with Robin stumbling back to the trees in disgust, shouting the payoff line, 'All right . . . all right . . . but it's the last time I'll ask you to do anything for me!'

Within a short time Tommy was sent overseas and the war became a reality. His section of the Blues was deployed to the western desert to a camp near Suez as a reconnaissance unit working with armoured cars and small tanks: 'We used to go out first, see the enemy and then come back – cos we were cowards!' He did not take kindly to having to sleep in a hammock – back home the army beds had been adjustable – but did develop a passion for hot climates that would inform his holiday habits for the rest of his life. He eventually received a gunshot wound in his right arm and ended up in Army Welfare. Tommy lost his A-1 rating, but his talents as an entertainer had not escaped the authorities. He was given the opportunity of auditioning – successfully – in Cairo for a travelling army concert party. In spite of the painful hard slog of his guards-

man's routine and a minor injury into the bargain, it is tempt-
ing to suggest that only now did his service career become
serious. He had at last found a proper, albeit frequently makeshift stage for his talents. He was not the only member of his
generation of funny men to develop his skills entertaining his
comrades in this manner. The system also provided greater
scope for individuals who would not otherwise have visited a
theatre to see an act like his, although with the variety theatres
in decline it was too much to be hoped that they would culti-
vate the habit on a regular basis once Civvy Street reclaimed
them.

Tommy was now in his element, although there were those
in this newly acquired audience who might have had second
thoughts. In his exhaustive study of service entertainment,
Fighting for a Laugh, Richard Fawkes reported the recollections of the actor John Arnatt, under whose jurisdiction
Cooper the trouper at one point found himself in Cairo: 'In
one of John's shows was an unknown conjuror making a virtue
of the fact that his tricks didn't always work . . . he had not
done anything before . . . certainly not as a professional.'
According to Arnatt, 'He was a bastard to be with as an officer
because he delighted in getting you up on the stage to help him
out and then he would take the mickey out of you something
terrible. He had the entire audience on his side and if you
weren't careful you came out of it looking none too dignified.'
Interestingly in later years Tommy almost entirely dispensed
with audience participation on stage and left the mickey taking
– always a dubious form of pastime when members of the
public are involved – to others. For the time being the rough
and ready forces environment was the perfect setting for such
spectator sport.

He had the intuitive sense to deliver what the troops
required, making great play of the trick in which some of the

cards in the packet held by the officer on one side of the stage magically found their way into the packet held by the officer on the other, becoming distracted along the way as he kept breathing on their pips and shining them all the while. The crowd roared. In later years he never lost his disrespect for military authority. The magician and writer, Val Andrews recalls seeing him lose his temper with people who insisted on using their service rank outside the military environment: 'Colonel this! Major that! Tell everyone you've just met Sergeant Cooper!' Back at base, echoing his childhood, he remained paradoxically a man isolated in his own world, immune to the popularity his extrovert performing talent should have won him with the rank and file. His colleague, Jack Chambers is on record that Cooper remained a man it was hard to get to know: 'We'd be sitting together after the show – drinking cups of tea out of sawn down beer bottles – and he didn't join in. He never had a mate or anything like that.' All his personality was now diverted into his act. Had there been other magicians in the unit, I am sure he would have found a bosom pal for life.

When the fighting drew to a close he joined the Combined Services Entertainment Unit attached to the War Office giving shows for the troops left scattered throughout the Middle East. With a restless conscript army, morale boosting was as essential at a time of keeping the peace as it had ever been while the greater distraction of fighting was taking place. It was now that Tommy decided he wanted to dedicate his life to being an entertainer. It was also in Cairo that the performance took place that must come close to the one in the Hythe canteen for qualifying as the most defining of his career. As Jack Chambers has explained, it was a cardinal offence for a soldier to be improperly dressed, even down to not wearing your cap: 'So if you can imagine one thousand troops sitting there and onto this stage comes a chap wearing very scruffy shorts and socks down to his boots – well, it was a masterly stroke and he just stood there with this gormless grin on his face and then he'd do the laugh.' To add to the anarchy he wore a pith helmet, a cloak, and had the word 'hair' written across his chest. One night at the YMCA at RAF Heliopolis he forgot the pith helmet and at the expense of cliché the rest is history.

Tommy told the story a zillion times of how this night he mislaid the helmet and happened to pinch the fez from the head of a passing waiter. It is unlikely that the move was premeditated and it paid instant dividends, adding even further inches to his height. In the company of the Guards he would have become less self-conscious about his size anyhow. As he stood there, this gangling giant of good humour, he had no idea that before long his new headwear would, as a badge of recognition, rival the bowler and trilby to which comics as diverse as Chaplin, George Robey, Max Miller and Tommy Trinder held allegiance. In addition, Arthur Askey had his forage cap and Bud Flanagan his battered straw hat. Cooper would now forever be associated with the fez. The kind he wore was originally burgundy coloured and much taller. Some time around the Sixties Tommy came to favour a brighter, more compact version. In her years with Tommy, one of Mary Kay's unofficial duties was to serve as Mistress of the Fez. In a letter to me she wrote: 'The shorter ones were his favourites and the colour of the early ones was too dark. I must have made a dozen nice bright fezzes over the years, but they weren't easy to make and if you notice some are taller on one side than the other! I always secured the tassel into the top of the fez so that it didn't fling about when he bent down. Also the felt had to be a nice, pinky red.'

Different versions of how it all came about have been

recorded. In some early interviews he let slip that he got the idea when he was in Port Said: 'I bought one for ten piastres – about two bob then – and when I came home and needed a new one I had to pay thirty-five shillings.' Down the years more than a few reminiscing servicemen have claimed that they gave him theirs. None of this is necessarily untrue. He would eventually have bought his own and acquired others, while Port Said may have been the scene of his decision to run with the idea as a permanent fixture. What surprises so many is that he was far from the first magician to wear one, a detail of which he would have been well aware.

A conversation on this very theme at The Magic Circle one evening resulted in an impromptu competition to see who could come up with the most names to have beaten Cooper to the fez. In fact there was a time when it became an unofficial part of the uniform for every other small time magician and children's party entertainer. There were also more than a few acts with fezzes prominent on the variety circuits of the Thirties and Forties, although Tommy would not necessarily have known of them all. Among those who could have given his fez a run for its money from those early days was Eddie Songest – 'With a Couple of Tricks and Colossal Nerve' – who used to boast that his was 'a trophy won in a competition in which he consumed twenty-five boxes of Turkish delight in the world record time of thirty-seven and five eighths of a second'. Tommy would certainly have been familiar with Sirdani, with his 'Don't be fright!' catchphrase and a stage identity that was a strange hybrid of Arab and Jewish. He made a name for himself on radio during the war explaining simple magic tricks and puzzles as a regular feature on the programme, *Navy Mixture*; every publicity photo I have seen of him reveals the squat purple flowerpot hat. Len Gazeka from the Midlands had an unusual gimmick to go with his fez. He would enter with his magic carpet under his arm, which he then proceeded to unroll on stage. Whenever he stood on the rug the tricks worked; whenever he failed to do so he found himself in Cooper territory. Possibly predating them all was Ben Said who had played at Maskelyne's as a comedy magician in the early Twenties. He had known better days as an illusionist in the grand manner, under the name of Amasis. In the files of Tommy's manager, Miff Ferrie was a poignant letter from Said from the Fifties with a brochure attached asking for work. 'There is only one Funjuror', the publicity proclaims. Miff must have noted the fez in the photograph. Ali (of Ali and Yolanda), Alex Bowsher, Johnny Geddes, Chris Van Bern, Percy Press; all have their place in the roll call of fez honour.

As British magical stalwart, Pat Page has explained, 'Everyone had a fez.' By coincidence, at about the same time as Tommy came home from the war in 1947, the magician Roy Baker was starting to market his original version of the egg and bag trick in which a fez was substituted for the bag. It was named 'Abdul's Fez' and hundreds must have been sold over magic shop counters down the years, but there is no record of Tommy ever performing it or adapting his own fez for the clever variation of one of his favourite tricks, although in due course he did rise to the comic possibilities the hat offered him. There was the time he took it off and white chocolate drops cascaded over his shoulders: 'I've got terrible dandruff'; the occasion at a Royal Performance when he came on with a weather vane attached: 'I've been struck by lightning!'

Conceivably it would be harder for a young performer to come out on stage wearing a fez now had Cooper and the others not done so. In our politically sensitive world, football fans travelling to Turkey in recent years have been asked to leave their Tommy Cooper impressions at home. Apparently

Turks have regarded the fez as insulting since the wearing of such hats was banned by Kemal Atatürk, the founder of modern Turkey, in 1925. Bizarrely there was even one occasion in June 1967 when the organizer of a private function where Tommy was booked to appear requested that he leave his trademark headgear at home for fear of upsetting the largely Jewish clientele. Others have adopted a more practical attitude to it. Val Andrews told him early in his career that he should take the fez off at the end of his act: 'People will think you're bald and you have a great head of hair and this is an asset and when you reveal it, it's a surprise.' To Val's delight, he always did.

The Middle East also provided a milestone in his personal life. It was there that he met Gwen. They first came together on a troopship travelling from Port Said to Alexandria, or maybe from Naples. Her accounts vary, but the romantic detail remained precise: 'The very first time I saw him I didn't speak to him. I had a shocking attack of flu and I was sitting in a deckchair all wrapped up in blankets and I saw this big man in battledress – he was a sergeant by now – standing against the ship's rail with his back to the sea. The first thing I noticed was that the blue of the sea caught the blue of his eyes. He had the most magnificent physique I had ever seen. He was terrifically attractive in an ugly-attractive sort of way.' When she asked someone who he was, she was told, 'His name's Tommy Cooper and he's doing a show on board.' Because of the flu, Gwen watched the performance from outside through a glass door. She couldn't hear a word, but she saw enough to formulate an opinion: 'I thought he was the funniest man I'd ever seen. This man's got star talent, I told myself. One day he'll be a big name.' Upon arrival in Egypt Dove went her separate way to Cairo, not realizing that within days their paths would cross again. Gwen was a civilian entertainer attached to CSE and on Christmas Eve 1946 she found herself having to accompany Tommy on the piano at a concert in Alexandria: 'I said to him, "Let me see your dots." He didn't know what I meant. I said "Your music." He said, "Just play the first few bars of 'The Sheik of Araby'."'

On their way back in the army bus he sat next to her. 'Can I put my head on your shoulder?' he asked. 'Certainly not,' she declared. The relationship began at that point and two weeks later he proposed: 'I don't suppose you'd marry me, would you?' 'I suppose I will,' was the response. There is no reason to suppose that Tommy had been party to such a deep attachment before, but the affair was not without its emotional complications. Gwen had recently been engaged to a pilot killed during the air raids on Cologne. When asked what she would have done had he survived, she replied, 'I'd have broken off the engagement. I really fell for Tommy.' They married in Nicosia, Cyprus on 24 February 1947. Tommy was so poor she had to buy her own wedding ring, although he made up for it later with a diamond eternity ring. Their honeymoon was a single night snatched at the Savoy Hotel, Famagusta. When they walked through the door the man at reception called out, 'Ah, Brigadier Cooper!' Their friends in the concert party had booked them in as Brigadier and Mrs Cooper as a joke. Without an inkling of embarrassment she would admit they had not slept together before that night, which with characteristic frankness she always described as 'bloody wonderful'.

Throughout their life together he called her 'Dove'. With her full-bodied figure she used to joke, 'Anything less like a dove!' Their daughter thinks the term of affection came about after a few drinks when 'love' turned to 'dove' and stuck. Maybe it came out of 'lovey-dovey'. Whatever the derivation, there is unlikely to be any deep magical significance to the word, since Channing Pollock, the suave American deceptionist who popularized the manipulation of the birds in his brilliant stage act, did not arrive on the theatrical scene until the early Fifties.

Gwen was five months older than her husband. She had been born in Eastbourne on 14 October 1920, the daughter of Thomas William Henty, a blacksmith's assistant. The gift of a piano from her parents at the age of eleven was the defining 'box of tricks' moment in her own life. All who came to know her would identify with the irrepressible joie-de-vivre and sense of purpose that could have led her to personal stardom in her own right – a performer in the Tessie O'Shea mould with piano in lieu of banjulele – had she chosen that path. On her travels in the Middle East she had fast been gaining a reputation as an entertainer. Ragged press cuttings pasted in her scrapbook before she met Tommy reveal that she had a far wider range of talents than her known skills as an accompanist would suggest. Working under the ENSA banner in the touring show, *Sunrise* in 1945, she is reported: 'The girl of many faces is something of a phenomenon. As the moth-eaten old charlady, she rocks the audience with laughter. As herself a few minutes later, she provokes that peculiar whistle which troops reserve for what they usually describe as "a bit of all right". She more or less runs riot through the show.' Another review, from Beirut, tells us, 'She gets right to the hearts of the audience. She has a Gracie Fields personality, her character sketches have 100 per cent entertainment value, and her vivacious singing at the piano of a charming satire entitled, "Men – men – men!" produced roars of laughter.' In Baghdad she is described as putting over 'her own sophisticated Mae West-ish solo act, but she isn't afraid to discard the glamour and paint her nose red in real slapstick stuff.'

In the concert party she had been partnered in the 'slapstick stuff' by one Jimmy Murray, 'an extremely good young comedian with a smooth and pleasant style.' Upon marrying Tommy it was inevitable that they would contemplate a double act together. A large buff regulation notebook – emblazoned with a crown and 'GR Supplied for the Public Service' – that Tommy kept up around this time provides some intriguing glimpses of their brief partnership on stage:

Tommy: Hello, darling. Is dinner ready?
Gwen: (Starts to cry)
Tommy: What's the matter, my sweet?
Gwen: Y-you d-don't l-love me any more.
Tommy: Don't be silly. What gave you that idea?
Gwen: Well, we've been married now for five weeks and this is the first time you've been worried about food!

One routine they worked on was a pastiche on American Broadcasting with its leaning towards product placement:

Gwen: Hey, bighead. Get out of that bed. We've got a programme to do.
Tommy: Will you quit yapping! Six o'clock in the morning. Who's to listen to us? Some burglars, maybe. Oh boy, I'm tired.
Gwen: Why don't you stay home some night and try sleeping?
Tommy: Sleeping? On that Pasternak Pussy-Willow Mattress? Pussy-Willow? It's stuffed with cat hair. Every time I lie down on that cat hair my back arches!
Gwen: Oh, stop grumbling! Here's your tea!
Tommy: It's about time. (Sips) Phoo! (Spits) What are you trying to do? Poison me?
Gwen: It's that McKeesters's Vita-Fresh Tea! It won't kill you.
Tommy: It won't? Why do you think the government makes

them put that skull and crossbones on the packet?
(Tommy screams)

Gwen: What is it?

Tommy: Your hair! It looks as though you just took your
head out of a mixer.

It was obviously an act in progress. Gwen recalled in later
years that they were once rehearsing in a room in Cairo. The
slanging match was so convincing, the caretaker wanted to
call the police. Later they tried a softer, kindlier, less negative
approach:

Gwen: Good morning, Tommy dear.

Tommy: Good morning, Gwen angel.

Gwen: Sweetheart, I must say you look refreshingly well-
rested this morning.

Tommy: Yes, thanks to our wonderful Pasternak Factory-
Tested Pussy-Willow Mattress. The mattress that takes
all the guess work out of sleeping. So soft and restful.

Gwen: Yes, sweetums. Here's your tea.

Tommy: Thank you, doll. (Sips) Ahhh! What tea!! It must
be –

Gwen: You're right, lovey. It's McKeester's Vita-Fresh Tea,
the tea with that locked-up goodness for everybody.

Tommy: Quick, darling. Another cup. Ahhhhhh!!

Gwen: Oh, peach-nut! You've spilled some on your vest.

Tommy: Good. Now I can try some of that Little Panther
Spot Remover. No rubbing. Just slap some Little Panther
on your vest and watch it eat the spot out.

Gwen: And imagine – a big two-ounce bottle for only three
pence farthing.

Tommy: Or, if you are a messy eater, you can get the handy
economical forty-gallon bottle.

Gwen: Angel eyes, I have so much to say this morning.
Tommy: Stop. Don't move, Gwen.
Gwen: But, darling!
Tommy: Your hair is breathtaking. That sheen. That brilliance. What did you do to it?

And so on . . . ! After the war there is evidence that they tried out the act before a civilian audience at the Theatre Royal, Margate, but it was a non-starter. According to Gwen, Tommy wanted to stay together as a team, but she had never lost faith in that first impression of her husband as a single act through the glass partition on the Alexandria ferry. Her devotion and dedication to the man and his career would endure until the end of her days.

Cooper was quintessentially a solo performer. In recent years the claims of one Frankie Lyons to have been part of a double act with him back in 1946 during the CSE years have to some people's minds been exaggerated out of belief, not least when they were given additional importance when formulated in the mid-Nineties into a stage play by his son, Garry. An army concert party is by nature an informal organism, a makeshift showbusiness world in which all the members are expected to work alongside one another in sketches, musical numbers and passing exchanges of corny humour known in the trade as crossovers. Tommy's exercise book provides us with examples. The initials could refer to 'Cooper' and 'Frankie', but more likely stand for 'comic' and 'feed':

C.: Hello there. Maybe you can help me. I've got a problem and I don't know whether to go to a palmist or a mind reader for the answer.
F.: Go to a palmist. You're sure you have a palm!

And again:

>   C.: You'd love the dimple in her chin though. You'd love
>   the dimple in her chin.
>   F.: Why twice?
>   C.: Double chin!

Out of such brief exchanges a permanent double act is not
born. Besides, they evolve out of genuine warmth and respect
between the two partners, never at the suggestion of some
would-be producer with officer status playing fanciful games
with his cast of conscripts. One is reminded of Steve Martin's
classic comedy sketch of the failed Hollywood agent pairing
off his make-believe charges: 'Laurel, you go with Costello;
Abbott, you go with Hardy.' It just doesn't work that way.
Cooper and Lyons never got past first post. Even had they
been in line to become the next Flanagan and Allen, the new
Jewel and Warriss, Lyons quite obviously lacked the drive and
self-sacrifice at the core of true star talent that not only
Tommy, but Gwen on his behalf, showed once they returned
to home shores. In later life Cooper pondered the quality in a
reflective moment: 'I often wonder what separates the amateurs from the pros. Being persistent, I suppose. There are
bound to be tough times and a lot of people give up. But I was
determined. Besides, there's a great streak of optimism in me.'
In other words show business has its own Darwinian structure.

Tommy set his sights on the London Palladium and got
there. Frankie settled for an honourable other existence with
a modest, but skilled job in engineering. With all the good will
in the world, Tommy would never have reached the top variety
theatre in the land with him in tow. Had one been casting
Lyons alongside the likes of William Hartnell, Michael Medwin, Harry Fowler and company, one would have to settle for

Sam Kydd, the chipper insignificant sidekick of a hundred service movies, but never a star. In his later years Tommy found himself lined up against a handful of dependable British character actors as occasional straight men. They all floundered in the shadow of the fez. Terry Seabrooke, one of Britain's foremost professional magicians, acted as a technical consultant to a production of *Frankie and Tommy* and formulated his opinion: 'It showed Tommy as a nasty type with a terrible, ruthless temper. It certainly was not the Tommy I knew for so many years.'

Inevitably the play attracted tabloid scrutiny. In addition, as if to rub salt into wounds a story was brought into the open by Lyons concerning the discovery of illicit drugs on a truck transporting CSE theatrical props that had been overturned on a road in Palestine in early March 1947. A British driver and a British sergeant were arrested and half a ton of hashish and opium was supposedly seized. It is an acknowledged fact that throughout the Middle East at that time demoralized soldiers were profiteering on the black market. Lyons alleges that rumours started to circulate around CSE headquarters in Cairo that Tommy was the sergeant implicated. On 27 August 1947 *The Times* reported that a lieutenant, described as the manager of a road show called *Juke Box*, had been acquitted of conspiring to smuggle the drugs that had been seized. At the beginning of March, just days after his marriage, Tommy had been on tour starring in the *Juke Box* show, but any evidence that he may have been implicated is circumstantial, his possible involvement beyond belief. His mind was now on other matters. Within a month or so he would be on his way back to England. He already had a strategy for entertainment success back home and could look forward to his new wife joining him soon after. It is also hard to think he was bright enough to figure as a criminal mastermind and had real suspicion fallen upon him, his return would have been curtailed. As for drugs *per se*? Magic *was* his drug. He had no need – as yet – for other substances. In later years, as we shall see, he would become prey to alcohol abuse and the mood swings that came with it, as susceptible to pain and anger as any other human being. It is jumping the gun to intimate he may have been accountable to such demons so early, as Lyons' whole treatment of him suggests. Eventually the stage manager and an Arab accomplice were charged and convicted, and in their embarrassment the British authorities were happy to draw a veil over the incident.

Meanwhile, with or without Gwen or Lyons at his side, the embryonic version of Tommy's comedy magic act stayed sacrosanct. As he wrote in his notebook at the time: 'Spoon Gag – Rope Gag – Fifteen Card Trick with Assistants – Egg Bag – Finis.' Professional show business beckoned. It may be appropriate to give Frankie Lyons the last word: 'He was determined. No matter whom, no matter what, he was going to get there.' And – happily for us all – he did!

FOUR

Life Gets More Exciting . . .

Upon his return to England, Tommy headed straight for the parental home at Langley. Gwen still had professional obligations to fulfil for the CSE in the Middle East and any semblance of a normal married life remained on the horizon. The drafts of letters he wrote to her from 'Devonia' provide an insight into those early days of readjustment at all levels, professional, domestic, and emotional, as well as trite but touching testament to his undying love for her: 'Have I told you I love you today? Well, my sweet, I do. I can't live without you, longing for your arms around me. I love you, my beautiful wife. I'm thinking about you every minute of the day.' He bounces her along continually with holiday camp enthusiasm – 'Keep smiling and your chin up! It won't be long now' – and goes out of his way to allay the anxieties Gwen obviously nursed regarding her family's feelings *vis-à-vis* their marriage – possibly without their initial knowledge – so far from the white cliffs of Dover: 'I told them all the news and put the matter to rest. So, my sweet, you have nothing to worry about as they are all happy and longing for your hasty return.'

It seems a typically cockeyed Cooper way of doing things

that he should meet his in-laws without first being introduced by his wife, but the self-motivated initial bonding experience went well on a fleeting one-night visit to Eastbourne, during which he met her mother, father, brothers, and grandma, as well as being treated to a pub crawl, a car ride to Beachy Head ('But boy was I cold up there!') and a visit to his father-in-law's metal works. The latter provided the red letter opportunity of the whole trip as he suffered withdrawal symptoms for the metal shop at the Hythe boatyard: 'I must admit your father has a nice workshop indeed. He's a very busy man. Then I broke up the work by showing some tricks for ten minutes. Your brothers were delighted with them and kept asking the time as they made sure they didn't work after one o'clock. Ha! We all went back to lunch.'

He wasted no time in testing the shallows of full time show business: 'This week I'm going to London to see an agent called Tommie Draper. Wish me luck, my sweet. How I miss you. With you here I wouldn't be half so scared! Ha!! I know what you would say, "Now go out there, bighead, and kill 'em." So roll on Friday.' No record survives of his first civilian audition in Gerrard Street. Within weeks the happy couple are reunited and inevitably set their sights on a home together in London. But not before Tommy has written asking for another audition at the Windmill – not at this juncture forthcoming – and, more importantly, a further one at the BBC.

On 2 June 1947 he wrote from Langley to a Miss Cook at the Corporation requesting that he be given a chance: 'My act consists of cod magic and comedy, which I think would be quite suitable for television.' He received a response almost immediately. On 5 June he was summoned by the Television Booking Manager to attend a 'preliminary audition' at 25 Marylebone Road the following Monday, the ninth, at 11.45 a.m.: 'Your performance should not exceed ten minutes in length.' The outcome was negative in the extreme, recalling the notorious report given Fred Astaire's initial screen test at Paramount: 'Can't act; can't sing; slightly bald; can dance a little.' Cooper was disparagingly immortalized as an 'unattractive young man with indistinct speaking voice and extremely unfortunate appearance'. His act had taken seven minutes of their time. In truth his bizarre persona and anarchic approach defied classification among the starchy Corporation bigwigs of that time. As a postscript, the report card filled out on the day added, 'nonchalant approach, but poor diction and unpleasant manner'. Someone wanted to add insult to injury. Not that Tommy saw this at the time. A courtesy letter arrived at his parent's home a week later simply advising that his performance was deemed unsuitable for 'our TV variety programmes as at present planned'. It is the irony of ironies that by the end of the year he had made his television debut, almost certainly with his audition act – it *was* his act – on a gala Christmas Eve variety show hosted by the musical comedy star, Leslie Henson. However, such a prestige booking belied the reality of the struggle ahead for the Coopers as they tried to come to terms with life on the first rung of the show business ladder in a shabby London town befogged by austerity and a Pyrrhic sense of peace.

It was impossible to meet Gwen in later years without understanding intuitively her contribution to her husband's eventual success. Whatever reassurance he had expressed in his letters to her, she now reciprocated in the flesh, her cheerful, forceful personality being exactly what was needed to keep him on track: 'There were times when he could be bloody difficult, sitting in the same chair all day, saying nothing, making cards and coins disappear. Then I would have to give him one of my pep talks.' The idea of persisting professionally as a twosome was never on the cards: 'I remember telling him that marriages in show business can easily fold up. So I told him to forget the double act and do the magic act on his own. Then you've got no one to fall out with but yourself.' She constantly endorsed his decision to play the magic for laughs. She also insisted that his forty-eight pounds or so demob pay went on a decent Savile Row suit for the act. In addition he splashed out on a Crombie camel-hair overcoat with a tie belt: it seems that back then you couldn't be taken seriously in show business without one. As he later claimed, 'I was the best dressed out of work act in London.' It is unlikely that he would have made it without her. She brought a smart editorial sense to the act that he had been quick to acknowledge when he was on the CSE circuit. He knew that if he wanted to be up there with Max Miller, Sid Field, and the rest of the greats he would be foolish to ignore it.

Work for a dysfunctional magician of whom no one had heard was sparse. Gwen acknowledged with typical forthrightness, 'We were so poor, we hadn't a pot to piss in or a window to throw it out of if we had!' In fact, they found a furnished room in Victoria for ten shillings a week and a landlady who bled them for every penny they had. She admitted that at one stage she used to scrub steps for other people, 'but I was so proud I did it at midnight so nobody would see me.' At a time when newly married wives were not necessarily expected to go out to work, Dove found more regular employment putting the eyes in dolls at a toy factory and then serving behind the counter in the gloves and leather goods department at Bourne and Hollingsworth, where she progressed to the rank of buyer. Their weekly luxury was a Sunday stroll into the West End for half a pint of bitter apiece at a pub in St Martin's Lane where show business folk gathered. One night they went mad, had two halves each and then realized they did not have the bus fare to get back home. They were by now living in a meagre flat in Lavender Hill. Gwen in a sudden fit of expediency dashed into a shop doorway and whipped off the stockings she had just received as a present from overseas: 'Nylons were like gold dust then and Tommy nipped into a pub and sold them for thirty shillings.' It would not be the only occasion his ability as a salesman helped to save the day.

For Tommy the daily routine took in the hard slog of the agents' offices. The legendary meeting place for out of work pros was the old Express Dairy in Charing Cross Road, where tea and consolation flowed in equal measure. But he showed more enterprise than most. As the others continued to bemoan the state of the country, the industry, their own careers, Tommy would suddenly bounce up and head for Leather Lane, Portobello Road or any of the countless markets in and around London. Four hours later he'd return to find the others still there with hardly a penny to their name, while his own pockets were considerably fuller. The magician, Bobby Bernard saw it happen.

The world of the street market trader enjoys its own mystique and has often overlapped that of the magician. Street entertainers like the legendary Charlie Edwards – they were more dignified to be dismissed as mere buskers and interestingly he sported a Crombie overcoat too – were a constant attraction at these affairs. One of Edwards's specialities was the flick or 'blow' book, a small volume, the pages of which were cut at the edge in an ingenious way so that you could flick the pages to show them blank, or covered in letters of the alphabet, musical notes, crosswords, drawings or whatever. Having dazzled the crowd with his handling of this simple novelty, he would pitch them to all comers together with the secrets – as concise as the mottos in Christmas crackers – of his other miracles, tricks with playing cards, glasses, and knotted handkerchiefs. Many years later Tommy presented a deft demonstration of the flick book on one of his television shows. So adroit was his handling, one knew he too must have performed it many times in its natural outdoor environment all those years ago.

Tommy's own *al fresco* speciality was a nifty little item called the Buddha Papers. A series of small paper packets with a penny in the innermost one were folded around one another. When they were unfolded the coin had disappeared or changed into a shilling. Much midnight oil was spent by Tommy and Dove cutting out, folding and sticking the gaily coloured tissue papers that gave the trick added carnival appeal. In addition there were packs of cards known as Svengali decks, one moment all different, the next all the same – a distant cousin of the flick book – and probably the money machine, the miniature mangle that printed your own pound notes and continued to hoodwink people long after Laurel and Hardy gave it wide exposure in the movie, *A-Haunting We Will Go*. For the first few months of his career the marketplaces of London provided his main stage. He had the personality and he got by. It is not an easy task holding a standing crowd, but he was impossible to miss in one, and the experience to be gained before a non-paying public was priceless, not least the knowledge of how people react to different actions, phrases, gags, and bits of business. The result is behavioural psychology at its most basic and most valuable. It is the inner secret of magic as a performance art.

Much of his market work appears to have gone in phases. There was a reasonably profitable period when he teamed up with an old stager who sold red Cardinal polish for doorsteps. Between them they could make three to four pounds a day. There was the less profitable occasion he acquired a handbag concession. He never forgot the spiel as long as he lived: 'I had to sell them at twenty-five shillings a time and used to say, "I can't tell you the name of the firm I represent, ladies and gentlemen, but it's an important one. If I told you, you'd recognize it immediately. I would tell you except that we are opening a new major store soon and I've been warned to keep everything secret because our many rivals are constantly on the watch." For all that the bloke who owned the stall only gave me four bob.' That assignment lasted one day.

The product with which he remains most readily associated among his mates from that time was the radio 'estabulator' [*sic*] or wireless fake. This was a gizmo that you attached to an old valve radio supposedly to improve its reception. High tech did not come into it. The 'interference suppressor' was little more than a cardboard tube with a couple of wires attached with sealing wax. It sold for half a crown. By moving the radio around it was never difficult to get a better reception for a short period and that was the window of opportunity upon which a sale depended. Frequently his brother, David would come along as the shill to start the buying. Del Boy and Arthur Daley had nothing on the Cooper duo.

Accompanying Tommy on many of his market escapades was his close friend, the magician and mind reader, Dennis Rawlins. One day they missed out at the last minute on a pitch at Hitchin market and desperate for cash decided to try their hand at an old street swindle inexplicably labelled 'Back of the Nut'. The following day was Derby Day. They bought a supply of small Manila seed envelopes, accessed a list of runners, and proceeded to write out the name of 'the favourite' on slips of paper that were inserted into the envelopes. Their knowledge of the racing scene rivalled what they knew about nuclear fission. They then took up position on the grass verge outside the nearby Vauxhall Motor Works. When the whistle blew, the workers spilled out and could not miss them. In the parlance of the trade, they 'worked the wagon and the whip', Tommy drumming up a crowd for Dennis who was mysteriously swathed in an imposing black blindfold, as befits the man who knows everything: 'This man is so fabulous he saved the life of Cecil Boyd-Rochford and C.B-R.'s niece!' Boyd-Rochford was the trainer of the time whose name the public knew. Once they had convinced everyone they had inside information on the big race, they had no trouble in shifting the tips at two shillings a time. They got out of town as fast as they could. The next day their recommendation failed to show in the first three and life moved on. After a while, by which time Tommy had secured a fledgling presence on television, he secured a lowly week's work in variety at the Alma Cinema in Luton. He found himself on the early morning train, anxious to make band call in time. As Dennis told the story: 'This other bloke got on. He looked at Tommy and said, "I know you." In his non-committal, mock bashful way, Tommy replied, "Possibly. Possibly." "I know you." "Quite possible." "Where, I wonder?" Then just as he goes to step off the train, he turns to Tommy and says, "Why, you're that bastard who sold me that tip!"' Tommy, one minute glowing incredulously in his new found television glory, turned instantly into a quivering wreck, saved by the slam of the door and the guard's whistle.

For Gwen the worst part was seeing her husband having to get up at five o'clock in the morning, even earlier if longer distances were involved. If he didn't arrive at certain markets between five and six he lost all hope of a stall for that day. The routine would have been even more tiring if he had performed a show the night before, but those who observed him in those days claim he was kept afloat outwardly by – in Bobby Bernard's phrase – a puppy dog enthusiasm. Larry Barnes, a contemporary of his in early variety, attempted to explain his special kind of energy: 'When you were in his presence you were always slightly worried that you were letting him down, that you were seen not to subscribe to his sunny side of life.' Much of this outward attitude was unquestionably down to Gwen's role as puppet mistress. There can be no doubt that she helped to bring out the extrovert in him in a social situation, triggering the ability to relax in other people's company *without* a trick in his hand. To many performers it can be far harder to walk into a crowded room – unprotected, unjustified, unnoticed – than walk onto a stage before a thousand people. Meanwhile she also controlled the purse strings, taking pains to ensure he did not fritter away what little money he did earn.

According to Val Andrews the first professional stage job Tommy had back in England was not performing his act but working as a stooge for Harry Tate Junior, the son of the great music hall sketch comedian. Val recalls how funny he was in the wan make-up and the flat cap, playing the tall gormless caddy with a wheel on a stick in the golfing sketch: 'Doing nothing, but doing everything', all for two pounds ten shillings a week. There was some sporadic film extra work and three humble bottom-of-the-bill weeks in variety, at the Manchester Hippodrome, the Brighton Grand, and the Playhouse, Weston-Super-Mare during the middle of 1947, but not much else. Morale was kept up by the camaraderie of many of those in the same predicament. Once a week he would get together with a group of ex-servicemen who had committed themselves to comedy as a profession, a prospect that before the war would have seemed as unlikely as turning base metal to gold or fighting Hitler single-handed.

The number who not only made it in a relatively short space of time, but also stayed at the top is staggering. Wisdom, Edwards, Emery, Bygraves, Bentine, Milligan, Secombe, Sellers, Sykes, Howerd, Hancock, Hill, they all contributed to a seismic effect on British comedy that has not happened since and may be comparable only with the revolution in popular music a decade or so later. They did not all achieve a similar success. The names of Joe Church, Harry Locke, Norman Caley, Len Marten, Robert Moreton – all stalwart pros – failed to register in the national consciousness in the same way. Luck as well as talent had a part to play in the longevity of a career, but at the moment they all shared the same heady dream of house-hold name stardom. It was certainly not the most congenial time to be contemplating such a future. The variety circuit was in a shaky condition, radio in spite of *ITMA* and *Band Waggon* had yet to find its golden age in comedy terms, and television had not established itself sufficiently before the service was curtailed on the outbreak of war for anyone to know whether it held out any lasting prospects at all.

Each of these now famous names needed his own personal Mister Sandman to conjure dream into reality. The key to this was being seen, a procedure with its own built-in Catch 22: unless you already had a representative, how were you to secure a decent booking where you could be seen in the first place? One answer was the Nuffield Centre, a club for ser-vicemen in Adelaide Street in the back of St Martin-in-the-Fields. A favourite haunt of agents and producers, it provided a free and easy showcase for many a comic emerging from the war. With or without this solitary oasis, talent would find a way and before long Norman had found a professional soul mate in an agent named Billy Marsh. Max discovered an advocate in Jock Jacobsen, Benny in Richard Stone, and 'the lad himself' in Phyllis Rounce. In each career one can point to one such strong individual working behind the scenes. As far as Tommy was concerned, Gwen could give him encouragement and guid-ance, but she did not have the professional qualifications to go the whole way. Miff Ferrie was waiting in the wings.

Miff was born George Ferrie in Edinburgh on 10 March 1911. A musician during his early life, he acquired his nickname in homage to the American trombonist 'Miff' Mole. The Thirties saw him recording alongside Roy Fox, Ambrose, Jack Hylton, Lew Stone and Carroll Gibbons at the height of the dance band craze, before deciding temporarily to set aside his trombone to form a permanent vocal trio. When *Band Waggon* hit the airwaves in January 1938, Miff Ferrie and the Jackdauz [*sic*] found themselves billed alongside comedy stars, Arthur Askey and Richard Murdoch as one of the resident vocal attractions on the series. Encouraged by this success, he then formed his own combination featuring the vocal group as part of a seven-piece orchestra, The Ferrymen. With regular radio work, a Parlophone recording contract and tours of Great Britain and the Continent in his date book, Miff was riding high. *Airs and Disgraces* was a short-lived series based around his talents. One imagines him as a chirpy little showman in a dour sort of way. Many years later brilliant Scots comic, Chic Murray made an art form of the contradiction. Then the war intervened. Invalided out of the army, Miff acted as Musical Adviser to United States Organization, Camp Shows. His USO work involved him in auditioning hundreds of musicians and other performers as well as production administration.

After the war Miff and his band became the resident attraction at the Windermere Club at 189 Regent Street, his activities extending to those of 'Entertainments Director', in which capacity he was responsible for booking the cabaret. One Friday afternoon in November 1947 a nervous Tommy Cooper went along to audition for the floor show. Few places can be more dispiriting than a performing venue without its audience, the cold emptiness a cruel champion of fear. Tommy later said, 'Unfortunately, the act I did that day was not suitable, but Miff made a few suggestions and told me to come back in a week or two. This I did, and to my amazement I made the musicians in the band laugh. I was working from then on.'

It is hard to know what he was thinking. His first audition act majored on a series of impressions of Hollywood stars, the comedy magic playing a minor role. The idea of the hysterical Cooper presenting a convincing parade of Jimmy Cagney, Charles Laughton and Edward G. Robinson defies belief. The route to show business as an impressionist was the most hackneyed of them all. Moreover, it was a difficult genre to burlesque. Accuracy was the keynote to success, unless you were Tony Hancock, a frustrated pretender and buffoon of a different kind, who made a big feature of his own lugubrious attempts to mimic these very names in his own stage act. Indeed he persisted with them into the mid Sixties by which time the originals were passing out of fashion. That he did so was criticized by some, but seen as an accurate reflection of what the quintessential Hancock character would purvey in a comically jaded variety act by others. Whatever, one does wonder whether somewhere along the way he witnessed the Cooper act at this stage and the idea was sewn.

The impressions aside, little did Miff know that the trick or two Tommy also managed to fumble that Friday afternoon were the tip of an iceberg of material already waiting in the wings. The return audition was not necessarily the challenge it might have seemed to the man requesting it. In later years Miff would himself take credit for suggesting to Cooper the idea of the burlesque approach to magic, to the extent of having Tommy apparently voice the claim himself in much early publicity, interviews that Miff in fact gave or provided copy for on his client's behalf. There may have been a genuine misunderstanding – Tommy was now too busy and too increasingly successful to be bothered – but the claim was not based on fact, as we know from the approach Tommy had already adopted in the services and at his BBC audition. More importantly, at that second audition for Ferrie the frenzied fellow in the fez achieved one of the most difficult feats in show business. He reduced the band to hysterics. Surveying the debris of imploded conjuring tricks, Miff had no option but to offer him a week's work at a salary of fifteen pounds, while thinking to himself, 'My God, if we could recapture that and channel it, we've got something that no one else is doing.' On and off Tommy played the Windermere for fifteen weeks over the coming year, initially as a supporting attraction to the exotic Marqueez – once described as the Pavlova of the music halls and now billed as the 'Glamorous Star of the East, featuring her famous Dance of the Seven Veils.' From that first booking, Miff continued to mastermind his career – through countless trials and tribulations between them – to the end of his life. At this early stage a surviving script suggests that he even muscled in on the act:

> *Tommy*: Well, Miff, what do you think of my magic?
> *Miff*: Your magic?
> *Tommy*: Yes, you know, the way I make things disappear.
> *Miff*: I haven't seen anything disappear.
> *Tommy*: You haven't? (Tommy hands wrist watch over)
>   Yours, I believe . . . (Then laughs head off)
> *Miff*: Mr Cooper . . .
> *Tommy*: (Still laughing) What's that noise? (Looks around)
>   Oh, it's you. What now?
> *Miff*: (Handing over a pair of socks) Yours, I believe . . .
> (Tommy pulls up trousers and displays bare legs. Registers
>   consternation, then off)

It took Miff a while to adjust to the spotlight favouring Tommy and his few other clients at the expense of his own ego. In the early years of their partnership, he could never completely ignore an opportunity for his own self-promotion, as shown by this gratuitous attempt at humour from a standard Cooper press biography:

> About a year ago, when coming from a rehearsal, he found a policeman waiting by his car. The following conversation ensued:
>
> *Tommy*: Yes, officer.
> *Policeman*: I shall have to book you for a parking offence.
> *Tommy*: Book me? Oh, you'd better talk to Mr Ferrie, my agent.
>
> His progress is indeed a tribute to Miff Ferrie, who brought Tommy into the business a little over three years ago and who has kept him working ever since.

As the years progressed and Cooper's good fortune headed for the stratosphere, Miff was able to come to terms with his own feelings of inadequacy, although, with his background as a minor star, self-effacement would never come easily to him. In fairness, there was not a moment around the clock when this short, bespectacled Scot with the shrewd eyes behind their tinted lenses was not prepared to fight Tommy's corner, but the relationship between them was never without its difficulties. Praise did not come as easily as reproach, while his comedy judgement proved little short of appalling, as epitomized by the time Miff sat stony-faced while Tommy demonstrated to him for the first time his classic routine with the cardboard box of 'Hats'. After that it became a byword of the Cooper household – as well as the production crew of many a Tommy television series – that, in Gwen's words, 'If Miff thought it wasn't funny, you can bet it was.' She used to smile, conceding that when Tommy wanted to upset Miff, he'd call him George. As we shall see, there were times when things became far more serious, Tommy conducting what amounted to a war of psychological attrition against him, but Miff – 'that little Scottish fellow sprouting red horns', as Tommy would refer to him – stood steadfastly firm with typical native fortitude. For the magician it remained a case of 'better the devil you know'. For all Ferrie assumed the notoriety of a *monstre sacré* as the power behind Cooper, and a short while later Bruce Forsyth too, he remained among his fellow agents one of the most respected players in the game.

This is the place to lay to rest once and for all the myth of the contract that existed between performer and agent. No arrangement in show business history has been more misrepresented. Tommy always claimed that Miff signed him unwillingly to a lifetime contract that guaranteed him a wage of twenty pounds a week for the first seven years, however many shows he performed. Gwen claimed she was livid when she heard he'd signed, guaranteeing Miff fifteen per cent – as distinct from the then standard ten – into the bargain. It became the most notorious agreement of its kind since the one that kept Sid Field out of the West End, a prisoner of the provinces, until he was nudging forty. However, even had the hearsay been true, it should be stressed that twenty pounds was a fair recompense at a time when the average supporting magic or comedy act was earning little more than ten pounds a week.

The original document as signed by T. F. Cooper over its pink and magenta sixpenny stamp on 28 November 1948, which is now in the possession of the author, is a totally honourable Sole Agency Agreement, as endorsed by the Council of the Agents' Association Limited. There is nothing to stipulate that Tommy should not receive the total earnings he has achieved in any one week, minus the commission that is set at the agreed fifteen per cent. The arrangement covers an initial period of five, not seven years during which Miff is expected 'to use all reasonable efforts to procure employment for me . . . and to guide and advise me with respect to my theatrical career and to act for me as Manager and Personal Representative in all matters concerning my professional interests whenever you are called upon to do so.' It granted Miff exclusivity in the area of 'Manager, Agent, and Personal Representative'.

Clause Six is a key one and certainly caused the greatest aggravation to Tommy over the years:

> The period of this agreement may be extended by you (i.e. Miff) from year to year by your giving me one month's notice in writing prior to the end of the said period or any extension of that period. Each extension and the determination of such extension shall be governed by the preceding Clause (5) except that the figure of earnings for such extended period shall be based on my earnings for the last year of the original period where only one extension takes place, or for the last extended period of one year immediately preceding the new extension, where more than one extension takes place.

As for Clause Five, there was no reason for Tommy to quibble. It was there to protect the performer as much as the agent, giving him the opportunity to walk away had Miff failed in his obligation to provide work in any four month period that failed in less technical language to reflect his average earnings in the previous twelve months. Here it is for the record:

> Should I at any time during the term hereof fail to obtain a bona fide offer of employment (sufficient to produce for me during the time this agreement shall have run a sum not less

than the equivalent of my average earnings taken over the twelve months immediately preceding the date of this agreement) from a responsible employer in a period in excess of four consecutive months, during all of which time I was ready, able and willing to accept such employment, either party hereto shall in such event have the right immediately to terminate this contract by a notice in writing to such effect sent to the other party by registered mail, provided, however, that such right shall be deemed waived by me, and any exercise thereof by me shall be ineffective if, after the expiration of any such four months period and prior to the time I attempt to exercise such right, I have received an offer of employment from a responsible employer.

Down through the years Miff religiously exercised his renewal option and the large stack of registered envelopes gathered in Cooper's files are their own testimony not only to the hold Miff undeniably held over him, but to the successful way in which he managed Cooper's career from a financial standpoint. From the moment Tommy signed with Miff his whole career represented a constant upward curve – helped not a little by the meteoric rise in fees triggered by the northern club boom – until the last few years when it became eroded by ill health. On this score the client never had reason to complain. Between the time of their first meeting and the end of the financial year in April 1948, Miff had secured Tommy work worth £223.00. The following twelve months, during which the agreement came into operation, saw him earning £738.00. By the time he reached April 1950 his earnings had more than doubled to £1,586.00, and by April 1951 almost doubled again to £2,987.00.

Tommy commenced his first week for Miff at the Windermere on 8 December 1947 and was held over for a fortnight.

Almost twelve months passed before the agreement was signed. Miff appears not to have been in a hurry. On 12 February 1948 Tommy, by now living in a flat at 105 Warwick Avenue in Maida Vale, wrote to Miff: 'I wish to thank you for all the engagements you have procured for me in the past, and would be happy if you would conduct my future business.' While Miff continued to find bookings for him, nothing was formalized until the end of the year. On 25 November, having moved yet again to a flat at 13 Canfield Gardens off the Finchley Road, he wrote to Miff a second time. After expressing again his gratitude 'for the help and care with which you have conducted my business in the past,' he continues: 'I would be very grateful if you would accept fifteen per cent commission, continuing to look after my interests in the future as personal manager unless this agreement should be terminated by mutual agreement. Hoping this is quite satisfactory and thanking you again, Yours faithfully, Tommy Cooper.' Two days later Miff wrote to Tommy expressing his satisfaction with this arrangement and the following day the situation was formalized. On the same day he dropped Miff a note, doubtless at the manager's suggestion, which stated, 'I hereby give you the authority to sign all or any contracts on my behalf.' Gwen claimed that Tommy told her he was shaking when he signed on the dotted line. There is no reason to suppose that this was anything more than the nerves of inexperience we all feel at formal turning points in our lives. It had not been a shotgun marriage.

Why he should have misrepresented the case against Miff so vocally in the years to come is a complex matter. He certainly came to dislike the man in other respects, feeling he treated him like a schoolboy and it is not difficult to imagine this prim Scots Presbyterian in the guise of some male Jean Brodie figure, although Mary Kay described him in a letter as possessing an additional dash of Uriah Heep: 'I recall the ghastly meetings with Miff in darkened doorways where he would pay his fees in old pound notes. He used to beckon Tommy with the first finger of his right hand and expect him to come running. He even expected Tommy to come over to him at parties where, perhaps, he was having a chat with the Duke of Edinburgh. Miff really thought he was the original Svengali and nothing pleased Tommy more than to totally ignore him.' Ferrie may have been insensitive, even loathsome to the performing temperament – surprising since he had been a performer himself – and he may at times have been editorially wrong, but in business matters he appears never to have been ethically incorrect. Whatever Gwen may have thought in the early days, his fifteen per cent was a fair enhancement on an agent's typical return if management duties were involved as well, and in a realistic moment towards the end of her life even she had to concede that Miff was as straight as a die.

Two of Cooper's early conjuring friends, Alan Alan and Bobby Bernard share a theory that Tommy spread the rumour about his contractual plight as cover for his own innate parsimony. It also explains why he never challenged Miff in the law courts as Bruce Forsyth eventually did. To do so would have exposed the lie of his own behaviour. Bruce never claimed he had been held to a punitive and restricted wage, only that his arrangement tied him unfairly to Miff for life. In the end nothing was found against Ferrie and Bruce paid £20,000.00 for the privilege of extricating himself from his clutches. Tommy would have thought twice about such expenditure. But the agent situation had its lighter side. The whole idea of paying commission to anyone preyed both on his mind and on his sense of humour. Enjoying a meal with Tommy in the late Forties after a Magic Circle show at, of all places, the Chislehurst Cricket Club, Michael Bailey saw that he was separating the cherry stones around the edge of his dessert plate. 'What are those for?' queried the future president of The Magic Circle, pointing towards the few set aside from the others. 'Oh, those are for my agent!' was the unexpected reply. It would appear that everything was viewed through the commission prism, even matters of life and death: 'I've got a clause in my contract that says I have to be cremated. That way my agent can get fifteen per cent of my ashes.' It matters little that Groucho had done the line before him.

Initially dates were sporadic. The Coconut Grove, the Panama and the Blue Lagoon were regular haunts, in addition to the Windermere. The names sound glamorous, but today alongside countless similar venues that he would play in due course, like the Bagatelle, Churchill's, the Embassy, the Colony, the Astor, Quaglino's, Kempinski's, they represent for the most part a litany of shallow sophistication and B-movie glamour, a world of Max Factor make-up, Lucie Clayton poise and Freddie Mills machismo brought down to earth by Soho smog. In contrast, August 1948 saw Miff dispatching Tommy on a five week CSE tour of Europe at fifteen pounds a week. The signing of the contract between them was celebrated by a drop in pay. The week commencing 29 November saw him working his first fully fledged week in an English variety theatre, bottom of the bill at the old Collins' Music Hall on Islington Green for a basic salary of ten pounds. Gwen, Dennis Rawlins and his wife, Betty, dutifully acted as unofficial claque in the tiny suburban hall. Tommy needed theatre experience and 1949 saw Miff targeting the provinces as the next step in his client's climb to stardom. It must have been dispiriting trudging around the country for a year playing the infamous Number Twos for a year at twenty pounds a week. Variety was on its last legs and these would be the first to go. To a travelling performer provincial theatre is still a world of smelly, Spartan digs and cold, grimy dressing rooms in strange, ostensibly colourless places. Away from the more glamorous Stoll and Moss circuits, the despair descending over acts who until now had regarded the halls as a modest, but constant source of livelihood must have added to the shabbiness. Food rationing would not have helped.

Tommy admitted many times that in those early days some audiences did not fully realize that his magic was supposed to go wrong: 'I remember one dreadful week. Top of the bill was the singer, Steve Conway, and I was second spot on. I went all through my act and there was not a titter from the audience. Nobody made a sound except me. I was laughing on the out- side but crying on the inside. That happened every night. People said, "There's a big feller up on the stage and he should be working down the pit. Our little Charlie can do tricks better than him." It got so bad I couldn't go out in the daylight in case somebody who'd seen the show recognized me. Even my landlady turned against me. It really unnerved me.' This could have happened at the Workington Opera House, the Barrow Coliseum, the Tonypandy Empire, the Maesteg New or one of a score of other less than glittering palaces of entertainment. But however depressing the venue, the experience was to prove invaluable and he soon developed the resilience to cope.

In November 1952, he had graduated to the Moss Empires circuit and was playing the dreaded Glasgow Empire, feared throughout the business as the 'Comics' Graveyard'. They didn't care for him at the first house. By the second open warfare had been declared. With a nonchalance he could not have mustered three years earlier Tommy simply came down to the footlights and told them all to 'fuck off'. He went straight to the dressing room, packed his bags and caught the first train back to London. Next morning, Cissie Williams, the highly respected booker for the Moss circuit, made her routine call to the theatre to see how the acts had fared the night before. The manager was forced to tell her that Cooper had returned to London. 'What happened?' she asked. He gave her the gist of the situation but was too embarrassed to use the exact words. Cissie Williams insisted: 'He must have said something that upset them. He couldn't have just walked off.' The manager bit the bullet and told it to her straight. 'Great,' she replied, 'it's about time someone told those bastards to fuck off!' One can hear every comic she ever consigned to failure on that stage cheering Tommy in unison whenever that story is told.

It is arguable that the nightclubs of the metropolis were no less difficult, not least because of the additional challenge of having to keep oneself and one's audience awake at two o'clock in the morning. What passed as conventional stand up comedy was out of the question if one was going to grab the attention of the crowd above the clink of glasses, the chatter of waitresses, the come-on of high-class call girls. A heady brew of alcohol, sex, and violence hung in the air. It was a heavy drinking environment with many clubs encouraging the consumption of liquor by promoting what were known as 'bottle parties'. Customers were served whole bottles of spirits which had a gauge fitted on the side. At the end of the night this showed how much had been consumed and their bill was worked out accordingly. The same bottle could also be kept in reserve for a customer on a future evening. To forestall violence among a partly gangster clientele some clubs, notoriously the Blue Lagoon in Carnaby Street, insisted that the bouncers on the door remove all guns on the way in.

He possibly came closest to his 'Glasgow Empire' experience in nightclub terms when he was playing the Bag of Nails in Kingly Street. Happily in that company he was more wisely restrained. The venue had a reputation for harbouring the real hard men of London. Most of the audience would have had a police record, or were coming close to acquiring one. One night no sooner had he stepped on stage than the heavy mob started to pelt him with bread rolls. His fez became an instant target. He was scared out of his mind, but had to say something and came back with a weak, 'Stop that.' As he described the occasion, 'The place came over all strange. "Stop what?" shouted this geezer. I said, "Why, stop throwing all these bread rolls at me." "And why should I stop?" he shouted back. "Well, because I haven't got an ad lib for people throwing bread rolls at me."' The audience were immediately on his side. As he said, things were never quite so hard after that, but you were never completely home and dry.

One advantage of the smaller clubs was the intimacy they allowed the performer to develop with his or her audience. The great American comedienne, Fanny Brice once summed up her relationship with a supportive crowd as 'much like sensing the presence of a friend in the dark'. The truly great British performers of the day like Max Miller and Gracie Fields had learned how to achieve this rapport however large the venue. Gracie herself referred to it as weaving a silver thread between herself and her audience. In time Tommy would join their company, although strangely, even at the height of his fame, he always refused to play a cabaret date in the vast Great Room of the Grosvenor House. For the moment though, every date played, every audience mood judged, every joke timed brought him a step closer to his own distinctive style, his unique tempo and the confidence required to drive him to the top.

Doubling clubs was not unusual, the Colony and the Astor being a frequent combination. One night in the spring of 1948 on his way between the Blue Lagoon and the Panama he was stopped in Regent Street by a policeman suspicious of someone walking through the West End of London with a couple of suitcases at such an ungainly hour. When he asked what he had in the cases, Tommy told him, 'Magic!' The officer was not satisfied and demanded he open them there and then. Slowly the sparkling spoils of his conjuror's routine spilled out onto the pavement: 'When he saw all the vases and rings sparkling under the lights he was still suspicious. He thought I was a burglar who had just done a job. At that moment, another copper came along and he happened to be an amateur conjuror, so to prove I was the real thing he made me perform one of the tricks. There I was in the middle of Regent Street at half past midnight doing "Glass, bottle. Bottle, glass."' Meanwhile Max Bygraves, with whom he was sharing the cabaret that week, was covering for him like crazy back at the Panama. By the time he walked on to do his act he appeared even more flustered than usual. He walked off shattered, turned to his friend and said, 'Max, I've had a frustrating day. Let's get pissed!' According to Max, they did.

His apprenticeship took a special turn and the provincial trek a welcome break at the beginning of October 1949. His dream of a Windmill audition had been brought to reality by Miff and at the fifth attempt he joined the distinguished roll call of contemporaries who had jumped this hurdle ahead of him, including Jimmy Edwards, Harry Secombe, Alfred Marks, Michael Bentine, and Peter Sellers. Tommy stayed for six weeks at this legendary temple of static nudity in the seedy shadow of Eros, earning thirty pounds a week. Disreputable and innocent at once, the venue had a reputation as 'The Comic's Dunkirk'. No one pretended that the predominantly male audience came for the jokes; they came for the girls. Johnnie Gale, the theatre's resident stage director, recalled how nervous the comic conjuror was: 'Occasionally we wondered whether the nervousness was entirely genuine. One afternoon he dashed into the property room in a state of agitation, grabbed a pudding basin and put it on his head instead of a fez. Then he went to take his cue. The basin was whipped off him before he got very far, but the stage staff laughed – and that seemed to please him.'

In the first week he doubled with an appearance at The Magic Circle's annual Festival of Magic at the Scala Theatre in Charlotte Street, enabling him to boast for evermore that in one week he had performed as many as fifty-two shows. At this time the Windmill (six days a week) had a 'six shows a day' policy, so how this was achieved may be something only The Magic Circle (six nightly shows and two matinées) can explain. Maybe there were some late night cabarets that did not get recorded properly, in which case he would have been moonlighting as far as Miff was concerned. The canny Scot was scrupulous in ensuring that everything that earned the merest penny was entered in the books. This included another diversion at the end of the year when he found himself spending Christmas at Morecambe playing an Ugly Sister in *Cinderella*. The comedy bandleader, Syd Seymour played 'Buttons'; 'Ermyntrude and Tinkle' were played by Tommy and Cyril Andrews, of whom nothing seems to have been heard since; and specialities were provided by Syd's 'Madhatters', Cooke's Pony Revue, Suzie the Cow, and Tommy Cooper – presumably divest of drag for a seven minute turn. Three weeks in Morecambe were followed by single weeks in Stockton and Oldham. It was the last time he wore a frock for an extended period on stage and began a love-hate relationship with pantomime that would ironically have an effect on his television career, as we shall discover.

After the Christmas season Tommy returned to the hit and miss pattern of the London cabaret circuit. The value of both the Windmill and the Scala engagements is that they had given him a chance to be seen in a conventional theatre by conventional theatre managements. On 22 May 1950 he was given his first bona fide West End theatre engagement by the producer, Cecil Landeau. It was the heyday of what was known as intimate revue, a now seemingly dated combination of whimsical musical numbers and ever-so-gently satirical sketches, with the opportunity for an act by a key solo performer here or there. The Cambridge Theatre was perhaps a little too large for the true intimacy the format required, but Landeau had had some success there the previous year with his production, *Sauce Tartare*. It featured a rota of names that were only just the right side of fashion, like Ronald Frankau, Renée Houston and Claude Hulbert. For his new show, *Sauce Piquante* he adopted a fresher approach involving many of the rising young Turks of the comedy establishment, including Norman Wisdom, Bob Monkhouse, Harry Locke and Tommy. All four shared a tiny dressing room. Bob recalled the huge man, whose props crowded the room, always trying to find the space to put on his shirt. One night Tommy handed Bob a dark stick of Leichner make-up and said, 'Write "B – A – C – K" on my back. Bob complied and Tommy said, 'That should end the confusion!' He then put on his shirt and continued in the confidence that he now really did have one thing less to worry about. With this insight into his own private madness, Bob loved the man from that moment on. Norman's recollections are much more basic: 'His feet smelled like rotting fish! Whenever his shoes came off, I would swish a newspaper frantically around the dressing room and moan. "Phew – Tommy! Your feet!" "What's wrong with them?" he'd ask. "Cor, didn't anyone ever tell you about Lifebuoy soap?" "Well, at least they'll keep the mosquitoes away," he replied.'

The distinguishing feature of both Landeau shows is that they featured an ingénue from the chorus who would go on to achieve a stardom greater than all the comics combined. At no point did she appear on stage with Cooper, other than in the finale of the show, but her chic and his gaucheness would have made an irresistible combination. Her name was Audrey Hepburn. She was on fifteen pounds a week, Norman well on his way to being the highest paid attraction in British variety was on a hundred, and Tommy was on twenty-five. The show folded after seven weeks. Tommy had joined only halfway through the run to replace an act that had failed to make the grade. By the end Norman took a drop in salary to fifteen himself, but Miff made sure that Tommy made no sacrifices.

He also refused to take his eye off the ball presented by the main challenge on the horizon, television. The records show that Tommy owed his debut in the 1947 Christmas Eve variety show to Miff. If he ever had cause to be grateful to the Scot – not as yet his sole agent – it was for the opportunity this gave him to cock a snook at the audition panel that had sneered at him a few months before. A few spasmodic appearances followed in the early part of 1948. At twelve guineas a time a career in television alone was not going to keep the wolf from the door. A suggestion from Miff to pioneer producer, Richard Afton in September 1948 for Tommy to star in a show called *Ferrie-Go-Round* in which Tommy played the part of a 'screwy steward' on board 'a *ferry*boat or pleasure steamer' with guest acts as the passengers and Miff supplying the band proved a non-starter. There was no further interest from the medium until Afton gave him a spot in a music hall programme televised from the Poplar Civic Theatre on 13 May 1950. In August he broadcast from Alexandra Palace in a show called *Regency Room* for another pioneer, Michael Mills. In November Miff decided to take advantage of a relationship from his radio days. Ronnie Waldman had produced several shows featuring Miff and the Jackdauz in his early days as a radio producer, including *Airs and Disgraces*. In January 1950 he transferred from radio to a position as Senior Producer, Light Entertainment, having already achieved a genial presence on the screen himself in *Puzzle Corner* in 1948. By October 1950 he was already Acting Head of Light Entertainment, Television.

Miff wasted no time in writing to his old colleague recommending Tommy as one of several artists of possible interest. On 28 November Waldman was able to respond: 'As you have probably gathered, there was hardly any need to remind us of Tommy Cooper, since we have now booked him for our big show on 23 December.' He was referring to the gala opening of their new studios at Lime Grove. Tommy's inclusion may have been prompted by the query scrawled on a memo to Waldman from Cecil McGivern, the Controller of Programmes, dated 13 November: 'I understand that some of the governors have asked when they are going to see Tommy Cooper on television again!' In the context of his original audition this represented true vindication. Miff managed to negotiate a special fee of twenty guineas. The show aired at 8.45 in the evening and featured Tommy as support to Dolores Gray, on the back of her triumph in *Annie Get Your Gun*, star ventriloquist Peter Brough with Archie Andrews, veteran droll Jimmy James, and assorted acrobats and ladder balancers.

Miff quickly followed up the situation with a meeting in Waldman's office on 2 January. A letter dated 23 January 1951 suggests they were treating this extraordinary talent with caution. With his variety and cabaret bookings Tommy was available immediately only for Sunday shows. These carried an added prestige. Ronnie made clear that the BBC was concerned that it could do Cooper more harm than good by launching him into a show of his own at such a time. They did not want to risk his reputation by using him in the wrong way. He was too valuable for that. Eventually 1951 would provide Tommy with only two occasions to shine on the small screen. In February he appeared as a guest of the wise-cracking violin virtuoso, Vic Oliver and in September on a programme, the title of which left no one guessing: *For the Children – Variety*. However, by the end of the year the pendulum of interest had swung from wariness through indifference to enthusiasm. On 4 December Waldman wrote again to Miff stating unequivocally that the sooner he can let him know when Tommy Cooper is free for a series the better it will be for all concerned.

The shift was inevitably due to the change in Tommy's theatrical fortunes. In July 1950 he had filled in as a replacement for Michael Bentine as the top comedy attraction in the *Folies Bergère* revue at the London Hippodrome. As a result he found himself in the running for a place in the second edition of the show. When *Encore des Folies* opened on 6 March 1951 the critic from the *Daily Telegraph* considered that the ensemble lacked inspiration and gave evidence of under-rehearsal, but conceded that 'the best individual turn was provided by Tommy Cooper as a hopelessly incompetent magician. I have never before seen anybody do as little as Mr Cooper and yet be so terribly funny.'

A transcript of the patter for his spot survives, courtesy of the lingering practice of having to submit all spoken material for such a show to the Lord Chamberlain:

I would now like to show you fifteen hours of magic and by way of a change I shall do my first trick first. Now you've all seen that very famous trick of sawing a lady in half, so to heck with it. (Throws saw over shoulder) A red silk handkerchief. I will now produce a bowl of goldfish . . . what . . . no table? (Makes 'bowl' disappear under silk instead) Every magician carries a magic wand. *I can do anything you like with this wand. You could tell me what to do with it, and I could do it.* There is a white tip here and a white tip there. Now the reason for the white tips is to separate the ends from the centre . . . I get worse! The magic wand clings to my hand. It can't fall down . . . (Turns hand) . . . because I have my finger there. Wake up fellows, I'm on.

I'll do my encore while you're still here. There is the bottle and here is the glass. The bottle will now change places with the glass. The tubes are empty. I feel very tired tonight. Been breathing all day! Bush! Bush! (Gesticulates with hands) Doesn't mean anything, just looks good. Music, please. (A single note or two) That's enough. And the bottle has changed places with the glass. (Failure) My next trick. This is called the Demon Wonder Box and was given to me by a very famous Chinese magician called Hung One. His brother was Hung Too. Box open . . . box empty. I now produce a blue silk handkerchief. I mean red. *See the way I stand. Well, what if I am!* I place the handkerchief in the box; say the magic words 'Hocus Pocus, Fish Bones Choke Us.' That's my best joke. Okay! And the handkerchief disappears from the box and makes its way into my left pocket. Please don't applaud. Just throw cigarettes. Place the handkerchief in the pocket so and produce it from the box. Go home, fellows. I'll lock up. The red handkerchief will now change to blue. In this racket you have to be crazy, otherwise you go nuts.

Yes . . . we now come to the bottle and the glass again. Music please. That's enough. (Failure again) This is the egg and this is the bag. You all know what an egg is and you know what a bag is. I will now make the egg vanish. Now I will make the egg come back. A child of three could do this trick. Wish he was here now! Where is the egg? (Places bag on table and audience hear egg 'talk') My next trick. I have fifty-two cards here. I will now make sure there are

fifty-two. (Riffles edge of pack to ear) Sorry, fifty-three.
Would you please think of a card? (To gentleman in audience) Two of Clubs? Correct! (Tosses card aside without
showing face to front) I will now restore the two pieces of
rope into one piece. I'm a liar. I expect you are wondering
what this is. (Picks up and discards strange object) So am I.
I can't help laughing. I know what's coming next. Here is
the skull of the magician who gave me that trick. And here
is the skull of the same magician when he was a boy. (Brings
out miniature skull) Watch! Watch! (Produces large clock
behind cloth) And now the bottle will change places with
the glass. The bottle has changed places. (Exposes two
bottles and two glasses) Oh, to heck with it! (Exit)

For an encore he came back to produce the bunch of flowers
from the empty 'vase or vayse', flicking the switch on the plinth
to produce the bouquet when everyone least expected it. The
band played a chord and jubilantly Tommy declared, 'I wrote
that music myself!' In his own typed version of the above the
words I have put in italics have been crossed out. One presumes that he would sneak them in for a nightclub show or in
provincial variety when the man with the blue pencil was not
around. The camp reference is, of course, a straight steal from
Max Miller's act, where it never worried a soul. But innuendo
was never Tommy's forte and it is significant to see him – or
the Lord Chamberlain on his behalf – refining his style at this
early stage. There were also variations during the run. At a
later date he would produce a large skeleton of a fish in lieu
of the goldfish bowl that never came: 'I'll kill that cat!'

The bottle and glass subjected itself to much business, not
obvious from the basic outline. For one of the transpositions
he gained considerable mileage from the old spotlight gag,
walking to the other side of the stage with the beam following

him, running back in the dark to switch bottle and glass around, then returning to the spotlight which was now frantically looking for him. At a later date for the third stage he would shriek, 'The bottle has now changed places with the glass' without lifting the tubes, then continue, 'The most difficult part of the trick is to make them go back again.' He'd then go into lightning reveals beneath the tubes of bottle and glass, glass and bottle, bottle and glass, glass and bottle again, before disastrously showing two glasses at one time, then two bottles, then in quick succession leaving all four objects in view on the table and flinging the tubes aside. The speed for the finish was incredible, while the words on the page can give no impression of the overpowering presence and nervous energy that drove the act along. As *The Magic Circular*, the magazine of The Magic Circle, reported, 'The skill with which he ruined his act was amazing.' Val Andrews also makes the observation that at this early stage in his career when he was relatively unknown to audiences it was something of a surprise when his tricks began to misfire. When he became famous the comedy had to come from another direction: no sooner had he picked up a prop than he would then laugh in anticipation of the disaster that was almost inevitable.

The Hippodrome season signified that he was on his way to the big time and Miff was determined Tommy should not spoil things for himself. He wrote to Val Parnell, the Managing Director of Moss Empires which owned the venue, asking for permission to pop into the theatre from time to time to view his client's act, since 'it is necessary, in the interests of his career, that I view his stage performance from time to time.' He made it clear he was not asking for complimentary tickets. Parnell replied stating that it was not customary for agents to make frequent visits to view their clients, but that in the circumstances he would have no objection to Miff looking into the theatre occasionally. For the eight minute spot, which with laughs could never have played for less than ten, Tommy was billed as 'Almost a Magician!' his most familiar billing from the early part of his career. His first ventures into variety had been tagged 'Six Feet of Fun', followed, when Miff came on board, by 'Television's Mad Magician'. The new label paid homage to that surreal ragamuffin of the halls, Billy Bennett, whose 'Almost a Gentleman' had gone out of service upon his death in 1942. One wonders if Tommy was also aware of the early bill matter of the suavely sarcastic American radio comedian, Fred Allen at an earlier career phase when he was known as 'Freddy James – Almost a Juggler'.

He was not receiving a lavish wage. Bentine in the previous edition of the *Folies* had worked his way up to seventy-five pounds a week, but Tommy's forty pounds was enhanced by frequent cabaret work at venues that now included the Savoy, the Dorchester, and the Berkeley, for which he regularly received an additional salary of seventy-five pounds. More importantly the press began to take notice. The most important young critic in the country, Kenneth Tynan went out of his way to eulogize him in the *Evening Standard*, describing him as our best new clown: 'Cooper is the hulking, preposterous conjuror, who is always in a jelly of hysterics at the collapse of his own tricks. Convulsed by his own incompetence, holding his sides, he staggers helplessly from trick to trick; no man was ever less surprised by failure. Cooper, you see, has a distinct attitude towards life; a stoic attitude, a gurgling awareness of the futility of human effort. And this is what raises him above the crowd.' No wonder Ronnie Waldman had pulled his enthusiasm up a notch or two. Even if Tynan failed to register fully Tommy's inherent panic, acknowledge the look that cried 'Help, what am I going to do next?', a perceptive person reading between the lines of his appraisal would have spotted something of crucial importance, namely that Cooper was capable of being more than a just a novelty act guaranteed to enliven an otherwise dull bill. Like Howerd, like Wisdom, like Terry-Thomas he need not be shackled within the confines of being a turn.

At the end of the run in February 1952 Miff punctiliously wrote to Parnell thanking him for his courtesy and cooperation during the run of *Encore des Folies*. The letter gave him an opportunity to tell Parnell that Tommy would be starring in his own television series commencing 12 March. On 21 December 1951 Waldman had written to the BBC Television Booking Manager, expressing his desire to build a new show around Tommy, in which he would not only give his usual perform-ance of lunatic conjuring, but also act as compère and provide the central core of the production by reappearing all the way through. The water needed testing with Miff from a money standpoint, but Waldman admitted to his colleagues within the Corporation that he was prepared to go up to a weekly fee of eighty guineas for eight shows. Eventually Miff settled for sixty. Tommy and Gwen could feel pleased with them-selves. Immediately after the *Folies* they flew off to Barcelona for two weeks' holiday. Around this time they moved to their most desirable residence yet, a two-guineas a week basement flat in a stately red-brick mansion block, Waverley Mansions, in Kenton Street, not far from Russell Square. Tommy could also boast his first car, a new Vanguard Estate, which he later claimed was the best vehicle he ever owned, dismissing in turn the Triumph Renown, the Ford Estate and the Mercedes that saw him through to the end of his days. Most importantly the combination of a long theatre run and a television series enabled him to be back in town with his mates, not only the comics whose trials and tribulations he shared, but also the magicians with whom he felt most at home.

The most vivid picture of Tommy the person at this point in his life can be gained from his magical cronies. Living near Russell Square he was only a short walk from the premises of L. Davenport and Company at 25 New Oxford Street. Every Saturday morning this mystical emporium – advertised as 'Where the Tricks Come From' – became the unofficial rallying point for a small group of young aficionados. Regular attendees included Bobby Bernard, Val Andrews, Billy McComb, Alex Elmsley, Cy Endfield and Harry Devano. It was not unknown for Orson Welles to add his weight to the gathering if he was in town. Between them they represented a motley bunch of professionals and amateurs bound together by a common enthusiasm. When they had outstayed their welcome at the magic store, the caravan would repair to a nearby Lyons' Corner House for the rest of the afternoon.

According to Val, Tommy was always on the look out for the latest novelty in the pocket trick line and was quite unable to contain himself from the headstrong demonstration of his latest acquisition as soon as they were in the café. He often had no idea how the trick worked and the Nippies, the Lyons waitresses in their short trademark aprons, would gather around in hysterics as he tried to master the intricacies of this newly purchased miracle. He once took great pride in genuinely fooling Bobby with a new version of the trick in which a coin was secretly concealed beneath one of three small red cups. In the old version you had only to look for the secret hair attached to the penny to announce where it was. Bobby had no idea what Tommy was up to as time and again he discovered the hidden coin. Cooper would register his excitement with what became a characteristic gesture, clapping his hands together like flippers and saying, 'Dear, oh dear! Dear, oh dear!' Except that in those early days the words were expletive based, a trait he had to purge from his behaviour when he started to mix with the Delfonts and the Grades. But as Bobby says, 'We all knew what he was really saying!'

For all his success he never bought a tea or a coffee for anyone. He used to say, 'You get the teas, boy' – a clue to his Welsh ancestry – 'and I'll get the chairs.' If the place was crowded he gave you the impression he was doing you a favour. It was a ploy he had developed in crowded NAAFI canteens. Then once you had brought over the teas that *you* had bought, he would launch into a lecture on how scandalous the charges were, working out the number of cups of tea that you should be able to extract from a packet for less than a farthing a cup. When he really had been broke, word got around that he had been unable to pay his Magic Circle sub-scription. According to Gwen he walked out on stage at one Magic Circle show and said, 'You can all stop talking about me – it makes no difference.' He turned around and there was a rubber dagger sticking out of his back. The audience was in uproar. When he became better off than most of his colleagues, it suited him to keep his hands in his pockets. Jack Benny kept up the pretence of meanness as a key trait within his comic persona; Max Miller, who supposedly never bought a drink for anyone, was a humanitarian by contrast when it came to secret good deeds. Alas, Tommy's behaviour was a psychologi-cal kink in his make-up that had no bearing on his comic perspective whatsoever.

Bobby can become quite agitated about his old chum. Put bluntly the Cooper of those early years was 'a ruthless oppor-tunist – he'd never pay for anything if he could find a way of getting you to give it to him.' Or pay you what you wanted if he could find a way of getting it for less. He became the acknowledged expert at discovering he had left his wallet or chequebook at home. In this context the Bill Hall story is legendary. Hall was an eccentric double-bass player on the variety circuit in the act known as 'Hall, Norman and Ladd'. In his spare time he was quite a deft caricaturist and had developed a sideline of reproducing sketches of his fellow pros as postcards for publicity purposes. One day Val spotted him in Lyons' clutching a packet of postcards for Tommy. Bill told Andrews he was charging him three pounds for the service. Val was sceptical, but Hall assured him he knew how to go about things. Tommy arrived and quickly got to the point, 'Bill, I've been thinking about the three quid . . .' 'That's right,' interrupted Hall, 'unfortunately I gave you the wrong quote. I forgot to include the price of the special bromide paper they were printed on.' Tommy took out his wallet and three pounds were extracted with the speed of jet propulsion: 'No, a price is a price. You said three pounds. There it is!'

For Val the vagaries of such behaviour were offset by the sheer dedication he put into his work, the midnight oil he would spend practising: 'He worked harder at perfecting his act than any other performer I ever knew.' The latest pocket tricks aside, he was a shrewd judge of the material that best suited him. And he was always fun. As Val says, 'He had many good qualities and could be great company and was fun to be with. But I always felt that his obsession about the cost of things spoiled things for himself and others. I was sorry for anyone who had a business arrangement with him.' Tommy used to get through three 'Electric Decks' a week, specially gimmicked packs of cards that create a convincing illusion of the cards flowing from hand to hand like a waterfall, until you take the lower hand away and they are seen to be strung together on a length of elastic. Val made these for the magic shops where they sold for seven shillings and sixpence. One day he told Tommy he was prepared to give him a special deal, bypassing the retailer on the way: 'I'll give you three at a time, twelve and six for three, or better still six for a pound.'

He wouldn't play: 'It seemed like more, it sounded more, and he couldn't make the mental leap to see the bargain. So he missed out. Or thought I had some devious plan to cheat him which he could not fathom. There were times when he was not too bright.' To an extent his caution with money reflected the hard times of his past, but was carried through to an extreme that bordered on the paranoid. Such may be the psychological fallout of having money sewn into your clothes as a child. It is a character trait that we shall need to return to before this story is over, but first there are further triumphs on stage and on television to chart, as well as the whole question of where he acquired his professional material.

FIVE

Mad About Magic

With typical self-deprecating charm, the American magician and humorist, Jay Marshall once told of the time a small child came up to him and said, 'When I grow up, Mr Marshall, I want to be a magician too.' In his quiet, kindly way he looked at the child and explained, 'Well, you can't be both.' In that sense Tommy, like Jay, never grew up. There was a sense that his act was a constant attempt to recreate the world of his childhood. Certainly without the magic Tommy would have been a dull man. To enter the consciousness of Cooper one needs to understand implicitly the world of the magician to which he gained admittance the moment he received his first box of tricks and where he remained happy, content and intrigued for the rest of his days. Patrick Page, who served for a spell behind the counter of Davenport's magic shop, recalls how he was like a child transformed, glowing with joy as he surveyed shelf after shelf of the glittering prizes that were the traditional magician's tools of his trade. Equally diverting was the vast array of practical jokes that would have taken him back to those comic paper advertisements of his youth: pencils that won't write, cigarettes that won't light, matches that

103

won't strike, cigars that explode, teaspoons that leap into the air, and sugar cubes that won't dissolve. Most important of all was something not obviously visible, the promise – conveyed so brilliantly by H. G. Wells in his short story, 'The Magic Shop' – that somewhere within these dusty walls must be the latest miracle, the ultimate marvel that will stamp your reputation as the 'wizardest' wonder worker in the whole wide world.

Tommy's innocence was witnessed on one occasion by the actor Richard Briers. Cooper blew a stream of bubbles towards the audience and reached out to catch one in his hand. It did not burst. He had secretly palmed an imitation glass bubble in the hand and created the illusion of picking one out of the air: 'The look on his face that he had done something that every child would like to do but never could, was exactly the look of my daughter, who was then three years of age, when she was blowing bubbles all about the place.' It never occurred to Richard that Tommy might have been acting, but, if this had been the case, he could only have achieved the effect through his own inner reserve of childlike naivety. Leslie Press, the Punch and Judy man was once booked by Tommy to entertain at the birthday party of one of his children. Cocooned within his booth he was puzzled why the audience laughter was dwindling away as the show progressed. When he emerged he discovered why. All the kids had given up on Punch's shenanigans, with the exception of Tommy, beaming like a lighthouse, and – it should be added in fairness – fellow comedian, Dickie Henderson.

I shall never forget an afternoon spent in his company at Ken Brooke's Magic Place. In the Seventies this informal studio, on the second floor at 145 Wardour Street, was the Mecca for the elite of the magic world. With its cocktail bar, capacious sofas and plush carpeting, it was, for Cooper, home from home.

Ken Brooke was a brash but endearing purveyor of material to professionals, highly respected as probably the best demonstrator of magic there has ever been. At the time one of his best sellers was a streamlined method for tearing up and then restoring a complete newspaper, devised by the American magician, Gene Anderson and popularized on Broadway by the top magic star of the day, Doug Henning. There was no way Tommy was going to pass by the opportunity of learning how to perform this latest sensation. The preparations for the trick embraced something akin to an advanced course in origami and Boy Scout proficiency with scissors, paste and brush. That is before you even came to apply the dexterity necessary to put the effect into practice. On this occasion I entered the studio to discover a floor that resembled a cross between an explosion in a newsagent's and one in a glue factory. It was difficult to know who was teaching who, Ken's high-pitched Yorkshire tones vying with Tommy's agitated West Country burr, as the latter made this point, queried that. Even allowing for the fact that they were notorious sparring partners, my most important memory is that Tommy was quite simply having the time of his life, matched only by the pleasure with which he would go home to perform the trick for Gwen at their dining room table that evening.

When Mary Kay first asked him what his hobbies were, she never expected him to reply, 'Magic'. Golf, photography, or fast cars maybe, but not magic. 'It was like watching a child play with a toy,' adds Mary, qualifying her statement immediately with 'but a very clever child.' Her idea of relaxation was to head off into the country with a well-stocked hamper for a picnic in some secluded rural backwater, but Tommy had no such idea of bliss: 'For him, the perfect picnic would be a small table in the corner of a magic shop, heaped up with an *hors d'oeuvre* of new tricks and washed down with a magic potion of unheard-of-power.' Magic was with him at every waking moment. According to his wife he even practised card tricks on the lavatory. He probably had a pack of cards under his pillow as well. He used to say that he carried so many tricks and props around with him – far in excess of what he really needed for his standard act – that it resembled 'a bloody circus'. At one count there were seventeen bags and cases full of magic and tricks on tour with him. He made no excuses: 'That's why I always have two rooms in a hotel. I use the sitting room as the practice room. I love what I'm doing, so when I try something new and it goes well, that's a great tonic for me. It's what I'm most concerned about.'

There comes a moment when enthusiasm shifts to obsession, as Gwen and Mary found. But, while his brain may have been disconnected from reality if by that we mean politics, sport and the world at large, there is no evidence to show that Cooper ever allowed his passion to betray his professionalism. Bob Hayden, a respected semi-professional magician from Southampton, recalls spending an evening back stage with Tommy during the run of the 1957 London Palladium panto-mime, *Robinson Crusoe*, a production that entailed many more entrances and exits than a conventional variety show. He is still impressed by the way in which throughout the evening Cooper would switch on and off between the pro-fessional job on the one hand and his total preoccupation with coin twiddling and the minutiae of magical technique the next. The pocket trick *en vogue* was one called the Okito Box, a small metal container along pillbox lines in which a coin could be made to vanish and reappear at will. While Tommy was fixated on learning from Bob how much dexterity was required to accomplish this without loss of face, he also knew to the nth degree how many footsteps were required to walk from dressing room to stage, the split second scheduling of this exchange with co-star Arthur Askey, or that with David Whit-field. The incident provides a valuable insight not only into his love of magic, but also into a surprisingly well ordered mind. In his case the line between love and lunacy, so often a by-product of obsessive behaviour, was kept distinct.

The fascination of magic, of course, is wrapped up in the secrets of the craft, on a level with the exhilaration in the pursuit of knowledge that has driven scientists and explorers from ancient times. To that can be added the capacity to appear to be doing what is clearly impossible, providing not merely enjoyment for others, but a considerable feeling of personal one-upmanship in the process. But, as the Hayden encounter may intimate, the most fun magicians have is in the company of their fellow magicians. For one thing magicians love to fool each other. In addition to the magic shops and the magic clubs a magic convention attracting anything from between 100 to 3,000 predominantly amateur and semi-professional registrants is probably staged in the United King-dom on an almost weekly basis, in settings ranging from the magnificence of the Blackpool Opera House to the cosiness of the lowliest village hall. It always surprises lay people to learn that at an international level, there is a circuit on which it is possible for a magician to earn his livelihood through per-forming, lecturing and selling his merchandise to other magi-cians without encountering a member of the public. These occasions represent a strange hybrid world where the mysteri-ous mingles with the commonplace. If the public were to be admitted to anything but the performances of the classier acts the image of the genre would plummet considerably, but redeeming the whole atmosphere is an extraordinary bond of fraternity and friendship, only occasionally undermined by the feuding that will exist in any tightly knit community.

Tommy had a hilarious skit that he used to act out at parties, often enhanced by wearing a bowler hat to represent the man who came through the door. It went like this: 'Mind you, I could do without some of the visitors I get back stage. It's Monday night. Knock, knock. "Come in." "Good evening, Mr Cooper, I'm from the Doncaster Magicians' Club." "Oh yes?" "Yes, and I just want on behalf of the Doncaster Magicians' Club to wish you welcome." "Thank you very much." He'd go out and the next night, the Tuesday night, he'd come back. Knock on the door. "Come in." "Well, you remember me, Mr Cooper, from the Doncaster Magicians' Club. I was in to see the show again tonight. Great fun, Tom. The way you did that trick with the silk handkerchief. Wonderful!" And on like that. Same the following night, the Wednesday, but no knock this time. Straight through the door. "Great again, Tom. But you didn't have the handkerchief in tonight, did you Tom?" He's got his wife with him now too. Thursday night, again, the door opens. You've guessed it! "Hang on a minute, Tom. Here, Gladys, Jim, Pete, come here. I want you all to meet Tom." By the end of the week all his bleeding relatives are in here drinking my best whisky. It's not on, is it?' It was so funny that in June 1956 the comedian Digby Wolfe, who eventually went to America and became a writer for *Rowan and Martin's Laugh-In*, sought to recreate it for one of his own television shows. Needless to say Tommy did not grant permission. Had his name been attached to it, the airing would have lost him many friends within the brotherhood of magic. More importantly, he knew that as he toured the country, whatever the name of the provincial society, when it came back to the basics of the hobby they all shared, he was as bad as the worst of them.

He was totally accepted within this world. With one notorious exception, when an official attempted to refuse him entry to a major magic convention in Brighton in the mid-Seventies, his celebrity never stood in the way of the privacy he craved at such events. He never minded signing autographs, but for most of the time he was allowed to mingle in the crowd, sounding out items for his act among the 'Dealers' – the indispensable trade fair where you could buy anything from an 'Atomic Vase' to a 'Confabulation Wallet', from a 'Nudist Deck' to a 'Nemo Card Castle' – and genuinely appreciating the subtleties of the performers in the stage and 'close-up' shows, envying their inventive acumen and advanced manipulative skills as much as they revered his comedic gifts. And then at the end of the day, when he had a chance to share and show tricks among his peers in an informal setting over a drink or two or three, he came alive.

In the Cooper mind the landscape of central London was defined not merely by nightclubs, theatres and the memories of sentry duty. As the Forties became the Fifties Tommy would spend every minute at his disposal rattling around the loop of the magic supply houses like a ball bearing on a bagatelle board. In addition to Davenport's, there was Harry Stanley with his Unique Magic Studio in Wardour Street, Max Andrews in Archer Street, Oscar Oswald on Duke Street Hill and Jack Hughes a few stops along the Northern Line at Colindale, supplemented by the flagship magic departments within the larger stores like Hamleys, Gamages, and of course, Ellisdons. In due course Ron MacMillan would open his International Magic Studio near the top of Leather Lane, Alan Alan would be forever identified with his 'Magic Spot' in Southampton Row, and Ken Brooke would move into Wardour Street, by which time Harry Stanley had relocated via Frith Street to Brewer Street. They were not all glamorous abodes. Tommy kept up a perpetual trek up dingy flights of stairs and along drab corridors, but as his reputation grew the men who purveyed the magic became all the more pleased to see him, knowing that the inclusion of one of their items in his act could well result in increased sales, not least with television exposure. In the Sixties Tommy often dragged his friend, Eric Sykes along with him on these expeditions. As Eric has pointed out, they were so pleased to give him the latest novelty on their shelves that money seldom changed hands.

The most influential of these dealers was Harry Stanley. A sometime musician with the Jack Hylton band, he and Miff Ferrie shared a common ground that made him especially interested in the young entertainer's progress. It was never Harry's mission merely to sell the artefacts of the magician's act. As an entrepreneur in his own right he promoted the craft in the eyes of the general public through West End shows and his involvement in the pioneering days of Commercial Television. More than any other individual, Stanley, through his publications and ability to spot a trend, shaped the British magical culture of the Fifties. One Sunday a month he would stage a small, intimate magic convention for magicians and their families at the Conway Hall in Red Lion Square, an event readily accepted by Cooper in his formative years as a platform upon which to try out new material without embarrassment. Harry certainly spotted the Cooper potential and was happy to spread the name by using Tommy's endorsement of several of his lines in his early catalogues, the pages of which proclaim 'Tommy Cooper enjoys using the Unique New Comedy Clock' and *à propos* of 'Playing Cards' (a small harmonica concealed in a dummy pack of cards), 'I sold the first one to Tommy Cooper and he has had plenty of fun using it.'

In time Tommy also struck up a rapport with Edwin Hooper. Known throughout the trade simply as 'Edwin the Magician', he kept a magic supply house in the unlikely venue of Bideford on the north coast of Devon. In a relatively short time this small time children's entertainer built his business,

'The Supreme Magic Company', into the largest postal service for magicians in the world. No sooner had Tommy received the latest Supreme catalogue or sales sheet than he would phone Edwin, usually with the instruction, 'Send one of each.' Hooper would then point out to Cooper that he had already purchased some of these items and that besides some of them would not suit his form of presentation. He used to reply: 'Never mind. Send them anyway. I'm just a big kid and it's like Christmas when I receive your parcels!' On one occasion Edwin even put pen to paper to spell out his dilemma: 'You ask us to send the "Three Stroke Ball Production" – two sets. We are *not* sending these until we have your confirmation to do so . . . this is not an easy trick to do . . . so I thought we had better warn you first.' However fair or unfair his assessment of Tommy's digital skill, perhaps he had visions of his famous customer ruining the trick before the gaze of millions on live television and curtailing the prospect of further sales in the process. Edwin need not have worried. Tommy's acquisitive tendencies never clouded his editorial judgement in knowing what was right for his act. The majority of his purchases were never performed in public, which not surprisingly – and perhaps mercifully – is the fate of most magic traded by catalogue, over the counter or, today, by means of the internet.

Cooper had an unerring instinct for the material that would suit him best. Into this category came the many variations of the so-called sucker trick, that genre in the magician's repertoire that allowed him to tease our expectations like a monkey on a stick, only to reveal at the finish that we were no nearer the true explanation. For example, over many years he taught audiences how to change the colour of a green handkerchief to red by concealing a red one secretly in the hand beforehand. When you pushed in the green, the red one emerged. Then when he opened his hand, the green handkerchief, contrary to all expectation, had disappeared. In an item like this digital skill and the comic situation combined to make a whole that was greater than the sum of the parts. Otherwise Tommy was true to his Magic Circle code and remained firmly against exposure, conceding in his defence that the secret of the bottle and glass trick that he did give away had been disclosed by clowns for years. So called secret threads being pulled obviously from the wings fell into the same category. Otherwise, as he claimed to magical supplier, Derek Lever towards the end of his life, 'I would never buy a trick from a dealer and then expose it because I know I am ruining that man's living. I am against exposure.'

Orson Welles, speaking from a more artistic point of view, once described a magic trick exposed as being 'as publicly attractive as an unmade bed'. Of course more magical secrets have been divulged through bad performance than in any other way, so in one respect Tommy, while anxious to stay on the side of the magic fraternity, could be said to have been acting against the grain of the burlesque ideal in adopting this attitude. On one occasion there was a hiccough in his relationship with Edwin Hooper when he revealed the working of a vanishing clock trick on one of his television shows. In the form sold by 'Supreme Magic' it was a lousy trick, something that probably attracted Tommy to it in the first place – clocks just do not resemble wooden cubes like dice with a two-dimensional face stuck on the front – but he conceded the error of his ways, agreed that the 'accident' should have been edited out of the show, and never made the same mistake again.

So many 'Unique' and 'Supreme' items found their way into the Cooper act that one might have been forgiven for thinking Tommy had shares in both businesses. He didn't. Instead, he set up his own magic shop. The enterprise would appear to have been a meeting point for his own fantasies and the need to find something practical for Gwen to do. Premises, if that is what they could be called, were found in Shaftesbury Avenue: those who recall going there in the Sixties remember the shop as little wider than a corridor with a counter across and the only exit through the front door. 'Magic and Fun Shop' went up on the fascia and Alan Alan, yet to establish his own shop, was installed as manager, with Gwen looking after the business side behind the scenes. It never had serious pretensions to be anything but an outlet for selling jokes, masks, novelties and simple tricks to the public, but it did well. Gwen once confided in me that it was nothing for her to drive up on a Saturday afternoon and be handed five hundred pounds in readies for the week's takings, and that was after Alan had taken his share. She consulted Miff whether they should put Tommy's name above the shop. Miff demurred and she agreed, the venture being considered not prestigious enough at a time in his career when his star was rising high. That conversation in November 1961 ended with her expressing admiration for Eamonn Andrews and his involvement in Commercial Television in Ireland. Miff reported, 'She would like to get some shares!' In contrast, the shop appears to have been the only business opportunity in which Tommy became involved during his whole career. In time interest waned and Alan, who also happened to be the world's top escape artist, moved on to other career opportunities.

Tommy's personal popularity was sublime and magicians readily conceded their best bits to him – a form of 'I surrender' in the face of his prodigious talent. One such was Peter Newcombe, an insurance executive by day and sometime secretary of The Magic Circle, whose own act acted as the slipway for some of Tommy's best. Magicians in the know always acknowledged Peter as Cooper set light to the 'flash' paper in the chromium prop known as the dove pan: 'Just a flash in the pan!' Or when he produced three coins and dropped them into a can, 'One, two, three,' at which point a jet of water squirted upwards and Cooper said with similar matter of fact-ness, 'Three Coins in the Fountain!' Ian Adair, a prolific ideas man and second lieutenant to Edwin Hooper at 'Supreme' in Bideford, kept Tommy supplied with a veritable stream of gags including 'I've had a pain here all day', 'Bagpipes', and 'Light Ale', words that only become funny when accompanied by Tommy taking a pane of glass from inside his jacket, throwing two pipes into a paper bag and causing the glass of beer in his hand to illuminate from inside. The current Magic Circle president, Alan Shaxon recalls the occasion at headquarters when member Len Blease demonstrated an effect in which his underpants ended up secured to a length of rope. The evening concluded with a session in the Gents with Len, Alan, and several others rigging up Tommy, his trousers round his ankles, for this extraordinary feat of topology. Len's diminu-tive stature up against the Goliath Cooper only underlined the missed opportunity for a television sketch that should have materialized but never did.

His obsession fed his persistence if he saw a piece of business he had to have. In the early Seventies, Paul Daniels was appear-ing as a supporting act to Michael Bentine in Jersey. Tommy came to see his old friend from the Windmill days and in the process caught the Daniels act, a highlight of which featured a cardboard puppet frog that found cards chosen by the audi-ence. Come the early hours of the following morning Tommy was still in Paul's dressing room begging him to let him have the frog. The more Paul explained that it represented a good eight minutes in his act and couldn't be replaced, the more Tommy kept at him: 'Go on, give me the frog.' Finally he said, 'I tell you what. I'll tell you a good joke.' He did more than a joke. He walked out on to the empty stage and did a routine about a conjuror and his assistant in which he played both the parts, the magician constantly admonishing the girl, 'Not yet, not yet.' Paul was reduced to hysterics as Tommy rushed back and forth across the stage acting out this charade. He then walked back to his seat, sat down and said 'Now, give me the frog.' Paul, privileged to have been an audience of one at a special showing of a routine Tommy does not appear to have performed at any other time, gave him the frog.

It is no surprise that holidays were also focused on magic. Wherever he went in the world he would be drawn like a magnet to the nearest magic shop. There was the infamous occasion when the Coopers had no sooner arrived at their Manhattan hotel than Tommy went in search of his favourite New York magic emporium. By the time the session ended he had forgotten the name of the hotel and after several hours of tramping the streets of the Big Apple finally had to phone home to their housekeeper, Sheila to find out where he was staying. He arrived back in the room as though nothing had happened, with Gwen considerably agitated. It was 1980 and he had not long been out of hospital. Las Vegas with its overriding air of make-believe was his favourite destination. Even before it became the unofficial capital of stage magic on the back of the success of master resident illusionists, Siegfried and Roy, its surreal environs offered magic stores and demonstrations of close quarter wizardry galore. Gwen was content to stay by the pool.

His closest friend in America was the brilliant prestidigitator, the 'Amusing and Confusing' Johnny Paul. A pioneer of the interest in close-up magic from the time he performed regularly behind the bar of his Magic Lounge in his native Chicago, he moved in the Fifties to Las Vegas as the Entertainments Director of the Showboat Hotel and Casino, in which capacity he was also expected to perform for the patrons. In the artificial atmosphere of the neon neo-polis his presence proved as genuine and as engaging as the sunset over the Nevada Mountains. In many ways he could have been Tommy's secret American sibling. A big burly man with large floppy hands, only the spectacles stood in the way of instant comparison. One of his standard lines was 'Don't applaud. Keep drinking. The more you drink, the better I get.' In interviews Tommy used to use a line that may well have been personalized from the original: 'I never drink before a show. If I did, my tricks might start to go right.' Paul's carnival sense of humour was exactly on Tommy's wavelength, although he did not set out to burlesque magic, merely to cloak conventional magical mysteries in the funniest dressing possible. To this he brought a sheer technical brilliance that was awe-inspiring, the envy of Tommy and all his fellow professionals. When Johnny came into London, as he frequently did, to make an appearance on British television, he would invariably end up at the Cooper abode in Chiswick for a late night session. One of his signature tricks was the effect in which a signed and chosen card finds itself pinned to the wall or ceiling when thrown into the air. Tommy managed to get his guest to show him the basic workings of the miracle. His daughter, Vicky recalls the aftermath: 'I remember Dad was really jealous about this trick. He spent the whole day practising and when I came home from school he produced a pack of cards and said "Pick one." I did and he threw them against the wall. They *all* fell down. We looked at each other and just started to laugh hysterically.'

When members of the public discover you knew Tommy Cooper, the one question they always ask relates to his magical ability: 'Was he any good as a magician?' It is not an easy question to answer for a layman. His technical competence –

if by that we mean manipulative skill – certainly lagged behind the likes of Johnny Paul and could probably be placed on a par with Woody Allen's self-assessment when it comes to playing jazz clarinet: 'no more seriously than a Hollywood star hacking at a golf ball in a pro-am match'. However, there is no doubt that he was far more committed to the skills of his craft than most members of the 'buy it off the shelf' brigade. The come-on lines used by dealers to sell their wares in the catalogues reveal how essentially lazy the average conjuror is – 'No Sleights . . . Easy To Do . . . Ready To Work Right Away!' – although what satisfaction could accrue in such a situation is probably more baffling than the trick on offer could ever hope to be. Because a routine did require serious practice did not rule it out of the Cooper repertoire. In the Sixties Harry Stanley brought out an item called 'The Indiana Rope Trick'. It enabled the magician to tie a knot in a length of rope under impossible conditions and then to slide the knot along the rope and off the end to throw it into the audience. Without giving too much away it involved considerable dexterity to get the knot to appear in the first place and then a deft handling of a complex little gadget named a 'locking finger reel' to send it on its way into the crowd. From the catalogue pages it looked just the kind of trick that dealers like to sell to amateurs, a fleeting novelty to be played with until another little miracle comes along. No one would ever have imagined it as an item in a top professional act, not least because there were almost certainly other simpler, more practical methods with which to achieve a similar effect. And yet within a few weeks of the trick being advertised Tommy Cooper was performing it with total assurance on the *Sunday Night at the London Palladium* television show.

But there is another level at which quite simply Tommy may be seen to be the greatest magician of them all. As top contemporary British wizard, Geoffrey Durham has pointed out, if the *sine qua non* of being a magician is the ability to express your personality through your magic, then no one expressed himself better through the medium than Tommy Cooper. There was no one to touch him because there was no one who had a personality more all-conquering than Cooper, no one who radiated until the end of his days a greater personal sense of wonder or of fun, as tissue papers changed into flowers in his hands, a wooden duck attempted to find a chosen card – 'You may have seen a duck do that before,' he would screech, 'but, to be fair, blindfolded?' – and, in later years, bottles of Martini reproduced like rabbits as an unexpected conclusion to the bottle and glass trick. No one left a Tommy Cooper performance not liking magic: his enthusiasm was contagious. When you establish communication with an audience as the criterion of greatness, matters of technical difficulty take on a different aspect. It no longer matters whether the trick has just been bought off the shelf, because in the hands of a great performer the presentation wrapped around it renders any hint of method irrelevant anyhow. Tommy himself once said, 'You can buy a simple trick from a magic shop and you can know how it's done. Yet a great magician can work on that particular trick and make something out of it and you'll think it's not the same trick you've got.' Tommy proved this every night of his working life when he made a small silk handkerchief disappear in his bare hands using the most elementary of methods that has been exposed to the public thousands of times; but always the audience burst into wild applause.

During the Thirties, Murray the Escapologist was a headline act throughout the world. He used to tell an anecdote about a special escape he performed on board ship in Cape Town with George Bernard Shaw on hand as a member of the super-

ABOVE: Tommy's parents, Thomas and Gertrude Cooper, circa 1920s.

ABOVE RIGHT: Three years old and ready for play.

Eighteen years old and
ready for the world.

Enjoying a bottle and a glass off duty in Egypt in 1947.

Gwen (far left), star of her wartime concert party.

Tommy and Gwen, just prior to their wedding in Cyprus, 1947.

The early publicity pose
that defined an image.

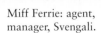

Miff Ferrie: agent,
manager, Svengali.

Later publicity pose when
success was assured.

Baby Vicky seems unimpressed (above) and with baby Thomas (below)
in the garden at Chiswick.

'Frankie and Bruce *and Tommy's* Christmas Show', 1966.

'Do you like football?'

'Bucket, sand! Sand, bucket!'

Time to relax with
the famous feet up
at home.

A sensation on the
Ed Sullivan Show,
New York, 1967.

'When autumn leaves
start to fall…'

'And ven zey are caught
everyone vill be shot…'

Funny bones: with
Anita Harris,
promoting
Tommy's Palladium
show, 1971.

A rare private
moment backstage.

visory committee to see fair play. When interviewed by reporters later, Shaw said, 'I found the man more interesting than the trick.' That is how it should be. Writing from the perspective of another performing discipline, the dancer Mikhail Baryshnikov summed up matters thus: 'When a dancer comes on stage, he is not just a blank slate that the choreographer has written on. Behind him he has all the decisions he has made in life . . . Each time he has chosen, and in what he is onstage you see the result of those choices. You are looking at the person he is, the person who, at this point, he cannot help but be . . . Exceptional dancers, in my experience, are also exceptional people, with an attitude toward life, a kind of quest, and an internal quality.' The same is true for all the legendary magicians in magic's history, the roll call that includes Houdini, Cardini, Dante, John Calvert, Robert Harbin, Channing Pollock, Siegfried and Roy, and Tommy Cooper.

One further quality that registered him as a great magician was his intuitive understanding of the great psychological block that holds so many magicians back from genuine personal popularity. It has been bluntly labelled the 'showing off' syndrome and unless mitigated by the personality of the performer can have an excluding effect on audiences. The original premise of conjuring is to defy the laws of nature and to do so in such a way that no one knows how you achieve the task. If a magician can find a way of letting his audience in on his act without of course divulging his methods, then a bridge is secured that might allay the worst excesses of the syndrome. No one surmounted this hurdle more effectively than the great Thirties manipulator, Cardini, who presented his sleight of hand with cards, billiard balls and cigarettes in an apparently slightly tipsy haze, as if these impossible phenomena were happening *to* him, entirely outside of his control, rather than the result of his incredible technique. In a similar way, by adding comedy to their juggling acts, first W. C. Fields and then 'Monsewer' Eddie Gray of the Crazy Gang found that audiences warmed to them as characters in addition to marvelling at their dexterity. When Tommy succeeded with his magic, it was as much a surprise to him as to his audience, who subsequently shared in his delight. He brilliantly developed an attitude that enabled him to connect with the public through hocus pocus without ever seeming to challenge them with it, to force it upon them, the habitual curse of so many of the magic profession. When he failed to join the metal rings and then found one inextricably linked through his buttonhole or when he discovered that the goldfish bowl he had produced from a metal tube would not go back inside the same tube – until in a sublime moment of inspiration he squeezed it between his hands – he took things one step further, entering a truly magical universe that was beyond anyone's control.

His friends retain their cherished memories of intimate sessions when he would perform tricks purely for their own amusement. At times like these he was allowed to show off, but his congenial nature always steered well away from conceit. Eric Sykes was once taken aback when Tommy caused a facsimile of the chosen card that had just appeared on his forehead to replicate itself in the same position in the minuscule photograph embodied in the Cooper identity card that had been under Eric's supervision since the start of the trick. Johnny Speight recalled the occasion he caused a shoal of little silver fish – albeit imitation ones – to materialize in his hands: 'These fish piled up on the bloody bar and I was that close to him and I couldn't see how he did it. It looked like real magic to me.' According to Alan Alan, there was one trick that technically Tommy performed better than anyone else. It is known in the magic business as 'Squash', a descriptive term for an effect in which a shot glass of whiskey held on the magician's outstretched palm instantly vanishes when covered by the other hand. For once Tommy's extra large hands proved an asset rather than a disadvantage. Another favourite party piece, often paraded at press interviews, was to cause a mark of ash from his cigar to appear inexplicably in the clenched fist of a journalist. But he was never less than honest with himself, as he admitted to a writer from the Sunday Express in 1981: 'Childish, isn't it? But I love it. I only wish I was better than I am. Mind you, who knows, if I were better, I might have become just one more struggling magician and you wouldn't be sitting here wanting to talk to me now.'

In his own eyes one of the high points of his career in magic was the day he was appointed to Membership of the Inner Magic Circle at its highest level with Gold Star. He also joked, 'As a matter of fact, I belong to the Secret Six. It's so secret; I don't even know the other five!' There is no doubting the prestige of the larger organization that in 2005 celebrated its centenary year with a Royal Mail special stamp issue and the endorsement by its most famous member, the Prince of Wales, of a unique four day celebration attended by the international elite of the magic world. But while many of the world's top professional magicians are members, it is not – as it is perceived by so many – an organization of professional qualification. Its membership, hovering around the 1,500 mark, consists predominantly of devoted amateur and semi-professional performers, who down the years have included Orson Welles, J. B. Priestley, Rudyard Kipling, and Lord Mountbatten.

Upon his promotion, Tommy wrote to John Salisse, the secretary at the time: 'As a young magician I dreamed of this, but never thought I would ever possess this great honour.' The organization is in many ways its own magic trick, embodying a paradox whereby the most successful magical performer in British history – and other prestige magic names like Cardini, Pollock, and Siegfried and Roy – should be so much in thrall to it. But top professional that he was, of its entire membership Tommy possibly best embodied the elements of amateurism – in its original and best sense of the word – that first fired its founding fathers a century ago. There was one other level at which he might be considered on a higher plane than the average rank and file of the society or, for that matter, any of the smaller provincial magicians' groups around the country, some of them designated as 'Circles' but with no legitimate affiliation to the top organization. To master sleight of hand and the mechanics of misdirection is one thing. Comedy is a far more elusive skill. It certainly cannot be bought over a shop counter, being the product of inclination, instinct and alchemy. Here, among his magical peers, Cooper was unquestionably king.

It is proper that the worlds of comedy and magic should share a special relationship. The mechanism of a joke and that of a magic trick have a decided kinship, with their mutual reliance on timing and surprise. Moreover, both comedy and magic play tricks with our perception of the world, one favouring the quirky representation of reality and the other turning that reality on its head. We accept gravity as a fact and when the clown accidentally turns the milk bottle upside down, the milk slops all over his shoes to our amusement; when the magician turns the milk bottle upside down, the milk stays in the bottle to our amazement, or it is supposed to. Both need an essential element of surprise to be fully effective. In the clown's case it is all the funnier if we do not see the action coming; in the magician's case we suspend disbelief but are still pleasurably taken aback when the impossible happens. Such reactions may become dulled with repetition but the skill of the performer can instil an essential freshness to maintain our interest and recreate the original sense of wonder. When the magician and the clown become one, an exceptional double whammy occurs, the milk its own testament to both the basic reality and the failed aspirations that attempted to subvert it. The special relationship, however, is not dependent on the burlesque approach. Conjuring has proved a convenient peg for many a comedy talent over the years, not least Johnny Paul himself. One has only to note the number of comedians, most notably in America, who began their performing careers as magicians, including Johnny Carson, Woody Allen, and Steve Martin, or those who maintained an interest in magic long after their comedy reputations were established, like Cary Grant, George Burns, Milton Berle, and Steve Allen. In England, Bud Flanagan and Peter Cook provide an unlikely pair with boyhood magical roots.

The first 'name' comedy magician was possibly the German–American Imro Fox, who became successful in vaudeville and in British pantomime as Abanazar around the beginning of the last century. A rotund man with a bald head and a handle-bar moustache, he mined an especially rich vein of self-deprecation: 'Yes, I'm a magician like the programme says. If you hadn't been looking in the programme, I know you would have taken me for a delicatessen proprietor. That's only my sideline. Wait and see . . .' He would trip over his feet as he walked on stage, glancing over his shoulder to admonish the imaginary culprit, 'Don't push!' Many years later Tommy would cut just such a trip out of his act, when some audiences began to credit the stumble to alcoholic influence rather than carefully rehearsed technique. Much of Fox's humour came from the running instructions he gave the orchestra leader as the act progressed: 'Waltz me, Professor. A little slow music. No, that is not what I want. I do not wish villain music. I want something soothing.' And then as a trick reached its climax: 'Now, professor, waltz me again.' Selling his personality – 'I have no hair to deceive you with' – was far more important than any of the tricks.

The first burlesque magician is harder to pin down. Frank Van Hoven – encountered earlier in this volume as 'The Man Who Made Ice Famous' – was the first to achieve anything like a star reputation with the genre, but there were others who merged wand with slapstick during the early years of the century. At this time Walton and Lester were billing themselves on the British music halls as 'the World's Worst Wizards'; Wally Walton then progressed to performing as a single in the Twenties, the same decade in which Lapp and Habel found themselves amusing audiences with their own travesty of the dancing spoon in the jar, long before Tommy was intoning 'Spoon, jar. Jar, spoon,' in his own act. Nor should it be overlooked that the magic act that self-destructs had been a staple of the circus clown's repertoire long before music hall welcomed magicians onto its stage, the fragility of eggs, the waywardness of livestock and the exposure of the 'Passe Passe' bottle and glass trick so cosily at home in this environment.

The only native performer on the halls to rival Van Hoven's success with comedy magic was Carlton. Billed as 'The Human Hairpin' he presented an eccentric appearance dressed in skin-clinging black bodice and tights, his already tall, thin stature elongated by the addition of a high-domed bald wig and elevators in his shoes, raising his height to almost seven feet. It is not inconceivable that Max Wall derived the ludicrous black tights of his own garb as the grotesque pianist, Professor Walloffski from watching Carlton. While, like Cooper, he was intrinsically funny in his appearance, his approach to magic was more subtle. As he performed his intricate card manipulations, he carried out a disembodied commentary on his own actions: 'Is there no limit to the man's cleverness?' A favourite exchange eavesdropped on a mother and child in the front stalls: 'Oh, Mummy, I know how it's done – I can see the wires.' 'Quiet, dear. Those are not wires – they are his legs!' 'Where's he gone to now, Mummy? He's disappeared.' 'Hush, my dear. He's only turning sideways.'

In the teen years of the century Van Hoven and Carlton were two of the highest paid performers on the British music halls, their salaries far surpassing those of the average magic act and rivalling those Cooper would one day achieve on the Northern club circuit, maybe even surpassing them in real money terms. It was nothing for Carlton to earn five hundred pounds a week. He was once featured in five top London music halls simultaneously. Towards the end of the decade Van Hoven could boast of earning one hundred thousand dollars in one hundred and ten weeks. In time Carlton put on weight and fell on hard times. Van Hoven died prematurely of pneumonia at the age of forty-two in 1929, his latter years beset by alcohol and womanizing. He predeceased Carlton by thirteen years. He was his only rival, although their approaches to comedy magic came from different directions. Cooper brilliantly straddled the two styles, tricks refusing to work one moment, and others succeeding beyond his wildest expectations the next. Contemporary magician, Ian Saville feels that this ambivalence within his act contributed greatly to his popularity: 'Lay people feel that if he really wasn't all that good, they have somehow been fooled (in a bad way) by being made to laugh at him messing things up. They feel easier laughing at someone acting incompetent rather than at someone who really might be incompetent.'

Cooper's impact for a new generation was such that when you tell his fans that he was not the first comic conjuror they are surprised. However, Van Hoven and Carlton aside, no one had attacked the role with such charisma and spontaneous *joie de vivre*. As the Second World War came to a close there were, in fact, others who had a head start on him on the British variety circuits. Claude Williams, billed as 'The Great Claude', made great play of the medal gag, awarding himself a gong if his tricks worked, and at one opportune moment in his act throwing a bouquet over his shoulder as he went to the table for his next prop. Turning, he expressed surprise at the generosity of the crowd. Fans will recognize the business as resurfacing eventually in the Cooper act. When Tommy turned to the audience and queried, 'For Me?' no one ever acted sheer self-deception for greater comic effect. Williams also performed a version of the bottle and glass trick using one tube and a rolled-up newspaper.

Donald B. Stuart, billed as 'Variety's Longest Laugh', appeared seven feet tall even without a high-domed wig. His elongated top hat made him seem even taller as he made great play of stepping over especially low tables to reach the other side of the stage. He would hang his hat on the edge of the proscenium arch and later ask someone from the audience to take it down while he proceeded with the act. What had been no height at all for Stuart was way out of reach for the spectator and produced a hilarious audience response. He too featured a version of the bottle and glass trick. Whereas Stuart was dry and debonair, Arthur Dowler, 'the Wizard of Cod,' was more down-to-earth. The magical equivalent of a sturdy Northern comic in the mould of Les Dawson or Robb Wilton, he fumbled and flatfooted his way in baggy suit and bowler hat from the prosaic to the surprising, all the while going back to attend to a birdcage that wouldn't vanish, until an alarm clock went off at the end of his act and released him from the responsibility. To the best of my knowledge he didn't perform the bottle and glass trick, but the bit where he threw three linked metal rings off stage, only to have them thrown back still linked but twisted out of all recognition a short while later eventually found its way into Cooper's act, as did – upon his death in 1953 – his comic *pièce de résistance*, the table that revealed two shapely female legs when its front legs fell off.

The doyen of British variety magicians, Mark Raffles has fond memories of Chris King, a Cockney who following an apprenticeship in America may have been the first in Britain to produce the bowl of goldfish under the large scarf and then make it 'disappear' for lack of a table to put it on. King's billing – 'You take two pieces of paper' – referred to the catchphrase that gathered comic momentum throughout his act as he unsuccessfully attempted to restore two torn pieces of tissue back together again. Mark recalls, 'Then looking puzzled, he turned them round and about as though unsure what to do next, giving the impression of having forgotten the trick. He then put the pieces back on his table and carried on with the next item. When he finally restored the papers, they changed into a party hat and he went off to a storm of applause.' Mark is convinced that Tommy must have seen King work at a formative stage: 'He had a totally different style and appearance, but the way he'd put down one trick that wouldn't work, go back to the papers, then back to start again with yet another prop, I can see how Tommy applied all that to his own personality.'

To peruse the trade papers during the late Forties there is nothing to suggest that Cooper was then either better or worse than any of these acts. They were all modestly successful, but at the end of the day they remained supporting attractions, representing an engaging sub-genre of the magic profession. Within a few years, in a career festooned by royal perform-ances and star billing, Tommy would take the genre to heights achieved not even by Carlton or Van Hoven. In terms of stature as a comedy conjuror, the only serious competition he ever had was on the international scene. Bob Monkhouse once asked Tommy if he had seen the act of Russell Swann, a top American entertainer, who, like Cooper, combined the burlesque approach with a capacity to succeed some of the time. The answer was negative: the prominent seasons Swann played at the Victoria Palace, the Trocadero Restaurant and the Dorchester Hotel in London in the Thirties would have been outside his social sphere as a boatyard apprentice. A genial man with a large moon face, Swann played the best cabaret venues throughout the world for three decades with a hilarious act in which, with hotel towel for turban, he turned purple as he blew a flute to coax a toy snake out of a basket to find a not-so-freely-chosen card, as well as walking off half way through to grab a bag of tools with which to mend a vanishing flower pot that refused to function. However, if Tommy did not see Swann he did see Carl Ballantine, arguably the nearest equivalent to Cooper in the United States in recent times.

People in the magic world who wish to detract from Cooper's success always cite the names of two performers, insinuating that he copied his act from both. Let us take Ballantine first. The foundation of Tommy's act was put in place in his boat-yard and service days and Ballantine did not appear in Britain – at the Empire Theatre, Leicester Square – until December 1949, by which time Tommy was already established in the profession, if only in a small way. Cooper had little conscience when it came to appropriating material from other performers, but he always claimed that specific items he used from the Ballantine act were legitimately purchased by him for his use in the United Kingdom from one Abbot Lutz, who claimed to be their creator. Magnanimously Ballantine confirms the account. According to Carl, Lutz had accompanied him to

London as general assistant and dogsbody and then stayed in England by means of the American GI Bill, which helped the military to study and to find jobs. Lutz became a teacher and somewhere along the line met Tommy and sold him the rights to the material to make ends meet. Ballantine claims Lutz couldn't have invented a gag if his life had depended on it. The material probably included the most immortal line ever addressed to a rubber chicken, 'Get dressed'; the studiously torn paper that is never restored, simply used to level up an uneven table or chair; and most memorably, 'Now from this empty bag I shall produce a real live dove,' followed by an explosion of feathers when he goes to burst the bag. Also prominent in the Ballantine act was the surprise spring-loaded production of a bouquet of flowers from the plinth. Other items like the tape measure watch – 'It's twenty inches past four' – and the musical 'playing cards' would appear to have been *bona fide* dealers' items accessible to all.

As a performer 'The Amazing Mr Ballantine' was as hyper-active as they come, a magical Jimmy Durante on speed, an intensity he has maintained with bewildering gusto throughout a distinguished career that began when he switched from straight magic to comedy in 1940 and has lasted over sixty years. His season in Cine-Variety at the Empire was not a success. The cavernous cinema was considered too large for the comic rapport he required with an audience and a fear of flying has confined him to America in recent years. Tommy is on record as having been disappointed at a performer whose reputation preceded him, although he was sympathetic enough to understand why the visitor failed to register in an audi-torium adapted for movies and not solo variety turns.

While Cooper bounced on full of confidence that one day he might become the world's greatest magician, Carl started out with the premise that he *was* 'The World's Greatest

Magician'. The banner on his table said so. He then saw his claim fall to pieces around him. With his darting eyes there is a raw nerve to Ballantine's work that always reminds me of the nervous energy that Spike Milligan, not a natural stage performer, could engender in a live situation when truly on form. With that he projects a satirical intelligence – 'They're catching on – no magic, just a charming personality!' – that plays off against the keynote of magical failure, as distinct from Cooper's skilful portrayal of fumbling incompetence. Not that the Ballantine act doesn't build to a similar shambles as props litter the stage and, on the line 'you probably wonder what I'm gonna do next,' a stage hand tosses Carl a broom to sweep up. To Americans he will always be better known as Seaman Lester Gruber, the character in the successful Sixties naval sitcom, *McHale's Navy*, a kind of 'Sergeant Bilko' of the ocean waves. Unfairly American television never gave him the platform to exploit his vaudeville skills in a show of his own and, unlike Tommy's, his act stayed static through the years.

While British and American audiences respectively laughed at Cooper and Ballantine, the French endorsed their own personal comedy magic favourite in Mac Ronay. Before becoming established as an almost resident Parisian attraction at venues like the Lido and the Crazy Horse, Ronay did make a tour of the provincial British music halls during the late Forties. There is no record that Tommy saw him perform at that time, although he did once discuss the Frenchman not too generously with Bob Monkhouse, who like me admired him. While the Cooper act was joyous and positive, Ronay displayed a magnificent mournfulness with which Tommy did not connect. If Ballantine was Durante writ large, then Ronay was more akin to Buster Keaton or even Tony Hancock, his every move underpinned by solemnity, a lingering sense of tragedy in the air. That was his intention and it kept audiences laughing through a career that lasted almost fifty years, his diffidently spasmodic pathos as one trick after another went wrong brilliantly conveyed by the constant dipping movement of his head that at times seemed almost disconnected from his body.

Perhaps Cooper was disconcerted that Mac also wore a fez – albeit a squatter version with a tuft like a beret rather than a tassel – and, although he hardly spoke in his act, traded in an infantile silliness that was so much a part of his own style. At one point Ronay would hold a lit candle and an electric torch a few inches apart. Blowing out the candle and switching on the torch at the same time produced the illusion that the light had travelled across. It was daft, but it was effective. When a short length of rope refused to stand erect in his hand, his answer was to hold it taut between his hands for a considered pause, turn both hands through 180 degrees and then let go of the now bottom end. To the best of my knowledge Cooper kept both items at bay, although with the magician's repertoire as stereotyped as it is there were inevitable echoes of material between the two acts, as pieces of rope failed to join together in the hand and a pencil rose out of a bottle – Tommy used a rose: 'Rose, Rose, Arisen!' – only to be left dangling on a thread. More interesting is the evidence of body language that Cooper could have adapted subliminally to his own purposes: the inability to close a box without trapping his fingers under the lid, to handle scissors without trapping the thumb in the handle, the deft footwork to kick away the incriminatory evidence of a trick gone wrong, the hand that proves less resistant to the candle flame than bravado first supposed. Indeed, when Ronay flexed the empty fingers of first this hand on one side, then that one on the other, one almost expected to see subtitles accompany the mime: 'Non comme ça! Comme ça!' But then Ronay also made great play of Claude Williams' medal motif! In this way what comes around, comes around.

It has always been assumed that in order to burlesque magic, or any performing skill for that matter, one has to be accomplished in the discipline in the first place. That such skill need not be a prerequisite can be shown by the large number of comedians who have taken it upon themselves to portray the role of the inept magician, quite as much as by Tommy's own hilarious attempts at ventriloquism and 'song and dance'. Attempts by comics to parody the hocus pocus man in the movies are numerous, including Chaplin in *The Circus*, Laurel and Hardy in *The Hollywood Revue of 1929*, Victor Moore in *Swing Time*, Jerry Lewis in *The Geisha Boy*, Fred Astaire in *Three Little Words*, even Gracie Allen in *International House*. But these were single outings conjured up for the cinema. Within the British variety tradition there are several top comedy names who devised a magic pastiche that became an established part of their repertoire as they toured in revues and summer shows.

Sandy Powell developed his own burlesque as an item to follow on in satiric counterpoint to a conventional manipulator booked to appear on his stage tours. Anyone who saw his benign incompetent getting his fingers burnt as he plucked cigarettes out of the air, or trying to rid his fingers of the vanishing and reappearing billiard ball secretly attached by a loop of thread, will still laugh at the memory. Albert Burdon, another giant of North Country comedy between the wars, became identified towards the end of his life with a single routine featuring a single illusion. Wearing a grandiose turban that appeared two sizes too big for his squat physique, he proudly announced, 'Ladies and gentlemen, I have here a magic cabinet that cost thousands of pounds.' His attempts to present the trick were constantly frustrated by an irksome 'volunteer' from the stalls and a stray walking stick that kept turning up in all sorts of places when he was least expecting it. The act ended with a physical whirlwind. His declared intention 'to show the cabinet the same all the way round' was the cue to hold on for their lives as the simple structure spun around possessed like some whirling dervish, the legs of the sorcerer and his apprentice lifted off the ground by the centrifugal force created. It was one of the most exhilarating moments in variety and very funny. Funnier still was the moment in the repertoire of Tommy's friends, Eric Morecambe and Ernie Wise, when they allowed audiences the privilege of watching them portray Marvo and Dolores.

It was never difficult for Eric to upstage his shorter partner, but here the stakes were raised several notches as Ernie portrayed the cliché girl assistant bedecked in tutu and fishnets, a distant cousin of many a principal boy that ever slapped a thigh in pantomime. However, once one had taken in this spectacle there was no taking one's eyes off Morecambe, upholstered to high heaven in an oversize tail suit that released a steady stream of tell-tale feathers as he stumped around the stage, interrupted only by the alarming bird-like noises that emanated from the innermost recesses of his person. The boys, as they were affectionately known, brilliantly extended their burlesque into reality, taking out trade advertisements for the magic act that announced they were 'Vacant' for January, February, March, April, and so on monthly throughout the year, with the exception of August, which was reserved for 'Holidays'. At no point were their own names mentioned in the ad. In a similar vein theatre programmes printed the act as just another speciality act on the Eric and Ernie show, giving no clue at all to audiences that this was the comedy bonus of all time.

Cooper took the device of the failed magic act to even higher levels of humour and observation. The side of him that never missed a cue during a hectic London Palladium pantomime was the side that acknowledged that for all the enthusiasm that kept magic alive, much of its world was threadbare, substandard and anachronistic. Props that had once been perfectly acceptable because they corresponded to kitchen utensils and table furniture of the time were hopelessly out of date. The patter that accompanied performances was similarly jaded, lines that had been refreshingly witty when first uttered by the greatest of British magicians, David Devant at the turn of the century, reduced to the status of cliché: 'We give the cards two taps – one hot, one cold!' The prefacing of each effect with 'And now', the naming of each prop as 'ordinary', the surprise-defeating description of what will happen before it does, the giveaway 'blink' when the secret move is made or the gadget released, all cohered into a general picture of mediocrity. The paradox is that much of this was due to the high visibility of substandard amateurs anxious – try stopping them – to show off their miracles at every platform offered by village hall, church social, or children's birthday party. Tommy had been there himself, but now with consummate professionalism he was on the outside looking in, tapping into peoples' subconscious horror stories of magic in the cause of laughter.

This is not to say that in the late Forties when Tommy arrived on the scene there did not exist a public face of excellence in magic, personified as it was by the swallow-tailed elegance of the likes of Cardini, Jasper Maskelyne, and John Calvert with their Ronald Colman moustaches and fashion plate looks. The style had been epitomized for a wider audience by David Niven in his portrayal of the magician, the Great Arturo in the 1939 movie, *Eternally Yours*. The Danish–American illusionist, Dante provided a more story book version of a wizard, but was essentially from the same mould.

They were all slick and sophisticated, neat and necromantic in the nicest of ways and the contrast could not have worked better in Tommy's favour. Suddenly there appeared someone with the hands of a labourer and the legs of an ostrich who looked nothing like the regular model. As such he had the edge over all the others who guyed the innate self-importance of the magic profession.

He never lost his love and respect for the mystique of the magician's craft, but was savvy enough to accept that his comedy skills shoehorned him into a public approach that needed to be kept separate from his private enthusiasms. Once early in his career he was spending the afternoon with Bobby Bernard in the Archer Street emporium of Max Andrews. His latest magic sensation was, according to Andrews, right up Tommy's street. Max talked Tommy through the presentation he envisaged for his star customer: 'You crack some gags and get a few laughs, then have a card chosen, tell a few gags, have the card shuffled back in the pack and tell a few more.' Gags and magic business continued to alternate until the chosen card was caught amid a shower of cards in the jaws of a large rat trap, about as unlikely an object as one might associate with a card trick. Tommy was unimpressed. With his deadpan stare he turned to Andrews and said, 'Never mind the fucking trick. Where are these gags that get all the laughs?'

SIX

Comic Ways and Means

The family tree of comedy has always intrigued me, the way in which the great performers take aspects of those they have admired from preceding generations and by a process of osmosis intuitively mould them into aspects of their own personalities, as if they belonged there and nowhere else. The impact of Max Linder on Chaplin, Harry Tate on W. C. Fields, and Little Tich on just about everyone who ever essayed a funny walk is well documented. Possibly the most influential British comedian of all was the Forties revue star, Sid Field. For seven glorious years between 1943 and 1950 his almost unbroken tenure at London's Prince of Wales Theatre acted as a honey pot for the new breed of comedians emerging from the services, his multi-faceted persona a revelation to those raised on the more stereotyped approach of the average stand-up of the day.

In an earlier volume, *Funny Way to be a Hero* I catalogued his legacy (and in part that of his occasional straight man, Jerry Desmonde) in this regard: Frankie Howerd's wheeze and surrender to amazement; the give and take between Morecambe and Wise; Max Bygraves's warm directness; Tony Hancock's despair; Terry-Thomas's genteelism; the spiv-like quality of Arthur English; Jimmy Edwards's musical mayhem; Norman Wisdom's frenetic incoherence; Dick Emery's coy effeminacy; Harry Secombe's genial daftness; Benny Hill's moon-faced innocence; even Olivier's archness as Archie Rice. Moreover, the impact he had is not to say that Sid himself had not been influenced in turn by those guiding lights of comedy that inspired him as a malleable young performer. It has always surprised me that virtually alone among his generation Cooper appears to have remained impervious to this chameleon among clowns. In that respect he stands tall as the most original of his colleagues. At one level his own comic persona was entirely its own invention, and yet nothing develops in a vacuum; it would have been impossible for him to have functioned as a comedian without many outside influences, among which the love of magic and the decision to burlesque it were only part of the story. There was very little original in what he actually did. His special talent was always in the presentation. Along the way he showed good taste in those he cultivated along the path of comic apprenticeship, most notably Max Miller, Bob Hope, Laurel and Hardy, and a few more.

Superficially his comedic roots can be traced back to the *Commedia dell'Arte*, the stylized comic form that emerged in Italy in the mid-sixteenth century, many of whose stereotypes – Harlequin, Pantaloon, Pulcinella – linger in the popular imagination. The analogy would appear less pretentious if in translation the *dell'Arte* readily conjured up its proper meaning, not 'of art', but 'of craft or skill'. With its emphasis on broad anarchy, apparent spontaneity and dependence on the mask as a short cut to characterization the form appears tailor-made for Cooper, the fez its own shorthand reference in the identity department, like Charlie's hat and cane and Groucho's strip moustache. The bedrock of the genre was provided by the '*lazzi*' or comic set pieces – anything from an isolated visual gag to an extended comic routine. Here more than any of his contemporaries Tommy would have had a superabundance of material to qualify for acceptance. But even contemporary *Commedia* expert, Barry Grantham concedes that it is difficult to assign one of the traditional masks to him: 'He has not the bragging, cowardly traits of the Captain, the pompous word-play of the Doctor, or the foibles of Pantaloon. Punchinello is celebrated for his total contempt for all accepted standards of moral and social behaviour. The choice of a *Zanni* – one of the lowlier comic roles – is not that obvious either. Most of them betray a fundamental baseness of character that seems to be totally absent in Cooper.' Not even the magic link with Harlequin is of help, since his tricks never went wrong. Grantham has to conclude: 'If he had been around at any point during the seventeenth century, we would today be richer by one more major Mask of the *Commedia dell'Arte*.' The readiness with which he was impersonated in his lifetime and the eagerness of so many to carry on doing so more than twenty years after his death, suggests that the Cooper Mask is established regardless and will endure for years to come.

Cooper's most obvious beginnings are in the world of the British music hall, an institution that shared one abiding quality with the *Commedia*, namely the inclusion of the audience as part of the performance, acknowledging its presence both directly and by means of the comic aside, the so-called fourth wall that exists between straight actor and clientele reduced to invisible rubble. The process fed the affection that existed between audiences and the stars of the day, principally the comedians. That the institution endured as long as it did after the heyday of Dan Leno, George Robey, and Little Tich is perhaps surprising, but Cooper and one or two others managed to ride the waves of such popularity into the radio and television era. Among these was the first enduring comedy star of the wireless medium, Arthur Askey.

There could be no greater contrast between the two comedians, the one gargantuan and gauche, the other impish and neat. It was put to effective comic use by Val Parnell in the 1957 London Palladium pantomime, *Robinson Crusoe*, in which Arthur played the dame and Tommy her sidekick, Abu ('a kind of magician'), and on one memorable television appearance for Thames during 1976 in which they partnered each other in a 'Me and My Shadow' song and dance routine, Tommy behind a screen providing the ludicrous silhouette of his guest star, whose nifty little skips were in hilarious counterpoint to the other's lumbering steps. The show was recorded at a time when Tommy's ill health was hard to conceal and age-wise they appeared to meet in the middle of the twenty-one years that separated them, but the affection of the younger performer for the elder statesman was palpable. That Tommy should literally shadow the veteran star on this occasion carried its own irony. He once professed his love for Askey to Arthur's Fifties scriptwriter, Bob Monkhouse: 'He never stops moving. I love that. All that energy. He goes this way. He goes that way. He's walking towards you. He's walking away. And the hands are always moving.' It was quite obvious to Monkhouse that Cooper had himself assimilated these essential traits of the tiny Liverpudlian. There was seldom a time when Cooper was not in motion himself, stepping from this table to that, picking up this prop, putting down that, feeding his audience an energy that kept it as alert as himself. I am also convinced that the influence was more than physical. Arthur was not a natural stand up comedian, unable to tell a joke without following through with a trademark chuckle that seemed to express apology, explanation and personal enjoyment at the same time. It bore little vocal resemblance to the throaty Cooper guffaw, but served a similar purpose nevertheless.

Cooper's admiration for Laurel and Hardy extended in a pre-video age to taking a projector on the road with him so that he could play their films. Tommy often reminisced about being part of the general hysteria in the West End on the occasion of their visit to Great Britain in the late Forties, the only time, he claimed, that he had ever queued for an autograph. It is not difficult to see why their work appealed to him with its brilliant use of anticipation in the cause of comedy. As Tommy explained: 'I always treasure a picture of the thin one standing there minding his own business and the fat one lecturing him. "Stanley," he says, "If you want a job done right, then you have to do it yourself." Then the fat one goes off to do it and comes crashing through a wall.' Just as we always knew he would. Tommy only had to touch a magical prop and let out his throaty laugh to trigger in all of us the same comic mechanism. He came to absorb aspects of both performers to the extent that he embodied both Stan and Ollie in one human frame, the figurative equivalent of one of his absurd half-and-half portrayals. One moment he could be exultant on tiptoe with all the misguided self-assurance of the fat man, the next awash with tears like the thin one. The combination was never better displayed than in a sequence where he attempted without much success to restore a bundle of tissue papers he has just torn to shreds. When, triumphantly, the tissues eventually transform into a posy of flowers, the sense of comic surprise in his accomplishment is worthy of them both.

John McCabe, the first biographer of Laurel and Hardy, whose work played a large part in restoring them to public recognition, summarized the three essential elements of their comic philosophy. In so doing he also acknowledged that Stan, as the creative half of the partnership, would have had no truck with any such thinking. The qualities were 'a strain of high nonsense; positiveness; innocence.' What was daft was there to be celebrated and guile had no place in their optimistic view of the world, that of 'the English pantomime where everyone did live happily ever after.' Tommy was no philosopher either, but it is hard not to read this essential three point pattern between the lines of his comic persona. He represented that contradiction in terms, a magician without guile, blithely assuming that the trick would work somehow and often oblivious that the method of its accomplishment might be in danger of exposure in the process. With Ollie he shared a sense of overwhelming satisfaction when things went right, with Stan a helplessness underlined by his almost infantile delight in those distractions from reality that the magician's art presented: anyone who like Stanley can ignite his thumb like a match, smoke a fistful of tobacco through his thumb and pull down the *shadow* of a window blind has to be accounted a magician too.

Stan's actual magical skills were less in evidence when they attempted the formal presentation of a magic act in *The Hollywood Revue of 1929*, one of those vaudeville-inspired attempts beloved by Hollywood studios to package as many of their leading players as possible in a single vehicle. In a gambit that resonates with the quintessential Cooper the curtain rises on the famous pair with their backs to the audience, still hurriedly arranging their props on the table. Ollie as the magician is alert to the situation and acknowledges the master of ceremonies by tipping his hat; when assistant Stan repeats the gesture, a dove flies out. Recrimination escalates into Stan being shoved into a bowl of eggs, thus ruling out a second miracle. The act proceeds. Ollie's genteel smugness as he presents an unimpressive parade of anaemic mysteries is brought back to earth when he slips on a stray banana skin, the residue from another ruined trick, and half-somersaults into a giant cake just placed on the table by Stan. Although he was only eight when the film was released, there has to be a possibility that it was seen by the young Cooper.

Rarely did Tommy pay outward homage to his heroes in his act, although in one of his television series from the Seventies an Oliver Hardy look-alike kept wandering disconcertingly into shot. Hero-worship was paid more effectively when it was paid more subtly, as when Tommy asked the musical director for some music. No sooner had a few notes been played, than he would abruptly cut it short: 'That's enough.' The significance is not the hoariness of the device, but the fact that the music was 'Love in Bloom', the signature tune of another comedy great, Jack Benny, who played the master of ceremonies on the occasion Laurel and Hardy essayed their magic act. A few years before he died, Benny's legendary comedic skills went on show for the last time at the London Palladium. Watching him enter to that music with his distinctive spring-heeled, arm-swinging stride was worth the price of admission. He concluded his act by announcing, 'And now – for a real treat – I am going to play for you.' He looked into the wings and called for his violin. A model with million dollar looks brought the instrument to him. He tucked it under his chin and asked, 'Are you a fan of mine?' She replied, 'No, but my mother is.' She then turned and walked off stage. Benny just stood there, staring in silence for what must have been four or five minutes. We'll call it the Jack Benny effect. Only one time since have I seen a performer milk silence for a laugh as big and that was Cooper himself, playing a member of the public deserted on stage by a make-believe magician who has left Tommy in the lurch, the latter's hat the receptacle for the broken eggs – that ever-recurring motif of comedy magic – that he has no intention of magicking back into their shells.

In interviews Tommy was more vocal about his admiration

for Bob Hope than for Benny. In later years he would stand on the same stage as Hope during the finale of a Royal Variety Performance and had difficulty reminding himself that it wasn't a dream. His radio broadcasts on the American Forces Network had been an essential part of morale boosting during the war and for no one more so than Cooper: 'I used to sneak away from duty to listen and was always getting caught by this sergeant major called Thompson. Great fellow. He usually let me off.' As a young man back in Civvy Street he paid homage in the crowd to Hope too, waiting among the thousands anxious to see him step out of his car in Leicester Square. On the surface there was little in common stylistically between the two performers on stage. However, aside from a shared penchant for snappy one-liners, albeit of vastly differing timbre and subject matter, one *does* thinks of Tommy's furtive beckoning of the fingers with his arm hung loosely by his side, a last desperate attempt to chivvy the audience when a joke falls on stony ground. 'Ripple, ripple, ripple,' he semi-pleads as he identifies where the laugh should be. Accompanied by a sneaky peek into the wings, it is a decidedly Hope ploy, signifying Bob's often dismissive attitude to much of his own material: 'I found that joke in my stocking. If it happens again, I'll change laundries.' For all Hope's outward display of self-assurance as joke after joke was fired across the footlights, there were moments when material, delivery and persona combined to make their own comment upon the guts and determination needed to become a stand-up comedian in the first place. One recalls the way he would hit the front cloth as if to find the quick exit for escape if needed and the subconscious nervous tic of constantly adjusting the handkerchief in his top pocket. Both can be discerned in Cooper. It is unlikely that Tommy ever rationalized these similarities on his own account, but, as we shall discover, he succeeded in bringing off the same effect in even more spectacular fashion. He may have begun his career guying the conventions of the magician's act. What few have noticed is that before long he was guying those of the comedian's trade as well.

If there was one comic for whom Tommy reserved the lion's share of his adulation it was the doyen of British stand-up performers from the middle years of the twentieth century, Max Miller. More than anyone in Cooper's youthful experience he set the standard for which to aim. No one has since surpassed the self-styled 'Cheeky Chappie' for the sheer brilliance of his technique, matched as it was by a personality that sparkled like the crown jewels. His mastery of stage craft was unerring. Max Bygraves, whose early impersonation provided him with his stage name, described to me how before he made his entrance Miller would have the electrician black out the stage for ten seconds. The music would cut out and quietness fell over the auditorium. People would be wondering why the show had stopped – ten seconds is a long time in such a context – but then all of a sudden the band would launch into his signature tune, 'Mary from the Dairy', the lights would go full up, the spotlight would hit the prompt corner and then at the precise moment for maximum applause Max would saunter on grinning from ear to ear in all his peacock splendour. The music would keep playing as he took off his coat to reveal one of his dazzling suits of floral chintz. Let's imagine it depicted buttercups or daffodils. He directed his gaze at a woman in the front row, 'D'you like it, lady? I've just had a mustard bath!' Only on the end of the gag did the music stop, at which point the audience suddenly heard the volume of its own laughter. To use Tommy's word, he was 'electrifying'. As Max used to vaunt of himself, 'There'll never be another, lady. No, there'll never be another!' There was scant conceit to the remark, because it was true.

Max remains acknowledged as the master of direct communication with an audience. He possessed the most expressive pair of eyes in show business: as he leaned across the footlights they cast their beam around the theatre like a lighthouse. His skill enabled him to reduce the most cavernous auditorium to the intimate surroundings of your own front room. He used to say, 'You need to be close enough to them so that you can nick a shilling from an old girl's handbag without her knowing.' Tommy certainly learned from Miller the technique of addressing the one lady in the house with an irrepressible titter, wherever she might be. Laughter is contagious and people with Miller's skill knew how to maximize this to their best advantage, working on the single outlet until the whole house echoed in the same way. There are times when one listens to some of Cooper's television appearances and wonders whether just such a titter had been planted or fed in on audio-tape. If this was the case, it was – as homage to the man who epitomized the variety profession – excusable. Miller had as shrewd an insight into his profession as anyone, as he showed when he described comedy to a young Bob Monkhouse: 'Comedy, son, comedy is the one job you can do badly and people *won't* laugh at you, but it's the one job you can do well and they will.'

Tommy would go to watch Max time after time and admitted to learning wide swathes of his patter off by heart, even though ostensibly their styles were far apart, Miller majoring on a self-conscious innuendo that never intruded into Cooper's more innocent routine. He was, after all, the man once described by John Osborne as 'a saloon bar Priapus'. Only when I came to survey Cooper's own material in transcript form did the echoes leap off the page. It is surprising that one had missed the obvious given the skill with which Miller stamped his verbal copyright on any joke he told. Jokes I had heard both comics tell on frequent occasions had not previously connected on the same wavelength. The misdirection had been in the delivery. Max's fluent cadencies linked to his knowing persona were in total contrast to Tommy's more matter of fact intonation. If Miller could be perceived as the Gielgud of spoken patter, Cooper had aligned with Richardson. It was through listening to the speech patterns of Miller and Groucho Marx that T. S. Eliot drew his parallel between the worlds of the music hall comedian and the poet. Among British performers there was no one to touch Max in this area because he *was* so easy to listen to, adroitly using emphasis and repetition within a line to communicate with maximum effect. Not a word was wasted, not a phrase longer than it needed to be. His speech took wing. The subtleties of his delivery would have been lost on the young Cooper when he was learning those lines, material that usefully stayed lodged in his subconscious to the end of his days. To my knowledge he never tried openly to imitate Max, unlike so many others – both Tony Hancock *and* Sid James included – who first trod the boards as Miller impersonators. He merely told the jokes as if straight off the page, in time making them his own through the curious expedient of being unable or uninterested in replicating the distinctive rhythms of his hero.

Today audiences hearing lines like the following will automatically think of Tommy first: 'I was talking to this girl the other day and I said to her, "Are you familiar with Shakespeare?" She said, "As a matter of fact I am. I had dinner with him last night." I said, "What are you talking about? He's been dead for years." She said, "I thought he was quiet!"' Then there were the wife jokes. It possibly excused them in Gwen's eyes that Miller had delivered them first: 'I've got the best wife in England. The other one's in Africa!' and 'The other day I came home and the wife was crying her eyes out.

I said, "What's wrong?" She said, "I feel homesick." I said, "This is your home." She said, "I know. I'm sick of it."' Miller – and Cooper by default – had millions of them: 'My wife came in the other day and she said, "What's different about me?" And I said, "I don't know. What is different about you? Have you had your hair done?" She said, "No." I said, "Have you got a new dress on?" She said, "No." "Have you got a new pair of shoes?" She said, "No." I said, "Well, I don't know. What is different about you?" She said "I'm wearing a gas mask."' Cooper was still making audiences cry at the latter almost forty years after the gas masks had been stored away.

At one point Tommy's reverence for the two master gagsters fused. Miller used to tell the joke about coming home to discover his wife with another man – 'not a stitch on!' It is not a joke Tommy would ever have used, but it is perhaps fitting that tucked away under 'Song' in his extensive file index of gags we discover the tag line incorporated in a parody of Bob Hope's memorable signature tune:

> Thanks for the Memory
> Of the night when I came home
> And found you not alone
> You said he was a nudist
> Who dropped in to use the phone
> Oh thank you, so much . . .

Max would have understood. A few years before he died in 1963, he had befriended the younger comic and bestowed upon him his trademark white snap-brim trilby. Tommy considered it his most cherished possession and regarded Max as his guardian angel for the rest of his days. The year after Max's death he scored a resounding personal triumph in the 1964 Royal Variety Performance. Among the botched tricks and the

'Hats' routine the Shakespeare gag was given a successful airing, while the aside, 'A lady over there's got opera glasses on me – she thinks I'm a racehorse' had given Max stalwart service. Cooper's friend, Val Andrews phoned the day after the television transmission to convey his congratulations. Tommy was out and Gwen took the call. Val explained how he had experienced a strange feeling while watching: 'I could almost see Max standing there.' For a moment there was an electric silence, before Gwen asked Val if he had been talking to Tommy. He hadn't. 'It's strange,' continued Gwen, 'he came back from the show as white as a sheet. I asked him what was up and he said he had turned round in the theatre and seen Max standing there. It must have been Max's ghost.'

There comes a stage when jokes, to the reluctance of their originators or those who make them famous, pass out of copyright and into oral tradition far in advance of any set period defined by the copyright laws. It was a process with which Cooper was more than familiar, extending to major set pieces in his act. When I was attempting to establish with Gwen the copyright of the 'Autumn Leaves' routine wherein Tommy, playing the melody at a grand piano, is smothered by a gradual avalanche of leaves fluttering down from the flies, I received the frank answer: 'I think we saw that in Vegas. We nicked it, like we nicked everything else!' Scriptwriter Brad Ashton has recalled the wonderfully funny takeoff on *Candid Camera* that Tommy would often perform in summer season. As a birthday present one year Brad surprised him with a video of the same routine being performed by Mickey Rooney on *The Ed Sullivan Show* on American television in 1963. He said, 'You bastard! Where did you get this?' Brad replied, 'The same place as you did!'

The lifting of comedy material was an accepted aspect of the downside of the variety and vaudeville circuit, a situation hard to understand at a time when on the comedy circuit today the idea of a performer telling a joke that is not of his or her creation is tantamount to a request for a refund. In that sense Cooper was never a creative animal, although this is not to take away from him and his peers another form of creativity that underpins the act of any great comedian as he works the audience, editing the act on the balls of his feet, cutting this material, adding that, throwing in an ad-lib that he may never remember again. Maybe the task is so challenging that the whole matter of where the material originated pales into insignificance, if it is performed effectively and the audience does not latch on. Nevertheless, throughout his career he had to give assurances to broadcasters both here and in America that he had rights in the material that they had not commissioned themselves. There must have been many a white lie told to see him over the hurdle.

Sometimes Tommy *would* ask for permission to use items from the acts of others, even if he could be depressingly misleading in the face of generosity. When magician, Peter Newcombe presented Tommy with the gags mentioned in the last chapter it was on the understanding that he wanted them for a party. He didn't explain that the party was the BBC Television *Christmas Party*, a festive transmission capable of reaching more than three million households as early as 1954. At other times jokes or pieces of business that today represent shorthand references to the man with the fez filtered through into his act without a 'by your leave' of credit. Nor Kiddie was a fairly inconsequential figure in British stand-up comedy in the Thirties and Forties, but according to Bob Monkhouse, a much missed walking encyclopaedia on such matters, he may well have been the first to tell the joke about finding the violin and the painting in the attic: 'So I took them to an expert and he said, "What you've got there are a Stradivarius and a

Rembrandt. Unfortunately – Stradivarius was a terrible painter and Rembrandt made rotten violins."' Another defining Cooper joke involved meeting a police constable after dark. It eerily echoed Tommy's actual experience of being stopped in Regent Street with two suitcases in the early hours, something that may qualify him for some kind of distorted ownership. The officer asks Tommy what is in the bags: 'I said, "In there, I've got sugar for my tea!" He said, "And what have you got in the other one?" I said, "In that one, I've got sugar for my coffee." And then he took out his truncheon and went "Boom" – "There's a lump for your cocoa!"' The slang use of the shortened form of 'coconut' for 'head' gives no clue to the fact that it was written by the driest of American radio comedians, Fred Allen, for a 1924 Broadway revue. It is similarly appropriate to use this paragraph to accord credit to 'Silent' Tait, an early novelty magic act on the halls, who was the first to make surreal use of a portable white gate through which he, like Tommy, would stroll for no apparent purpose whatsoever. However, what Cooper did not filch from anyone was the skill that enabled him in the Stradivarius gag to achieve a laugh on a pronounced pause after 'unfortunately', before he even reached the punch line; the panache of his pantomime as – 'Boom' – he saw stars the moment he struck his head with the imaginary truncheon; the proficiency with which according to Mary Kay he used the gate as a device to measure the receptivity of the audience in this venue or that.

When Tommy and Gwen were not conducting their own comedy research in Las Vegas, whether in the hotel showrooms or by watching the television in their room, they were fortunate to have a friend living in Denver, Colorado who would monitor the airwaves for them. A contact from early variety days in Great Britain, Norma – there is no record of her surname – had obviously married an American and set up home in the United States. Her copiously detailed letters, summarizing the comedy she thought would appeal to Cooper's style and trading domestic trivia at the same time, provide a means of coming to terms with her own homesickness during the latter part of the Sixties. In this way Tommy was educated to the cod magic routine of comedy actor, Dom DeLuise, although to his credit he appropriated nothing from the account. Other letters convey a detailed breakdown of what Mac Ronay did on *The Ed Sullivan Show*, while three words that became a Cooper cliché – 'My teeth itch!' – are attributed to Shelley Berman, a more sophisticated performer altogether. Norma questions whether Tommy would be at all interested in Jackie Gleason's sitcom-style sketches featuring, 'The Honeymooners': 'I wouldn't have thought so, although I will gladly watch for good ones, if you like.' She concedes that the incoming *Rowan and Martin's Laugh-In* does not appear to hold out much promise and by the end of the decade, when the correspondence appears to stop, a note of gloom has set in: 'The other shows have turned to politics and the rebel youth for their humour, it seems.' For these observations Gwen sent gifts from the old country and enough dollars to treat her kids with toys from time to time. It was a useful arrangement for both sides and kept Cooper in touch with the American scene.

One performer who came under close observation in her letters was the master clown and pantomimist, Red Skelton. As one of the top comedy stars on American television during the Fifties and Sixties he performed literally hundreds of solo pantomime sketches on his show. Today his legacy is perpetuated in a special theatrical tribute by the comedy performer, Tom Mullica, who was able to identify for me most of the mime routines that surfaced in Cooper's act as being of Skelton's creation. Gwen Cooper herself had hinted that Tommy appropriated much of this material while watching

151

Red in Las Vegas. There was the bit where he played a cowboy using an oilcan to oil an invisible door, only to discover eventually that it is his elbow that needs lubrication; the hen-pecked husband accompanying his wife to the top of the Eiffel Tower, where in manoeuvring her into position for a photograph he nudges her over the edge; the fool with the feather – he sucks air in when he should blow out and chokes in the process; the tennis player playing in slow motion who eventually gets the ball stuck in his open mouth; the old man vaunting himself in the company of young girls – only to revert to decrepitude when they have left. There were more, some in fairness not identified by Mullica, like the one where Tommy gave an impression of a man guiding the planes in on an aircraft carrier with a paddle in each hand, then realizing they are coming straight at him: anguish fills his face as first he attempts to bat them away and then ducks in horror throwing the paddles in the air. Tommy justifiably prided himself on his miming skills – the studied approach to make-believe is an important aspect of any magician's technique – and while not in the Skelton class, he always incorporated a brief mime sequence in his act when time allowed. The items carried the advantage of requiring little in the way of props.

It is perhaps surprising that at no point did Norma mention another colossus of American television comedy, although at the time she was writing his presence was certainly not as dominant on the small screen as it had once been. It is equally surprising that for all his eulogizing of Miller, Askey, Hope, Benny, Laurel and Hardy, Tommy is nowhere on record in admitting his admiration for the same performer. And yet of the comic generation that preceded Cooper he conceivably exerted the biggest influence on the crazy young conjuror. His name was Milton Berle, acknowledged as the principal pioneer of comedy on American television. In any discussion of comic copyright his name must loom large. Known unashamedly throughout the business as 'The Thief of Bad Gags,' he qualified unequivocally as the prime exponent of comic appropriation. So outrageous was his approach it became part and parcel of his all-consuming geniality: 'What has Bob Hope got that I won't do two years later?' It is the greatest of ironies that he of all comics should be responsible for possibly the most influential day in the career of the young comedian. Berle never played London in person, but Val Andrews and Bobby Bernard both remember the ecstasy shown by Tommy when introduced to his talents in the 1949 film, *Always Leave Them Laughing*, bouncing up and down like a kid who has discovered Santa Claus really does exist. In the movie Berle essentially plays himself, an ambitious young comic who is criticized for rising to fame on the back of other performers' material and then gradually forges his own style. One doubts if Cooper ever gave a second thought to the fact that as he watched the movie he was caught up himself in a process similar to what was being played out on screen.

When *Always Leave Them Laughing* opened in London, the reviewer for the *Monthly Film Bulletin* reported of its star: 'He is a comedian for whom no joke is too old, and who can only be funny when surrounded with an apparatus of stage comic paraphernalia.' To Tommy, Berle represented an epiphany. Watch the film today and it amazes as an archaeological reference guide to so much that became solidified within Tommy's own act: we can only be left wondering where Berle acquired the stuff in the first place. Here we find the gentle ribbing of the crowd: 'I can always look at an audience and tell whether they're gonna be good or bad. Good night!' The targeting of a make-believe individual for comic effect: 'This gentleman down here – your head is shining right in my eyes.' The remorseless literal-mindedness: 'A man came up to me in the street. He said, "I haven't had a bite in three days." So I bit him.' Even comedy magic. Throughout his life Berle too was a magic addict, a trait he acknowledges in the movie as he approaches a member of the audience and instructs him accordingly: 'Take a card. Now tear the card in halves. Tear it in quarters. Tear it in eighths. Tear it in sixteenths. Now hold the little pieces in your left hand and throw them over your head. Hah hah hah. Happy New Year!' It stood Tommy in good stead down the years. At another moment Berle tosses a ping pong ball under his hat and after a split second spits it out of his mouth. The illusion is so strong that it looks like the most skilful bit in the magician's handbook and is funny into the bargain.

One can see the young Tommy now, scribbling away co-cooned in the dark of the cinema through several screenings of the film, the light-fingered Artful Dodger to the magnificent Fagin of the comic craft. But the influence of Berle extended far beyond anything the Cooper pencil would entrust to paper. While Tommy's personality was essentially his own, there are aspects of his presentational approach that are pure Berle. No comedian was ever more 'in your face', his introductory 'Thank you. Thank you. Thank you,' achieving immediate contact with his audience, as it did for Tommy so many times later. Physically big like Cooper, he radiated action, as Arthur Askey did too, but on a more grandiose scale. Berle's confidence energized the young Cooper like nothing before, providing a road to Damascus moment on a level with the day the milk cascaded out of the bottle and the one when he planted the fez on his 'cocoa' for the first time. It may conceivably have been the catalyst that led to his commitment to succeed as a comedian beyond the limits of the self-contained comedy magic act, where as we have seen the spoken comedy sprang out of the props and the conjuring.

His jottings from service days reveal that any early attempt to perform straight stand-up had been tentative to say the least:

Ladies and gentlemen – and members of the audience . . . I'm very happy to announce that just before I came out on this stage, I signed a two-year contract with Paramount. (Wait for applause) Now I'm waiting for Paramount to sign . . . But I could have been in *The Yearling*. The only trouble was they didn't ask me . . . I'm really happy tonight though. I just received a little bundle from heaven (wait for applause) my laundry. But now at this time I'd like to . . . Hmmm, I'd like to! I have to. It's in my contract . . .

And so on. There is no indication that Tommy didn't write – or at least compile – this himself. Equally, it may be a transcript of a Hope radio monologue. At least the punctuation shows a rudimentary evidence of the understanding of timing. On the opposite page he has flagged the remnant of another routine, 'Comedy Script by Tommy Cooper':

For a number of years we were deliriously happy – but then we met each other . . . She was an odd-looking girl. She had a big heart and hips to match . . . But I didn't care . . . I just worshipped the ground her father struck oil on. Whenever I looked at her, time stood still. In other words she had a face that would stop a clock. But it was a face men go for. 'Gopher-face Sally' they used to call her, the pride of the London stockyard. But I never was that cruel. I just used to call her 'Melancholy Baby', because she had a head like a melon and a face like a lolly.

Underneath he has written, 'Finis. The poor man's Bob Hope.' Did he seriously think Hope wrote his own words, or was he merely projecting himself onto his idol's reputation as a performer? Even Berle would have tiptoed around material like this. By the time he returned from the CSE tour of Germany that Miff booked for him in 1948 his writing style had changed to become more narrative-based. A mere fragment of a script survives, of which the following is a part. There is no indication that he ever worked it for a paying audience. It was certainly not what Miff was selling to managements when he booked the man described as 'Almost a Magician':

I've just returned from a tour of Germany. As you know you have to be inoculated before going abroad ... The doctor studied me for a few minutes and finally shook his head. I exclaimed, 'Unbelievable, isn't it?' The doctor picked up my arm and took my pulse. You can't trust these doctors. They'll take anything. I told him so. He raised his eyebrows. Have you ever tried raising eyebrows? It's more fun than raising chickens. The doctor brought out a needle about three feet long. 'What are you going to do?' I screamed. 'Spear fish?' He said, 'Now this won't hurt a bit.' And he was right. He didn't feel a thing. The last thing I recall saying was, 'What's the purpose of all this?'

Perhaps for 'purpose' he meant to write 'point'. It might have rescued a line left hanging in the air with no prospect of a laugh. He had yet to learn how performers like Berle were able to force the laugh regardless. Yet to arrive were the snappy staccato style of a hundred disconnected doctor jokes and an ability to trump Berle at his own game. It is not hard to understand why professionally he adhered to a magic-based structure for the time being.

Watching *Always Leave Them Laughing* during the research for this book was an illuminating experience. It was also an

emotional one, in a way that has nothing to do with the creaky
sentimentalism of a plot with lines like 'How many years do
you think a comic has to knock around before he can learn
his trade – the broken-down joints he has to start in and
sometimes finish in too?' Shadowing Berle's character in the
movie is an ageing burlesque performer played by the great
Broadway comic, Bert Lahr. No more perfect casting could
have been found for someone whose job it is to show Berle's
character the ropes and, more importantly, to reveal the dignity that can exist in the tradition of the clown. The film
culminates in Berle beckoning a far from well Lahr up onto
the stage. They go into a soft shoe shuffle. Lahr falls. The
audience is expectant. It could be part of the act. It is not.
Lahr's character dies with Berle hastily bringing down the
curtain. The parallel with Cooper's own end is tear-jerking.
Little did Tommy realize that at the very moment his essential
comic self was crystallizing, he was also witnessing a simu-
lacrum of his own demise. When I described the outcome of
the film to his daughter, Vicky she was visibly struck with
emotion. Then after some reflection, she spoke: 'Perhaps he
looked on that as a secret prayer, the way he always wanted
to go.' The stark reality is that he saw a version of his own
death played out before him.

Within a short time Tommy discovered Berle's best-selling
book of humour, *Out of My Trunk*. It was his introduction
to joke book culture, embracing a search for comic material
that covered every single joke book he could lay his hands on.
Most familiar at this time were the slender pamphlets of
Robert Orben. Published principally as patter books directed
at magicians and masters of ceremonies, they achieved a much
wider audience among laughter makers, many comedians lifting whole chunks of copy to fill the need of a stray radio

broadcast when something fresher than their standard act was required. No less than Max Wall has been singled out in this regard. Normally the books were considered worth their weight in gold if they came up with one new joke for the purchaser. How much was original with Orben has long been contested. Oral tradition runs havoc again. There was nothing subtle about their titles: *Comedy Caravan*, *Patter Parade*, *Bits, Boffs and Banter*, and *Screamline Comedy*. In one of the most bizarre leaps of career advancement in history, by the mid Seventies Orben, an amateur magician, who had worked as scriptwriter for Jack Paar and Red Skelton, was installed as special assistant and speech writer to President Ford at the White House. Long before this connection immortalized Orben, Tommy realized that he possibly needed something a little more exclusive than what could be bought for a few coins over every magic shop counter.

He found the answer in New York, where he met Billy Glason, an ex-vaudevillian who had performed an act billed as 'Just Songs and Sayings' that interspersed patter with popular songs of the day. In an extensive career on the boards he had collected trunks full of jokes that he had written on file index cards and upon retirement set to and ordered the material into some kind of shape, modernizing where necessary. He claimed he could breathe new life into any gag. 'Who was that lady I saw you with last night?' became transformed into 'Who was that lady I saw you with at the sidewalk café last night?' – 'That was no sidewalk café. That was our furniture!' Steve Allen, Johnny Carson, Ed Sullivan, even Bob Hope availed themselves of his services. Tommy was one of the privileged few granted purchase of his twenty-six part *Fun-Master Giant Encyclopedia of Classified Gags*. Only a very few sets were home-produced on the thinnest paper available, 'to make it possible to make as many carbon copies we can!' One source says that it sold originally for three thousand dollars, not that Tommy paid that! An undated postcard to Chiswick shows Glason trying to clinch the transaction with Cooper: 'It's been five months since I first spoke of the Giant File and I've been trying desperately to get you to be the first and *only* proud possessor of this tremendous encyclopedia of classified gags in England. You keep saying, "in due time," but I think now is the time. How about it, Tommy? I did give you a good concession of $900.00 for the twenty-six volumes, so won't you please say the good word? Stay well. Best wishes, Billy. PS Write & make me happy!!'

Over the years Tommy purchased not only the Encyclopedia, but also the *Book of Blackouts* in five volumes, the *Book of Parodies* in three volumes, the *Comedy and Emcee Lecture Book* in nine lessons, the *Humor-Dor for Emcees and Comedians*, all published under Glason's Fun-Master imprint. They constitute thousands of pages, some mimeographed, some carbon-copied onto paper so flimsy it is surprising it survived the typing process. In addition he subscribed to a monthly sheet also issued by Billy entitled *The Comedian*. To peruse Tommy's personal copies is tantamount to looking over his shoulder as he scrutinized this gag here, that one-liner there. Those that appealed were marked accordingly. They averaged out at about one a page, maybe a page and a half, but hardly any found their way into his act and if they did I have yet to find one that achieved classic status as a Cooperism, unless you include the line he (and Milligan too) claimed he wanted on his tombstone: 'I told you I was sick.' He also subscribed to regular bulletins of gag material issued by the British scriptwriter, Peter Cagney and two more New Yorkers, Art Paul's *Punch Lines* and Eddie Gay's *Gay's Gags*. Tommy may have thought he was purchasing new material; he was really buying a comedian's extended security blanket for the day when his bankable material was taken away from him and audiences stopped laughing. The nightmare was real for every comic.

There was one extended piece of business in Glason's pages that Tommy performed time and again. It was one of those gags that came perilously close to pre-empting itself every time it was performed, but constituted a highlight of the Cooper act as night in, night out he pushed against the obvious. Tommy had switched the basic premise from the juggling stunt detailed by Billy to the device, more appropriate to a magic act, of scaling a playing card into a hat a few feet distant. On the first attempt he fails: 'Missed'. On the second attempt he fails: 'Missed'. He announces that if he fails a third time he will shoot himself. He fails again. At this point he picks up a revolver and strides into the wings. A gunshot is heard. He walks back on: 'Missed!' Tommy used it to bring the house down during his appearance at the 1953 Royal Variety Performance. Ironically, he could not have met Glason until his first visit to America in 1954! Indeed, records place their initial transaction in March 1962. The basic premise must have been rooted in clown tradition, but had Cooper not been acquainted with it before, it would assuredly have been worth all the hundreds of dollars Glason was able to cajole out of him.

Perennial Cooper props like the flower that wilts every time it is watered and the sword that recoils on itself when he pretends to swallow it, as well as many of his cod juggling bits – like timing the third (soft) cannon ball to reach his forehead at the precise moment he brings together with a resounding crack the two other hard balls in his hands – were all part of the same clown legacy. A more short-lived bit of business with a similar pedigree from the late Fifties was what Tommy called his 'Goofus' routine, one of the few musical sequences in his repertoire, again almost certainly spotted on a trip to America.

A thousand clowns before Cooper had donned a long overcoat stuffed with motor horns. Only Tommy could announce 'Please notice I have absolutely *nothing* concealed about my person' before revealing the horns for all to see: 'This is note F, this is note G. This next one – I don't know what that one is . . . Huh huh huh!' The title of the routine relates to an early hillbilly number by Gus Kahn. The item might have been more effective with a tune better known to English audiences, not least Kahn's more memorable and more appropriate, 'Toot, Toot, Tootsie!'

When it came to acquiring strong original material Tommy never realized how lucky he was on his own doorstep. Aside from the massed ranks of the television writers, many of them familiar names, commissioned by the television companies to provide him principally with sketch material – names that we shall encounter again in the chapters on his television career – there were three writers who should forever be guaranteed their place in the roll call of honour attached to classic Cooper comedy gems. Their names are Val Andrews, Freddie Sadler, and Eddie Bayliss. According to Vicky Cooper, Eddie was probably her father's favourite writer. He had no links with show business or the literary world, was a lorry driver by trade and came to Tommy's attention when out of the blue in the late Sixties he submitted some material to Miff Ferrie. His reluctance to give up his day job kept him outside the cabal of the top television comedy writers of the day, in whose company he could well have held his own. To his credit Ferrie spotted that he had a sure grasp of the conciseness that hall-marked a great Cooper gag and Tommy's fondness for a literalism that could go to surreal extremes, as in these:

My feet are killing me – every night when I'm lying in bed they get me right round the throat like that.

161

I had a ploughman's lunch the other day – he wasn't half mad.

'When you walk in a storm, hold your head up high' (singing) – I did and fell in a puddle.

Eddie was also responsible for the memorable visit Cooper made to the doctor the time he lost his voice:

He said, 'Open your mouth,' and then he said, 'A little raw.' So I went, 'Grrr . . .' He said, 'I'm gonna test your ears, cos sometimes when you lose your voice it affects your hearing.' I said, 'Right.' He said, 'I'm gonna go down there and I'm gonna whisper something to you. And if you hear me I want you to repeat it.' I said, 'Right.' So he went down there and I went down there and he said, 'How now, brown cow?' And I said (softly) 'How now, brown cow?' And he said 'Pardon!'

Bayliss gave Tommy the basics of his fly routine, the miniature newspaper – 'a fly paper' – upon which the fly would alight for Cooper to sneak up behind and annihilate it with an almighty mallet and – once he had convinced us he was only kidding – the best method of getting flies out of the room: 'I use this. Instant starch. It doesn't kill them, but they glide out the window like that.' At this point Tommy, arms outstretched, would perform an effortless glide around the stage himself. Eddie had as sure a grasp of the visual as of the verbal, as also shown on the occasion of the 1977 Royal Variety Performance, upgraded by Lew Grade to Royal Variety Gala in recognition of the Queen's Silver Jubilee, when Tommy with one eye on the royal box took a sword from his table, carefully laid it on the ground and knelt expectantly in the direction of

162

Her Majesty. After a few seconds he stood, replaced the weapon and shrugged, 'Well, you never know!' By then, however, the Palladium was in uproar. According to one reviewer, 'the Queen, who doesn't always laugh too easily, literally shouted' at the joke.

If Eddie was his favourite writer, Cooper still owed Val and Freddie a considerable debt of gratitude for devising his most memorable routine, for which neither of them has ever been given proper credit. I refer to the 'Hats' sequence. Both Sadler and Andrews had been around Tommy from virtually the start of his career. Freddie was by night, as his letterhead proclaimed, a 'Comedy Impressionist and Compère' on the concert party circuit, trying to eke out an existence by doubling as a scriptwriter by day. Val, the only survivor of the trio, was and remains in his eightieth year respected throughout the magic community for his achievements as an author, dealer and light comedy performer in his own right. In those early days both were paid what might be deemed less than modest amounts to pen material for their friend. Freddie had some success with a burlesque of the 'catching a bullet in the teeth' routine that would crop up in the Cooper repertoire until the end of his days. Perhaps more memorably, he gave him the gag with the skipping rope: 'Here we have a skipping rope – so we'll skip that!' Anything that gave Tommy an excuse to sling something to one side without fear of breakages had an additional cachet.

In the early Fifties Val advertised himself as 'The Magicians' Scriptwriter – at your service for a complete act, routine, or patter for a single effect, written to your own style.' One night he had been performing himself and was aware of his friend grabbing him as he came off stage: 'Who writes your patter, boy?' Val replied that he did. 'Well, I want you to write something for me.' In time Tommy professed his interest in a standby of the magician's repertoire from an earlier time. Chapeaugraphy was virtually an act in itself, in which a large circle of felt with a hole in the centre was twisted into a variety of different hats. The French magician and entertainer, Félicien Trewey had scored heavily with the device during the latter part of the nineteenth century, his presentation being one of the very first performances captured – by the Lumière Brothers – on film. At its fullest extent his routine presented a parade of as many as thirty-two characters 'under one hat', including toreador, miser, drunkard, costermonger, priest, schoolmaster, a whole sequence of nationals, including a Turk in a fez, and a Salvation Army 'lassie'. The idea can be traced back to the early part of the seventeenth century when in more limited form it featured in the act of Tabarin, a popular charlatan and farceur who performed on the streets of Paris. Since Trewey's heyday it had become relegated to a large extent to the amateur stage and lecture platform. Tommy had recently seen a performance in which the different hat shapes were linked to an accompanying story line for the characters represented.

For a man who never wore hats in real life, the comic potential of the actual article had long intrigued him. In 1970 Tommy confided to the journalist, John Dodd that he first discovered he was funny when he was wearing a hat. He was seventeen and standing at a bus stop with a hat on his head when people began to laugh and snigger. At first the circumstances must have been daunting for the developing teenager, but with a pith helmet and a fez behind him he would in adulthood turn the discovery and embarrassment of his teenage years into comic gold, as first shown by the early routine in which he went back and forth between the theatre tabs in a series of daft impressions – each signified by the hat he was wearing – of 'famous people of the past, the present, and the future'. He featured this as a second spot in the show, *Paris*

Comic Ways and Means

by Night at the Prince of Wales theatre in 1955. In the original sequence he paraded, in quick succession, Uncle Sam; John Bull; Napoleon; English sailor; American sailor; 'Two sailors at once'; Napoleon again; 'We should not have lost the war! (Nazi helmet); 'Why?' (British Tommy); the King of Norway; 'the other way' (turns hat through ninety degrees); Nelson (with a hand over his right eye); Half Nelson (same as before, but down on bended knee); and so on. Sometimes he would become hopelessly entangled with the tabs, sometimes completely out of sync with the invisible assistant backstage readying each hat for him. With this in the back of his mind Val devised the concept of using a box of different hats instead of the disc of felt to tell a continuous story. Tommy brought in Freddie to add some ideas of his own and the routine that stopped the show for Cooper on more occasions than any other was born during the run of *Paris by Night*.

His effortless ability to switch with lightning speed from one to another of a whole procession of characters that included tramp, sailor, banker, cowboy, soldier, little old lady, fireman, pilot, policeman, and a few more along the way – while keeping order for himself in the box that belied the confusion experienced by the audience – would alone qualify many a lesser performer for a place in comedy's hall of fame. The words of the doggerel that began

'Twas New Year's Eve in Joe's bar, a happy mob was there.
The bar and tables were crowded, lots of noise filled the air.
In the midst of all this gaiety the door banged open wide.
A torn and tattered tramp walked in. 'Happy New Year, folks,' he cried.

were largely inconsequential – and sometime incomprehensible – but provided a springboard for his gift for comic looks like

165

no other routine in his repertoire. It is hard for Val to be specific about who was responsible for what detail other than, 'I can safely say 50 per cent of it was Sadler, 50 per cent Andrews.' He is also gracious enough to concede that what enabled the routine to grow in stature and remain fresh over so many years were the occasional *faux pas* on Cooper's part that proved so funny he kept them in. It is great testimony to his acting skills that night after night they continued to come over as entirely spontaneous. Tommy would be hardly a dozen lines into the script when in a moment of excitement – 'Them's shooting words,' a cowboy said. 'Are you aimin' to be shot?' – he forgot the words and had to backtrack to the beginning, muttering the whole sequence again *sotto voce* and switching hats around at a great pace while he caught up, all the while insinuating to the audience that it will be business as usual soon, as if nothing had happened. Val recalls that when this first happened – during a dressing room rehearsal – he had to spend half an hour convincing him how funny it could be on a regular basis: 'His reaction was, "Yes, but they'll think I really have forgotten!" There were times when Tommy was not exactly a mental giant!'

Such lapses proved the making of the routine. Inevitably at one stage he can't find the hat he needs: 'I've got to get a bigger box! Where was I up to?' Then it is time for the fireman to have his say, but Tommy brings the helmet up so sharply, he hits himself accidentally with considerable force on the forehead. Registering pain as only he can, he appeals to the wings: 'Now that's dangerous, that is. You should have padded that a bit. I could have cut my head open on that.' The poem concludes with the bar-room brawl getting so out of hand – 'in rushed an Indian; a little schoolboy; I don't know who that is!' – that the law has to intervene:

In the middle of all this fighting you could hear the
   knuckles crunch,
When all of a sudden they heard a policeman's whistle . . .

It doesn't come.

They heard a policeman's whistle . . .

No luck this time either.

They heard a policeman's whistle . . .

At last we hear the sound effect from the wings. Tommy peers
out at the disgraced stagehand with disdain and utters the line
that sums up amateur theatrics everywhere:

Isn't it marvellous, eh?
That's all he has to do.
And he's wearing make-up as well!

Then a policeman came in and pinched the whole damn
bunch.

In a more expansive moment Val confided to me a more
detailed account of the circumstances surrounding the birth of
the sequence, acknowledging in addition the burlesque monologue style of the comedian Billy Bennett, the low comedy
laureate of the music halls, as a further source of inspiration.
The verbal structure of 'New Year's Eve in Joe's Bar' started
out as a conscious Bennett-style parody of 'The Shooting of
Dan McGrew' by the Edwardian balladeer, Robert William
Service. In addition, working away in Val's mind was the
memory of an extinct double act, Tom Payne and Vera Hil-
liard, in which the comedian played a door to door salesman

with a number of hats in a suitcase. The many strands became plaited together to produce a classic. Over the years other writers with Cooper's consent took the basic premise to rewrite other words and characters around it. It was always a futile exercise. Audiences would never tire of the original. Why should they, let alone the performer, settle for second best?

Tommy never relinquished his interest in the piece of felt itself. In later years the writers John Muir and Eric Geen came up with the approach that suited him best and, more importantly, did not clash with the now established pattern of 'Hats'. For all his skill in switching hats back and forth at breakneck speed in and out of a cardboard box, he had proved less adroit at twisting the ring of felt into a series of specific complex patterns while following a set patter line. The new angle was an incidental one, taking away any such worries as he reminisced about the lady who had approached him before the show to enquire how serious a person he was in his private life. Tommy is anxious to stress that at home he is nothing like the buffoon she sees larking about on the stage, that he reads a lot of serious books, attends a lot of serious plays. All the while he is twiddling the cloth into an inconsequential series of bizarre headpieces that hilariously disprove the assertions of the moment.

It is doubtful if Sadler received the remuneration that was his due for his part in the 'Hats' routine. Val, who wrote for Tommy on a fairly regular basis from 1947 until the mid Sixties, certainly never received what his contribution was truly worth. Only economic necessity kept him in the loop for so long. There were times when he might have been forgiven for walking away. Around the time when 'Hats' came into being he submitted to Tommy a sketch based on the idea of Cooper as a penniless restaurant owner forced by circumstances to play all the staff himself, doubling as commissionaire, head waiter, chef, even the performers in the cabaret that included a Russian violinist and an adagio dancer. When Val asked Tommy whether he had had a chance to study the sketch, the reply was non-committal: 'I haven't had a chance to look at it yet.' He thought no more of the matter until a few months later he was watching an episode of *The Tony Hancock Show*, the early 1956 series for commercial television that featured the star before *Hancock's Half Hour* cemented his television reputation on the other channel. A carbon copy of the original sketch was played out before him. At one point he turned to his mother and said, 'If the next character to come through the door is a Russian violinist, this has gone beyond coincidence.' It was! As he says today, 'I rest my case. I worried considerably about it. Thought I was going out of my mind. When I mentioned it to Tommy – I wasn't aggressive – it was his defensive attitude that worried me. He was like Billy Bunter: "No, Skinner took the cakes." It was nothing to do with him.' Val, a modest and unassuming man, refused to have anything to do with Cooper for several months, but the need for a few shillings, the camaraderie of the magic profession and the fact that Tommy could be such good company brought them together again. But he remains quite clear about what happened: 'He would have sold it. Thinking it was not suitable for himself in the first place, he didn't want to give me any money for it and thought I would just dismiss it. If it was no good for him, it was no good for anybody. Did he seriously think he was brighter than me in that regard?'

John Muir also testifies to Tommy's less than straightforward manner in dealing with scriptwriters when money was concerned. For one Blackpool summer season Muir provided him with a routine that burlesqued the skills of Percy Edwards, the well known animal impersonator. When he asked how it was working out, Tommy replied, 'It died. Not a laugh. I tried it out and had to drop it.' That put paid to any suggestion of payment. However, when he mentioned the matter to another act on the bill it transpires it was getting huge laughs each night. A short while later John caught Cooper doing the routine on one of his television shows for Thames. When he approached the company they told him that Tommy had claimed the material as his own. The broadcaster smelled the proverbial rat and wasted no time in paying him. Andrews, Muir and Brad Ashton all testify to his cheeseparing habit of delaying the use of material submitted by them until he could perform it on television, thus shifting any financial obligation from himself to the production company. That he might continue to use such material in his stage performances in perpetuity was something that was always pushed to one side.

From a myriad of sources the Cooper comic repertoire slowly came together. In the early days his energy was indefatigable as he went out of his way to try out material that was new to him. David Berglas, Pat Page, and Bobby Bernard all share fond recall of him popping into meetings of the smaller London magic clubs, like the Thursday sessions of the Institute of Magicians in Clerkenwell and the Friday ones of the London Society of Magicians in Red Lion Square, to test new stuff *en route* to a late night cabaret booking. At other times he would test gags by springing them on friends or family in anxious anticipation of the reaction. 'Usually he bursts into the kitchen with a funny hat just as I'm putting the joint in the oven – and is hurt if I don't laugh,' Gwen once said. Jokes were like tricks, things to try out with renewed excitement whenever he found one to his liking. Backstage or at rehearsals he never lost an opportunity to try out a new gag, as Bob Monkhouse reminisced: 'I once saw him in a dressing room dangling a bath tap on a piece of elastic. I asked him what he was doing. "It's a gag," he said. He was going to come on, dangle it up and down a few times and then say to the audience, "Tap dance!" I thought the idea was terrible, the worst joke I'd ever heard. "Don't do it," I said. "They'll attack you." Of course he went ahead with it and brought the place down.'

The final arbiter always had to be Cooper. Once he had convinced himself that something was funny, there was no stopping him. One tires of the times ones sees his jokes dismissed as 'old'. Billy Glason hit the nail on the head in his sales pitch: '*There are no old gags!* The only thing old about old gags are the ones who've heard them before and the answer to those who want to admit their age when they remark that a gag is old, is "Say, you don't *look* that old!"' Tommy once confided his feelings on the issue to magical friend, David Hemingway: 'It doesn't matter how old the gag is. It doesn't matter how many times the audience has heard it before. If it's funny, it's funny.' Anyhow, public memory is so short that what an audience is capable of forgetting is remarkable, until the point when familiarity does set in and a joke assumes the status of an old friend. Who would not have attended a Cooper show and come away disappointed at not hearing lines like these?

I said to the waiter, 'This chicken I've got here's cold.' He said, 'It should be. It's been dead two weeks.' I said, 'Not only that, he's got one leg shorter than the other.' He said, 'What do you want to do? Eat it or dance with it?' I said 'Forget the chicken. Give me a lobster.' So he brought me a lobster. I looked at it. I said, 'Just a minute. It's only got one claw.' He said, 'It's been in a fight.' I said, 'Give me the winner.'

When Davenport's magic shop had its premises opposite the British Museum, the joke used to be that Tommy went to one for his tricks and the other for his gags. Barry Cryer has a theory that Cooper was fully aware of the awful quality of much of his material and was entering into a conspiracy with his audience: 'He knows it's a terrible joke and he knows they know it's terrible. They were laughing less at the joke itself than at how bad it was, not to mention his effrontery in sharing it with them.' My contention is that there is no such thing as a bad gag, if it is well told and the personality of the teller can surpass its inherent triteness. That may amount to the same thing. Certainly, one of Cooper's skills was his ability to spot what would work for him in this regard, to recognize the innate structure that would connect effortlessly with his delivery.

Someone once commented that the best Cooper one-liners had an almost haiku-like quality. I doubt if the theory would hold water if subjected to the many rules of this most compact, most complex literary form, but one senses what they were trying to say. No one understands the mechanics of the process better than current comedian, Tim Vine. Had he been around in Tommy's time, providing the master with material, he would have been the one writer Cooper made sure he paid properly. Without impersonating or making any overt refer-ence to his hero, Vine keeps alive the logical illogicality that underpinned so much in the Cooper joke compendium. Like-wise had Tommy been alive today he may well have had a harder time on the circuits that Tim plays, since he could not claim to have been the comic auteur that modern audiences expect in such situations. In a curious twist of time warp, jokes by Vine published indiscriminately on the internet have been wrongly attributed to Cooper's repertoire. When through a horrendous series of misunderstandings one of them found its way into my stage tribute, *Jus' Like That!* it achieved as loud a laugh as any of the gags Cooper had told in his lifetime:

Apparently, one in five people in the world is Chinese. And there are five people in my family, so it must be one of them. It's either my mum or dad. Or my older brother, Colin. Or my younger brother, Ho-Cha-Chu. But I think it's Colin.

It has all the Cooper qualities. It is succinct. It has a rhythmic three part motif tucked away inside – just think of 'lump for your cocoa' – that occurred time after time in his material. It has a strong visual, almost cartoon-like quality that again is so often present. And, like a great magic trick, it exploits the sheer joy of surprise. Even the most familiar gags in the Cooper canon kept this intact. The nearer he got to the punch line, so at the moment of telling the joke became reborn. When asked by David Hemingway to explain his humour, Tommy simply replied that the two funniest things were a surprise and a funny picture. His entire repertoire is a cartoon gallery of the unexpected.

Tommy was often at his most surprising when driving home a literalism, the headlights of which we didn't see coming. Study the cross talk routines of Flanagan and Allen, Sid Field and Jerry Desmonde, Norman Wisdom and Desmonde again, and the device appears played out to the point of tedium, redeemed only by the charm of the performers. Tommy kept it on its toes, in the way Harpo had done at an earlier time when he produced an axe and split a table on overhearing a gambler say, 'Cut the cards.' Cooper took it to brazen extremes not encountered since Ollie forced Stan to eat his hat in *Way Out West*:

I slept like a log last night. I woke up in the fireplace.

Sometimes I drink my whisky neat. Other times I take my tie off and leave my shirt hanging out.

Someone actually complimented me on my driving the other day. They put a note on my windscreen that said, 'Parking fine'. So that was nice.

My dog's a one-man dog – he only bites me. I say to him 'Attack' and he has one. He took a big lump out of my knee the other day and a friend of mine said, 'Did you put anything on it?' I said, 'No. He liked it as it was.'

He could draw the obvious to your attention with such wondrous incredulity that you forgave him for it. The slightly demeaning word 'pun' never entered your mind as Tommy went through his roll call of crazy props: two gloves sewn together: 'Look, second hand!'; a toy plane suspended from a coat hanger: 'Aircraft hangar!'; a golf club that separates into two pieces: 'I joined a golf club last week. It keeps coming apart!' He even had a wild tendency to carry the trait into real life. Those not in the know might have wondered whether he was subject to Asperger's syndrome. Robert Agar-Hutton has recalled his visit to a tailor's shop in Shaftesbury Avenue where Tommy had come to buy a suit. Checking himself out in the mirror, he turned to a member of staff and asked, 'Do you mind if I take it for a walk round the block?' With a client so famous, how could they object? At which point Tommy took from his pocket a small block of wood, placed it on the floor, walked around it once, and then agreed, 'Fine, I'll take it.' There's also the occasion he walked into a library, asked for a pair of scissors and proceeded to cut the bottom off one of his trouser legs. He went up to the librarian and announced, 'There's a turn-up for the books!' The latter incident may be apocryphal. It is warming to think it may actually have happened.

Not far removed in his personal comic spectrum was the

fascination for 'doctor' jokes, his habitual poor health lending an ironic quality to their status. A book could be filled with them. When a Sunday newspaper ran a competition for original Cooper jokes in 1975, they outnumbered all the others submitted. Possibly the first one he ever heard was a Max Miller original: 'I said, "Doctor, I've broken my arm in several places." He said, "Well, you shouldn't go to those places."' Many others were almost certainly buried in the depths of time: 'So I said to the doctor, "How do I stand?" He said, "That's what puzzles me!" "Doctor, I feel like a pair of curtains." "Then pull yourself together." "Doctor, doctor," I said, "There's something wrong with my foot. What should I do?" He said, "Limp."' In effect they were interchangeable. To be acquainted with one today – whether he told it or not – is as vivid a reminder of the man himself as the fez or the catchphrase.

As he traded in such nonsense – in the best Carrollian sense of the word – he tapped into something that related to the child in us all. He made us laugh again at what we had chuckled at in the *Dandy* or *Beano* when we were eight years old. The innocence manifested itself in other ways. His table of props resembled nothing more than a children's play area. And the act was totally suitable for children of all ages. In spite of his admiration for Max Miller he completely belied the old W. C. Fields adage, 'Nothing risqué, nothing gained.' Gwen is on record as saying that if he ever told a dirty joke she would divorce him: 'He didn't need to. He could still make people laugh.' In truth such humour would have been too knowing for his own persona and when he did come close to it in his regular act it was with the naughtiness of the playground, as when he produced from his pocket a brassiere with three cups: 'I met a funny girl last night.' But he was not above the tendency to resort – ever so rarely – to smuttiness when occasion demanded. Brad Ashton recalled the time he saw Tommy struggling against a tough Geordie club audience, reduced to telling uncharacteristically adult gags in an attempt to hold the crowd. The management was not best pleased. On a stray occasion in May 1966 Miff received an admonitory call from a management requesting that Tommy 'tone his act down a bit' for the second night of a convention of oil executives at Brighton. When the agent asked for more specific information, the reply came that the client would like Tommy to cut, 'The Tarzan joke, and the one about when he performed in the USA in a nudist colony and a lady said, "Well, he isn't a Jew anyway!"' The complaint is hard to comprehend. Miff demanded that it be put in writing and doubtless the headmaster served summons on his pupil in the standard manner.

They were rare incidents, not least because Tommy knew what he was doing. Survival is one thing, habit is another. He once said, 'Once you tell the first dirty joke you tell another and before you know where you are, you've got a blue show and I don't want that. It's very difficult to get back from blue material to clean material.' His friends, Morecambe and Wise had once featured a routine in which it was hinted that Ernie might have been responsible for an illegitimate pregnancy. The postbag groaned with letters of protest for several days. The nearest Cooper came to a racist gag, the Brighton reference notwithstanding, was when he asked a Chinese waiter if there were any Chinese Jews: 'He said, "I don't know. I'll go and find out." So he went and came back. He said, "No. There's only apple juice, pineapple juice and orange juice."' The closest he came to a sick joke was his confession that he always travelled in the tail end of an aeroplane: 'You never heard of one backing into a mountain.' A perennial routine called 'Souvenirs', in which he produced objects from a box to signify places he had visited – The Isle of Man (a dummy trousered leg held in appropriate position); Holyhead (a sprig of holly on a headband); Leatherhead (an old boot held on top of his head); Bath (a bath cap); East Ham (a ham joint held accordingly); West Ham (switched to the other hand); Oldham – Phew! (same joint held to his nose)' – was first written to include a gag where he blew up a pink rubber glove and inverted it to represent the lower regions of a cow: 'Huddersfield!' Even that was deemed by Cooper to be somewhat near the knuckle.

Miff made sure that the merest sexual or lavatorial reference was blue-pencilled in any material sent by him for Tommy's consideration. Inevitably the demarcation line differed between them, but Tommy was his own best judge. It is hard to believe that in 1965 Ferrie went out of his way to have the following, now accepted as a quintessential Cooper classic, edited out of a television show: 'I went to my doctor and said "I keep dreaming these beautiful girls keep coming towards me. These beautiful girls keep coming towards me and I keep pushing them away. These beautiful girls keep coming towards me and I keep pushing them away." He said, "What do you want me to do?" I said, "Break my arm."' It all seems so harmless now, but perhaps back then did send out a frisson not in accord with his image. If Tommy did commit the occasional indiscretion it was almost certainly mitigated by the fact that on no occasion did cynicism or malice intrude into his humour. He made fun of nobody but himself.

There were times when his material hinted at a curiously philosophical tone, situated in a strange no-man's land between ignorance and a higher mental power:

Somebody once said that horsepower was a very good thing when only horses had it.

I think inventions are marvellous, don't you? Wherever they put a petrol pump they find petrol.

It's strange, isn't it? You stand in the middle of a library and go 'Aaaaagh!' and everyone just stares at you. But you do the same thing on an aeroplane and everyone joins in.

Whether Tommy and his writers or more learned people rooted in academia were the first to make such topsy-turvy observations I do not know, but the fact that he was prepared to acknowledge them is significant. Deep down they profess to a questioning of the way the world works that gets close to the higher level of conceptual or representational humour exploited so successfully by Spike Milligan in *The Goon Show*, going beneath the level of language to the fundamental structures of thought and life itself. Milligan could have written Cooper's apparently simplistic comment – made to Bob Monkhouse while discussing hobbies – that while other people paint apples, bananas and oranges, he paints the juice, not to mention the one about the Rembrandt and the Stradivarius.

Perhaps it is not surprising that occasionally he hit a macabre streak. Roy Hudd describes seeing him strike up an imaginary conversation with a guy threatening to jump from the theatre balcony: 'Why? Please don't jump. Think of your family and your friends. Everything's gonna be alright.' He said all he could in an effort to avert the tragedy. There followed a pause while Cooper pretended to listen to the other point of view. He then responded, 'Oh, I understand. Throw yourself off then!' A radio discussion programme hosted by Robert Robinson once decided on a Tommy Cooper joke as the greatest gag of all. In its barest form it involves a man knocking on a door and asking for Charlie or Fred or whoever. 'Charlie died a couple of hours ago,' is the response. 'He didn't say anything about a tin of paint, did he?' comes the reply. Many will not find that funny at all. If you are a comedian or a philosopher, you almost certainly will. It sums up the ridiculousness of life itself, the human condition pared to its barest bones. When Milligan elected to cast Cooper in a god-like role he was in part acknowledging this aspect of the man.

It is unlikely Tommy would have thought through the seriousness of this himself, although serious is everything he professed to be in his approach to comedy. According to Mary Kay he was a great admirer of Woody Allen: 'Tommy liked his dead seriousness. He always maintained that humour came out of very serious, very macabre situations. You have to be dead straight in order to make people laugh.' When writer and film director, Michael Winner temporarily took over the *Sunday Times* 'Atticus' column from Hunter Davies in June 1977 he was determined to give Cooper some coverage. He invited himself along to Chiswick and asked Tommy to nominate a joke that he could quote the following weekend, without realising the pressure he was placing on the comedian's shoulders: 'It was as if I had asked him to explain atomic fusion. He sat there agonizing over what one would be right. I saw a serious man applying himself to his job.' In the same way, the more extensive his repertoire became, so the choice that existed behind the scenes of each appearance became more daunting. He once gave voice to another aspect of the constant challenge that faced him: 'Simplicity is the hardest thing in the world to achieve. I suppose that's what I'm aiming for.' He never professed to understand his own talent, nor did he want to know, recognizing that self-consciousness could cause it to implode on itself. In that sense comedy and life were one. As Woody once said, 'When it's all over, the news is bad.'

But Tommy was essentially an optimist and knew how to stay that way. 'Never mix with miseries, because they'll bring you down to their level,' he was fond of saying. In this vein he shared with his fellow countryfolk, Harry Secombe and Gladys Morgan a propensity for laughing at his own jokes. It is something comedians are not supposed to do, but with Cooper was excusable at two levels. Firstly he always gave the impression that the gag – 'Here's a quick joke. I want to hear it myself!' – was new, even more surprising to him than to the audience. Secondly, it was an integral part of his amazing, almost totally unrecognized gift for subverting the whole art of comedy itself. Frankie Howerd had most obviously flouted the conventions of the genre, his speech a garbled string of interjections and asides that made mockery of the fluency of the monologue comedian. His wheezes, his fidgeting and his overall discomfort were a constant distraction to the task in hand. No one obviously thought of Cooper in this regard. He was adept at messing up magic, but as the years progressed he became funnier still getting the basic business of being funny wrong as well. It is a trait he leaned on increasingly as the years progressed and his delivery became more slurred and strangulated.

The inept comedian made a powerful partner for the bumbling magician. As Levent Cimkentli, a spiritual heir to Cooper among the new generation of American comedy club performers, has pointed out, he will often use his catchphrase to fly in the face of comedy technique, delaying the punch line and affecting the compactness of the gag: 'There's this fellow and he's rowing up the road like that. (Does rowing action) Not like that. Like that. So he's rowing up the road like that, and this policeman comes up to him and says, "What are you doing?" And he says, "I'm rowing up the road." And the policeman says, "You haven't got a boat." And he says, "Oh, haven't I?" (Starts swimming for his life)' The tag is delayed by fourteen syllables, but in spite of the irrelevant information

Cooper has added, the joke gets an even bigger response, because it is even more ridiculous. With Levent's observation in mind it is interesting to revisit a sequence already quoted in this chapter. As transcribed above it does not reflect an accurate version of what Tommy actually said. This is a more faithful account:

> I said to the waiter, *I said*, 'This chicken I've got here's cold.' He said, 'It should be. It's been dead two weeks.' I said, 'Not only that,' *I said. I said – I said it twice – I said,* 'He's got one leg shorter than the other.' He said, 'What do you want to do? Eat it or dance with it?' I said 'Forget the chicken.' *I said, 'Forget the chicken.* Give me a lobster.' So he brought me a lobster. I looked at it. I said, 'Just a minute.' *I said, 'Just – a – min – ute.'* I said, 'It's only got one claw.' He said, 'It's been in a fight.' I said, 'Give me the winner.'

The repetitions, the curious cadences are italicized. With a lesser comic they would have impeded the flow considerably. With Cooper they enhanced it.

As he wreaked havoc on the art of magic in his attempt to emulate the great illusionists of his youth, so he turned comedy on its head in his attempt to mirror the slick professionalism of the likes of Miller, Askey, Benny and Hope. Both the magicians and the mirth makers were representative of an ideal he knew, subconsciously at least, that he could not attain. The greatest paradox of his achievement is that he drew level with them. In so doing he was able to defy all the conventions, like repeating a piece of business – catching the ball in the cone, for example – several times in his act, when the rule book made clear that, unless it was intended as a running gag, you left well alone after securing the initial laugh. He would get sidetracked by talking to people in the wings. Miller had acknowledged their presence with conspiratorial glances as part of a conversational flow with the audience. To Cooper, the distraction was more real: 'What do you mean come off? I've only just come on.' Or, thinking the audience wouldn't notice, he would look down under his table and mutter, 'Well, you shouldn't have been under there in the first place.' There were also the echoes of Bob Hope's own insecurity; the cough that was never cured, unashamed punctuation pause to cover all inadequacies; and the jokes that maybe were old and sub-standard – 'Here's another one you may not like!' – giving an added fillip to Barry Cryer's audience conspiracy theory. 'Funny enough – is it funny enough?' he would ask. He was even pre-pared to repeat a joke if he felt it had let him down first time around: 'I've got a cigarette lighter that won't go out. (Pause) I've got a cigarette lighter that won't go out.' Like Frankie Howerd's whole act, it was of course perfectly calculated: this was the only line he used in this way.

The unorthodox approach led to him taking calculated risks that none of his contemporaries would have dared. One night he walked on stage and said, 'It's lovely to be here.' He paused, moved a few paces sideways and said, 'It's lovely to be here as well!' On one occasion I saw him take the same device to even braver lengths. The venue was the Bournemouth Winter Gardens, the permanent home of the Bournemouth Symphony Orchestra. For three months of high summer the classical musicians moved out to make way for the star entertainers of the day. In this profit-maximizing process many performers found themselves playing a stage not best suited to their talents, one which, New York's Radio City Music Hall ex-cepted, qualifies as the widest I have ever seen. I can visualize Tommy's entrance now. Looking as if he had just been pushed on, he came from upstage to the centre of the apron, paused, looked to one side and then the other. He hardly said a word.

His doubting expression told all. Fancy putting a comic on a stage like this! He then turned and taking all the time in the world – he might have been walking the dog – strolled to one end of the vast orchestral platform. He fired a salvo of one-liners at the audience on that side of the theatre. For about three minutes the laughter swelled. He then turned again and walked all the way to the far end of the stage on the other side where he embarked upon exactly the same sequence. The audience now laughed even louder. You knew it was coming, which made it all the funnier.

In time the audience came to expect something out of the ordinary from him. It reached its zenith with the device where he found himself locked in his dressing room, which may have had its origins in the earlier one where only his feet appeared beneath the curtain. As the tabs were flown with the spotlight centred on his shoes, his bewildered cry for help told all: 'Where am I? Where am I?' In later years a working off-stage stand microphone became a requirement demanded of all club and theatre managements. No sooner than his name was announced, the audience could sense something was wrong. First a sigh was heard over the loudspeakers. As Lenny Henry once remarked, 'If you can get a good laugh just by breathing out, that's serious comedy.' Then the words followed: 'Oh dear! What's going on now? I can't get out. I'm locked in. I'm still in the dressing room. Now all the lights have gone out. Where's the door?' When he does get out, 'It's darker out there than it was in here. What's this? It's my suit. It's another suit. Huh huh. You'll laugh at this. I'm in the wardrobe!' Eventually he does find his way to the stage – 'Right, can we go?' But when the tabs are drawn we see him facing away from the audience, talking to the wall. The laughter eventually provides him with his bearings and the act proper begins.

Television producer, Royston Mayoh swears that he was

once present at a Birmingham club where Tommy kept up this invisible pretence for forty-one minutes, by which time he had lost and found his trousers and probably done a circuit of the Bullring in the attempt. I think it is likely that somewhere down the line a set of tabs jammed and he improvised the entrance from there. In time the device also became magnificent cover for his late arrival at a venue, the get-out with many an exasperated stage manager: 'You're late, Mr Cooper.' 'It's alright. Don't worry about it.' 'Look, we've only got five minutes.' 'It's alright. Start the band.' Lee Evans recalls witnessing Tommy extemporizing into the microphone as he dressed and set up his props on one such occasion, only going on stage when he was ready.

It is no wonder that when he died the way he did, people thought it was a joke. It is no wonder also that he was the object of awe and admiration in his fellow comics whose routines were meant to show the results of rigid discipline, careful rehearsal and accurate timing. Not that this excluded Tommy from their company. Only a performer with strong technique and immense confidence could successfully enter the forbidden territory he appeared to tread. On one occasion he was featured at the Shakespeare Club, a converted theatre in Liverpool. One night the hydraulic stage played up as Tommy was rising into view. Comedian Pete Price remembers that it stuck halfway and wouldn't budge an inch: 'In fact the audience could see only Tommy's head and fez, yet he went right through his forty-five minute act and held them all the time.' One speculates that had hydraulic stages been more commonplace, he would have been tempted to repeat the circumstances.

It must come back to self-belief. He once discussed telling the corniest joke in the world: 'You have to have such innocent faith in it that the audience just *has* to laugh.' Perhaps this was the most important thing he acquired at the college of Milton Berle, class of 1949. Bob Monkhouse once described to me an impromptu lesson in comedy he had been given by the American. Berle asked Bob to cite any joke he had ever heard him tell, also to give him an unrelated phrase consisting of a couple of words. His claim was that he could go on that night and substitute the two new words for the established punch line. In this way, 'This suit is made from virgin wool. It comes from the sheep that runs the fastest,' became 'This suit is made from virgin wool. It came from a sheep last Thursday.' At the end of a string of progressively shorter one-liners, Uncle Miltie, as he was known to the American public, did the new version. According to Bob, the audience roared: 'He was completely the master. He had them hypnotized.' He could have been dangling a tap on a length of elastic. With both men the power of suggestion was helped by eyes that lit up to signal a joke; with Cooper it was aided further by an intrinsic physical funniness that not even Berle possessed. Eric Morecambe once asked Barry Cryer, 'Why is it that he goes on stage and they start laughing immediately and when I go on stage I have to start working?' He said it with great love. But with Cooper there was always a high level of the art that conceals art. Deep inside he was working as hard as the magnificent Morecambe ever worked.

Tommy once spent an afternoon with Eric and Ernie during which they got around to discussing and trading ad-libs and heckler stoppers. A few nights later Eric was present at a cabaret club where many other influential show business people were in the audience. Cooper was halfway through his routine when the unforgivable happened; a waiter right in front of him dropped a tray of drinks. All the pros looked at each other expectantly, not least Morecambe. Of all the lines that had been thrown around among the three of them, which, he wondered, would Tommy consider most worthy of the occasion. After a suitable pause during which his eyes took in a grand tour of audience, culprit, tray and audience again, Cooper stared at the offender and said 'That's nice!' He then continued with his act as if nothing had happened. The simplicity of the response was more powerful than anything from Orben or Glason that might have been tucked away in the innermost recesses of his mind. But about the incident I have a theory. The anecdote has been told by more high profile Cooper aficionados than any other. They all remember where they were and who they were with at the time. And it is always a different venue. Taking into account the clause Tommy invariably had built into his contract when he was playing a club, that waiter service would be suspended for the duration of his act, I wonder whether the incident wasn't repeated on more than one occasion to Tommy's specific mandate. We are back to the art that conceals art and an artist as great as Eric Morecambe didn't spot it. Moreover, Cooper's response was the right one for a man whose humour was never judgmental or cruel. If my theory is true, one wonders whether the idea was his own. To return briefly to matters of authorship, the Broadway composer, Harold Arlen refused to draw a dividing line between composer and lyricist. 'It's the collaboration,' he would stress. Perhaps that is what counts with Cooper. Scarcely any of his material was original, but the thousand secret collaborations he engendered with this original writer here, that pioneer ideas man there achieved something alchemical. He made their often pedestrian creations his own. And he always left them laughing.

SEVEN

The Steady Climb

Encore des Folies brought Tommy more than recognition. It revealed the patronage, in association with Moss Empires, of one of the more important new impresarios on the West End scene. As a speciality dancer Bernard Delfont had once been part of an act himself and had an affinity for backing distinctive variety talent, as well as a love of all that was spectacular in show business. At this time, Norman Wisdom was on the verge of a major career breakthrough as a result of Bernie's ability to spot a rising star, while thanks to his affectionate promotion Laurel and Hardy and the legendary Danish–American illusionist, Dante, had been enjoying great success in Britain during the swansong stage of their careers. The combination of comedy *and* magic, in a more vigorous mix than ever before, made Cooper a natural in his eyes. With the exposure from the television series, *It's Magic* in the spring and early summer of 1952, it was inevitable that before long Tommy would progress to a better class of provincial booking. Following a two week debut appearance at the London Palladium in July, low down on a bill topped by forgotten American comedy team, Peter Lind Hayes and Mary Healy, he embarked in the autumn on his first tour of the prestigious Moss Empires circuit. He received a weekly salary of eighty pounds for the Palladium booking; with an assist from Delfont, Miff was able to command £125.00 a week in the country, as his client zigzagged his way from Liverpool to Glasgow, Birmingham to Brighton, Newcastle to Finsbury Park and all points beyond, with a few weeks in town for Christmas to take advantage of the lucrative cabaret season.

He would formally arrive back in the West End for the week commencing 25 May 1953, compromising at ninety pounds a week to take part in the two week bill at the Palladium that coincided with the Coronation of Her Majesty the Queen. American comic, Danny Thomas, who was in some ways the poor man's Milton Berle, was top of an otherwise lack-lustre bill. Where was Bob Hope when birthright, if not citizenship, called? It was then back to the provincial grindstone, until the beginning of December when Tommy found himself deputizing at the Adelphi Theatre for Tony Hancock, previously – and incongruously – committed to pantomime duty, during the last two months of the revue, *London Laughs*, in which he appeared alongside Jimmy Edwards and Vera Lynn. The weekly salary of £150.00 was more in line with Tommy's new co-star status. Delfont could not have been happy to look on as Cooper made an impact in a revue presented by three of his main rivals, Jack Hylton and George and Alfred Black. He became determined that in little more than a year he would have the mad magician back in the West End working under his banner. However, before Tommy opened in his new *Folies* production, *Paris by Night* at the Prince of Wales Theatre on 9 April 1955, for a run that would extend for seventy-four weeks through to September 1956, Delfont kept him under his wing with summer season at Southport and pantomime at Dudley. In both shows he co-starred with radio comic, Derek

Roy and 'Sugar Bush' vocalist, Eve Boswell. In the latter, *Humpty Dumpty*, he played King Yoke of Eggville, presumably finding renewed opportunity for egg tricks and poultry jokes.

Any gaps were mostly taken up by single weeks in variety under the herald, *Bernard Delfont Presents*, although a more significant opportunity presented itself in the immediate wake of the Adelphi engagement in the form of a further opportunity to appear with Vera Lynn. In a press statement issued during the previous year, Ferrie had stated that 'So far no fewer than eight offers to appear in the United States have been refused.' It was now time to accept. Miff zealously collected the eight affidavits required by the authorities, rallying among others Ronnie Waldman, Val Parnell, and Delfont to the cause. On 31 March 1954 they set sail on the Queen Elizabeth *en route* to Las Vegas, where Tommy was booked to appear with the singing star and a predominantly British company in the revue, *Piccadilly Revels* at the Flamingo Hotel. In the desert resort show business was fast asserting itself as something more substantial than the fly-by-night accompaniment to so many jangling slot machines, the Flamingo – built by mobster 'Bugsy' Siegel – regarded as one of the classiest venues in town. The trip would provide a major challenge for all concerned, even if Tommy seemed a natural for a nation described by James Thurber as one 'that has always gone in for the loud laugh, the wow, the belly laugh and the dozen other labels for the roll-'em-in-the-aisles of gagerissimo.'

In its review *Variety* asked of the show, 'Whether it can sustain itself at the turnstiles satisfactorily for the five weeks booked may be open to question. Although fairly diverting, opus moves somewhat heavily. Tightening should improve it.' Of one thing the newspaper was certain, 'Tommy Cooper proves high spot of the revue,' to which Tommy joked, 'No wonder. I'm six feet four, the rest of the cast are three feet six!' *Variety* added, 'The unexpected climaxes to his tricks are smooth prestidigitations tailored for laughs.' Miff wrote home to his wife, 'Jack Benny was in last night, and it was not until Cooper came on that he applauded.' The show folded after two weeks and a night. According to Gwen, who did not accompany her husband, the Americans couldn't fathom the appeal of our so called 'Forces Sweetheart': 'They thought she looked like a horse eating an apple through barbed wire and, besides, the war had been over for almost a decade.' Kay Starr, a singer they could understand, was rushed in to replace the package show. In the *Daily Express* an aggrieved Miss Lynn was reported as saying a little ungraciously, 'I just felt my colleagues weren't up to my standard.'

Tommy never lost his love of America, the vitality of this Land of Hope, Milt and Benny. Not a gambling man himself, he could not stop laughing at the garage that advertised 'Petrol, free aspirin and sympathy!' for those that were. However, the debacle of the show left him a wiser man. He told Val Andrews how before the opening night everyone was 'all over' the company, nothing too much trouble for the crew backstage. However, when the singing star failed to register, attitudes changed. When he came off on the closing night he discovered the whole stage plunged into darkness: 'As far as they were concerned we were over and done. They didn't even say "goodbye".'

On his return via New York Tommy was offered a season at Radio City Music Hall. Miff has always been made the scapegoat for the fact that he did not accept, but in simple language to have done so would have been to have fallen out with Delfont. Prior to their departure *The Performer* had announced, 'He goes with the happy knowledge that on his return he will be solidly booked for the next two years. This, of course, is part of a carefully thought-out plan of campaign by Miff Ferrie who has so successfully helped to steer the lanky comedian to his present enviable position.' That Tommy was in such a strong situation is actually because of Delfont's commitment to them both. The two solid years of bookings constituted a contract between them by which the impresario guaranteed the performer £150.00 a week (for a two year period) for a minimum of forty weeks in any one year. It is conceivable that the myth of Tommy being shackled to a set weekly salary hatched out of the shell of this agreement, even if he was now guaranteed £150.00 a week – according to the retail price index the equivalent in today's terms of almost £3,000.00 – far removed from the pittance that he claimed was his dole from Miff in the early years. For the record the Vegas deal had guaranteed him $1,250.00 a week in a contract that also carried the clause, 'It is a condition of this Agreement that the Artiste is to be accompanied by his personal manger, Mr Miff Ferrie.' It added that all transportation and living expenses for the two were the responsibility of the performer. It may read like a 'freebie' for Miff, but was an arrangement that was totally justifiable in light of the relative inexperience of the performer. On the collapse of the show, Miff, on behalf of his client, settled for a total of $5,000.00 as joint payment for work done and compensation, the equivalent of £1,750.00 in sterling. The process, although disappointing, was relatively straightforward, unlike the situation that had been brewing between artist and agent.

On 4 January 1954 Tommy had instructed his solicitor to question Miff's right to a fifteen per cent commission. Miff wrote up the situation, thus giving us an insight into his client's somewhat roundabout way of confronting a problem: 'At midday Tommy Cooper telephoned me and said he was going to see his solicitor that afternoon as he was having trouble with his income tax. I asked him why on earth he was going to a solicitor about his income tax, as this was surely a matter for his accountant. He then said his accountant was in Malta, but that his solicitor wanted to know why he was paying fifteen per cent commission. I asked him what his commission had to do with income tax and he said that his solicitor wanted to see his agreement with me. I said I still did not get the reason for this and asked him if he was unhappy about anything. He said he was perfectly happy about paying fifteen per cent and then asked me what I thought he should do. I said that as he was perfectly happy paying fifteen per cent the obvious thing was to tell his solicitor so and once again told him that I could see no reason why his commission had anything to do with his income tax. He then asked me once more what I thought he should do, as he was going to see his solicitor that afternoon. I told him to do whatever he wanted to do, but that I could see no useful purpose being served, as the Agreement was perfectly in order as he well knew, having taken it to Equity and another party, namely, his accountant in the past.'

After a terse telephone conversation between Miff and Cooper's solicitor, Tommy later in the day summoned up the courage to tell Miff that he did regard the fifteen per cent as too high and that whilst he had not objected to paying this in the early days, when he was earning only twenty pounds a week, he thought that now he was earning hundreds, Miff was getting too much. The situation unleashed a profitable series of exchanges for the legal profession with demands to survey the Agreement and Miff's letter of extension exercising his right to continue handling Cooper's affairs from the first date of renewal, 28 November 1953. Miff was only too happy to provide not only these, but the correspondence from more than five years earlier in which Cooper had expressly stated his wish that Ferrie look after his interests as Personal Manager for the agreed commission.

When Miff's solicitor got to the root of the immediate problem, it hinged on Tommy's unhappiness with a situation whereby he found himself responsible for paying his manager's expenses on the American trip. In his naive eyes, dragging up the old commission ploy provided a possible route to discrediting Ferrie and cutting him out of the trip altogether. At the same time there was an opportunity to rake over old ground and Cooper's growing dissatisfaction with the 1948 agreement. Tommy went behind Miff's back and took the issue to Leslie MacDonnell, a director of Foster's Agency, which was packaging the Vegas show. MacDonnell subsequently confided in Miff that he told Tommy's solicitor 'that he thought Cooper's case rather dubious, and that Mr Ferrie had done very well for Tommy Cooper.' On 23 February, Cooper's solicitors wrote to Miff's representatives, giving notice 'terminating your client's agency six months from the date hereof. Our client, of course, cannot restrain your client from going to America, but we are instructed to inform you that if your client does go it will certainly be at his own expense.' As cold comfort the letter ended with the information that Cooper was prepared to enter into a sole agency agreement on a ten per cent basis, 'which is the usual commission payable on this type of contract and determinable thereafter by either side giving to the other three months notice in writing.' There was no case against Miff whatsoever. Eventually his solicitors advised Ferrie to adopt a policy of no further comment and for the time being life went on as usual.

Having put his signature to the original Las Vegas contract with Foster's Agency dated 4 December 1953, Cooper subsequently signed again what in essence was the same agreement with Foster's American partners, the William Morris Agency on 10 March 1954. On 30 March, the day before they sailed, a letter from Ferrie's solicitor to Cooper's suggests that Cooper was threatening to take the matter to arbitration. The response was that if Cooper persisted in his claim that there was no binding contract, it could only be decided in a Court of Law. There the matter was allowed to rest for the time being. The conjuror did not have a leg to stand on, but he was an optimist. The following day they set sail together. The episode had not provided the best of climates for such an odd couple to contemplate a trip together of such high professional significance, whoever was paying. Tommy, of course, had one trick up his sleeve. He could always withhold his commission, something he did callously from February 1954, until Miff was forced to initiate legal proceedings against him on 21 July 1954. Cooper was forced into a corner. Instructions were written up for Council, but forestalled by payment from Cooper for all amounts outstanding by the end of the Southport summer season. The title of the show, *Happy and Glorious*, must have sounded a hollow note to them both.

Meanwhile it was back to work for Delfont. In *Paris by Night* he was given second billing to a rising television comic named Benny Hill. There was no doubt who stole the show. For all his ingenuity and charm Hill was not a natural stage performer. Every night he would walk down in the finale to less applause than the performer who preceded him, an experience that would have done nothing to boost his theatrical morale. To make matters worse, *The Times* declared Tommy's contribution to be 'the evening's one first-rate thing.' In *The Observer*, Tynan wrote that Hill's comic technique was not yet assured enough for the theatre, before adding that the revue was saved by Cooper, adding this telling description of him, 'picking his way through the debris of fumbled conjuring tricks like a giant stork pecking for sustenance in a morass.' More down to earth was David Marsden, a business associate of Miff, who phoned during the run with his assessment:

'Tommy stole it, but Benny was bad and blue, looked effeminate and clothes bad!'

Benny was a gracious man and would reminisce affectionately about his co-star in later years. They had adjoining dressing rooms. Hill's habit was to arrive early before the show, enjoy his cup of tea and a Marie biscuit and attempt to get some rest on the *chaise longue*. Cooper would arrive at the last minute, usually with a group of mates in tow, cracking gags as if the show had already started. According to Benny, the one person who did get a bit agitated was his dresser: 'He'd knock on the door and say, "Mr Cooper, it's nearly time." Tommy would say, "No. It's alright. Huh huh huh. Relax. Relax." And Joe would say, "But, Mr Cooper, you're on." This sort of exchange would go on for several minutes until the dresser had no choice but to hammer on the door and shout, "Mr Cooper, they're playing your music." Tommy screamed, "Why didn't you tell me? I'll be late. I'll be late." He was just as funny off as on.'

The careers of Hill and Cooper would crisscross with amazing irony over the years. Hill had been born and brought up in Southampton less than a mile from where Tommy's parents moved to open their fish shop after the war. Both had idolized Max Miller, and while Cooper acquired his stage attack, it was Benny who translated his lecherous flair for the risqué into something that would appeal to audiences for another generation or two. During the Seventies they were the two undisputed laughter stalwarts for Thames Television. When American distributor, Don Taffner was looking for material on the Thames shelves to package for American exploitation the sheer bulk of the Hill catalogue chose itself for the eventual process of editing into the faster paced versions of *The Benny Hill Show* that justifiably won the cherubic clown international recognition on a scale for a British performer not experienced since Chaplin. With his wicked flair for mimicry, he was almost certainly the first star comedian in the country to be made entirely through television. Had he been a more successful theatrical performer he may have dedicated less time to the medium and missed the international opportunity.

In the late Sixties, long before Taffner appeared on the scene, Miff, with the blessing of Thames, had taken a couple of tapes of Tommy's television programmes to show to the powers that be at the Desilu studios in Hollywood. In the viewing theatre the executives could not restrain their laughter. According to Miff, 'When the lights went up everybody was wiping the tears out of their eyes and getting their breath back and the head writer, a guy called Lou, said, "Gee, that was terrific. But who we gonna get to play the parts?"' Not that Tommy was without success on American screens. In 1963 and 1967 he made two trips to America to make a total of five appearances for *The Ed Sullivan Show*. When in 1962 Mark Leddy, respected agent and booker for Sullivan, first tracked Tommy down in Blackpool on the recommendation of American magician Jay Marshall, he wrote back to Jay in Chicago, 'This is a very funny man. In his next to closing spot, he had enough funny stuff to do three Sullivan Shows. In my humble opinion he is much superior to Ballantine because Ballantine does the same damn act all the time.' When he got to New York, Sullivan described him to his audience of millions as quite simply 'the funniest man ever to appear on this stage.' Afterwards Leddy wrote to Miff that he was 'as happy as hell with the results.' Sadly, Cooper's international potential was never fully realized. As Barry Took pointed out, a large proportion of the *Paris by Night* audience consisted of foreign tourists, to whom much of Hill's material in those days remained a mystery; with Cooper, instant impact was guaranteed.

As submitted to the Lord Chamberlain, his comedy magic

spot had by now been almost entirely revised, the bottle and glass appearing only fleetingly, and a similar device, known as 'Elusive Rabbits' – once a major part of Arthur Dowler's routine – promoted to central position. This involved two wooden cut-out rabbits of different colours within two tubes, referred to as boxes. At the end of the sequence, the rabbits were turned around to reveal two entirely different colours from those that commenced the trick, proving the lie to any audience theory that all Tommy had to do to make them change places was to turn the tubes back to front:

Good evening. I would now like to show you about ten hours of magic and for my first trick we have here a white handkerchief with black spots. I shall now make the spots disappear. There you are – a white handkerchief and there are the spots. (Shakes handkerchief and spots fall to floor) I have here a small piece of rope. For this I shall need the assistance of a gentleman in the audience. (Flings rope to member of audience in stalls) Thank you, sir. Would you now be so kind as to tie a knot in the centre of the rope? Right. You've done that? Now tie another, if you please. And another. Have you done that? Good. You may keep the rope. I've been trying to get rid of it for weeks. Now here we have two rabbits. This one is the white rabbit – white hat on box. And this one is the black rabbit – black hat on box. Right. White rabbit. Black rabbit. I shall now make them change places. Say the magic word (gibberish) and the rabbits have now changed places. The most difficult thing now is to get them back again!

Now here we have an ordinary small frying pan. Piece of paper in it. I light the paper and what do we have? Just a flash in the pan! Now my next trick is really mystic. Yes, absolutely mystic. Genuinely mystic. And here is my stick!

And now with the help of the boys I should like to play a solo on the harmonica. Sorry. I forgot to take it out of the box. Now we have a tray with four glasses on a cloth. I shall now whip away the cloth without disturbing the glasses. I whip it away *just like that* – or even quicker. On the count of three I shall whip the cloth away and the glasses will remain. One. Two. Two and a half. Three. There. (As he turns, glasses are seen to be stuck to the tray, the cloth slit accordingly for easy removal) I've done it. I shall now produce from this opera hat a live rabbit. I say the magic word. (Gibberish, followed by explosion) It *was* there. You have all heard of Houdini, the famous escape king. Here is a picture of him. (Takes photo out of envelope and surveys empty card) He's got away again! Have you seen these? (Plays) Playing cards! Here is the white rabbit and here is the black rabbit. To make them change places. Huh huh huh.

My next trick. Here we have a brass bowl. I now drop three coins in the bowl. One, two, three. There you are. Three coins in the fountain. 'Oh, That Old Black Magic Has Me In Its Spell'. (Sings for few bars unaccompanied) 'Honeysuckle Rose'. (Ditto) (Business with bottles and glasses on table – no dialogue) Have you seen this record? (Holds up black square with a hole in the middle) For square dancing. This magic wand was given to me by The Magic Circle. It's the only one of its kind in the world. Absolutely priceless. (Snaps it over knee) Look at the grain! Here we have the white rabbit and here is the black rabbit. See the white hat on the white rabbit box and the black hat on the black rabbit box. Now to make them change places . . .

Now Tommy builds to his big finish. After much shifty fumbling that he deigns the audience not to notice, he shows that the black rabbit is really blue and the white one yellow.

'Howzat?' Again most of the material would stand him in stead for the duration of his career. Peter Newcombe's extended generosity is in evidence – perhaps in return for the plug for The Magic Circle – and we see the first mention of a catchphrase in embryo. Appended to this transcript, under the heading 'additional material for possible use', was the material he had previously submitted for use in the Hippodrome show. In this way the act was evolving constantly.

However, for the billing he commanded in a show like *Paris by Night* he had to work harder than within the confines of a mere ten minute solo spot. The brief experience of a single summer show had enabled him to develop as a revue comedian, although in the approach to the London production he was churlish and short-sighted enough to enquire of Miff why he was doing three spots for the price of one! Miff's response can be left to the imagination. West End audiences were now treated to *A Few Impressions* and the sequence that saw him volunteering out of the audience to assist another 'conjuror'. The 'impressions' spot was prefaced by what may be the first extended story-style joke that he performed at an important professional level, the one about the three bears: after father bear and baby bear have enquired, 'Where's my porridge?' the mother bear comes down and says, 'I don't know what you're making all this fuss about. I haven't made it yet!' The parade of hats was tagged by Tommy quickly donning a coat for the finish: 'Nelson – Half Nelson – It's me all the time! Do you like the coat? Genuine camel hair. You don't believe me? Look.' When he turned, the coat was seen to have a hump on the back.

The third spot was billed in the theatre programmes as *It Never Fails*. It is inconceivable that in Cooper's hands this old piece of burlesque business ever did. After the initial surprise of the bowler-hatted Cooper stepping up on stage as one of two spectators conscripted by a magician of the old school, the routine settled into traditional slapstick fare. In the Prince of Wales show the other volunteer was played by Ronnie Brody, a short, staunch supporting comic of the period who, unlike Ronnie Corbett, who began in a similar mould, never built on the early promise he showed. Both Cooper and Brody were instructed to hold their hats in front of them. From the moment the magician broke an egg into Brody's hat, it was totally obvious which way the sequence would go. Tommy found it quite hilarious, only to have the smile wiped off his face the instant a second egg was broken into his hat.

Magician: I will now say the magic word . . . Abadaba . . . Abadaba . . .

Tommy: You've abadabad my hat.

Magician: (to Brody) Is the egg still here? (Brody nods) (Then to Cooper) Is your egg still there?

Tommy: It's here, but it's not still. (Worriedly he swills it around in the hat)

Magician: I shall now say the magic formula. Abracadabra. Sim Sala Bim. Shazam. Betty Grable. Betty Grable. BETTY GRABLE.

Tommy: Forget Betty Grable. What about the egg?

The magician admits failure and departs the stage amid histrionics that portend a nervous breakdown. From that moment the routine is played out in silence as both volunteers stand stranded on the stage, looking first into the wings, then with a start at each other, then into their hats, at the audience and back again. The comedy is played out entirely in looks with Cooper milking that Jack Benny effect for all it is worth. Brody is the first to take the initiative, coming over to Tommy to deposit every last drop of the egg in his hat in that of his colleague, before leaving him to his own devices. Tommy continues to stare with a stoic submissiveness that belies any initial disgruntlement, a lone figure on the vast stage, unsure of how to resolve his predicament until mischief takes over and he contemplates throwing the contents at the audience, then thinks better of it, puts on the hat, and walks off, the eggs having disappeared. Davenport's supplied him with a special gimmick to insert in the hat for the purpose. The finish is a small detail in the wider significance of the routine.

When in 2005 I was invited by the National Film Theatre to select thirteen favourite moments of film and television magic for a presentation to mark the Centenary of The Magic Circle, the choice of a Cooper moment presented the widest options, but without hesitation I homed in immediately upon this routine, recreated by Tommy possibly for the last time on an episode of the Thames variety series, *London Night Out* in the late Seventies. By now his son, Thomas was playing the magician, scriptwriter Dick Hills was filling Brody's shoes, and Betty Grable had been supplanted in the sex appeal stakes by Brigitte Bardot. I chose it because the seven minutes represent the most concise lesson in visual comedy technique I know. At no point does Cooper over-react, his facial and bodily reactions a compendium of how to survive the worst extremes of the comic universe. Throughout the pace remains unhurried in the best Laurel and Hardy tradition, the self-conscious stance of his pear-shaped torso on its jittery legs feeding off the truth of every poor soul coerced into such duty by a mediocre magic act. Only the ending had changed. By now the Davenport's prop had gone the way of a hundred other rust-coated gimmicks and he simply pulled out a flat cap and walked off in style. Walking back with the hat – quickly switched in the wings – he was now in a situation to bombard the audience with confetti when the right moment came.

At three spots for the price of one Cooper had proved that

he amounted to more than what Miff must have feared he'd become, a solid supporting speciality act incapable of acquiring star billing. It was a dread that haunted Ferrie down the years. When in 1958 he was called by the *TV Mirror* for a comment from Tommy whether he thought there was a future for magicians on television, Miff snapped back, 'Tommy Cooper is not a magician. He is a comedian.' Even as late as 1965 he was remonstrating misguidedly with ABC Television for wanting to send out photographs of his client in a fez, pictures that branded him as 'what I can only describe as a speciality act,' adding, 'It is the image of Cooper the Comedian that must be projected and not Cooper the Conjuror.' By the end of the Fifties Tommy had more than consolidated his reputation as a comic in the broadest sense, having experimented with similar routines for other revue shows, principally in Blackpool and Coventry before returning to the West End under the aegis of Bernard Delfont at the Prince of Wales in *Blue Magic* in February 1959. In the process he built up a repertoire that stood him in good stead in later life when they provided – like the 'Eggs in the Hat' – sure-fire, but seldom seen material, with which to refresh his television appearances. Most popular in this supporting repertoire were 'The Buffalo Routine' and 'Hello, Joe'. Sadly the names of the writers of both sketches have been lost to history.

The former was a pastiche of *Candid Camera*, the routine which came back to haunt Cooper when Brad Ashton spotted it on American television. Set in a sport's shop, the buffalo refers to the buffalo's head in which the camera is hidden. Audiences also have to imagine a tennis racquet containing a secret microphone. Tommy plays the unsuspecting customer who enters wanting to exchange a pair of tennis socks, but who becomes increasingly riled as with each exchange he is told to 'look at the buffalo': 'Once and for all, I didn't come here to look at the buffalo. I don't like buffaloes. I don't want anything to do with buffaloes.' Things only become worse when he is told to talk into the tennis racquet at the same time. Tommy is dispatched to the cashier and the shop assistant eats a clove of garlic in his absence. This is not the most subtle of routines. Tommy returns and things get further out of hand. In the tradition of the programme, the salesman eventually concedes what has been happening. As the news sinks in, he cannot believe the change in his good fortune, delirious at the fact that he is on television: 'You've been having me on then. This is a joke. I'm on TV?' It had to be seen. The great Swiss clown, Grock had a catchphrase, '*Sans blague!*' which translated as 'Get away!' It would have been perfect here, had Cooper's expression not said it all.

'Hello, Joe' teased the limits of reality even more so, as Tommy is interrupted on stage by what appears to be a distraught refugee from a shipwreck. Peering into the horizon he spots his imaginary long lost friend: 'Hello, Joe.' At first Cooper is puzzled, but is soon drawn into the fantasy, addressing the invisible man himself and sharing an invisible drink for old time's sake, even brushing down his lapel when it splashes against him: 'Careful – you spilt it all over me!' The situation builds melodramatically with the intruder shooting Joe, the stage becoming a pool of blood and Tommy escaping to the refuge of a stool like a young girl fleeing a mouse. Tommy then spots the equally invisible Fred: 'Put that gun down, Fred. I've got a knife. Take that, take that, take that.' He 'stabs' him three times accompanied by three rim shots. Tommy is miraculously confused by the sound effect: 'How come I shot him with a knife?' Two invisible corpses now litter the floor as gingerly Tommy tiptoes his way over them. His mime was so good you could almost see the blood on the stage. The sketch took the conceptual humour that often crept into his act – 'My wife got this fashion book and she opened the page and she said "I want that." I said, "What?" She said, "I want that fur coat." So I cut it out and gave it to her' – into another dimension.

For *Blue Magic*, which ran for thirty-eight weeks, Tommy had Shirley Bassey, scarce out of Tiger Bay, as a co-star. The second 'Hats' routine received its full dress West End première and his salary advanced considerably to £350.00 a week. However, during the latter part of the decade relations had become somewhat strained between the Delfont office and Ferrie. There were the trivial matters where Miff had to intervene on Tommy's behalf, most often his obsession with who paid for the eggs and the stooges used in his additional spots. In fairness to Bernie, he almost invariably picked up the tab for the latter, but Cooper still thought he was getting a bad deal. The cost of forwarding telegrams from one venue to another on the Delfont circuit became an even more unreasonable *bête noir*, to the point where Tommy forbade the practice rather than dip into his own pocket. In the run-up to the 1957 London Palladium pantomime, for which Delfont leased his contract to Val Parnell and Moss Empires, Miff put Bernie in an invidious position by asking him to intervene between himself and producer, Robert Nesbitt, when a clash occurred a few days before opening between a high profile cabaret booking, for which Cooper was already contracted, and a full scale dress rehearsal called for that night.

Miff pleaded he had no idea an evening dress rehearsal would be held three whole nights before opening. Then, just at the point he is asking for favours from Delfont, he sends him a letter hauling him over the coals for allowing his client to participate in a BBC sound broadcast from the Palladium to publicize the pantomime without his knowledge. In a telephone exchange Bernie deemed that Miff 'was making a nuisance' of himself. In his precious manner Miff retaliated that he was in no way going to deviate 'from the usual way in which I conduct my business,' in which everything appertaining to his client had to be drawn to his full attention before a decision was made. The schoolmaster tendency was showing. These were hardly the circumstances in which to plead with Delfont, in the same letter, to try again to secure Tommy's release for the cabaret. The all powerful Nesbitt won the day, as he always would, and Bernie felt bruised.

Further cracks began to appear in the relationship in the autumn of 1958, Delfont claiming – probably with some justification – that Miff did not discuss things sufficiently with his artist. The telephone log for 7 October records: 'Blew his top! *He* (Delfont) is going to say where he will work. He either does six television shows or none at all. Would like to be released from contract. Banged phone down.' The six shows were a series of programmes, *Cooper's Capers*, that Delfont had decided to produce for ATV, the company run by his brother, Lew Grade, in a display of one-upmanship over rival broadcaster, Associated-Rediffusion, which had featured Cooper in a series during the previous year, and the BBC which was showing interest at this time. Whether Cooper did not wish to record a series at all at this stage of his career or whether he thought he should be entitled to twelve shows as in the previous A-RTV run is not known. Ferrie found himself dealing less and less with Bernie direct, more and more with his two lieutenants, Keith Devon and Billy Marsh. Indeed, it was Devon who called with the news that Tommy was going into *Blue Magic*, a peremptory month before the opening.

On the back of Cooper's success at the Prince of Wales matters were smoothed over. As Max Miller once said in another context, 'People have a remarkable way of forgetting when you make money for them.' In August 1959 Bernie and

Miff were back on telephone terms, the impresario wanting to discuss Cooper on the basis of a £350.00 guarantee (his enhanced salary for *Blue Magic*) with the chance to make £500.00 for a guarantee of 40–45 working weeks. The offer does not appear to have been taken up. *Blue Magic* closed towards the end of 1959. After a short pantomime season in *Puss in Boots* with Edmund Hockridge, Derek Roy, and Petula Clark in Southampton, Cooper entered into an uncertain six-month period of stray cabaret bookings and the occasional television guest spot before opening for the summer as second top to Frankie Vaughan at Brighton Hippodrome.

The institution of weekly variety was fading fast and Delfont would have to concede that in the restricted theatrical environment of British show business there was no way he could monopolize the Cooper career in the Sixties as he had to a large extent in the Fifties. This did not stop discernible unrest when an offer to play the Palladium with Cliff Richard during the summer and autumn of 1960 was seen to clash with a commitment made by Miff for a Christmas season for Howard and Wyndham co-starring with Jimmy Logan and Eve Boswell at the Manchester Opera House. On 23 March Miff recorded an exchange with Billy Marsh: 'Thought Mr Delfont had first refusal. Very upset, etc. (Delfont in the background nattering)' Marsh threatened taking the matter to solicitors and a furious Delfont rang Stewart Cruikshank, the boss of the Howard and Wyndham circuit, who reported back to Miff: 'Said Delfont came on rather excited, but as far as he was concerned he has no right to think he owns every act in the country.' The upset didn't stop Tommy playing the 1960 summer season in Brighton for Delfont, nor a seventeen week run for him in Torquay the following summer. But Miff sensed that to sustain the quality of Cooper's bookings he had to diversify with other managements, a fact that deep down the impresario to whom

Tommy owed so much must have understood. It should be added that his salary for the Howard and Wyndham show was £515.00 a week, giving Miff the opening to negotiate a percentage deal over and above the Delfont standard £350.00 for the Torquay season.

Cooper would continue to work successfully for Delfont for the next decade, but only on an intermittent basis, most notably in two seasons with Frankie Vaughan, with whom he achieved a considerable rapport. Tommy idolized this most British of troubadours and his blundering burlesque of Vaughan's song and dance act – a melange of every gag with a cane and a top hat ever conceived – became another staple of his repertoire. Not surprisingly, it became even more effective in close proximity to the elegance of the original when they shared the bill together. The 1964 London Palladium summer revue, *Startime* also featured Cilla Black, The Four- most, and the world's greatest juggler, Francis Brunn. It broke all records, until Ken Dodd made his single-handed assault on the venue the following year. The success of the Frankie and Tommy combo was repeated for Bernie in a short ten-week season at the Bournemouth Winter Gardens in the summer of 1967. In the three years his salary had shot up from £400.00 to £800.00, indicative of the steep rise in his popularity on the back of his growing television success.

Throughout the new decade Cooper would play seasonal shows for all the top entertainment managements, including Harold Fielding, Tom Arnold, S. H. Newsome, George and Alfred Black, and Richard Stone. It is significant, however, that not until he worked for the latter two, at Blackpool Winter Gardens during the summer of 1968 and at Scarborough's Floral Hall the following year respectively, did Tommy achieve sole star billing above the title of the show in which he appeared. There had been an occasional week in variety when he had topped the bill, and a stray pantomime here or there, but they were the exceptions. At all other times he was featured as mere second top or in a co-starring role alongside names like Nina and Frederik, Jewel and Warriss, Millicent Martin, Ken Platt, Alfred Marks, Beryl Reid, Hylda Baker, even Freddie and the Dreamers, in addition to those already mentioned. Even shared co-star billing seldom led to his being featured in the all-important spot prior to the finale. By contrast, from the mid Fifties there had been no question over the sole drawing power of many of his comedy contemporaries, names like Norman Wisdom, Tony Hancock, Al Read, Harry Secombe, Max Bygraves, and a little later Dodd and Charlie Drake. Besides, of them all, only Dodd would have been strong enough to follow Cooper on an all-comedy bill. Tommy's progress to such star status entailed a steady climb, even though he was firmly established as a national figure assured of instant recognition by this time. In the early days part of the situation may have been contingent upon his being perceived as a novelty act, but he soon outgrew that. The state of affairs throws light both on his opinion of his own talents and on the possible dexterity of his manager and agent in manipulating his career to their maximum advantage.

For all his ups and downs with Miff, billing never appears to have been an issue with Tommy. When I drew the matter to the attention of his daughter, Vicky, she was not surprised, adding that her father never had a high opinion of his talents in the first place. The fact that he always stole the show appears to have been irrelevant: 'He never thought of himself as being good enough to be top! He always thought the others were so much better than him. And I think it comforted him to know that he did not have the responsibility of the name billed above him.' This would have explained his resistance to forcing the issue with Ferrie when it came to top of the bill status. The situation was epitomized by a television scenario which took place in the mid Sixties when ABC Television hit upon the bright idea of featuring Frankie Howerd, Bruce Forsyth and Tommy together in a major Christmas special. All three comics enjoyed approximately equal stature at the time. The broadcaster knew it was taking on a major feat of diplomacy by even thinking about it, not least because two of them, Cooper and Forsyth, shared the same agent. In the Thirties a similar tussle over billing had resulted in Ethel Merman and Jimmy Durante having their names crisscrossed on a Broadway poster, with the proviso that the posters were changed monthly with the names swapped around. Part of Cooper's popularity in the business always resided in his basic humility. Barry Cryer testifies to the fact that he had no malice, no sense of competition towards other comics. When the ABC show hit the schedules the billing told the same story, 'Frankie and Bruce's Christmas Show, starring Bruce Forsyth and Frankie Howerd, with guest star Tommy Cooper.' If Tommy was happy with such an arrangement, why should Miff have cause for concern? Besides when it came to his own series on television there was never any question that he was the star.

A cynical view could suggest that this was exactly the situation that most suited Ferrie at another level. Bigger theatrical billing at an earlier time in Tommy's career may have caused it to nose-dive prematurely in a way that led to a drop in income, thus giving Cooper justifiable excuse to walk away from their sole agency agreement, according to which Miff was obliged to maintain the level of his client's earnings from year to year. When one studies the pattern of his annual income from the beginning of the Fifties, Miff achieved his obligation with the resourcefulness of the best Chancellor of the Exchequer this country never had. The figures that follow – and similar amounts to be specified later – are based on documents in my possession that were kept scrupulously by Miff over the years, but are not officially certified sums:

1950–1: £2,410
1951–2: £4,508
1952–3: £5,694
1953–4: £7,569
1954–5: £7,827
1955–6: £9,465
1956–7: £9,237
1957–8: £13,980
1958–9: £14,605
1959–60: £17,157
1960–1: £15,523
1961–2: £17,293
1962–3: £16,980
1963–4: £15,548
1964–5: £22,947
1965–6: £25,036
1966–7: £25,849
1967–8: £45,927
1968–9: £61,500
1969–70: £61,592
1970–1: £84,510
1971–2: £115,098
1972–3: £114,728
1973–4: £125,955
1974–5: £149,770
1975–6: £155,000
1976–7: £169,589

These amounts represent gross income, but exclude VAT that became payable from 1973. After 1976 a decline set in, but –

as we shall see in greater detail later – this was due principally to Tommy's health problems. In the above sequence, in those years where growth was not maintained, there are justifiable reasons, which Tommy would have been the first to acknowledge. His income for 1956–7 was compromised by loss of earnings caused by illness during his autumn season at Coventry and four weeks of holiday not taken during the previous year. The dip in 1960–1 marked the only time in his career when there might have been cause to worry, but came in the wake of the Delfont wrangles without the useful weeks in provincial variety to fill in the gaps between pantomime and summer show. Miff held his nerve and the inflated Howard and Wyndham fee for the ten week Christmas season would have flattered his client's ego. As for 1962–3, the diary did incorporate five weeks of holiday by specific request of Tommy and for nostalgia's sake two weeks' work for CSE at a token fee of £100.00. The following year there were thirteen weeks set aside for vacation. Whatever the criticisms Cooper levelled against him, Miff never stood in the way of Tommy taking time out. In 1968–9 there were fifteen free weeks by request, the following year twenty-one. In 1972–3 additional holidays to compensate for a long theatre run in 1971–2 similarly accounted for the minor shortfall.

That year saw Tommy's earnings pass the £100,000 mark, a milestone in part achieved by his one undisputed starring appearance for a season at the London Palladium in the revue, *To See Such Fun*. By now he was too much of an institution to be anything but top of the bill. Physically the late Sixties represented his peak as a performer, his skills refined by the constant drudgery of repeated experience, his health still on top of his performing skills. It was fitting he should play the Mecca of vaudeville at this point, although sadly on a disappointing bill that did him no favours. Miff, fully appreciating the support

Tommy had given many other star names, held out for more quality, but to no avail. He particularly objected to the inclusion of piano player, Russ Conway, whose chart-topping days were way behind him, but impresario, Leslie Grade, brother of Bernie and Lew, was adamant. Conway's particular gift was an ability to make a finely tuned concert grand sound like your neighbourhood pub 'Joanna'. Following a heated telephone conversation with Grade a full two months ahead of opening, Miff scribbled down: 'Is booking Conway regardless. If I want Cooper released they will tear up the contract. Was very rude!' Clive Dunn and Anita Harris, a last minute replacement for Clodagh Rodgers, were the other principal performers on a bill that reflected the television culture of the day. Tommy received a standing ovation on the opening night. In fairness to all concerned the day of this type of show, bedecked with ostrich feathers and sequins, was fast drawing to a close.

Miff negotiated a deal that guaranteed a salary of £2,500.00 per week plus a percentage of 10 per cent of box office takings over £18,000 in any one week of thirteen performances. It was a fabulous deal: although Ken Dodd had raised the ante in the meantime, the standard star's money at the Palladium for names like Secombe and Hancock during the early Sixties had been around £1,000 a week, worth only £1,500 in 1971. The show opened traditionally in the spring, but ran for only twenty-four weeks, unlike the thirty-one week run of Cooper's previous excursion at the theatre with Frankie Vaughan in 1964: *Startime* had played right up to Christmas. Tommy attracted a small percentage bonus in only two of those weeks. The disappointment raises questions about Cooper's own box office potential. Veteran variety agent, Norman Murray once told me that Tommy was never considered 'box office' in the manner of names like Dodd, Wisdom, Bygraves or Secombe.

The view is endorsed today by Michael Grade, who played a peripheral role in the booking of his father's production: 'Norman was right. You would be taking a huge risk topping the bill with him anywhere in the conventional big theatre circuit – summer season, pantomime or other between season revues.' Herein resides another possible explanation why it took so long for him to headline in his own right. Part of it may have something to do with the fact that he had less appeal to women than the other names cited. It is difficult to use phrases like 'sex appeal' of people like Dodd and Secombe, although Wisdom and Bygraves certainly had that. All four performers were capable of tapping into a romantic undertow with the fairer sex through the success of their singing. The mothering instinct that a Harry, Norman or even Charlie Drake could engender cannot be discounted either. None of this put a stop to any claim that Tommy might be the funniest man in the world. Women had seldom been fans of W. C. Fields, or Groucho for that matter, although Harpo and Chico had compensated in his case. On the other hand, the great Max Miller had projected a curious ambivalence that had appealed equally to both sexes. J. B. Priestley mused that many women might not have warmed to Cooper's act, 'which is altogether too daft for them', adding that in person his manic presence might even alarm them. One can begin to understand why few wives would drag their husbands to the Palladium to see a berserk conjuror in a fez, irrespective of the fact that by the time he reached star status at the theatre he may have been so familiar to the audience it catered for that the 'must see' excitement had gone.

Not that *To See Such Fun* was an out and out disaster. For that one has to go back to the beginning of 1971 when Tommy found himself starring in a Christmas revue at the Coventry Theatre. The management had the 'too clever by half' idea of running three shows a day, a pantomime starring Ted Rogers in the afternoon, and a twice nightly – 6.00 and 8.45 – variety spectacular with Cooper in the evenings. Tommy was joined on the bill by the comedian and impressionist, Peter Hudson. The previous summer they had played to capacity business together in Torquay, and been extended by a week. In contrast, Peter will never forget the evening in Coventry when there were only eighty-four people in the 2,000 seat house. As he says, 'At six o'clock in the industrial heartland they're all having their tea.' The theatre manager came round and announced, 'That's it.' Tommy said, 'What's "That's it"?' 'An all time low,' came the reply, the manager taking almost perverse glee at entering the record books in such a negative fashion. Tommy became quite depressed. Later that night Cooper and Hudson went for a Chinese meal to take their minds off the problem. A couple came into the restaurant, spotted the famous man and went up to his table: 'Tommy, what are you doing here in Coventry?' He gave his trademark sigh and proclaimed, 'Just passing through.' The wry understatement was the perfect accompaniment to his fortitude in the face of insurmountable odds.

Apart from television appearances and special gala performances, *To See Such Fun* represented Cooper's last appearance in the West End. Miff might have been worried, but a new trend in entertainment had been fast developing that would play like a dream into his strategic hands. I refer to the phenomenon of the predominantly northern social clubs. The neatness with which the old established order of the working men's 'Club and Institution Union' (the CIU) entered a marriage with show business as the last embers of the variety circuit were reduced to ashes proved to be an example of convenience writ large. Private enterprise, often driven by the breweries, expanded the basic concept with its cloth-capped image into glitzy palaces of entertainment, even though in essence they remained vast beer halls with delusions of grandeur, as sophisticated as package holidays and fake Burberry labels. Although audiences were mixed, the culture was masculine-led. Spike Milligan instantly saw why Tommy would be in his element here: 'When he played a club all the men knew they were better looking than him, they had better figures than him, they could talk better than him. They just immediately fell for him right away.' On this circuit there was no doubt that Cooper was a box office King. With tongue in cheek Tommy phoned Miff from one such provincial outpost in April 1968: 'I don't want to upset you. Business is wonderful. "Sold out" notices every night.'

The applause that – however enthusiastic – had been functional in theatres was now joined by cheers of 'Good old Tommy' and 'Give us more, Tom.' In the drinking environment the downside was provided by the hecklers, but they were mostly good-natured. A standard Cooper gambit was silently to agree with them, then to do a double take to the rest of the audience as if he didn't know what it was all about. He was expert in using the situation, resisting any attempt to play against it. Once at the start of a joke – 'I was standing on this quay, see . . .' – someone in the audience stood up and began to play the mouth organ. Cooper simply started the joke again, 'I was standing on this quay, see . . . playing the mouth organ . . . I forgot that bit before!' Only when the cheers had subsided did he complete the gag. All the experience of the early years performing in pocket-size London nightclubs now boomeranged back in good stead.

That Miff should contemplate putting his star client into such a setting was initially met with snobbish dismay in some theatrical circles. The first interest had been shown as far back as June 1960. Producer Dick Hurran, understandably wishing to protect the interests of Howard and Wyndham, for whom Tommy was scheduled to appear at the Manchester Opera House during the forthcoming Christmas season, wasted no time in phoning Miff when a club appearance by Cooper was announced in the area. The log reads: 'Hurran very upset that T. C. is playing the clubs. Cruikshank is on holiday, but would be very annoyed. They are really the dregs – beer and skittles – advertised all over the place.' The following day brought matters to a head: 'Cruikshank forbids T. C. to work Stockport club. They are dumps with wrestling and all!' Cruikshank had his way. No further approaches of this kind were made to Miff until 1963. The first full week played by Tommy in such a venue was that of 29 April at La Dolce Vita in Newcastle for a salary of £350.00. The following week he played Mr Smith's in Manchester and the money was already rising. This time he received £400.00.

The club circuit provided Miff and Tommy with a lifeline to continued prosperity that neither of them could have envisaged at this point. In 1964 and 1965 Cooper returned to La Dolce Vita and Mr Smith's as gaps in his theatre and television schedules allowed, sometimes playing double weeks. In 1966 the Club Franchi in Jarrow and the Club Fiesta in Stockton were added to the itinerary. In this very short time he was commanding £1,000.00 a week for these forays out of town. Like Jack's beanstalk the remuneration spiralled to giddy heights as venues competed for the biggest names in the land. Gracie Fields was coaxed out of retirement and Louis Armstrong coaxed over from America on the back of the money-spinning club machine. After *To See Such Fun* closed in October 1971 the clubs would become his principal form of livelihood apart from television. There would be only two more summer seasons, in Margate (1972) and Skegness (1973), and no more pantomimes. A four week spring season at the New Theatre, Oxford in 1972 was not a success. Venues like the Golden Garter, Wythenshawe, the Fiesta Club, Sheffield and the Wakefield Theatre Club now replaced the top resort towns as the desirable places to revisit. Before long the new trend spread southwards to accommodate, among others, the Lakeside Country Club at Frimley, Cesar's Palace at Luton, and Bailey's at Watford. The Double Diamond Club in Caerphilly even lured Tommy back to his roots.

The club boom allowed Miff to keep abreast of his targets to stay in Tommy's good graces financially. In 1968 the comedian received a staggering £4,750 for two weeks work at Batley Variety Club and the continual rise – helped in no small presence by his increasingly high profile on television – became inexorable, far surpassing any reasonable adjustments that inflation might have dictated. By the same token Miff saw the bookings as a wonderful opportunity for keeping his client on the *qui vive* with live, grass roots contact with his public between the relatively sterile spells dedicated to the demands of the electronic medium. By 1969 Tommy was able to command a minimum of £2,500 a week, the following year £3,500. By 1972, £4,000 was the norm, 1974 £5,000. By a weird paradox, as his health forced him to take life easier he found himself earning more for working less. 1975 saw him settle into a loose routine of two weeks on and one week off. In January of that year his fee shot up again to £6,000. In August 1976 £7,000 became his standard fee. After a health scare in that month Miff also began to consolidate a pattern that embraced split weeks and one night stands for even higher amounts on a *pro rata* basis. As late as 1982 when he could still manage a complete week near to home he could command £8,250 for a week from Bob Potter at Lakeside. By this time the wider club bubble had inevitably burst, but on his death Miff had engagements in Tommy's book for weeks at Bailey's in Watford and the Night Out in Birmingham for £8,500 and more than a few shorter dates at this rate. At the height of his client's career he had been able to boast to one newspaper, 'If I told you how much Tommy gets, the other comedians would turn Communist overnight!'

Tommy would have said that he earned every penny. As he grew older the new working pattern with its constant travel was far more exhausting than the resident summer and winter seasons. There were echoes of the old variety days, but conditions backstage were often lacklustre by comparison. Mary Kay recalls just one instance: 'There had been an electricians' strike and the dressing room at the club was unheated. Worse by far was the fact that this particular dressing room had a door leading directly outside. In order to reach the stage, everyone else had to pass through this area.' Tommy quipped, 'I've never thought much of open-plan building.' Like all good pros, he felt he could surmount any obstacle thrown across his path. The clubs also required that he performed for an hour at a time, as distinct from the two or three shorter spots that theatres required.

As his star and his fees skyrocketed, one might have been forgiven for supposing that Tommy's initial discontent with his contractual situation with Miff would have gone away. In fact their relationship would continue to decline. Occasionally there would be a period of remission, only for the helter-skelter process to start all over again. As far back as the beginning of 1960 Cooper had used Las Vegas as an excuse to open up for a second time the hornet's nest that was the sole agency agreement. Leslie Grade had offered him an eight week season in the desert commencing 19 February. Tommy called Ferrie on 29 January to state his case. Miff recorded, 'Grade can get him out of commitments!! T. C. then says he does not like my interfering with his business. Will just pay me fifteen per cent so long as I don't interfere. Says he is definitely going.' Miff countered that Tommy had contracts at home that kept him in the country. This was only partly true, since, as we have seen, that period in question was a relatively fallow one. The main sticking point appears to have been a week in cabaret for £300.00 at the New Royal Restaurant, Liverpool. In the normal course of events, it should have been easy to shift. Unfortunately it was the week of the Grand National and Tommy was a premium attraction, although if anyone could have got Cooper released it was Leslie Grade. Things were complicated by Grade, without Miff's knowledge, inviting the Coopers at his own expense to Paris for a weekend to meet the Las Vegas producer. Once again Miff felt slighted. He chronicled what followed in a letter to Grade: 'Since then I understand from the Artiste that you have made further direct personal contact with him in an endeavour to persuade him to go to Las Vegas notwithstanding his commitments in this country. Such conduct on your part is most unusual and I am therefore obliged to ask you to refrain from soliciting any Artistes who are exclusively represented by this office.' It was typical Miff-speak with his self-importance standing prima donna fashion in the path of common sense. Mark Leddy in a note to Jay Marshall, following some minor kerfuffle about a request for publicity pictures for an Ed Sullivan appearance, had summed up the more irksome side of the agent and manager: 'The guy that handles Tommy is not only ten-percental, he is temperamental and he likes to be consulted on everything.'

In the wake of the disagreement, Tommy took himself along to Equity on 1 February with his copy of the agreement, thinking there may be some loophole that justified his independence on the matter. Ferrie's solicitor, Oscar Beuselinck was brought on board. On 4 February, by which time Tommy's wrath had subsided, he wrote to Miff on the outcome of the Equity ruling:

'They have pointed out to him that he cannot accept the Las Vegas commitment and he is not going to do so. They also agree with me that it reflects credit on both Mr Cooper and your self that you have been associated for twelve years, but that inevitably after such a long period of time, as with marriage, there must be a few ups and downs. They also agree that Cooper has no legal right to seek to break his contract at this stage.' It is possible Cooper had been goaded to go to Equity by Grade himself. The Grade Organisation was fast becoming the most powerful agency in the land, if it did not already hold that accolade. Lew and Leslie would have been delighted to have reined in the recalcitrant Cooper to augment their already spectacular client list.

At times client and agent appeared like a couple of kids playing a sadomasochistic game of cat and mouse. The more successful he became, so Tommy seemed to take perverse delight in giving Miff a harder time. And as each year came around so Miff, like some ghostly Old Father Time figure with his scythe, came round the corner to extend the agreement between them for another twelve months. The worst excesses of his client's behaviour will be chronicled at a later stage, but aborted telephone calls and insults to Miff like 'Your wife was only a chorus girl,' became the order of the day. Here is the record of a typical call from May 1966: 'Has his accommodation been fixed for tonight at Brighton? I said, "No." He had never asked. He said, "You should have asked me!!" I told him he had always made his own arrangements for Brighton, as he had his connections there. He got rude and slammed phone down.' Miff's peeved schoolmarmish tendency did not help matters, as in this letter from April 1968: 'Your note with unsigned contract for the cabaret engagement on 10 June has just arrived. I must insist, Tommy, that in future, if you wish to turn down work, which I think is a great mistake, that you return contracts immediately, and not sit on them for five weeks, as has happened in this case. You must surely realize that this only creates a most embarrassing situation all round, and does not do the Cooper image any good.'

When, in August 1968, Dick Hurran mentioned casually to Miff that he had seen his client taking part in a midnight matinee for charity in Jersey the previous Sunday, Miff wasted no time in writing to Cooper, who he has assumed was tucked up in bed in Blackpool where he was appearing for the summer season: 'Would you mind telling me what is going on? When I spoke to you on the telephone last Monday and asked where you had been over the weekend you made no mention of this, but merely said you had been "dashing about". Apart from this deceit, you must be mad to do such a thing, especially when George Black Ltd have agreed to cut the Buffalo routine in order that you may have some rest during the Blackpool shows. In any case, why was I not advised of this Jersey charity? You know that all offers (paid or unpaid) must be referred here in the first instance, and to have to write this here to you after twenty years of successful management is something I never thought I should have to do. An explanation from you will be appreciated.' Tact and diplomacy were not Miff's strongest cards. A smoother operator like Billy Marsh would have tiptoed more gently in confronting the situation. The word 'deceit' was ill advised. Tommy scribbled a reply: 'A polite letter will always get a reply. But I will not answer any letter that is set out to upset me.' Miff never received an explanation for Jersey, but there was no doubting the sincerity contained in another letter he penned to Cooper at this time: 'Our successful association has brought you from ten pounds a week to the present position when you can talk of turning down £2,500.00 per week – just try to remember who has *always* been on your side.'

221

The beginning of 1969 represented a nadir in the relationship, Cooper writing to Miff on 5 February, 'Dear Little Caesar, The tone of your voice and your conversation last night was very aggressive indeed and I advise you not to speak to me like that again.' Matters had been getting out of hand with regard to payment for his appearances, with cheques handed direct to the performer becoming mislaid. Two weeks later Miff attempted to remedy the situation in writing: 'I suggest that fees or remittances for all your professional activities be made to this office. We have discussed this point recently and you agreed with the logic of it. As you know, on many occasions in the past I have chased up managements and clients for fees only to find that you had in fact received payment, which is a most embarrassing position for all, particularly your image.' In his obeisance to that last all-important, five letter word, Miff was a spin doctor before his time.

On 8 May 1969 a significant event occurred. Tommy bought Miff lunch. As the guest wrote to his host afterwards by way of acknowledgement, 'That makes it only three meals you now owe me.' Unfortunately Gwen could not be present. Miff added in his letter, which again set out the goalposts of their business arrangement, 'Believe me, Tommy, I could not have been more serious when I said to you today that I am very concerned about the way things have been going lately.' At the time there was a disagreement over a proposed guest appearance by Tommy and his son on a Thames pilot show called *Whose Baby?* that had been agreed without Miff's knowledge and approval, but he had not been referring to this specifically. Notes made prior to the meeting found in his files reveal quite simply that he had reached the limit of endurance and was now prepared to bring matters to a head:

You have said in the past, when you do not accept my advice, that I demoralize you. Brother, it is I who am being demoralized. I am on the receiving end of the phone. Either
1. I conduct the business without interference and with full cooperation from you.
Or
2. If you still persist carrying on the way you are, I shall just continue to book you till you peter out.
Or
3. You can buy yourself out of your agreement.

With dour Scots fortitude Miff *was* prepared to hang in there. In a footnote he has added as a morale booster: 'History repeating – e.g. the Forsyth situation – what has he done since he left me?' In the two years since they parted in 1967, very little indeed. Now Tommy was his only client of substance. He would never be able to replace him at this relatively late stage of his career. One theory says that he cannily cultivated Forsyth in the early Fifties as a sword of Damocles to hang over Tommy's head. He had first spotted the entertainer doing an impression of Cooper at the Windmill in the early Fifties. Bruce was almost certainly the first in the line of Tommy impersonators, fully capable of doing his whole act if required at a time when the magician had yet to achieve national fame. The impression was funny, whether you identified it as Cooper or not. Miff actually forbade Forsyth to perform it on television at an early stage. Had Cooper reneged on their agreement, he would almost certainly have promoted this one aspect of Bruce's multi-talented repertoire above all the others.

The lunch with its semblance of conviviality might have appeared to have smoothed things over in favour of the first option on Miff's scribble pad, but not for long. On 15 May

Miff was writing to Tommy again with reference to his telephone call of that afternoon: 'Your recurring insults, groundless accusations, culminating in your latest statement, "I am too big for you to handle," I now find intolerable. You say that you intend to take legal advice in order to get out of your agreement with me. As it would appear that my achievement in building you to your present status is now being completely disregarded, if not forgotten, by you, I should suggest, in these circumstances, that you proceed without delay.' As a performer Tommy did not possess a big ego, but, by way of mitigation, he was at this stage showing an increasing tendency towards alcohol that may have prompted the uncharacteristic comment. On 17 May he rang Miff with the news that he would be hearing from his solicitor, also sending him a telegram with instructions to have the sole agency agreement standing by. The following day he called again, 'I hope you have a very unhappy holiday' and rang off.

Miff went on holiday and nothing more appears to have been said on the matter. Tommy's drinking would plunge him into even more abusive behaviour towards Ferrie in the decade to come, but the agreement *per se* would not appear to become an issue again until Miff raised it himself in a letter to his client of 4 March 1978, following the receipt of a disc that Tommy had made for Pye Records together with a contract signed by Cooper without Miff's knowledge to accompany the same. The recording, a comedy version of the old *Casablanca* standard, 'As Time Goes By,' was beset by copyright problems, as Miff had predicted, and was never released. Tommy had proceeded against Miff's advice. Miff conceded that in the circumstances he was prepared to waive any commission on the enterprise, but added, 'Should you contravene the terms of our agreement in like manner in future, there will be no alternative for me but to take, albeit most reluctantly, the necessary legal steps to protect my interests.' The agreement had been in operation for almost thirty years. It was most unlikely that things were going to change now. In truth he was indispensable to Cooper, whose faults and foibles a new agent coming fresh to the scene would not have tolerated at any price. Eventually a comedy version of Vera Lynn's 'We'll Meet Again' was released in place of the *Casablanca* number and Miff kept his distance on the matter.

At times Miff's daily routine appeared a non-stop round of excuses proffered for his client's lateness at rehearsals or for cars hired at the broadcaster's expense and kept waiting for inexplicably long periods. 'When a car is requested to pick up Mr Cooper at 8.15 a.m., it is 11 o'clock before he appears and when the car is required to pick him up at night, the driver and car are then put to use until 4.00a.m.,' was one such complaint. Tidying up the debris of unpaid bills was another chore, particularly hotel accounts, although keeping abreast of Tommy's wilful tendency to disregard the accommodation arranged by Miff in favour of somewhere else became too much of a challenge. This matter came to a head in November 1974, when Miff announced that he would no longer continue to provide this service for him. Tommy immediately jumped into the breach, interpreting the decision as a dereliction of managerial duty on Miff's part. The sole agency agreement was not mentioned in the letters that passed between them on the matter, but the reading between the lines was clear. Miff pointed out that the menial chore had never been part of his obligation to his client in the first place, but matters were smoothed over and he continued to book his accommodation on the road.

With Mary Kay now a permanent part of his entourage, he had obviously become nervous regarding the over-familiarity of his manager with his hotel arrangements. In March 1975 he wrote to Cooper: 'Apropos of your remarks about your hotel bills being sent here, it must be stated categorically that I do not request this, but, as it is your wish that I book your hotel accommodation, it is obvious that this is the reason why accounts are sent here. This is quite normal procedure. Nevertheless, if you wish to continue booking your hotel accommodation, the respective managements will be advised not to send your accounts here. I would remind you, however, of the occasions when I have settled outstanding accounts for you, which you have overlooked, in order to save you embarrassment and legal action. In conclusion your remark about "Secret Police" is entirely uncalled for and is strongly resented.' The cheap jibe is testimony to Tommy's sheer paranoia on the matter of his infidelity. The one thing he should have appreciated about Miff's character was that discretion was assured. He almost certainly disagreed from a moral standpoint, but business called for a different ethic. As he had said before, 'Just try to remember who has *always* been on your side.' As far as he was concerned, nothing would be allowed to tarnish the 'image'.

There were also the – seemingly – more trivial matters of a manager's routine, like the occasion when the Thames booking executive reported that Tommy had agreed to make a walk-on appearance to tag a sketch for Mike and Bernie Winters for a crate of Scotch. Miff was adamant: 'My acts do not work for cases of booze.' When he was told during another enquiry that Eric and Ernie had received payment in kind for a personal appearance, he replied, 'Told him if Morecambe and Wise cared to work for cameras [*sic*] that was their business, but my acts work legit.' Ferrie always heaved a sigh when he heard from a venue that Tommy wanted his bar bill made out to 'props'. And as Tommy's income soared, so he was prepared to lean on Miff for a certain kind of advice: 'Do I know anyone who could get him dear stuff (tape recorders) at a discount?' It was left to Gwen to be complimentary about their escalating good fortune. In April 1969, she dropped Miff a note, 'I'm glad to see my husband's money is going up. It won't be long before I get that new mink coat!'

On the debit side there was Miff's almost complete lack of understanding on the matter of comedy, compounded, as Bruce Forsyth has remarked, by the fact that he thought he had been placed on God's earth to produce great comedians. Gordon Peters, a comic who showed much promise within Miff's clientele for a few years, testifies to this defect: 'I was very down and he said "I've got a good idea for you." He reached under his desk and brought out this false leg with the comment, "I'm sure you can make something of this!"' The failing will become more apparent when we examine Tommy's television career in depth. For now let it be said that there *were* moments when in the context of the cosy, friendly image that he saw as so important to his client Miff was indisputably correct, on one occasion stopping him from holding a puppy over a candle flame for a television skit – 'Hot Dog!' – and on another chastising him for punching a teddy bear as a running gag in a stand-up magic routine.

Tommy's daughter is of the opinion that the tensions be-tween her father and Miff turned much of the time on a power struggle between Miff and her mother. Gwen had always com-manded Tommy's respect when it came to assessing comedy material. In the early part of his career she had more than held her own in other ways. According to Val Andrews, there was the modest charity show where they encountered another magician – Francis Keep, alias 'Uncle Boko' – with a fez like Tommy's on the same bill. Gwen went backstage and sorted him out: 'You won't be wearing that!' During the run of *Paris by Night* Tommy had wanted to feature a gag that involved throwing a paper dart through a window on one side at the back of the set. The idea was that it came whizzing back though the window on the opposite side, accompanied by the sound of a jet engine at full blast. Delfont protested that the gag was too expensive to stage, but Gwen stood her ground: 'If the plane gag isn't in on opening night, there will be no opening night.' It stopped the show.

It is not difficult to imagine Gwen, jealous of her husband, resenting Ferrie when there was so much she thought she could be doing for him herself. As Vicky said, 'Consequently she would wind Tommy up something rotten about Miff. Father would get angry and mother would goad him to get on the line to Miff. More often than not Miff would slam the phone down. Then five minutes later I'd be delegated to call Miff back so that the slanging match could continue. Father would get all hot and bothered, while mother sat impassive at the table with a stony face as things got worse.' It became a vicious circle as Tommy kept insisting to Miff not to phone Gwen when he was not there, protesting, 'It is bad for her health and upsets her nerves badly.' While all this may not sound the perfect recipe for happy Sundays at home, Vicky concedes today that Miff did get a lot of things right for her father and kept his business affairs in order in a way that would have defeated many a lesser agent.

In retrospect one of Miff's shortcomings was his inability to spot the occasional window of opportunity that could have enhanced the Cooper career at any given time, the 1960 Las Vegas offer being one instance. Openings that were slammed shut in other media will be detailed in later chapters, but it has always intrigued me that he refused resolutely for Tommy to have any involvement in radio. In 1955 Cooper was courted relentlessly by the producers of *Educating Archie*, the hit BBC radio show starring ventriloquist Peter Brough and Archie

Andrews that for ten spectacular years catapulted an incomparable parade of new British comedy talent to stardom. The list embraced Tony Hancock, Max Bygraves, Hattie Jacques, Beryl Reid, Benny Hill, Harry Secombe, Dick Emery, and many more. The combination of the cheeky schoolboy dummy and the ingratiating comedy magician ever anxious to educate his young friend to the sort of tricks and japes that characterized his own schooldays seems irresistible. The vocal contrast between Archie's high falsetto and Tommy's gruff tones must have constituted a radio producer's dream: Cooper had the most distinctive new voice in comedy. Even Brough's own powers of persuasion were brought on board by the BBC, but without success.

Ferrie's reasoning appears to have been that his client was a visual performer, a ruling with which Tommy does not appear to have disagreed. However, it contradicts Miff's desire to develop his client as more than a novelty act. His magical background had not stopped another performer, David Nixon becoming a superb straight man to Arthur Askey on radio in the Fifties. Peter Waring, a debonair, laid-back patter magician, who specialized in throwaway lines like, 'A bachelor is a man who's got no children . . . to speak of,' had stolen a march on them both until his suicide took him off the air in 1949. The greatest British wireless comedian of the Fifties was Tony Hancock. Watching thoughts flicker across his morose countenance on television tended to obscure the fact that his presence on the radio compelled you to imagine his expressions when you were listening. Max Wall was another visual clown who built for himself a substantial radio following. The final dampener to the argument would have been Peter Brough himself. The idea of a ventriloquist on radio was a non-starter, *until* one considers the medium for what it is, namely a theatre for the imagination, something understood as vividly as by the likes of Dylan Thomas and Francis Durbridge as by Brough's original scriptwriters, Eric Sykes and Sid Colin. Another approach in the same year for Tommy to appear as a regular team member on the panel game, *My Wildest Dream*, a precursor of *Does the Team Think?*, was more reasonably turned down. Whatever his ad-libbing powers, they were unlikely to hold their own among practised wits like Ted Ray, Tommy Trinder, and Jimmy Edwards.

A fragment found in Tommy's papers from around the late Forties suggests that he had not always been averse to the idea of appearing on the medium. Headed 'Radio Script by Tommy Cooper', it begins:

How do you do, ladies and gentlemen? As you know my name is Tommy Cooper. The reason I mention the name is that it may be necessary later to identify the body. For some reason I can't forget my school days. What memories! I may not have been the smartest boy in the class, but I wasn't far away from the smartest – about three seats away. Mathematics was easy for me. One and one is two, two and two is four, four and four is eight, eight and eight is sixteen, sixteen and sixteen – and then there's history – I should be on the stage!

It then segues into 'I have just returned from a tour of Germany' mode. Around the time of the Peter Brough enquiry, both Val Andrews and Freddie Sadler turned their hands to writing pilot scripts for a radio series for him. Sadler's began:

This is the BBC Light Programme. The time is seven o'clock and here is an important announcement. Due to circumstances beyond its control, coupled with the fact that all the other contract artists are appearing elsewhere, the BBC has no option but to inform you that the next half hour will have to be . . . *The Tommy Cooper Show*. And here is the cause of all the trouble, Tommy Cooper!'

The script held little promise. The idea of satirizing familiar theatrical and cinematic genres had been taken to new heights by Frank Muir and Denis Norden in *Take It From Here*. There seemed little point in building an entire thirty minutes around an extended sketch with Tommy as Frankenstein, although on the assumption that you knew what Cooper looked like, which most of the country did by the mid-Fifties, there could have been no funnier casting. Had Miff seen the script, he would have felt vindicated in his decision. On the other hand, had the *Educating Archie* opportunity been grasped, Tommy would have achieved a public relations boost to die for – with repeats the show attracted an audience of eighteen million – and resident star guest status with none of the responsibility of having to carry the show. The elegant and unassuming Peter Brough always managed that with no trouble at all.

If the golden age of BBC radio comedy could not claim Cooper's success as part of its glorious achievement, there was another British institution with which he would become inseparably and triumphantly linked. His appeal to royalty, quite as much as to the working men's club circuit, underlined his classlessness. Whenever he was billed to appear on the Royal Variety Performance, he would unquestionably steal the show. Today the annual event is a shallow celebrity-obsessed shadow of its former self. In an era when there *was* a variety profession and genuine respect both for real talent and the royal family, it was a true accolade to appear, as he did in 1953, 1964, 1967, 1971, and 1977. The challenge of playing a crowd that has one eye on the royal box most of the time is legendary. Few have the ability to cut through the ice to the

satisfaction of the whole house. In 1963 John Lennon succeeded with the line, 'Those in the cheaper seats clap your
hands. The rest of you just rattle your jewellery.' The following
year Tommy came close: 'I've brought the wife. I said, "How
much is a ticket?" They said, "A hundred pounds." I said,
"How much is a programme?" They said, "Six pounds." I
said, "Give us a programme. She can sit on that."'

Possibly more important to Cooper were the more intimate
occasions he entertained the royals, both in their own environment at Windsor Castle, and at a succession of Variety Club
luncheons when the presence of the Duke of Edinburgh sig-
nalled the occasion for an impromptu double act between
the pair. The first dates back to 1955. Television producer,
Richard Afton was involved in organizing the event and called
Miff excitedly on 20 January: 'Very Confidential!! The lunch
date for Tommy on 8 February is fixed. The Duke of Edinburgh will be there sitting alongside Tommy. When he heard
that T. C. was being invited he accepted with alacrity as
"Tommy Cooper is the Queen's favourite comedian."' Pathé
Pictorial was at the Savoy Hotel to film the event for posterity.
When he failed to make a beaker in a tube disappear on a
tray, he asked the Duke to stand with the request, 'You hold
it!' The Duke obliged, at which point the beaker vanished
right under his nose. 'You've done it! You've done it!' shouted
Tommy above the applause. He whipped off his fez to reveal
a smaller one underneath, presenting it to the Duke to take
home for Prince Charles: 'That's for a certain very small gentleman.' He repeated the formula in even more spectacular
fashion at a similar event in July 1964, this time asking the
distinguished guest to hold a bowl of water on a tray. Tommy
threw a cloth over the bowl, which disappeared without trace,
until in a brilliant piece of unrehearsed stage management
the onus of exposure was placed on the Duke as he showed

the bowl attached to the side of the tray the audience was not supposed to see. The publicity value of the event was enormous.

A personal hat trick was achieved when Tommy was the principal speaker at the sixtieth birthday party given for the Duke by the Variety Club in 1981. He rose to the occasion wearing a bizarre set of mouse ears, which he justified as an elephant deterrent: 'People don't know this but elephants are frightened of mice. If an elephant saw a mouse, it would run away. It would go. And it works, cos if you look around the room you won't see an elephant anywhere.' He then turned to Gwen by his side and muttered, 'A bit subtle that, wasn't it?' As the laughter built, he attempted to adjust his bowtie. It fell apart in his hands. 'What did I do?' For the entire world he looked as if he was besieged by demons from another planet, the nervous laugh his one last link with reality. He then coerced Gwen into a card trick: 'First take four cards, madam, and then give me one back. Now can you say out loud what is the difference between the first hand you had and the second hand you have now?' 'The Queen is missing,' came the reply. 'Well, you can't have everybody!' said Tommy.

When it came to delivering an after-dinner speech or similar there was no one to top him. Members of the Grand Order of Water Rats were treated to a typical display of his rugged wit when he delivered an unforgettable address at a lodge meeting in March 1981. Having referred to the true etymology of the title of the organisation whereby 'Rats' is 'star' spelled backwards, he went on to make the observation that 'air raid' spelled backwards was 'diarrhoea' and that his agent, Miff Ferrie was 'just as big a bastard spelled backwards as he is forwards.' Perhaps his irreverent streak was most in evidence in 1983 at a Variety Club function held in this country to honour Dean Martin. It is unlikely that Martin, an infrequent visitor to these shores, had ever set eyes on this man before. Nevertheless he would have felt the goodwill the man generated and, being the showman he was, Dino laughed along with the flow as Tommy got into his stride: 'I lie awake and think of the old Martin and Lewis films. And when you think of those two, it's amazing how things turn out. Dean Martin has become an international star known all over the world. I often wonder what happened to the Eyetie who used to do all the singing!' At this stage Tommy's physical condition was weak, but he still had the ability to punch home his humour to an audience. His ability to prick the pomposity of formal functions and lodge meetings contributed in no small measure to his popularity within the profession, aligning him with that earlier master of the revels and royal favourite, Bud Flanagan.

The most memorable line Cooper ever spoke in royal company remains the most controversial. There is no one who hasn't heard at some time what he said to the Queen in the line-up after a Royal Variety Performance. As legend has it, he asked Her Majesty if he could ask her a personal question. The Queen replied, 'As personal as I'll allow.' Tommy said, 'Do you like football?' She said, 'Not particularly.' He said, 'Well, could I have your tickets for the Cup Final?' The controversy surrounds whether the line was original with him. Max Bygraves attributes it to Bud Flanagan and Max certainly shared many royal stages with the leader of the Crazy Gang. Cooper never did. And yet others, not least court photographer on such occasions, Doug McKenzie, swear they were there when it happened. Jimmy Tarbuck, who was standing next to him, can even pinpoint the year, 1964, the occasion he shared the stage with Tommy, Brenda Lee, and Cilla Black. There is no reason to question the recall of any of these stalwarts, but the line is so much within the spirit of Flanagan, there can be little doubt that it was his origination. We shall never know what gave Tommy the gall to repeat it, although McKenzie has an interesting sidelight on the circumstances. Tommy was disappointed that the Queen hardly took any notice of him in the line-up. As she walked away, he gave his attention-grabbing cough to regain her attention – 'I say, your majesty,' – and then asked the question. It was typical of Cooper to do it on the downbeat, investing it with a surreal originality of its own, but it was not truly his. According to Max it was first delivered to the Queen Mother, which most probably sets the year at 1950, when the young Bygraves shared the bill with Flanagan and Allen, Jack Benny, and Max Miller. Bud had been one of the speakers at the July 1964 Variety Club lunch. It was now November. Perhaps the old stager had educated the new pretender to the original exchange on that occasion, maybe in reminiscence with the Duke himself. Let us only hope it did not change the Queen's opinion of him. Word has it that Bernard Delfont, one pace behind the Queen, glowered at the time. Tommy's interjection was tantamount to addressing the monarch direct, which you never did. However, there is no record that Miff received a complaint from the Palace the following morning.

EIGHT

Cooper Vision: Part One

When Tommy was given his first series, television comedy was still at a tentative stage. Arthur Askey's success was not wrongly perceived as little more than televised concert party. Richard Hearne, with his Mr Pastry characterization, was primarily a children's performer accorded bonus adult appeal by nature of the grown-up fascination with the medium that purveyed him. By 1952 it was generally perceived that the only show to have achieved any sort of breakthrough in presentation terms was Terry-Thomas's *How Do You View?* with its intimate approach and sketch comedy that scored visually. The star's bizarre appearance with his gap-toothed smile, elaborate waistcoats and exaggerated cigarette holder, once wittily purveyed as a television aerial, were made for the medium. The challenge that faced Cooper as he contemplated his first television series, *It's Magic*, was daunting, but the fact that magic was a visual performance form had to be in his favour.

A habitué of live performance, Tommy would have to adapt to the more exacting approach of a medium, where, as he admitted in later life, amid a welter of technical distractions the performer has to create his own atmosphere with the studio

236

audience situated on the other side of an enforced barrier of cameras, cables and the people operating them. That mood then had to filter into the homes of millions more. The number of people who have volunteered to me that Cooper is the only comic they have watched from their favourite armchair with tears streaming down their cheeks indicates that he was more than passably successful. However, when he looked back on his first series experience, he did so with a modesty that borders on the defensive. He always recognized it for the big break it was, but in interviews never referred to it as his own show, always as McDonald Hobley's: 'He had a show called *It's Magic*. I went in as a guest artist, but they kept me for the series.' Hobley, one of the defining faces of pioneer television in this country, was the debonair continuity announcer who acted as master of ceremonies throughout the programme and proved a perfect foil to Cooper. But the *Radio Times* billing (as well as Cooper's contract) left one in no doubt: 'Tommy Cooper in *It's Magic*'. Only then in humbler print do we encounter 'A miscellany of mischief, music, and mystery, introduced by McDonald Hobley.' The listings magazine also carried a credit, 'Material for Tommy Cooper supervised by Miff Ferrie.' There is no indication of who wrote what and one assumes that Tommy and Miff collated it from the usual ragbag of sources.

Miscellany is the spice of variety, but in this instance it almost certainly undermined the public's expectation of the programme. It was not a magic show *per se*, as its title suggests, but clung to the word 'magic' in its figurative sense as the key that locked all the ingredients into place. Tommy's burlesque interludes were interwoven with items that epitomized the 'magic' of music, of dance, of song, and so on. The slender assumption that each segment had a magic of its own was a dangerous one. An early format alludes to featuring the magic of art (backed by music 'while we look at it'), of 'the country-side in spring' (film backed by music), of the magic of detection (short whodunnit), of beautiful words (the balcony scene from *Romeo and Juliet*), even the magic of a piece of machinery. Very little has anything to do with the fez-capped giant on fast track to becoming a national figure, although – for all the wrong reasons – the threatened mishmash would have been totally in accord with the image of havoc and mayhem that he cultivated.

The format triggered an erratic response from Cecil McGivern, the Controller, Television Programmes. A week ahead of the first transmission he wrote to producer Graeme Muir, expressing his fears of a clash of bad taste and, with inflated self-importance more worthy of military regiment than television studio, issued his command: 'I rely on you to be utterly vigilant – and utterly ruthless – right up to the moment of transmission in cutting out anything and anybody you find to be in the least offensive. Putting, for example, Tommy Cooper in the same context as *Romeo and Juliet* is immediately a risk and you must accept considerable responsibility.' 'Offensive' is not exactly the first word that comes to mind in considering Cooper's humour and, as for Shakespeare, what a wonderful Bottom he would have made in the Dream. For all the flaws in the rationale of the show, McGivern reveals the paranoia that exists to this day in television commissioning editors with few if any credentials for the role. Nevertheless, it is surprising to encounter the insecurity at a time when the industry remained relatively cosy – because still experimental – and an Enid Blyton culture ruled.

A typical running order shows that Tommy contributed on average six appearances during a single transmission, all with Hobley and all brief, with the exception of his final six minute closing spot before the finale. Muir later commented pompously, 'I rationed him to thirteen minutes of each forty-five minute show. I felt that this was enough. People either dote on Tommy or can't stand him.' The balcony scene went ahead, with no evidence of interference from Tommy. Most of the reviews agreed that if you found Cooper funny you would not dislike the show, only the *Evening Standard* referring to him as being 'the odd man out all the time.' The *Daily Mail* maintained, 'He can produce more laughs to the minute on television than anyone else we have seen.' But McGivern remained jittery. After the second show he sent a memo to Ronnie Waldman, the executive responsible:

1. The Breughel picture was hopeless.

2. The last joke (mother and the walrus) was in doubtful taste.

3. The dancing again.

4. The programme had more ordinariness than magic.

Whether McGivern was happier with the parade of fire-eaters, table tennis champions, harmonica players, calypso singers, and other diverse attractions that Muir subsequently coaxed through his studio doors, we have no way of telling. Eamonn Andrews even read a poem extolling 'The Giant's Causeway'. To bolster the magic content, a guest magician from The Magic Circle was included each week. The show ran fortnightly from 12 March for eight episodes, an option for the final four being picked up along the way. Tommy was paid sixty and Miff twenty guineas a show. The true value was not in the worth of the contract, but in the avalanche of new enquiries for personal appearances that Miff received as a result. There was no rush to repeat the exercise of a series.

Writing in the Television Annual for 1953, editor Kenneth Baily was amazingly less than gracious about Cooper, given the populist fan-based slant of the publication: 'The result was a hotchpotch which could only have been redeemed if the starring comic had been liberal enough in the inventiveness of his material to keep it fresh and full of surprise each time he appeared. Unfortunately, Tommy Cooper had not that liberality of material.' In the circumstances, Miff must shoulder a large part of the blame. No recordings survive and the scripts are little more than running orders which give few clues to precise content. However, they do show that he mingled quick comedy sketches with the crazy conjuring and this would have added to the disjointed nature of the whole exercise. It was generally conceded that Tommy needed more experience as a comic to carry such a vehicle. He could only achieve that on the road. Thanks to Bernard Delfont, Miff was able to write to Waldman with a note of triumph in September 1954: 'You will be glad to know that Tommy has had a most successful summer season at Southport, where, apart from his act, he has been playing sketches and can now safely be classed as a 'production comic'.

Whatever the flaws of the production of *It's Magic* there was no doubting the chemistry that existed between Cooper and Hobley and every effort was made to secure Tommy's presence on the BBC's 1952 *Christmas Party*, hosted by the announcer, televised live on Christmas Day that year. Cooper always looked back on this one appearance as the turning point in his perception by the public. At the beginning of 1950 approximately 350,000 households had television sets; by the end of 1952 that number was fast approaching one and a half million. With only one channel to choose from, it is fairly certain that every single one of those homes would have been tuned into the festivities at Lime Grove at 7.30 that Christmas evening. Tommy would have had to play to capacity at the London Palladium for several years to have gained the audience that saw him most memorably magicking a block of wood – from ear to ear – through the long suffering Hobley's head. One reviewer wrote, 'The Television *Christmas Party* usually depresses me because the enjoyment seems so artificial,' but concluded that Cooper enhanced the situation. He stole the show in a bill that included Norman Wisdom, Arthur Askey, Frankie Howerd, Petula Clark, and many more.

For the time being high profile guest spots were his one means of staying in front of the viewing public. He teamed up again with Hobley on *Kaleidoscope* in February 1953 and with bandleader Henry Hall in *Face the Music* two months later, when he shared with the public his delight at the arrival of his baby daughter, Victoria a few days before on 2 April: 'I'm getting a big play pen with bars all round. Once I get inside she can't get at me!' Most talked about was the occasion in August 1953 when in *A Little of What You Fancy* he enlisted the services of Gilbert Harding. In a stunt reminiscent of his defining anti-gravity milk bottle trick, he filled a large can with water, covered the mouth with a sheet of cardboard and balanced the can upside down on the head of the provocative host. Tommy explained that when he removed the cardboard, the water would stay suspended in the can. The trick failed and Harding was drenched. The television personality was capable of beaming charm or scathing scorn. Fortunately on this occasion he was in a lighter mood and, when questioned on the incident afterwards, referred to his guest star as 'a delightful maniac'.

The next interest to be shown in featuring Cooper in a series of his own came with the arrival of Commercial Television in 1955. It is hard in retrospect to imagine the monopoly held by a lone broadcaster when it came to promoting talent. Had the second channel not arrived Cooper might have stayed for ever in series oblivion. Fortunately for Tommy many of the most powerful people behind the new enterprise, like the Grades, Jack Hylton, and Val Parnell, were tried and tested variety professionals who understood what he stood for, not – Waldman excepted – civil servants running an entertainment enterprise. The first enquiry came from Associated-Rediffusion Ltd, the company awarded the London weekday franchise, on 24 August 1955, although his theatrical commitments prevented a series from materializing until March 1957. However, his presence at the Prince of Wales Theatre for most of this time placed him in a perfect position to gain exposure on the new wave of variety spectaculars that would stamp their own hallmark on the new channel. He made the first of many appearances on *Val Parnell's Sunday Night at the London Palladium* on 16 October 1955. *Saturday Showtime* was another vehicle that availed itself of Cooper's talents during this time, a fast car between Piccadilly Circus and the studios at Wood Green just about making this an option in the days of live transmission.

When Miff eventually sat down to lunch with the executives at Associated-Rediffusion in April 1956, he had the uneasy memory of *It's Magic* at the back of his mind. Miff was less than impressed by the trial script written by John Antrobus and Dave Freeman. In the first place, although the new format would have more skilfully crafted sketches, it was still variety-bound with guest acts and singers. Script editor at the new company was David Croft, who would one day set his stamp on popular British culture with a string of situation comedies of which *Dad's Army* remains the most notable. Miff was adamant in a letter to Croft dated 16 May 1956, in which he emphasized how much thought he had given to the conundrum of presenting his artist on the small screen: 'That is why I suggested my idea for a series entitled *My Life by Tommy Cooper*, the copyright of which, incidentally, I should naturally retain. This idea is, in my opinion, the only way of presenting him to viewing audiences to the best advantage, as frankly I am not interested in any ordinary type of show for him. So unless the scripts are written around this idea a lot of everyone's valuable time will be wasted, and I can see no point in proceeding further.'

Miff's idea was to show 'what happens to Tommy Cooper during the course of an ordinary day,' opening in his home and closing in his theatre dressing room before making his entrance on stage, 'over which credits should run.' The main weakness was that it deprived audiences of seeing arguably what they most wanted to see, their hero in all his calamitous splendour on that very stage. However, Ferrie's tentative movement in the direction of situation comedy, or at least the comedy of situation – irrespective at this stage whether his client could cope with the genre or not – was prescient given that the two British pioneers in the field, Tony Hancock and Jimmy Edwards, had still – by a matter of weeks and months respectively – to bring the device to the medium. In addition he made one exceptionally astute observation to Croft about his client: 'Regarding the trial script, it is far too *frenzied*. One does not have to create a *frenzied* situation for Tommy. Just write it smoothly near-normal and he'll frenzy it up naturally.' As for his involvement and his paranoia about what he regarded as *his* copyright, these were drawbacks that television companies would soon learn to tolerate if they wanted Cooper on their screens.

The BBC must have heard on the grapevine of the commercial interest. On 30 April the Light Entertainment front office expressed interest in a one-off Cooper half hour to be included in a run of showcases for comedians that would also feature Jack Benny and Max Wall, but nothing more was heard of the project after a meeting with Miff at the Corporation on 2 May. Ferrie might have assumed that the Associated-Rediffusion interest was home and dry, but this was not the case. On 14 August there was cause to get jittery when a complication arose regarding technical facilities for a dummy run, leading Head of Light Entertainment, Michael Westmore to declare the project shelved for the time being. Miff wasted no time in rekindling BBC interest by dropping a line to Ronnie Waldman, emphasizing that he had 'finally figured out what is in my opinion the ideal format to enable him to be presented to the fullest advantage.' Nothing however came of a meeting with his old colleague and had it not been for David Croft's persistence at the new company Cooper's television future might have remained at a loose end. Energized by a visit to see Tommy in person at the Prince of Wales, Croft made sure by 10 September that not only had a dummy run been scheduled for 26 October, before Tommy headed north for his autumn season at the Coventry Theatre, but that a deal was in place for a series of twelve half hours at a fee of £350.00 a show to be recorded in the spring of the following year. Sadly Croft would leave the company before he could add his own signature to what he had championed.

By the beginning of 1957 Miff had changed his mind about the title, now endorsing *Cooperama*, with *My Life, Starring Tommy Cooper* as a fall-back. The company wanted to proceed with *The Tommy Cooper Show*. Miff resisted, citing 'lack of originality' in his defence: 'Mr Cooper is a most unusual personality and it is only logical that a series starring such an Artiste should have a title in keeping with such a personality.' A compromise was reached and the series was called, *Cooper, or Life with Tommy*. So much for originality! In the absence of recordings and scripts, one is left to imagine the outcome. All the evidence suggests that it was a debacle.

An ominous footnote had been appended to Miff's proposal: 'There should be no studio audience.' There is every indication to show that on this point he and the broadcaster were in accord. A letter from producer, Peter Croft listed the complications that arose if studio space had to be sacrificed. Scenery would have to take a stylized form, while only a small percentage of the audience would be able to see any one particular item. The same company's *A Show Called Fred* and *Son of Fred* – presumably shot in the same studio – had managed without during 1956, but Milligan's absurdist scripts starring Peter Sellers were so out of the ordinary that the absence of an audience did not seem to detract from their appeal. Tommy's whole motivation as a performer was audience-based.

On 11 May 1957, two-thirds of the way through the run, Miff wrote to John McMillan, the Controller of Programmes, that 'Mr Cooper is becoming increasingly unhappy at the prevailing state of affairs, particularly the scripts and the casting, with the result that he wishes an entirely new cast for the next programme.' Scripts were an uncoordinated affair, with Freeman, Freddie Sadler, Richard Waring, and Patrick Brawn contributing episodes singly or in pairs. Antrobus had wisely left the fold earlier. Miff hardly needed to add that 'such lack of cooperation was certainly never anticipated, otherwise this series would not have been undertaken.' A few days later Peter Croft put pen to paper to make a complaint – and a point – of his own: 'We have so far overlooked the fact that he is continuously late both for morning and afternoon rehearsals, resulting in a loss of approximately five hours per week of rehearsal time.'

As we have seen, Bernard Delfont took television matters into his own hands for the series, *Cooper's Capers*, that materialized for Associated Television Ltd the following year.

With the master showman at the helm we can be assured that Tommy certainly had the sounding board of an audience on this occasion. The inclusion of the singer, Aileen Cochrane suggests a return to something nearer a variety, rather than a pure sketch format, although again his comedy magic talents were downplayed. The transmission time of 10.15 p.m. on Fridays – a shift from 9.30 p.m. on Mondays – would not have instilled confidence in the star. The director had to be replaced after the first show. Artist and agent could derive some consolation from the fact that Commercial Television had still to reach large sections of the UK. He would not return to television screens in a resident series until 1966, by which time the whole country was immersed in the culture of ITV.

Miff did nothing further about the series situation until the end of December 1959, when he plucked up the courage to write to the Corporation's new Head of Light Entertainment, Eric Maschwitz about the possibility of a spring or autumn series for the BBC in 1960. The reply was prompt, but not promising, citing his commitment to a large number of series in those periods. As far as the Corporation was concerned Tommy's best hope for exposure resided at the level of producer, rather than executive patronage. Bill Cotton, by now producing his father's show, *The Billy Cotton Band Show*, sensed the chemistry that might exist between the jovial showman and the exuberant magical jester. He was right. Cotton Senior made a willing stooge as Tommy subjected the bandleader to the guillotine illusion – with all the gags he would perpetrate on Michael Parkinson on *his* show almost twenty years later – and used him as a special audience of one as he made a succession of paper balls disappear before Billy's very eyes. This sequence had been brought to perfection by the New York master of sleight of hand, Slydini. As the balls became larger, the laughter from the audience became louder.

The routine was a brilliant demonstration of applied psychology. Each time Cooper went to make a ball vanish, an upward flick of the wrist propelled it over the bandleader's head. Cotton had no idea what was happening until the magician asked him to get up from the chair and walked him round to show him the mound of tissue paper that had piled up behind.

Alongside *Dixon of Dock Green*, *Juke Box Jury* and *Perry Mason*, *The Billy Cotton Band Show* was a comfortable cornerstone of Saturday night viewing in the early Sixties before *The Generation Game*, *The Two Ronnies* and *Parkinson* redefined the face of weekend viewing a decade later. Between January 1960 and March 1962 Cooper made no fewer than four guest appearances with 'the old man' for fees starting at 250 guineas and rising to £325.00. Bill would get special approval for this sort of money, extending far beyond what the BBC had been accustomed to pay for guest artists in such circumstances, but inevitable in the face of increased competition from the commercial channel. Around 1960 £350.00 was his standard fee for an appearance on the Palladium show or another production of similar stature on the commercial network. As the ITV audience grew, regular appearances on *Val Parnell's Sunday Night at the London Palladium* became more important for his profile, although in actuality, in spite of the persistence of ATV's legendary booker, Alec Fyne, he turned down more than he did. For all Miff wanted to soft pedal his client's identification with the comedy magic routine, it did present a gift to a format like the Palladium show, capable as it was of immense variation, unlike so many set comedy sketches and novelty acts. Tommy constantly made the excuse that he never had anything new. The real reason is that when he did have something new he did not want to waste it on the television audience. In 1963 Miff asked Fyne for a fee of £500.00 and top billing. In television they deemed this kind of status more important than in the theatre. They settled for £450.00 and would have to wait until 1967 before achieving the star spot on a bill that also featured Al Read, Peter Nero, and host Bob Monkhouse. For that he received £1,000.00, but by then his television presence had taken a major turn.

In the overall context of his career the most significant enquiry for a guest appearance came in September 1960, for a cameo role as the Mad Hatter in a Christmas extravaganza loosely based on the Alice books. He did not accept the offer, although the idea of Tommy performing the 'Hats' routine at his own tea party might not have been as incongruous in Lewis Carroll's eyes as it first appears. The enquiry initiated a dialogue with ABC Television, a rival to ATV and A-RTV on the franchise map, where it resided as the weekend contractor for the North and the Midlands. In time it would merge with A-RTV to form Thames Television. Virtually ninety per cent of Cooper's remaining television appearances would be made for the company in one of its two manifestations. Initially they constituted guest star opportunities on ABC's own showcase spectacular, *Big Night Out*, but in June 1961 a less likely invitation was extended for Tommy to appear on *Thank Your Lucky Stars*, the pioneering pop programme that allowed teen-agers to give their verdicts on the latest releases.

The show was produced by an ex-radio producer for Radio Luxembourg, Philip Jones. His biggest coup in the role came in January 1963 when having heard over the phone an acetate of a number called 'Please Please Me,' he booked an emerging rock group named The Beatles for their first national television appearance. For the moment it was enough to know that Tommy Cooper had made a comedy record – 'How Come There's No Dog Day?' on the 'A' side, 'Don't Jump off the Roof, Dad' on the flip side – an excuse to add a touch of novelty to the standard fare of Alma Cogan, Michael Holliday, and The Temperance Seven. Within a short while Jones would become Head of Light Entertainment, first at ABC and then at Thames, and as such the most influential individual in Tommy's television career. A kind, unassuming man with total commitment to the talent he opted to promote, he was a show-man on the inside rather that the outside. Performers warmed to this, sensing that he – unlike so many executives and impre-sarios – had no wish to upstage them or exercise his own ego on the back of theirs. In matters like these Tommy was rela-tively easy-going, but even so he always appreciated the special quality of Philip Jones.

Meanwhile in September 1962 Miff received an unexpected enquiry from the BBC for Tommy to star in its pantomime, *Puss in Boots* for transmission on Christmas Day. Tommy was at first resistant. Pantomime had never been his happiest medium. Producers complained that he had difficulty carrying the plot. According to provincial pantomime supremo, Derek Salberg, he was 'very bad on lines; you could hear him for two or three minutes, then he just tailed away.' Cooper must have felt torn between this responsibility and the demand of having to do double duty as the obligatory speciality act in the ballroom scene as events reached their fairy tale conclusion. Nevertheless, of the seven pantomimes in which he had appeared so far, *Puss in Boots* had figured four of those times, mainly with Cooper as the King. Unfortunately the previous year the Bradford pro-duction had been fraught with calamity, beginning with major disagreements with the director, who in the opinion of the star had no sense of comedy, and ending with a smallpox epidemic that brought the run of twelve weeks to a close after eight.

In a letter of 14 September, Miff spelt out why he thought Tommy should forego the holiday he was contemplating at the time of the BBC project, in the process showing that he had not lost sight of further television horizons for his artist:

'In my considered opinion it would be a mistake for you to miss this opportunity which would enable you to become established as a "Production Artiste" and once and for all nail the impression that you can only be used in solo spots doing your own material in other people's programmes. This is a very important matter as far as your progressive career is concerned, and I do think that if you could postpone your holiday, you would be wise professionally to do so.' Tommy gave in and Miff negotiated a fee of £525.00 to incorporate the recording and two weeks of rehearsals. The producer was set to be Richard Afton, a friendly patron from Tommy's past.

What soon took on the aspect of a pantomime all of its own began late in the evening of 31 October when Tommy phoned Miff to complain about the script: 'Says King part is nothing.' Two days later Afton became ill, to be replaced by his colleague, Harry Carlisle. A flurry of telephone calls took place between Miff, Tommy, and Bill Cotton, now Head of Variety at the BBC. With Afton suffering a relapse and rehearsals due to commence on 5 November, the situation appears to have been resolved until the following day when Cooper failed to attend rehearsals. Holland Barrett, the Head of Artists' Bookings, was forced to write to Miff to announce that owing to the short amount of rehearsal time at the BBC's disposal, they had no option 'but to make alternative arrangements'. In other words, Tommy's services were no longer required. In a subsequent letter dated the same day, Barrett wrote: 'I understand that you are maintaining that in the course of a subsequent conversation with the producer, he agreed that Cooper could play either the King or Jolly the Jester according to his preference. I find this hard to understand in view of the fact that the producer had already asked us to engage another artist (Reg Varney) to play the jester.' Since Tommy appears to have raised his objection to the role of the King only two working days before the start of rehearsals, it all seems somewhat disingenuous. The BBC had apparent good reason to take Tommy to court for breach of contract. In the circumstances the contract was cancelled and David Nixon stepped into the breach as King. Very late in the day Cooper had his holiday, but he won no marks with the Corporation as a result of the incident.

The episode cooled any immediate interest the BBC might have had to exploit the comedian in the wake of his success on *The Billy Cotton Band Show*. Meanwhile Tommy had plenty of offers for guest spots and a full theatrical diary. It was not until October 1963 that he sat down to lunch to discuss the way forward with Philip Jones. Events seemed to move quickly, with an offer for a series of eleven shows with an option for a further two. However, the insistence of ABC that Russ Conway and Susan Maughan should be co-starred with Cooper meant the series was stillborn. Jones did not lose interest, nor could he. The following year would see Tommy's defining success in *Startime* at the London Palladium. The high profile of this show placed him in a category whereby television companies could ignore him only at their peril.

In 1964 the BBC returned to the fray. In April, Manchester based producer, Stan Parkinson – independent of the London-based monolith that was the Light Entertainment Group – came up with an interesting idea, a series of short programmes in which Tommy would be interviewed about all aspects of his life. Tommy's ability to have people in stitches in pubs and clubs as he recounted incidents from his childhood, his service career and more would thus be able to reach a wider audience. The idea of the comic interview was not new. Terry-Thomas had been featured in this way with veteran announcer, Leslie Mitchell on *How Do You View?* while Benny Hill would later come to make the device his own, but in both cases the interviews were staged, the subjects being outlandish characters drawn from their stars' repertoires of comic types. Parkinson was favouring a naturalistic approach. Again the idea went away, presumably because of the insignificance of the slot offered. A Manchester based production did not carry the weight of a London vehicle. However, Miff did not forget the device. A more substantial enquiry came in October when Executive Producer, George Inns – in that less politically correct age, he had devised *The Black and White Minstrel Show* – began to float the idea of a series of fortnightly spectaculars for the spring of the following year. The following day Philip Jones, with almost telepathic instinct, rang Miff: 'Any use in talking about another series for T. C?'

With reference to the *Puss in Boots* fiasco, if impresarios soon forget past sins when their perpetrators make money for them in theatres, the same also applies in television when they provide the key to high ratings. Philip laid low as the BBC embarked on a merry go round of bureaucratic uncertainty in which the project was passed from one producer to another and no one seemed sure whether Tommy Cooper came under the label of 'Variety' or 'Comedy.' The Light Entertainment Group was traditionally split between the two 'cultures' in this fashion. The rigid pigeonholing never helped anyone. Bill Cotton – a showman in his father's image and Tommy's true champion at the Corporation – unfortunately found himself as Head of Variety handing over executive responsibility to Frank Muir as Head of Comedy. Part of this was due to Miff's high-handedness on the format front – with an insistence that the show should not be a parade of guest acts and dancing girls – although at no point was a situation comedy being proposed. The sketch format under discussion came closer to the genre of revue – or 'broken comedy', to use the ugly, self-defeating phrase adopted in more recent years – and could conceivably have emanated from either side.

Tommy's own ideas – or, more probably, Miff's, shared by Tommy – complicated matters. In a letter to Cotton dated 12 December 1964, Miff became more specific about his client's stipulations: 'He would be happy to embark on a weekly series next autumn, provided it could proceed along the lines which I explained to George Inns, namely a thirty minute (or less) programme based on the interview idea, which could lead anywhere and tentatively entitled *Conversations with Cooper*, to be screened any evening except Saturday.' The success of his friend, Michael Bentine's *It's a Square World* had impressed Tommy and almost certainly played a part in this thinking. Sadly Stan Parkinson, stranded in the provinces, did not receive an iota of credit. At the end of the year when Cotton is about to hand over the baton to Muir, Philip Jones, again with prescient timing, dropped Ferrie a gentle note: 'I really think the idea of *Cooper Talks* with a (John) Freeman-type interview dissolving into flashbacks is excellent.' And then to show he really had thought the idea through, he continued: 'Bearing in mind Tommy's strength with a live audience, I feel the flashbacks/sketches should be live rather than filmed. Otherwise one is dependent on an audience laughing at monitor screens, which is not always successful.' He adds, 'We are just as interested in Tommy as ever.'

By now Miff was so far advanced with the BBC that he had gone along with Cotton's idea of a special to be recorded in May to act essentially as a pilot for an autumn series, but the relationship between Ferrie and Frank Muir quickly deteriorated. A script was commissioned – by David Cumming – with Miff irrationally demanding that 'his' idea of the interview device be taken out when he showed dissatisfaction with the first draft. It soon materialized that the contract for the autumn series would not be issued alongside that for the special: in other words the corporation was now hedging its bets. Miff should have become suspicious when the BBC began to speak of the one-off within the context of the *Comedy Playhouse* series, which was sufficiently well established as a lottery strand from which successful episodes were promoted to series status, of which *Steptoe and Son* had been the most successful. Muir claimed this had always been the case. Cotton, who would have been forced to concede otherwise, stayed away from the curious game of *Call My Bluff* that resulted.

Eventually Tom Sloan, their mutual boss as Head of Light Entertainment, had to agree with Ferrie in a letter dated 10 May 1965 that the single programme had always been part of an overall understanding. By reneging on the gentlemen's agreement, the BBC had played straight into the hands of ITV. On 26 March Philip had phoned Miff, who used the opportunity to explain the BBC situation to him – as if Jones didn't know. Ferrie fairly stated that he was 'in no way haggling or putting one against the other, merely endeavouring to do the right thing for T. C.' He mentioned that the BBC had agreed a fee of 'around £1,000.00', which was the case, and that he would put a brief synopsis – a revision of the interview concept – in the post. Philip replied, 'I am certain we could have a very happy association with you and Tommy.' Allowing for the hazards of defining happiness, he was substantially – although not entirely – correct.

In no time the interview device hit a snag. With less than three weeks to recording the pilot at Teddington Studios on 19 September, Philip, doubling his executive remit with the role of producer for the show, phoned Miff: 'Cannot get Malcolm Muggeridge, Eamonn Andrews or Cliff Michelmore. Will have to settle for a good straight actor.' Securing the services of an actual interviewer of substance was never going to be on the cards, thus weakening the comic contrast between star and interrogator. Perhaps it was an omen. ABC Programme

Controller, Brian Tesler wasted little time in telling Ferrie what he thought of the pilot: 'I know that the audience laughed (at most of the show anyway); I know that by some people's criteria the show was by no means a failure. But as a *Tommy Cooper* show, as a way of harnessing the talent of this very funny man, it *was* a failure; a disjointed, uncomfortable, old-fashioned failure.'

While admitting that Philip Jones and his director, Mark Stuart shouldered much of the responsibility, Brian was anxious to stress that Tommy was even more accountable, since it was in order to assuage him that their mistakes were made in the first place. 'The Convict's Return,' a sketch from earlier times pushed by Cooper and rejected by Miff at every possible opportunity somehow found its way before the cameras. The writer, Frank Roscoe had been out of his element. No attempt was made to integrate the musical guest, Petula Clark, into the scheme of things, Tommy simply introducing her in the manner of a stage compère. Moreover, the interview device had not worked satisfactorily, the high energy comedy level required by the show dipping at those moments. In other words, Tommy should not be given a straightforward invitation to ramble on about one of his experiences, however funny that might be on a conventional magazine programme. Tesler was happy to retain the presence of an interviewer, but more in the role of straight man and compère, wasting no time in cutting to the action of a sketch set up by the chat with a snappy question and answer exchange. Ad-lib conversation in itself was deemed too downbeat for such a production. Brian also stipulated the most challenging requisite he made of the star: 'We must ensure that Tommy, once he puts his fate in our hands, will have enough faith in his director's assessment of what will work to cooperate with him willingly and whole-heartedly.' The first show of the series was recorded on

12 November. After viewing the results, Tesler was buoyant enough to write to Miff in more positive mood. Aside from the inevitable glitch here and there, he admitted, 'This was a very funny show and Tommy was revealed as a very funny man who is not restricted to comedy magic.'

All was set for consolidating Cooper's television career, but the first series would be a fiery ordeal. As Tesler stressed in his letter to Miff of 6 December 1965, 'Personality problems (some of which you have been coping with for many years) inevitably made the process painfully slow, but I think ultimately rewarding.' Recording dates were rearranged several times to accommodate the search for better material, leading to a team of six writers comprising Brad Ashton, John Muir and Eric Geen, John Warren and John Singer, and Austin Steele. Philip Jones reverted to his executive role, leaving Stuart in charge as producer and director. The run would not be completed until the beginning of March, dashing Miff's original hopes for a transmission in the autumn of 1965. It would eventually air on Saturday evenings in the World Cup dominated summer, the run being interrupted for one week by the game between England and Mexico. At least he could be happy that his favoured title, *Cooperama* finally won the day. His 'based on a format by' credit was secure and two weeks before the first transmission he was already discussing recording dates for a second series. On a less happy note, George Brightwell, the genial ABC Programme Administrator, with whom Miff had established the friendliest of associations, left the company at the end of January.

A surviving episode of *Cooperama* from 1966 reveals actor Derek Bond in the role of the suave interviewer. He is blandness personified and lacks the essential disciplinary edge of the great straight man. Nothing can disguise the fact that for the major part of the first half of the show Tommy is performing solo material that would be delivered more effectively in stand-up than perched on a stool. A reference to Paris segues into the mime routine based on a visit to the Eiffel Tower – for which he has to stand – and then, courtesy of a mention of the famous Lido cabaret, into a sketch involving Tommy with two acrobats. It is the traditional variety fare of a thousand Palladium shows and Tommy, preening around in tight-fitting pants and bolero, is very funny indeed, but it hardly represents the original breakthrough upon which Miff had his sights. A quickie that led into the commercial break involving Tommy as a street trader who ends up smothered in paint and whitewash is puerile in concept – he is peddling lucky charms! – and in execution.

Part two begins with Tommy's interview presentation of the 'Chapeaugraphy' routine with the ring of felt. A short semi-silent sketch with the comedian being recognized in a restaurant by a fan who can't stop laughing at his hero and then, by way of the last laugh, departs with Tommy having to pay his bill has a bizarre credibility and showcased Cooper's own trademark laugh to great effect. Then it is back to more stand-up material with Derek Bond as Tommy 'impersonates' vaudevillians Al Jolson and clarinettist Ted – 'Is everybody happy?' – Lewis. On the back of the Lewis routine with the clarinet, Acker Bilk makes a guest appearance and holds up the comedy with traditional jazz in traditional light entertainment guest star fashion for three minutes. The final item, an extended sketch in which Tommy finds himself mistaken for a bank robber in a police station might have been what Miff had in mind as he attempted to lure Tommy's image away from the manic magician, but still ends with him plying the police constable with Milton Berle's 'Happy New Year' playing card gag. The half hour comes over as relentlessly contrived and is directed with no understanding of physical comedy. We never see Cooper in a proper long shot when it counts, as in the mime sequence. One desperately longs for someone to invest in new stand-up material for this great clown and then leave him to his own devices.

By the time his second series for ABC came around at the beginning of 1967 *Cooperama* had been renamed *Life with Cooper*. The tedious device of the straight man interviewer had been discarded and each episode began on more secure ground with a short stand-up sequence of comedy magic and gags, a characteristic that now identified almost all of Tommy's television shows until the end of his career. This was always what he did best and if all else failed, the shows had one segment that was worth switching on for. In another change, the exit door had been shown to guest musical acts. The programmes were even more sketch driven with filmed quickies used as punctuation. The pedantic hand of Ferrie behind the scenes remained discernible from the manner in which all concerned clung to the old contrivance of allowing viewers to eavesdrop on a day in the life of the star. It was as if the comedy had to be excused or justified. In this way viewers were treated to whole episodes detailing the misadventures that befell Cooper when he went to have his passport photograph taken, when he was waylaid by fog *en route* to Birmingham, or when he ran out of cash to reclaim his left luggage. Much of it was tedious, but nothing dented the popularity of the star.

Tesler and Jones appeared to treat Miff as an *ex officio* executive producer, although he would not formally be recompensed by ABC until the second series of *Life with Cooper*, when he received a flat £1,000.00 fee for format and £250.00 per show as script consultant. Tommy, who earned £1,000.00 a show for *Cooperama*, was now earning £1,500.00 per programme. Miff had no qualifications for his role. It would not be the last time – although it may have been the first – a television company elevated an artist's manager to editorial status, chiefly to flatter his ego and substantiate the bonds that tied the star to the company. Today, the moment their clients have been identified as star potential, agents and managers simply set up shop as independent production companies in the first instance and work their persuasive powers on commissioning editors who understand no better. At least Tesler and Jones were accredited television professionals whose own understanding of how to handle distinctive and sometimes difficult comic talent like Hancock, Howerd, Forsyth, Hill, not to mention Cooper, went before them. Unfortunately Tommy, for all his own comic judgement, did not possess the added intellectual clout that enabled performers like Benny Hill, Ronnie Barker, and Stanley Baxter to play a major part in the production of their own shows, although they were not openly credited for this.

Almost as if to prove to himself and others that he was earning his money, Miff was never contented. His constant carp that 'a good idea is not being executed properly' seemed to place the entire onus on the writers and none on *his* so-called format. When he complained that material for an entire run of six or seven shows was never signed and sealed in advance of the first recording, he couldn't grasp that an ongoing television series of this kind relies on the necessary creative give and take between star and writers, and that subsequent episodes grow organically out of the success or failure of the previous one. Specific writers came in for special condemnation, namely John Muir and Eric Geen, whose work Tommy especially prized. Miff chided his client, 'If you wish to be seen on any television screen doing such old-fashioned material, then all the progress we have accomplished so far will be wasted.' According to Muir, he and his partner could never reason why Ferrie was so adverse to Cooper performing stand-up on television or wallowing in the ludicrousness of his persona, all the time wanting him 'to stop playing the idiot and become a light comedian'. When they produced a script which they considered their best ever, Miff threw a tantrum and walked out of the meeting. Muir and Geen did not stay around for the last series of *Life with Cooper*, taking some consolation from the fact that they were able to add some creative dignity to the final flourish of Hancock's performing career for Philip Jones and ABC Television before his tragic end in 1968.

There was never a time when Miff did not need convincing. Things might have been different if Cooper had enjoyed a monogamous relationship with a single writer or writing team. Since Cooper's first excursions into television comedy in the Fifties, the bar had been raised by one man, Tony Hancock. His career was now in sad decline, but the result of his earlier achievement – and the more lasting one of his scriptwriters, Ray Galton and Alan Simpson – had been to challenge those engaged in producing comedy for the box with a greater sense of responsibility for quality. Miff and ABC Television had rightly set their sights high for Tommy Cooper, but in doing so had tended to overlook the essential nature of their own star, an innately funny man with the vigour of variety in his veins as distinct from the more contemplative actor's approach that Hancock brought to his work. Hancock was a realist *in extremis*; Cooper was a fantasist caught up in the net of his own clumsiness. In the passport episode, for example, there were sketches that demanded him to be arrogant and argumentative, which suggested they might have been written with Hancock rather than Cooper in mind. Typical Tommy was neither. Moreover, put him in a sketch involving a real doctor's surgery or a real airport and he came to earth with a thud. Even when a true life incident was dramatized, as in the falling asleep on sentry duty episode, the results were relatively flat when contrasted to Tommy's animated telling of what happened. On the other hand portray him as a waiter in a high class restaurant threshing around in a fish tank with a mallet to catch a customer's chosen trout – 'I'm tickling him – he's tickling me – huh huh huh!' – or as a desperate television repair man forced to sit Punch and Judy fashion in an empty screen enacting all the programmes – news, weather, drama, cricket, volume control and picture distortion included – and the laughter reached new decibel levels. At times like these his sketch comedy was – quite as much as Milligan's – *Monty Python* before its time.

To have sustained an ongoing situation comedy he needed a permanent writer partnership capable of exploiting his absurdist take on the world and, like all successful examples of the genre, a well-defined fixed milieu in which to operate. For one brief moment there was a possibility that Ray and Alan could have come together creatively with Cooper. In 1966 they had written the book for *Way Out in Piccadilly*, the successful revue starring Frankie Howerd and presented by Bernard Delfont at Tommy's old haunt, the Prince of Wales Theatre. In December 1966 Delfont approached Miff with the possibility of Tommy starring in a similar vehicle to follow on from the Howerd show in the autumn of 1967. The fact that Cooper's friend, Eric Sykes had directed the original show could have been an added incentive. Had the stage partnership worked, one can only surmise what might have been achieved in television terms by the three – or four – of them. It was not to be. Miff chose the option of further cabaret dates and the recording schedule of the second series of *Life with Cooper*. ABC had always been flexible in its approach to recording dates and would surely have welcomed the prestige that would have accrued to Cooper as a result. The series would not air anyhow until the spring of the following year, 1968. Of all Miff's misses, it was arguably the biggest lost opportunity of them all.

Tommy expressed to journalist David Nathan, in an interview for his book *The Laughtermakers*, the wish that he might have found a Clouseau-like mantle as Sellers had done. Had he done so, it would have embodied his greatest gift, the apparent clumsiness which conceals perfect timing. The nearest he came to finding writers who could reliably capitalize on this was the partnership of Johnnie Mortimer and Brian Cooke, who joined the *Life with Cooper* team for the second series at the suggestion of script editor for that run, Barry Took. Their sketch where he played the fiancée visiting his prospective in-laws contains at its core a prime example of what Galton and Simpson had achieved with Hancock on a much grander scale, namely taken aspects of the performer's own personality and built upon them for comic effect. They always admitted that they never invented the character of Anthony Aloysius St John Hancock, merely enhanced what was already there. At one level the sketch is a monstrosity of comic misunderstanding. The parents visited by Tommy are not those of his fiancée at all. A bystander has misdirected him to 56, Ladbroke Grove, not, as he requested, 56, Ladbroke Avenue. Much of the dialogue between Cooper and the supposed father-in-law to be, played by the redoubtable Robert Dorning – a reliable character actor who in the mid-Sixties was almost interchangeable with Arthur Lowe in the roles he played – betrays a total lack of understanding with his persona. Tommy, in answer to a question about his intentions towards the daughter, would never have declared, 'Well, between you and me, I'd like to drag her into a shop doorway and with a bit of luck . . .' However, the sequence in which sitting on a settee he juggles the growing burden of hospitality offered to him by prospec-

tive mother-in-law and father-in-law betrays a brilliant observation of Cooper in real life.

Notes made while watching the sequence do scant justice to
this mounting comic *tour de force*: 'Takes cup of tea in right
hand; takes glass of whisky in left; balances plate of sandwiches on right forearm; receives cigar in mouth; "You're not
eating your sandwiches"; swivels cigar to left side of mouth;
turns to move mouth down to sandwiches; fails to connect;
holds whiskey in right hand with cup of tea; takes plate of
sandwiches in left hand; crosses legs; balances plate in crook
of right foot; takes glass with right hand; mother-in-law looks
the other way; pours whiskey into tea; balances cup and saucer
on glass in left hand; puffs on cigar with right hand; "And *do*
have a piece of my homemade cake."; right hand already waiting to take second plate; etcetera.' The rhythm of the piece
and Cooper's look of consternation and embarrassment
throughout contribute to a comic highlight of his television
career.

Significantly the third series of *Life with Cooper*, recorded
during the opening months of 1969, employed the services of
Eric Merriman as script editor and appears to have placed far
greater emphasis on the fantastical. Miff no longer figured in
the credits, having advised Philip Jones and new producer,
Milo Lewis as early as 1 June 1968 that he was now forced to
disassociate from any script involvement. His decision led to
a more open format in which sketches shed their ties to the
'day in the life' motif. Tommy and the writers must have felt
like caged birds restored to flight. A few days later Miff wrote
to Cooper from his creative ivory tower: 'What is now being
proposed as programme material is so far removed from the
original format, which was agreed and accepted by ABC and
yourself as the best means of projecting your natural comedy
talent on television, that I simply cannot allow my name to be

connected with it.' In Walter Mitty fashion he goes on about 'making a breakthrough in the world of television comedy programmes', completely overlooking the fact that the only way in which the term 'breakthrough' could ever possibly be applied to Cooper was in relation to the idiosyncratic nature of his personality and his comic technique. His persona was its own god-given innovation. As Morecambe and Wise would show, it should not matter how hackneyed the so-called format might appear if it allowed the comic sunshine to permeate through. Not that Miff's 'format' had ever been anything but pedestrian. Moreover, if one were going to approach the challenge of a true British comedy breakthrough from the benchmark of Hancock's greatest achievement, it is arguable that no such thing occurred until Ricky Gervais delivered *The Office* in 2001.

Miff continued to brainwash Tommy on the issue. On 8 August 1968 he wrote to Cooper following a discussion in Blackpool the day before 'when it was decided that you were in agreement with me regarding the unsuitability of the script material submitted so far by ABC television and that in order to have this matter dealt with properly, it will be necessary for you to write me to this effect. I enclose herewith a draft letter which you may care to sign and return to me.' Two days later he heard from Tommy, but it was not the letter he expected: 'Dear Miff, Regarding the six shows for Thames, after a lot more thought I cannot lie to myself – to me they are still funny! So with that in mind, I must do them. Sorry you don't feel the same about this, but I must be true to myself. Best wishes, Tommy.' Only Miff would argue against the instinct of a great performer. In so doing he deprived himself of credit by association with some of Cooper's greatest comedy moments.

It should not be forgotten that in the heyday of the music hall and the variety theatre the career of a sketch comedian like Harry Tate or Sid Field would have been founded on a repertoire of not much more than the contents of two or three television sketch half-hours. Add to the volume of Cooper's accumulated television material the copious array of stage and stand-up stuff he had mastered down the years and it can be seen that his total comic arsenal was considerable to say the least. The Thames series of *Life with Cooper* that aired in the spring of 1969 does not survive in its entirety but, in addition to the priceless encounter of Tommy with his supposed in-laws, featured many memorable moments that do. Dudley Foster played an aggrieved Cooper neighbour in a preposterous 'over the garden wall' sequence by Mortimer and Cooke, in which a lone apple overhanging Foster's side of the fence on a branch belonging to Cooper's tree gives cause for dispute. Hostilities build to ludicrous extremes as sunflowers on one side with roots on the other are visibly tugged through the ground and a heavy roller is thrown in fury at Tommy's prize-contending marrow. Whereas Hancock would have argued his way through the sequence, Cooper, with Foster, jubilantly confronts the crisis with a succession of visual gags, until a policeman comes along to settle the matter. He idly plucks off the apple in question, munches into it and settles down to listen.

A semi-silent sequence, attributed to Eric Merriman, George Evans, and Derek Collyer, in which Tommy strolls purposefully into a gentlemen's washroom adorned with bowler hat, brief case and umbrella quickly escalates into chaos as he negotiates a minefield of plug-less washbasins, recalcitrant taps, scalding water, eye-squirting soap dispensers and a wayward roller towel unit. The piece brilliantly exploits his intrinsically funny way of walking, each foot poised for that briefest of split seconds as it makes its own decision where next to tread before it plants itself back on the ground. As he moves from one hazard to the next, the effect is enhanced by much of the camera work that makes him appear even taller than he actually is. The location of the sketch must have made Miff squirm, but at no point is it played at a cheap lavatorial level. Possibly at his insistence, there is not a urinal in sight! In a similar slapstick vein Barry Cryer joined forces with Eric Merriman to produce the sketch in which Cooper played a toastmaster officiating at the top table of a stuffy banquet. This showed his ability to transform the most ancient slapstick ritual into something orgiastic in dimension, as gavel, food, furniture, microphone cable, fire extinguishers were orchestrated into a comic set piece from which no participant emerged unscathed and the toast to absent friends ended with Tommy saturated by the collective contents of every single glass. The whole sequence is played out by Cooper with a seriousness that belies the seeming inanity of the material and that is why it works so well.

The two television sketches from this period that probably linger longest in the memory of those who saw them are both essentially solo pieces, although the first is adorned by a group of suffering extras sitting at tables who are subjected to the rigours of the Thames special effects department as it conjured up the conditions of a storm at sea in which Tommy, courtesy of Cryer and Merriman again, took the established device of the burlesque ventriloquist to new levels of absurdity. The set literally teeters from side to side on a rocking mechanism as Tommy staggers this way and that on the tiny cabaret stage. Watching the sequence is enough to make one queasy, if one were not already laughing out loud. The chair, the table, the performer and his dummy slither back and forth as Cooper attempts in what is essentially a burlesque of a burlesque to prove that he is as fine a technician as the best of them: much of the basic business where the head of the dummy becomes detached from the body and the head disappears derives from the comedy vent act of Sandy Powell. Cooper battles on against all the odds, coaxing the little fellow to sing for us – 'Gye, Gye Glues!' – and engaging in a frantic wrestling match as he attempts to restore the doll to its suitcase. This becomes a losing battle and as he concedes an encore to the doll water starts to burst through the first of four portholes in the wall at the back of the stage. No sooner has he closed this than water gushes through the second, then the third, then in pairs and so on, until in defiance of his efforts to stem the flow, it is cascading through all four at once. All the while the stage is rolling to and fro, the magician and dummy drenched to desperation levels as they continue to slither in whichever direction gravity dictates. At the conclusion Tommy is literally poured into the wings. Had it been a sequence in a movie, the routine would have been talked of today with the same reverence with which cineastes discuss the scene in the stateroom where the Marx Brothers manage to compress more people in a confined space than is humanly possible. At one point a stray life belt rolls across the tiny stage as if in wistful comment of this very fact.

The sketches in which he appeared to work the best were those that showed him fighting against the tricks played by fate, not least the caprices of inanimate objects. It is appropriate that the other unforgettable sequence from this time should make verbal acknowledgement of this, although it fits less obviously within the mould itself. Merriman, Evans, and Collyer are formally credited as scriptwriters of Cooper's pastiche of the Hamlet soliloquy, but Val Andrews recalls working at an earlier stage on the premise for Tommy. The sight of our hero in doublet, hose and flaxen wig confirms our gravest suspicions that the boards at Stratford East and not Stratford-upon-Avon were his rightful habitat:

To be or not to be, that is the question.
Whether 'tis nobler in the mind to suffer
The slings and arrows of outrageous fortune . . .

Breaking off he immediately shifts into stand-up mode: 'I had
a bit of bad luck yesterday. I was pinched for parking. I said
to the officer, "But I'm in a cul-de-sac." He said, "I don't care
what kind of car it is. You can't park here."'

Or to take arms against a sea of troubles . . .

'I usually travel by sea . . .' And so the verse of the original
is brought up against the dire reality of the comic's lot, a
double-edged comment on the two performing traditions.
Other aspects of variety are brought into the mix, with Yorick's
skull the pretext for further bad ventriloquism, this time in
open parody of the brilliant Arthur Worsley, who allowed his
dummy, Charlie Brown to do virtually all the talking as he
stood there bemused and – a technical *tour de force* – tight-
lipped, the almost unsmiling butt of a thousand quips, daring
the audience to catch the merest lip movement. Tommy keeps
his teeth clenched in defiance as with a nod to Worsley's
catchphrase he attempts to coax words from the grotesque
papier-mâché head: 'Look at me, son. Look at me. Here's a
joke. Here's one for you now.' But the jokes are incidental.
Before long the real laugh becomes the impossibility of knowing who is supposed to be speaking to whom at any one time.
The routine culminates with a song and soft shoe in obeisance
to Ophelia, a re-working of an old Max Miller number:

> Oh, Oh, Oh, Ophelia,
> Oh please reveal – y – a
> In love with me.

You have such appeal – y – a,
That's why I kneel – y – a
On bended knee!

This is the cue for Tommy to adopt an Al Jolson pose and round off proceedings with a parody of 'Mammy': 'Hammy! Hammy!' According to Mary Kay, he had great difficulty learning the routine, but the relish he showed in performing it and the ovation it received must have compensated for the difficulty of juggling the contrasting vocal patterns in rehearsal.

Whatever the quality of his material, Tommy was carried along by the immense public affection shown towards him. By the third show of the first series, *Life with Cooper*, transmitted on Saturdays from the beginning of 1967, had reached seventh in the ratings. By the time of the second series in the early part of 1968 it regularly dislodged *Coronation Street* at the top of the ratings, being watched in something like 8,750,000 homes. A repeat of the same series during the summer months attracted equally large audiences. ABC was quick to realize it was on a winning streak. When it became clear the company would be metamorphosed into Thames Television as the London weekday contractor, making it the most powerful component of the federal ITV system, it decided to put on hold the transmission of the third series of *Life with Cooper* until after the new franchise came into force. It did not air until the spring of 1969. In order to leave no one in any doubt that its intentions towards Cooper were honourable it boosted his and its own profile by going into production with two Tommy Cooper specials to herald the opening of the new company.

NINE

Cooper Vision: Part Two

Much of the promotion of the new ITV was tied to Cooper's presence. *Cooper King-size!* was scheduled for transmission on the opening night of the new era on 30 July 1968. It appears to have grown out of a suggestion by Miff to repackage between new covers a selection of Tommy's most popular routines extending back to the beginning of his television career. In addition to a stand-up comedy magic spot, viewers would be introduced to or reacquainted with those building blocks of his expertise as a production comic, namely the 'Hello, Joe' routine, the *Candid Camera* 'Look at the Buffalo' sequence, the 'Eggs in the Hat,' 'Autumn Leaves' and, of course, the 'Hats'. The presentation took the form of a nostalgic chat between Tommy and Deryck Guyler in his crusty old man role as Tommy's dresser. Resurrected from earlier television shows were the squeaky shoes sketch and the 'Zoo' routine. In the former Cooper followed up an expedition to a shoe shop with a visit to a musical soirée: he arrives late and has to tiptoe to his seat in the telltale footwear. In the latter sequence he stood facing the camera contentedly with a sign that said 'monkey house' behind him. Marvelling at the joys of nature as he snaps away with the camera around his neck, he starts to throw food to the animals. Before long the peanuts are being pelted back in even greater quantities. As the battle escalates Cooper's aggrieved expression tells all. Almost defeated he crosses over to another side of the set. The sign behind him now reads 'Gorilla'. The pay off came when a gorilla's arm extended from behind the television camera, grabbed Tommy's own camera and ended up taking a picture of the star.

The title of the special was not cleared with Miff or Tommy, causing them some disquiet in the event that reviewers might attack the programme for going over old ground. *Cooper Classics* or *Vintage Cooper* had been their preferred options. In the circumstances it did not matter. As Tommy understood only too well, public memory is very short. The show became a high profile exercise for the star who now automatically found himself branded the face of comedy on the reinvigorated channel. Unfortunately the recorded transmission fell off the air after twenty minutes when on the opening night of the new service the Thames technicians went on strike. It was shown in its entirety at a later date. Sadly like so many shows from that era it does not survive, even though the packaging of so much classic material qualified it as the Cooper show most deserving of longevity. It happened to commit the sin of being recorded at a time when reusable videotape and shelf space were deemed more valuable commodities than the intellectual property they were serving.

The other programme with which Thames used Cooper to celebrate its launch was a more original affair. Not transmitted until November, *Cooper at Large* was the brainchild of producer and director, Mark Stuart. Loosely based on the 1960 French film fantasy, *Zazie dans le Métro*, in which a young girl is subjected to an *Alice in Wonderland* experience on the Paris underground system, the project focused on Tommy meandering around the fantasy world implied by a television studio. It was a brave attempt to achieve something different and in more imaginative hands might have taken him into a Jacques Tati observational dimension. Instead it became a series of sketches triggered by the remnants of scenery discovered by Tommy in the studio: a Fred Astaire ballroom, a Western saloon, an orchestral rostrum and so on. The show did little to live up to the claim of its publicity to 'add another dimension to the star's character as he breaks fresh ground in a world of fantasy where his versatility is given free rein,' while the sound of audience laughter in a supposedly empty studio became a disconcerting anomaly. When it did come to life it was on those occasions when the star ventured into tried and tested territory, as when he adapted his Frankie Vaughan business to the Fred Astaire routine. A short sequence where he discovers an isolated camera and self-consciously explores its ability to capture a wide range of expressions provided a hint of what a creative mime in the tradition of Tati or Red Skelton might have made of the premise. A moment where he walked into a projection screen and found himself embroiled in the action of a World War Two drama, although executed well technically, left one pining for the inventiveness of Buster Keaton in this area. But in one regard Miff would have been pleased. There was not a magic trick or a fez in sight.

Ironically in July 1968, the very month that saw Thames Television taking to the air, Miff received a call from his old friend and ex-ABC employee, George Brightwell, who as General Manager was now helping David Frost run his independent production company, David Paradine Productions Ltd, henceforth to be referred to as Paradine. Frost was keen to discuss with Ferrie the idea of selling Cooper in a colour package to America. A meeting was arranged and there is no reason to suppose that any disloyalty was initially felt to ABC/

Thames by agent or performer. The focus was on America, Tommy still had six shows to be recorded for the ITV company for UK transmission, and at a time when independent production was slowly taking off in this country, who was to say whether a production for Paradine could not also be offered to Thames? Miff may or may not have overlooked Frost's role as head of the London Television Consortium that had been awarded the new London weekend franchise. He was in effect the progenitor of Thames's principal rival, London Weekend Television. Regardless of any residual loyalty to Philip Jones, if one thing could be assured of bringing Tommy running to Miff it would be mention of exposure in James Thurber's land of 'the roll-'em-in-the-aisles of gagerissimo'.

Correspondence between Brightwell and Ferrie from the beginning of August mentions the possibility of an exclusive contract for Tommy's services relating to *both* the UK and the USA. Miff had wasted no time in grasping the upper hand creatively when one reads of their shared intention 'to eliminate the frailties of production that have beset Tommy in the past'. Frost's enthusiasm for the comedian was unstinted. All involved had high hopes of international recognition for Cooper 'as the funniest of men'. From the first Frost was envisaged as executive producer, Ferrie as associate producer of the enterprise. Full consultation would be accorded Tommy and Miff on all creative and personnel matters. The first show would air in America under an arrangement Paradine had with Westinghouse for a series of programmes under the title of *David Frost Presents*. It was proposed that this should be a pull-together of classic Cooper routines! *Cooper King-size!* had aired only seven days before Brightwell summarized all the points in his letter to Miff. It is additionally ironic that in a short while Thames would become the most successful exporter of British television product to America. Had he

continued to perform in more shows for the ITV broadcaster, Tommy could well have stood a better chance of emulating Benny Hill in the international marketplace. The
Paradine venture almost totally failed to deliver in this arena
and even on the domestic front soon became bogged down in
the dissatisfaction and acrimony that seemed to follow Miff
around.

The existing contract with Thames and the commitment to
record the last series of *Life with Cooper* in the opening
months of 1969 meant that both parties had to tread nimbly.
Brightwell stressed the caution of not rushing into their new
domestic series and stressed that when it did materialize it
could be offered to any of the ITV companies or the BBC. This
time around, Tommy would not only be receiving £1,800.00
a show for a series of thirteen, an increase of £300.00 over his
last Thames rate, but was also entitled to fifteen per cent of
net profits, with Miff on five per cent. Miff also received a fee
of £300.00 per show. However, a note scribbled by Miff ahead
of a key meeting revealed why he had taken this route: 'Purpose of agreement is to exploit the talents of Tommy Cooper
and particularly to enlarge his image in the USA and other
foreign countries.' The American showcase, in which David –
pace Vera Lynn and Ed Sullivan – introduced Tommy to US
audiences, was recorded in London on 18–19 December 1968.
The full agreement was not finalized until the first day. The
contract gave Paradine the option rights for two further consecutive series after the first.

With a typical quirk of fate other companies now began to
make enquiries about possible American exposure. Alec Fyne
at ATV rang Miff twice during January 1969 to explore the
prospect of Tommy appearing as a guest on shows starring
Engelbert Humperdinck and Liberace, both being packaged
by Lew Grade for international consumption. Philip Jones,

who by now was obviously aware of something afoot, had already phoned to investigate the option of re-shooting *Cooper King-size!* in colour as ITV's entry for the Golden Rose competition at the 1969 Montreux television festival. Should it win, it would be guaranteed sales in all territories. Moreover Pathé, working as distributors for ABC/Thames, had just sold the first two series of *Life with Cooper* to the Netherlands and were looking for production opportunities of their own with guaranteed network distribution in the USA. In the event it is conceivable that ATV, Thames or Pathé could have done more to advance Cooper internationally than Paradine. Paradine had no network deal and there was little interest at syndication level. During the last week of April 1969, the special aired in only five territories, namely Boston, Baltimore, Pittsburgh, Philadelphia, and San Francisco, but these were the major cities within which Westinghouse had their own television stations, so their interest should have been a foregone conclusion anyhow. Nothing appears to have been achieved at the level of syndication.

On 31 March Brightwell rang Ferrie to announce that they were now trying to interest LWT on the domestic front. On 2 April Miff informed George that he had now formally made Thames aware of the Paradine agreement adding: 'I also advised them that I should think if they wished to participate in the production of these shows then this would simply be a matter for discussion and negotiation.' Philip Jones had replied that Thames would 'certainly consider and discuss any suggestions you may have for future Tommy Cooper shows'. Inwardly he must have realized that as far as LWT was concerned the matter was a *fait accompli*, although in July Paradine did go through the formality of discussing the project with the BBC, courtesy of Cooper champion, Bill Cotton. The news travelled fast. On 29 July the *Evening News*, prompted by what it regarded as the excesses in advertising levy that the new ITV companies had to pay to the government, ran an article headlined 'Catastrophe at ITV', in which melodramatically it reported that 'the stricken competitor could not afford to keep its horse-jumping or even pay for the Tommy Cooper package series made by none other than David Frost.' The report had no foundation other than the fact that Cotton and Ferrie had been spotted together at the Paradine office. Jumping to conclusions in the media is nothing new and a retraction was published. Before the week was out Brightwell was discussing with Cyril Bennett, Programme Controller at LWT, studio dates for a series of thirteen recordings that allowed for transmission during the early months of 1970.

At the end of shooting the last successful series of *Life with Cooper* Tommy requested that Milo Lewis, about to leave Thames, be contracted, making the sound observation, 'Working with someone I know well must be an ideal way to start.' The American special had been produced and directed by Gordon Reece, later to achieve notoriety and a knighthood as image maker and media adviser to Margaret Thatcher, but he had moved on to pastures new, possibly to Tommy's relief. In a catalogue of Cooper complaints some leap off the page:

In the James Bond quickie the point of the whole thing was to see the arm come around the wall and hit me in the face with the pie.

In the juggling routine the dropping of the pile of plates was out of frame.

In some shots I was either out of frame or the vital point was missed completely.

Unfortunately, unlike Hancock (with Duncan Wood) and Morecambe and Wise (first with Colin Clews at ATV, and then with John Ammonds at the BBC and Thames), Tommy never had an enduring creative partnership with a single producer. Nothing sinister need be read into this, the inevitable result of the vagaries and unpredictability of the freelance work ethic that was more prevalent in ITV than the BBC at the time. The request for Lewis was not – or could not be – granted and Bill Hitchcock, the trusted veteran of many an Arthur Askey or Dickie Henderson show, joined the team. Having wisely consulted Miff, the first move he made at the beginning of August was to bring in respected American scriptwriter, Dick Vosburgh as script editor. Their combined presence did not forestall Miff on 24 September – six weeks ahead of the first recording – dropping a note to Brightwell that had about it a decided air of *déjà vu*: 'Frankly, I am becoming increasingly disturbed at the lack of preparation for these shows.'

Miff could not come to terms with the success of the ABC/ Thames association and did his unintentional best to drag Tommy back to times past. The opening stand-up routines were maintained, but the device of the interviewer was resurrected. Vosburgh and a team of writers headed by Barry Cryer worked hard to make the restrictions work. Revue comedian, Peter Reeves was an imaginative choice as the interviewer and fulfilled the brief more successfully than anyone so far. The device was happily taken away from Cooper talking about his own life and given a historical skew to give free rein to Tommy's penchant for dressing up. Both the carnival atmosphere of sketches like these and the comedy conjuring were enhanced by colour for the first time. Hitchcock worked hard to ensure the shows had a slickness of pace that the Thames shows often lacked. In this regard greater emphasis was placed on pre-recorded quickies – it was the era of *Rowan and Martin's Laugh-In* – although these were often a hit or miss affair. The series was simply called *Tommy Cooper*, LWT missing out on the fun their graphics department could have had during the show's opening titles with the abbreviation of 'Life With Tommy'.

The historical segment is now remembered as a highlight of the enterprise, providing some of the defining moments of Cooper's television career and adding weight to Barry Cryer's premise of how you wrote for the man: 'The perfect Tommy Cooper sketch is one that says, "Tommy enters tailor's shop – does trousers jokes – then exits."' The roll call of history was summoned to provide excuses for jokes, jokes, and more jokes. Old jokes were brought back into service, as in the Dr Livingstone episode where he brought forth 'the skull of a very famous witch doctor – and here's the skull of the same witch doctor when he was a boy!' Some were excruciatingly awful, like the time he dragged up as Florence Nightingale – 'Call me "Sir"'? 'Why?' 'I'm a night nurse!' Others were visually inventive, like the three cornered Dick Turpin hat that spun around on his head. Cooper fell in love with the device like a child with a new toy. Other comics would have left well alone after the first revolve, but Cooper in his usual way must have repeated the business at least seven times getting bigger laughs all the while. As Cryer says, 'He had that flair. You'd say he was overdoing it, but then you heard the laughter he got.' Tommy was fully aware he was breaking the so-called rules: 'I just slipped that one in there. I wasn't gonna do that. I wasn't.' But there was more to the gag than the mechanics of the prop. Cooper's increasingly giddy look of disorientation as it spun around made it far more than a fancy dress shop accessory.

Throughout these segments he displayed a newfound relish

in the absurdity of what he was about, as in the Toulouse-Lautrec sketch when down on his knees, which had shoes attached – 'Mini Cooper!' – he launched into what at the time must have been an extremely painful dance version of 'Happy feet, I've got those happy feet' and then discovered a way of levering himself up on the arms between two chairs to convey the illusion that he really had lost eighteen inches. When he portrayed Henry VIII he had the same fun heaving up his upholstered stomach onto his chest every time he leaned back in the chair. When the Julius Caesar sketch flagged he launched into a song on the zither: 'Oh, how we danced on the night that we wed. We danced and we danced cos the room had no bed.' Over the laughter Tommy shouts, 'Listen to that, see,' as if to remonstrate to Miff that he was the one who knew what made people laugh, before incongruously invoking the name of his hero, 'Miller's the name, lady. Here's another one!' Funniest of all was the infamous Robin Hood sequence when he shunned Lincoln green for Lincoln pink. It is hard to imagine that he reached the end of rehearsals before realizing that a costume was being prepared for him in a colour that superstition forbade him to wear. Dick Vosburgh remembers it was the day of the show. He had never seen Cooper more agitated: 'I'm *not* wearing it!' The wardrobe department rose to the emergency and, long before Mel Brooks deconstructed the Sherwood myth in *Robin Hood: Men in Tights*, quickly made him another in the new colour. Again a funny hat came to the fore, this time with extended peak and long, adjustable feather used to impersonate a railway signal to the sound of an express train – 'The Golden Arrow!' Reeves provided a natural audience – one could almost have believed that he had not seen a script – but like a fine straight man had the improvisatory skills to rein in Cooper as he wandered off on yet another flight of playful fancy.

One major feature that distinguished the LWT shows from those at Thames was the high level of guest stars attracted to work with Cooper in the other sketches. In moving across from ATV to the BBC in 1968, Morecambe and Wise had raised the stakes in this regard. LWT was anxious for Cooper to be seen to give them more than a run for their money. The resident repertory company of British sit com stalwarts that had adorned Tommy's previous series, including Deryck Guyler, Robert Dorning, Dudley Foster, Arthur Mullard, Bob Todd, and Dandy Nichols, was now supplanted by a more glittering array of guest performers that embraced Ted Ray, Arthur Lowe, Bernard Cribbins, Richard Briers, Thora Hird, Vincent Price, Eric Sykes, and the Ronnies, Barker and Corbett, though not together. However there was a fundamental difference in the dynamic between star/stars and guest. On *The Morecambe and Wise Show* visiting artists queued up for a chance to be ridiculed by the comedy duo and, before the show was over, to upstage them: one has to think only of Leonard Rossiter, Angela Rippon, Peter Cushing, and Glenda Jackson. However, as Eric Morecambe was the first to admit, nobody upstaged Cooper.

According to Dick Vosburgh, Price was already a fan ahead of the occasion, his fascination for the *Planet Cooper* prompting the query, 'Where *is* it in this galaxy?' He was so carried along by the spirit of the show that he even perpetrated a card trick on the star that misfired by one digit – 'Well, what's a spot among friends?' – at which point the missing spade mysteriously slid into position. He also took part in a Mississippi river boat melodrama in which Price played the gentleman gambler anxious to marry off his ugly daughter to Tommy's banjo-strumming hayseed character. When Cooper accuses Price of cheating, it ends in a duel with the two combatants measuring out their paces. Tommy fires.

Price: You were supposed to wait for the count of three.
Cooper: Well, one and two is three. (Price slinks to the
  ground)

Michael Bentine was featured in one episode, bringing with
him some of his tried and tested material, which lost nothing
in the translation to Cooper's way of working. In one sketch
he played a Soviet spy forced by officer Bentine to photograph
indelibly in his memory the crucial information he must take
into hostile territory and then to eat the source. Diary, plans,
microfiche, even the model of a top secret rocket, all became
Tommy's diet in the line of duty. For most of the sequence, he
remains silent, his expression veering tellingly between disgust,
satiety and, courtesy of a salt cellar that happens to be in his
pocket, relish as he is force-fed every unsavoury mouthful.
Another sketch saw Michael in a favourite role as an obscure
Middle Eastern sheikh subjecting Cooper's plume-helmeted
British emissary to a drinking ritual before negotiating an oil
treaty. Tommy is forced to imbibe increasingly large measures
of a lurid, steaming cocktail that was certainly not Orangina.
Peter Reeves recalls that Tommy acted quite prudishly towards
this item, although on this occasion Miff did not appear to
demur, happy for his client to utter the payoff: 'You must have
an awful lot of camels!'
  The least likely guest was the distinguished husky-voiced
actress, Joan Greenwood. She commented afterwards that she
found the experience 'incredible, madly chaotic, and absolutely frightening', adding that she 'would not have missed it
for anything'. The surprise of the television audience at seeing a smoking-jacketed Cooper joining forces with the svelte
seductress in a Noël Coward pastiche was only matched by
Tommy's reaction when at the end of a spirited rendition of
'Knees Up, Mother Brown', the tag to the sketch, she launched

into a somersault and a full throated, 'How's your Father!' According to Vosburgh, when in the spirit of fun she took it upon herself to stand on her head at rehearsals, Cooper – stereotyped in his attitude to the way women should behave – had trouble dealing with it. There were times, of course, when his own outré behaviour had a similar effect on others. Perhaps they were kindred spirits after all; Greenwood did list 'circuses' as her hobby in *Who's Who in the Theatre*.

If anyone did manage to upstage him, Greenwood did, not that he had a problem with the situation. However, according to Vosburgh and fellow scriptwriter Garry Chambers, at another level Tommy always became self-conscious when working with women. Moreover, his persona made it impossible for him to achieve a sexual chemistry with any of his occasional leading ladies. Garry recalls how when Diana Dors appeared on the show in a daringly low-cut outfit, Cooper found it difficult to achieve a rapport with her at all. In Dick's words, he was 'frightened out of his skull'. A routine in which single-handedly he attempts to deputize for Diana's disposed dancers and backing singers, gesticulating with a pink feather boa up, down and around as she sings her song, becomes a supreme display of comic embarrassment and the funnier because of it. Always, of course, there was the threat of Dove hovering in the background. With Thora Hird as a guest there was less of a problem.

In spite of the fun that often burst through the screen, it was not a happy series. Tommy became increasingly exasperated about finding enough material for his stand-up spots, while his growing health problems were beginning to make inroads on the smooth running of the schedule. When because of a combined lung and throat condition he had to miss a show – subsequently rescheduled – for the first time in twenty-one years, even the equable Brightwell had difficulty expending sympathy: 'He is of course his own worst enemy and I have no doubt that even during this period of enforced idleness, he will still be smoking his wretched cigars and talking when he should not be.' In addition his legs were a constant cause of concern.

As for the writers, Vosburgh still recalls the dread his team felt when Miff descended upon them like a miasma in studio or rehearsal room. In the end his obstreperousness became so overwhelming that Cooper insisted he be banned from all television studios thereafter. It had long been established between artist and manager that he absent himself from the theatres where Tommy was working for fear of upsetting the star. Dick still bristles at the mention of the Scot's name and recalls a sketch that provided the defining moment of his own antagonism towards him. In this Tommy played the part of 'Fingers Figgins', a burglar complete with mask, crowbar and bag of swag over his shoulder, who enters a labour exchange – now a job centre – looking for work. When the script was circulated a telephone conversation ensued between Dick and Miff, during which Vosburgh asked, 'Are you saying it isn't funny?' Ferrie replied, 'Being funny has nothing to do with it.' Dick, who thought his own reputation was on the line for no other reason, pressed him on what was wrong. To this day he curses him roundly and often for his response: 'I have spent the last twenty years keeping Tommy Cooper in gainful employment. He would *never* be seen entering a labour exchange.' It reads like a sketch itself, but Ferrie was nothing if not serious.

At Thames, Mortimer and Cooke constantly came up against a similar barrier. As Brian Cooke explained, 'Ferrie didn't understand comedy, constantly saying "Tommy wouldn't *do* that!" Since all that Tommy ever *did* do was appear on stage or television, it somewhat limited our scope. We navigated our way around it by having him do fairly mundane things that he (Tommy) had to do, such as buying a suit or having a meal. "For heaven's sake, Miff, he has to *eat*!" "But people would recognize him," said Miff.' "Er, not in *this* restaurant. They're all Chinese. They've just come over. They've never watched television in England."' And so the battle waged. It got easier as Miff realized that Cooper could handle sketches where *he* portrayed a waiter or a chef or whatever and still get big laughs. As Brian adds, he always played himself anyway and was always likely to whip a bunch of feather flowers out of his sleeve if he thought the sketch was not going as well as he hoped.

The concluding shows of the LWT series reveal a raggedness that suggests under-rehearsal and too few ideas too late. The old pattern asserted itself with Ferrie, perhaps now with some justification, claiming that scripts were being finalized and guests booked without consultation with Cooper or himself. With one show left to record Miff wrote to Tommy on 10 April 1970 expressing his dissatisfaction with Paradine, not least at the level of overseas exploitation: 'As you know, the primary object was "to produce and develop ideas and projects for feature films and television programmes directed towards the promotion and enhancement of the talents of Tommy Cooper throughout the world," the main foreign target being the USA.' He also expressed concern for Tommy's health with specific reference to the additional stress of 'all that goes with the making of a television series'. Tommy never presented less than a genial front, but Miff was sympathetically aware of the pressures beneath the surface: 'From my long experience of you I know only too well how you have to put the act "on and off", and I fully realize that it is sometimes just not humanly possible for this effort to be maintained throughout.'

Cooper's continued high presence in the ratings ensured that there was even greater interest in him as a live attraction. Miff recommended a return to club and stage work, to which he readily agreed. It would be three and a half years before he returned to television screens in a new production. The only exception was a stray episode of the LWT series – so bad it was not originally aired – transmitted as a 'special' in March 1971. In later years he made comic capital out of the gap by saying that by then so many people were impersonating him that nobody knew he'd been away. In truth the repeats of his past shows saw to this anyhow. The real underlying cause of his exile, however, was the fallout from the Paradine situation.

Four days later on 14 April Ferrie wrote to Brightwell disturbed 'at the way this project has disintegrated'. Notwithstanding, Paradine was keen to exercise its option for a second series – the contract provided for a total of three series in all – but was happy to have the date by which it was due to exercise the same deferred by a month to 1 August. In acknowledging this Miff wasted no effort in cataloguing the grievances between the two parties. Top of the list was the disappointment at foreign exploitation level. Then after a schedule of niggling housekeeping difficulties and a reiteration of the usual script and guest aggravations he added, 'Tommy Cooper's own personal feeling in this matter is "that he would not go through that again for a million pounds".' It was not the first time Ferrie had voiced the sentiment on behalf of his client to Paradine.

It is worth noting that on the same day, 23 June 1970, with that gift of timing with which he appeared so sensitive, Philip Jones called the office. The journal simply says: 'Very pleasant, etc.' On 31 July Frost exercised the option of Paradine for a second series. David added a sweetener, the offer of a whole week of guest appearances on his New York based talk show that had taken over from Merv Griffin on the American networks and would accord Cooper a level of exposure way beyond the small pickings achieved by the earlier special. As David explained this was a 'first' in talk show terms and could be publicized as such. Five days later Tommy, perhaps unwisely, declined. Matters quickly went downhill. In Miff's opinion, on the basis of the overseas failure, the contract was null and void and there was no option to exercise. Paradine had failed to fulfil its part of the undertaking and there was no way Cooper would work for the company again. To its credit Paradine refused to become litigious. All Frost wanted was to get Cooper back on screen, and time and creative energy were both being lost.

Many and varied were the ways suggested to find the best way out of the tangle. Miff offered Frost first refusal on all Cooper's television appearances in the USA; David rejected the somewhat meaningless proposal. At one point there was a suggestion that Thames might take over the baton from LWT in essentially the same arrangement with Paradine. Cyril Bennett at LWT attempted to break the stalemate by suggesting that Tommy's company, Tommy Cooper Arts Ltd, package the shows for Paradine with Miff as executive producer [*sic*], David's dedication to his own career as a performer having understandably prevented him from fulfilling that role satisfactorily himself. All efforts were made by Brightwell to insist that Tommy and Miff would have full creative control. More than a year went by. On 10 October, Tommy, not unnaturally exhausted as he approached the end of his Palladium season, wrote to Miff: 'I should like you to deal with the Paradine situation on my behalf as you think fit.' But there was no way this changed his opinion with regard to working with or for Paradine again. Miff had already taken legal advice, which accepted that there was an argument that the contract could be deemed invalid, although it advised restraint. Matters came to a head, however, when Ferrie discovered that Paradine, far from making attempts to exploit the LWT series in America itself, had in fact merely assigned all rights in this regard to LWT, leaving the broadcaster to arrange marketing 'at its discretion (without being under any obligation to attempt overseas sales)'. The point was enforced to Brightwell in a letter on 14 October 1971 which stated categorically on legal advice that the assigning of such rights constituted 'a fundamental breach of the contract which entitled Tommy Cooper Arts Ltd to treat it as having been repudiated by Paradine'. In other words Tommy was under no further obligation to the company. Significantly, on the previous day, 13 October, Miff had received a telephone call from Philip Jones enquiring of the situation and suggesting a series of six half-hours in the spring of 1972. Miff reported that the matter was '*sub judice*'. Jones asked Ferrie 'to keep his call also as confidential'.

Frost enlisted the help of his agent, Richard Armitage of the Noel Gay Organisation, to help fight Paradine's corner. For a while there would appear to have been a standoff. The situation was not helped by David's professional preoccupation elsewhere and the ill health of Brightwell, whose spells in hospital were sadly becoming as frequent as Frost's transatlantic trips. On 16 March 1972 Cooper's solicitor sent in a copy of his firm's fees, making the point that 'there appears to be nothing for me to do at present in this matter.' On 6 April Brightwell emerged from hospital again to write to confirm 'that we would wish to continue with the production of television programmes at the earliest possible moment contingent upon his club and theatrical appearances.' The letter was its own sad admission of failure. Miff returned from holiday to advise George that as far as he and Tommy were concerned the matter was closed. There was something of a rearguard action by Paradine's solicitors, Harbottle and Lewis, in July

1972 when they wrote to contest the claim that the contract was null and void. On 7 August Miff dashed off an emphatic reply: 'Tommy Cooper's position was set out in my letter of 14 October 1971 written to Mr George Brightwell of your client company following advice received from my Solicitors, Messrs Goodman, Derrick & Co. after consultation with leading counsel, Mr A. Leolin Price, QC. If your clients wish to discuss the matter further with me, I am quite prepared to do so.' They did not reply. Miff has scrawled emphatically on his file copy: 'No acknowledgement'. Possibly Frost was worried by the bad publicity an adverse legal action might have brought him. That Cooper of all people was prepared to take the initiative and stand to lose an estimated £25,000.00 if the ruling went against him is indicative.

Miff did not rush to pick up the phone to Philip Jones. Implicit throughout the entire saga had been the procedure whereby if Paradine dug in its heels, Tommy could simply remain off television and concentrate on theatre and cabaret in the hope that Paradine would eventually realize it was holding a worthless piece of paper. It remains an accepted truism of show business that you can never force an artist to perform. He had already been off the screen in new product for fast approaching two and a half years. It would obviously be circumspect to advance with caution. Not until the beginning of November did Thames make the offer of four one hour specials to be recorded in 1973. Within a week a deal was done whereby Tommy would be paid £18,000 for the quartet: in the words of Thames's booking executive, Iris Frederick, 'Believe me, Miff, we have never paid out anything like this before!' Recording would not commence until May of 1973. However, before 1972 was out, Frederick had come back to Miff with an option (eventually exercised) for a further four specials at £5,000 a show for production in 1974.

On 9 December Miff wrote to Cooper to confirm the news, but added a caveat that the long shadow of Paradine might threaten in the distance, that a court case – for all the advice of learned counsel – could still work against them, and that there was always the possibility of an injunction being issued to restrain him from appearing on television. Tommy sensed he had been off the box for too long and took the chance. Besides, he would be back home at Teddington Studios, the picturesque facility on the bank of the Thames where in its film studio days Max Miller and Gracie Fields had shot some of their more memorable movies for Warner Brothers. It was nearer to his Chiswick home and more congenial in so many ways than the cold hinterland of Wembley, the makeshift home in those days of LWT before it relocated to the South Bank. Paradine's solicitors made one last desperate play to make life difficult for Thames in the summer of 1973, but Lord Goodman's firm dashed off a sharp rejoinder that simply referred them back to the earlier correspondence.

The hour long shows transmitted under the banner of *The Tommy Cooper Hour* reverted to an extended version of the format of his earlier Thames programmes. Peter Reeves and resident actress, Clovissa Newcombe were not invited to return. Occasional musical guests at the level of Anita Harris, Dana and Vince Hill were welcomed back to the fold. The historical interview segment had exhausted its strongest potential and the pressure was taken off booking high profile guest names in favour once again of that second division of comedy support which at the time of the Ealing comedies enjoyed far greater prestige. Sheila Steafel, Hugh Paddick, Glyn Houston, an almost unrecognisably young Richard Wilson, veteran variety comic turned actor Tommy Godfrey, and Janet Brown – before her breakthrough to stardom on the back of her Margaret Thatcher impersonation – all graced the series.

More importantly Mortimer and Cooke were back as sole scriptwriters for the initial four shows, the first of which opened with an effective reworking of the 'Autumn Leaves' sequence. An elegantly clad Cooper and a chiffon-attired chorus of dancers gradually became enveloped in swirling mist as Tommy made his own attempt to sing the Streisand classic, 'On a Clear Day'. The Cooper cough took on a new logical purpose as, arms thrashing, he hacked his way through the fog. It would have been funnier still to someone who had not seen the leafy original. This show also contained the sketch already referred to in which waiter Cooper, wearing goggles and snorkel, turns the catching of a diner's favoured trout into a veritable aqua-display. Most memorable was the one-man play in which Tommy donned the half and half costume that portrayed a Nazi officer in one profile and a British brigadier in the other. Although at one point Bob Monkhouse intimated to me that Tommy had used a similar device on one of his early *It's Magic* shows, I have been unable to verify this. The idea itself is as old as Dan Leno's joke book and can be traced back in a rudimentary form to the *commedia dell'arte* where one actor would portray two characters not in profile, but with a mask on the back of his head and a reverse costume, requiring a turn from front to back to effect the change. Many years later a one-person tango was performed with success in the sexually ambivalent world of Thirties Berlin cabaret by the speciality dancer, Lela Moore. According to Italian quick-change star, Arturo Brachetti, who features his own version of the tango in which he plays both the sexy seductress in one profile and the trim gigolo in the other, the device was even used in fairground sideshows in the early part of the twentieth century as a serious 'half-man, half-woman' come-on amidst the dwarfs, fat men, and tattooed ladies

In the second one hour special new heights of lunacy were

reached in a sketch when Tommy encountered Adolf Hitler on an inter-city train: 'Do you know I never forget a face. That is a face, isn't it?' Frank Thornton played thespian Muswell Beamish, unbeknown to Tommy carrying his latest role into public places for his art: 'I like to work my way into the roles I portray!' Cooper's look of lost bewilderment as he recognizes the monster over the top of his newspaper suggests that the true actor was seated opposite. For the first time we see our hero display a social conscience as he inveighs against the supposed Fuehrer with a rolled up newspaper, belatedly trying to instil in him a sense of remorse: 'You've done some terrible, terrible things in your life.' Tommy discovers that he has spent his time since the war not in South America, but in a way no one could have guessed: 'For some years I was a bingo caller in Cleethorpes.' In today's tiresome atmosphere of political correctness, as affectionate an entertainer as Cooper might not be allowed to get away with the absurdity, although the concept was only two steps removed from his lop-sided caricature of the Nazi officer. In the years since we have been subjected to the tedium of *'Allo 'Allo!*, the edginess of Freddie Starr's Adolf and the continued comic exhilaration of Mel Brooks' evocation of the regime. And yet when Tommy hits Beamish over the head and declares, 'That's for Auntie Ethel! You frightened the life out of her in 1940,' he perhaps – through Mortimer and Cooke – came closer to the common truth than many another more passably fashionable satire.

The strength of items like these and the confidence that exuded from the star in his stand-up spots combined to make these glossy productions – enhanced for the first time at Thames by the new dimension of colour – some of the most engaging of his career. Indeed, the comedy magic openings were now allowed to take up most of the first third of the three-part shows. Unfortunately, beneath the surface Cooper's life was not so happy. Within days of the first recording Philip Jones was asking what they should do about Tommy's health, a euphemism that embraced his increasing dependence on alcohol alongside his worsening leg and bronchial conditions. Miff rather churlishly replied that it had been made quite clear to him by artist and broadcaster that, following the contretemps at LWT, he should have nothing to do with the shows, but he knew full well that he could not disassociate himself from his client's general wellbeing and that the remaining years of their relationship would be devoted as much to this aspect of his life as to securing his income and organizing his diary.

The second tranche of four specials was placed in the experienced hands of Royston Mayoh, but was less successful. Mortimer and Cooke had made the decision not to continue, realizing that their future resided in situation comedy where they were able to copyright the characters and storylines. The success of shows like *Father Dear Father*, *Man About the House* and *George and Mildred* suggests that they made the right move. Dick Hills, one half of the Sid Green and Dick Hills combination that first brought Morecambe and Wise to prominence, was invited to fill their considerable shoes. Sadly it was a job for more than one man and in retrospect, given the large teams of writers enjoyed by shows like *The Two Ronnies*, *The Frost Report* and earlier Cooper strands, it is odd that the Thames executives did not act on the matter. The specials were bereft of truly memorable moments outside of Tommy's stage sequences, with the flair for the absurd appearing to have been jettisoned for a more realistic approach. A regular item in which Tommy played a rather drab tramp reminiscing about his past exploits lacked the bravura one associates with the comic, while the interviews with Allan Cuthbertson based loosely on Tommy's life threatened to take him back to the dark ages. Cuthbertson had been brought in as an all-purpose straight man halfway through the first four shows. He would stay for the duration of the one hour specials, but throughout he betrayed an uneasiness that sat at odds with Tommy's sunny, relaxed approach. However much the straight man traditionally represented the cultural opposite of the comedian, beneath the behavioural veneer a certain kinship has informed all the important double acts in history. At times Cuthbertson seemed just too severe in a caricature way, not helped by the residue of his supercilious colonel image from countless movies and television plays.

A segment in which Cooper, Cuthbertson and a male guest standing at lecterns in scholastic gowns read in a monotone lyrics of popular songs of the day as if they were declaiming an academic text owed a lot to the cliché that someone like Cooper could read the football results and make them funny. It emerged as the unfunny and unimaginative indulgence that it was. Unfortunately the star did not recognize the triteness of most of the material and continued to endorse Hills's talent for a further series and frequent guest spots. Tommy found himself in the firing line of a bad press that panned him with barbs that were all the more painful because so hackneyed: 'Absolute drivel'; 'Insult to the intelligence'; 'Unadulterated rubbish'. The shows mostly came to life when he was left to his own devices in a fantasy land of carnival costumes and accessories, the most successful of which involved an encounter between Dracula and the Bride of Frankenstein: the business he managed to extract from the fangs of the former, which he almost swallowed, was funnier than anything presented to him on the page.

Although Tommy could still turn on the magic of his personality, the shows were losing their sparkle almost in direct sympathy with his off-stage problems. They often appeared to lack the defining stamp of the star they were celebrating,

Cuthbertson being given a presence on screen that at times would have led a visitor from another culture to surmise that it was his show. Links that should have been the prerogative of Cooper himself were entrusted to his stilted tones. A sequence in one show with the enchanting Italian puppet creation, Topo Gigio should have culminated in Tommy interacting with the little mouse in the way that Ed Sullivan frequently did on American television. The role was delegated to Allan. Mayoh is honest about the difficulties that confronted him and others as producer. By now the recognized 'banker' that redeemed any show was perceived to be his stand-up sequence. To protect the preparation of this, Tommy would only be called for rehearsal when absolutely necessary. To give this and other key sequences maximum time before the live studio audience, anything that did not *need* to involve him was pre-recorded. That way Cooper never even met Topo Gigio.

Irrespective of the problems, Jones was keen to discuss 1975. Miff initially stalled, but did agree a guaranteed fee of £7,500.00 for an additional special, for Christmas, to be recorded in 1974. This automatically came with an offer of the same amount per show for a series to be taped in 1975. Miff asked his client whether in light of his increasing health problems that might be too many. In response Tommy queried whether the shows needed to be an hour in length. The ratings for the hour specials, transmitted as *The Tommy Cooper Hour*, had been colossal, Tommy continuing to trounce *Coronation Street*, *Crossroads* and *This Is Your Life* in the Jictar Top Ten. Unsurprisingly Thames decided it would be better to have Cooper on screen in shorter bursts than not at all. Iris Frederick came back with an offer of £2,000.00 a show for a series of six weekly programmes at the new length, emphasizing that this was 'the most paid to any artist for a thirty minute programme'. Miff, alert to how much more Tommy could now earn in cabaret over a similar period of commitment, asked for £4,000.00. They settled for £3,500.00.

The series, called simply *Cooper*, was recorded during the late summer and autumn for October/November transmission. Again produced by Mayoh, with Hills at the scriptwriting helm, it represented an uneasy mix between vintage stand-up Cooper and Seventies light entertainment at its shallowest. Every attempt was made to make the shows even less arduous for their star. Fashionable piano-playing chanteuse, Lynsey De Paul was tacked on as a resident guest, but did not appear on screen with Tommy once during the series. David Hamilton was given duties as master of ceremonies that again should have been invested in Cooper. In the interview segment that now came even closer to the original Stan Parkinson concept one longed for Cuthbertson, Bond, or any thespian to make up for the self-consciousness of Hamilton's smug approach. The body language between the two is fascinating, Tommy on the left of screen openly facing Hamilton on the right, the latter's sitting position painfully contorted between his upper half acknowledging Cooper and his lower half pointing out of the picture in the opposite direction. Most of their exchanges are based on the weak premise of Hamilton hijacking Tommy's jokes or stories and completing them. There had been better uses for the exasperated Cooper look.

In consolation the series produced one classic Cooper sketch in which once again he played a waiter at a smart restaurant. This establishment, presided over by head waiter, Victor Spinetti, is unique in that it boasts a room behind the scenes where waiters can vent their frustration by smashing crockery out of the gaze of troublesome customers. As Tommy explains in an aside to the audience, 'Out there is the nasty room where I have to be nice, and here is the nice room where I can be nasty.' He was at the top of his form as he kept crossing the line between fawning politeness towards the diners one second and his own maniacal rage the next. The display of slapstick chaos was worthy of Laurel and Hardy at their most deliciously destructive. As the mayhem spiralled out of control he became hopelessly confused as to which room he was in. As he says, 'I ended up in both rooms – twice as nasty.' According to Mary Kay, the sketch had some foundation in reality, Tommy having heard on a trip to New York of just such a restaurant that gave waiters the opportunity of laying into a fully-dressed dummy in the kitchens. A clapped-out ventriloquist's doll with an orange fright wig is demolished in recognition of the fact as the sketch proceeds.

Conscious of the greater income Miff kept advising him he could earn in the clubs, of the dangers of over-exposure, and of his own physical deterioration – which will be discussed in greater detail in a subsequent chapter – Tommy, without wishing to close the door on subsequent years, held off from committing himself to a similar series in 1976, but eventually agreed to star in an hour special that was recorded in October of that year at London's Casino Theatre. This was christened *Tommy Cooper's Guest Night*, for which he received £7,500.00. Even allowing for the impetus provided by the inclusion of his hero Arthur Askey, the energy had gone out of his performance and the atmosphere that should have come as a bonus with the theatre setting was non-existent. But this did not prevent Thames wishing to pursue the idea of a series of six half-hours from a theatre location in the near future. However, before any commitment could be made, Tommy experienced a heart attack in Rome in April 1977. In the aftermath of the setback to his health, Thames offered a single one hour *Tommy Cooper Show* special to be recorded in studio in March 1978. As his condition improved, so he also committed himself to the earlier suggestion of the theatre-based series, now christened *Cooper – Just Like That*, taped at the New London Theatre in July and August of the same year. Both projects were transmitted in the autumn. For the first he received a whopping £7,750.00, for the second an equally impressive £5,000.00 per half-hour show. In addition by now virtually all of his Thames product could be expected to attract considerable overseas residuals from Australia, New Zealand, Eire, Sweden, Belgium, the Netherlands, and – for some reason – Swaziland!

The danger of any theatre-based series was that it would fall into the trap of laziness as far as material was concerned, and not merely from Tommy's point of view. Script writer Dick Hills sounded Tommy a warning in a letter dated 20 June: 'I get the impression that Thames are working on the principle that Tommy Cooper doesn't need writers, and all that needs to be done is to jog his memory . . . I think it is important that the show is based on your act and that it is what the people really want to see. But that is not the same thing as relying on your prop room to supply material for six half-hours.' Hills had a point, but he had done little himself to advance the cause of his profession in his service of the star. Dick was around for only two of the shows. George Martin and Eddie Bayliss were brought in for the duration. Yet another producer was taken on board and on the surface the choice could not have been more fortuitous. Peter Dulay, doyen of *Candid Camera* in this country, had started in show business as a stand-up comedy magician in the flagging days of the variety theatres. His father, Benson Dulay had been one of the last great magic troupers on the boards, with a comedy illusion act in which he too featured a hilarious version of the guillotine trick. With Peter at the helm Tommy was given a full-time magic consultant for the first time. With the backing of magical technician, John Palfreyman, Dulay fed Tommy's confidence with burlesque versions of some of the great set-pieces of theatrical magic, including filling the stage with livestock – 'And now I'm going to produce two thousand ducks in twenty seconds' – and the kettle that poured any drink called for by a member of the audience. However the idea of teaming him for some of the time with a wacky girl assistant intent on upstaging him – played by comedy actress, Sheila Bernette – was against the grain of everything he had achieved as a solo performer and went nowhere fast. The shows ended with a meaningless sing-along featuring Cooper surrounded by a sub-Nolan Sisters act known as the Sisters Duane. This item alone would have been good reason for everyone at Thames connected with the show to be dismissed. But there *were* moments – like his portrayal of Romeo and Juliet in cinemascope, taking his time to stride across the stage as he had done in another context at Bournemouth Winter Gardens all those years previously:

Romeo: Oh, Juliet, I hear there was someone in your chambers last night.
(Walk)
Juliet: Yes, there was.
(Walk)
Romeo: Who was it?
(Walk)
Juliet: D'you what?
(Walk)
Romeo: I said "Who was it?"
(Walk)
Juliet: It was me. I fell out of bed.

John Palfreyman recalls the anxiety everyone felt whether he'd manage to complete the walk from one side of the stage to the other. Even in fast forward it appears slow: one could almost be forgiven for supposing his feet had been anaesthetized.

The 1978 New London series saw the great comedian at the nadir of his form. For the most part good ideas backfired through lack of rehearsals and the physical condition of the performer upon whom they were dependent. John shudders at the memory of the humbling ritual whereby black coffee had to be poured down his throat three quarters of an hour before the dress rehearsal and again as recording approached. Classic bits of business were omitted from tried and tested routines; other lines were repeated for no apparent reason. For some time his slight incoherence had been funny, but now words were being left out of sentences with embarrassing effect. In one moment of desperation he interprets a laugh as a prompt to turn his back to the audience and check his flies. At times he even appears to lose his temper with the audience, berating a woman in the front row: 'Hey, watch me! How dare you look away over there!' Distracted by his nails, he then turns angrily to the back of the tabs: 'Stop talking. Somebody out here's dying.' There was a time when he could have made such comments funny, but that moment had passed. It is impossible to say how conscious he was of the shambles in which he found himself. According to Palfreyman, Cooper became increasingly introverted as the series progressed. His own enjoyment in his performance had deserted him. At the end of one show he is heard muttering 'Rubbish! Rubbish!' under the closing credits. There is an obvious tone of acrimony to his voice that no one on the production team picked up. If they perceived it as a variation of the Morecambe and Wise catchphrase they were chillingly mistaken. It is amazing that the shows were transmitted in the form they were. Perhaps there were no editing options left.

After the first recording Philip Jones called Ferrie with disappointment rather than censure in his voice to report that 'the magic is not what it was.' However he was prepared to keep his judgement open until he had seen more of the shows. His personal opinion did change, but no one could ever claim this was Cooper's finest hour. Nevertheless, the series was scarcely half over before Philip was agitating Miff to sit down to discuss the future. Possibly on the back of whispered interest from the BBC, Thames was prepared to follow through with one further series. The six episodes of *Cooper's Half Hour* were aired in the early weeks of the autumn of 1980. By now almost every permutation on obvious titles had been worked for him. It would be the final series he would record for television, whether for Thames or any other company. Everyone must have appreciated that Cooper was winding down both creatively and physically, but his health appeared to pick up and there was a noticeable improvement in form. It was especially touching that his son, actor Thomas Henty should be featured as a regular cast member, proving to be an astute partner to his father in what amounted to a weekly retrospective of many of his classic theatre routines. 'Hello, Joe', the 'Buffalo' sequence, 'A Few Impressions', the 'Zoo' routine and a cod hypnotic sketch that had also served Tommy early in his career were given a last airing and emerged surprisingly as fresh and funny.

The shows, produced this time by Keith Beckett, were designed with musical guests and dancers to give Tommy even less to do. There was little in the way of demanding new material, although from time to time he grasped the nettle of a new technical challenge as in a routine in which he attempted without much success to control the movements of a large ball floating through the air courtesy of the device known as chroma-key or colour separation overlay. On the spoken comedy front, there was even a hint of self-mockery that did something to redeem the worst excesses of the last debacle: 'The producer on the last show – I said to him, "What was it like?" And he said, "It wasn't very good." He said, "It wasn't you." And I said, "What d'you mean it wasn't me?" He said, "You didn't have any sparkle." He said, "You were down." He said, "You weren't bright."' The sequence rambles on until the producer leaves in a huff – 'Well, it may have been a Daimler!' At least the new writing team of Eric Davidson and Laurie Rowley, with support from Bayliss, was delivering to a standard, however little the prominence of Tommy's old material left for them to do.

Cooper's remaining television appearances would be confined to guest spots with Eric Sykes, Bob Monkhouse and the Dutch personality, Willem Ruis in the Netherlands. A special under the banner of *The Main Attraction* for the BBC in the summer of 1983 reunited him triumphantly with his old friend, Frankie Vaughan as Tommy's 'special guest star' – an instance of tables turned after so many years. Sadly a few years earlier he had been prevented from appearing in what might have remained in the archives as the crowning guest appearance of his career, when he was one of the few 'local' British acts to be extended an invitation to appear on *The Muppet Show* recorded under Lew Grades's banner at Elstree Studios. Editorially the idea was sound. Kermit, Miss Piggy and company had worked admirably with the young American illusionist Doug Henning. Both Bob Hope and Milton Berle had found their match in Fozzie Bear. Alec Fyne at ATV had made the approach with an enquiry for November 1978 three months previously. Miff's reply was that Tommy was not free. He did have cabaret dates in his diary, but nothing that, as Leslie Grade would have insisted, could not have been rescheduled. The request was renewed for January and was again refused. As things materialized by the time this date came around Tommy was incapacitated. In some ways Tommy Cooper could have been a Jim Henson creation, but alas the green felt and the red felt were not destined to come together and for that Ferrie has to take considerable responsibility.

One television show graced by Cooper as a guest on several occasions was *This Is Your Life*, in its halcyon days at Thames when Eamonn Andrews was the custodian of the big red book. Tommy steadfastly refused ever to be featured as a subject, unwilling to see himself made an emotional hostage to ratings, something with which Miff heartily concurred. This was a stand that went back to the show's earlier life at the BBC. Besides, according to daughter Vicky, her father absolutely hated surprises. Perhaps out of loyalty to Thames, however, he went out of his way on four occasions to pay tribute to people he especially admired. He never left without leaving subject, friends and family, not to mention the usually placid Andrews, in a state of comic turmoil from which it was difficult for the show to recover. He came from his sick bed to accuse fellow magician, David Nixon of stealing all his tricks and claimed on another occasion that he had no idea who actor Bill Fraser was. Bob Todd, the lugubrious sidekick of countless Benny Hill shows as well as the occasional Cooper programme, provided a third occasion to cut the bile of false sentiment as Tommy saw fit.

Most memorable was the show to celebrate Eric Sykes. Arranged in tiers above and alongside Eric and his family were many members of the British comedy elite, including Spike Milligan, Jimmy Edwards, Johnny Speight, Max Bygraves, Terry-Thomas, Hattie Jacques and Frankie Howerd. To witness this veritable first eleven reduced to hysterics was an amazing event, the sight of Milligan alone helpless with laughter as he wiped the tears on his shirt sleeve providing a genuinely touching moment. The show that set out to be a tribute to Sykes became by default a tribute within a tribute to Cooper. It said everything that needed to be said about the respect in which he was held by the comedy profession. His files show that these appearances were scripted by him with possible help from Eddie Bayliss. No one would have guessed from the sense of anarchy that prevailed, although the fact, if known, would probably have enhanced the esteem extended towards him by all present.

However inconsistent it had been, one thing remained constant in Cooper's television career. That was the tolerance and affection that was sustained on his behalf by those working with him. The excesses of his lateness have passed into folklore. Production crews and supporting cast members would curse and tear their hair out as the scarce seconds of studio or rehearsal time ticked away, but the moment he arrived with his plastic bags clinking away in each hand and that beaming smile plastered all over his face, all animosity dispersed. Among top comics he was not alone as a sinner in this regard. Perhaps only he got off so lightly. On one notorious occasion he walked in late for rehearsals in a bowler hat and pyjamas: 'I'm sorry. I couldn't get up!' Obviously he had changed in the back of the car for the gag, but as Eric Sykes, his director on that occasion, observed, 'How could you be cross with a man like that?' Producer Dennis Kirkland has added the observation that Tommy had been waiting at the top of the road in the hire car for nearly an hour watching everyone go in and waiting for the optimum moment in which to spring the surprise! Mary Kay recalls a different detail, possibly from another occasion, when Tommy arrived in dressing-gown and nightcap clutching a teddy bear.

At times like these he might have been a schoolboy back in the Fawley playground, although as Mary has pointed out his basic unpunctuality was a flaw that undermined everything he preached to others, namely 'that attention should be given to every possible contingency and problem. He knew it was a serious weakness. "I don't like it," he would say, "but it just seems to happen." ' In truth the years of playing in theatres and nightclubs had rendered mornings non-existent in the normal sense. As Dick Vosburgh joked, 'You scheduled him early for location at your peril. Even a bromo-seltzer was too much for him to handle!' Royston Mayoh tried to coax Thames into recording a cabaret show with him at midnight, the time when his body clock was most responsive, but unions and bureaucracy stood in the way. As Roy added, 'Ask Cooper to sparkle at eight, he'd only just finished scratching himself!'

Journalists and photographers kept waiting were possibly harder to placate, but overall conceivably more allowances were made for Tommy Cooper than for the average star. That he came with no side, no swagger helped to justify the privileges accorded him. He drew affection towards him like a magnet and that excused a multitude of misdemeanours. The rank and file on the studio floor doted on him as one of their own. He always had a trick to show them, a gag they could swap with their mates. Here he would allow himself to be a little off-colour, as on the occasion he sat on the set of *The Bob Monkhouse Show* during rehearsals. He went through the blocking of his material for the director, Geoff Miles, but the laughter conveyed from the studio floor to the control gallery bore no relationship to what Tommy was demonstrating for the cameras. Gradually the whole crew and production team became caught up in an avalanche of laughter triggered by the sight of a dummy sexual appendage of Sir Les Patterson proportions protruding beneath his left sock and trouser leg. If Tommy had seemed unnecessarily restless on the occasion, unable to keep his leg still, now we knew why. It took a considerable time for the studio to return to normality. But the outward display of bonhomie came at a cost. Dennis Kirkland, who worked with Cooper both as producer of his last special at Thames and as a floor manager throughout his career, insists like so many that he was the same off camera as he was on: 'You just get on with Tom. He's hysterical. He's everything that everyone wants him to be.' It was easy not to notice the pressure this placed on the man himself, something that, as we have seen, Miff Ferrie fully understood.

Directors and producers worth their salt – on Cooper shows the roles were usually taken by the same individual – knew how to make their own concessions. You were bound to flounder if you failed to acknowledge the spontaneous nature of the man. Royston Mayoh admits, 'To direct Tommy Cooper in the accepted sense was a nonsense. Tolerance was the key. My job was to give him his fences, tell him where not to exceed. He was never difficult, never vindictive. The only thing he seemed embittered about was Miff Ferrie's dog. "That fucking dog," he'd say. "I'll even eat that fucking thing!" And you were always alert to his health. When his legs were such a problem, if a script came in that required him to go upstairs, you made sure he never saw it, however funny it was.' The main frustration for all directors was attempting to contain a comic giant of six feet three and a half inches within a three by four frame. The moment they cut to a mid shot they often halved his comic value, but not to do so brought its own problems for the viewer preconditioned by grammar of this kind.

The abiding memory of so many who worked on the shows is the rehearsal of his solo spot. In the early days he complained that the time allowed for this was crowded out by that allocated to sketches and guest musical acts. Eventually an hour of every camera rehearsal was set aside for the purpose. It consisted of Cooper on stage muttering to himself – he never rehearsed gags out loud – then moving backwards and forwards between two tables all the while going 'Pitter, pitter, pitter' and 'Patter, patter, patter'. Mary Kay captured the process perfectly: 'Then he would suddenly say "Woof" and mutter some more and then say "Woof, woof" and gesticulate with his hands as though he was persuading us to do something. He looked as blankly at us as we did at him. Once more he'd move about and say "Patter, patter, patter" and "Big woof". That was it. He'd insisted on time for his stand up and hadn't shown us anything. The "Woof", of course, was meant to represent the laughter from the audience.' It was all over in ten minutes.

For the star, the exercise was valuable at a psychological level, part of what Mayoh described as helping to create the atmosphere in which he excelled, something in which he had the full support of the technical crew. As for sketches, Mayoh again held the key: 'The best you could do is arrange the supporting cast around him so that if he wandered off on some track of his own they could catch up. There was no point in telling him he was three inches off his mark. You just moved the mark and let him get on with what he did best.' As actress Sheila Steafel commented, 'You didn't really work with him. You were there. You worked around him.' When it came to the scripts themselves there is a half-myth among writers that he was bad at remembering their lines, but Mary Kay insists that he applied a schoolboy diligence to learning his words by rote. Audio tapes exist of the process. I think she can be believed that for the most part he would often be word perfect while others in the cast would arrive unprepared. Apparently he was fond of quoting Spencer Tracy on this point: 'All you have to do is know your lines.'

Writers, actors, producers, all come together in their memory of the moment when rehearsals had to stop for him to perform his latest magic trick. It had nothing to do with the show, unless he could find a way at a later date of giving it a comic twist, but obviously represented his own subconscious attempt at a bonding exercise with fellow team members. As actor Gordon Peters observed, 'You never got close to him any other way. He was totally obsessed in his own world.' Perhaps that obsession makes his success in such an essentially collaborative medium as television all the more remarkable. With a fully lit stage and a responsive orchestra, stage work came second nature to him. Television was always bound to be a bigger challenge.

I have left to last what may have been his funniest moment in a television studio. Sadly it was not recorded. It happened at a time when fellow comic, Dick Emery was hitting the headlines with the break-up of yet another marriage. Tommy was enjoying an after-rehearsals drink with Barry Cryer in the bar at Teddington Studios. He looked at his watch and saw it was fast approaching eight o'clock. He then remembered that Morecambe and Wise were taping their own show that night. 'Let's go down to see the boys,' said Cooper. Tommy had no difficulty getting past the flashing red studio transmission light. He sidled along the edge of the audience seating rostrum as Eric and Ernie forged ahead with their warm-up, which was in full flow. Barry held back as Tommy barged into the act. The place was in uproar as he grabbed Eric by the arm and went down on his knees, shedding tears by the bucketful. It took several moments for the laughter to subside. Eventually Ernie managed to say something: 'Tommy, what's the matter?' After a sob or two more, Cooper composed himself and said, 'Dick Emery has gone and left me.' At which point he stood up and left as suddenly as he appeared. As Eric would have said, had he not been rendered speechless by the incident, 'Well, there's no answer to that!' Perhaps Cooper did not need so many scriptwriters after all. For a man who did not like surprises, he never lost his knack for giving them.

TEN

Method in the Madness

All great performance is based on a finely tuned individual balance of skill, ego, and personality. In Cooper's case there can be no question that he possessed the latter trait in profusion, while, as we have seen, his ego – unless the word is qualified as the need for an audience's affection – was, for such a giant of comedy, a relatively low-key affair. However, in using incompetence as the peg upon which to hang his public image, he could not help but raise the question of the extent of the first attribute. The anatomy of a physical comedian of Cooper's accomplishment, like that of a soccer superhero, can be seen to comprise a framework of poise, agility, heart and mind. There were actually times on stage when he resembled a football star with his ability to change direction with amazing cunning, the feints and swerves of his body adding a balletic quality to the equation. The risks he took in the cause of laughter showed no lack of courage at a level worthy of a Victoria Cross in the front line of comedy. How rational he was is another issue.

I doubt if Cooper ever really stopped thinking about his work. His absorption in the preparations for a performance was legendary, never leaving a single thing to chance – ensuring that he had two, sometimes three of every prop he needed – and constantly preoccupied with the secret workings of a mechanical flower pot or an exploding cigar rather than a matter of deeper introspection. A stage hand once commented on his habit of treble-checking every prop before a show: 'Tommy's no fool. He knows where every single bit of gear is. It's like a space-launch countdown.' For a standard cabaret appearance, this amounted to over one hundred props distributed over three tables, not to mention free standing items like the gate, the table that disintegrated and the pedal bin with the shock-horror head that popped up from inside. Anyone who observed the process would have to admit that there was something Zen-like in his application to the task. Photographs and sketches made to help the process reveal the bird's eye view of his stage to be as fascinating as the most surreal version of Kim's Game. Hidden among the props were prompt cards – anything from postcards, shirt stiffeners and the dividers from packets of Shredded Wheat – containing new jokes to be tried and mistakes (plotted) to be made. His son Thomas, who in later years helped his father with this chore, once said that Tommy knew where everything was blindfolded.

For all this attention to detail, he had no wish to analyse his appeal: 'I honestly don't know what it is, and I don't want to know, because if I became self-conscious, I would lose the gift.' But neither, unlike Dodd or Morecambe, did he analyse his humour. Barry Cryer claims he never heard him utter a single analytical remark. His response to a gag would always be a simple 'Yes' or 'No': 'It was as if something went "Ping! I can do that." He would never explain a rejection, although he would always be very nice in turning something down.' Peter Reeves recalls the lunchtime spent in conversation with an intense lady journalist from the Swedish equivalent of

Radio Times. She went on and on about her theories of his humour, relating it to the bigger issues affecting society at the time and at last concluding, 'Is this the way you approach your work?' 'Well, I put something in and if it works, I keep it in. If it doesn't, I leave it out.' 'Very interesting,' was her reply. One longs to have seen the expression on his face.

His natural speech rhythms were such that he often repeated key phrases. The writers at LWT picked up on this. Dick Vosburgh recalled the read-through where one of the team launched into the material he was submitting for the opening stand-up, written as Cooper would say it: 'Good evening. Good evening.' Tommy looked at the words and was aghast: 'What's this? I can't say that. I don't say everything twice.' Everyone fell about laughing. The story manifests itself in another form with the young Alan Ayckbourn, no less, as the writer faithfully reproducing Cooper's speech patterns on the page. When Tommy read the four words aloud, he found himself delivering the greeting four times: 'Good evening. Good evening. Good evening. Good evening.' 'There are too many good evenings here,' he complained. On another occasion at Thames, Dick Hills included in his script the lines, 'And he came in like that – it could have been like that – but no, it was like that.' Royston Mayoh explains that Tommy genuinely didn't understand: 'Dick just didn't think. He had done the unforgivable. By holding a mirror up to his foibles, he ran the risk of exposing the myth.' All magicians are inquisitive by nature, but the ultimate secret Cooper did not wish to have explained was his own.

Unless he was taking his straight-faced penchant for teasing people to unheard of lengths, there are some remarkable instances of how dim he could sometimes appear. Val Andrews remembers the early time when the last five words of the line that went 'this trick was given to me by a very famous Chinese magician, Hung One – *his brother was Hung Too*,' emerged one night as 'and his brother was executed as well.' Tommy couldn't see what was wrong. Val said, 'He would argue, "But he still died." He could never grasp it.' Cryer cites the wrong emphasis he would place on the word in a line. Another joke went something like, 'A man walked into a bar and went "Ouch!" It was an iron bar.' Barry explained how important it was to put the emphasis on the adjective, not the noun. An argument ensued: 'Isn't the joke, 'It's an iron *bar*?' 'What are you talking about?' 'Did they laugh?' 'Yes.' As Barry says, 'He wasn't interested. But then *he* laughed.' Maybe it was funnier Cooper's way as long as Cooper was doing it, but as Andrews says, 'It was a pity his intellect didn't match his talent.'

But it could never be that simple. Inevitably, much of his success has been accounted to timing, that cliché of comedy appreciation. Spike Milligan once compared Cooper's verbal dexterity to a finely honed razor or a piece by Chopin: 'It was so magically correct. There's only one split second in a moment of time when the joke is right. Go left or right of that and it doesn't happen and he hit a bull's-eye every time.' On the other hand his magical colleague, Patrick Page dismisses forcibly the whole idea that he was born with some special gift: 'Bollocks. Tommy didn't understand the meaning of the word "timing".' He may not have had the intellectual grasp the term implies, but at an instinctive level there was something locked into his very being that with experience achieved the sharpness and exactitude Milligan held in such high esteem. Tucked away in a single sketch – the one set in the fish restaurant – is an exchange between Cooper and the difficult diner that encapsulates this verbal skill. Tommy continues to show remorse for 'his little fishy friend', the trout that the character played by actor, Anthony Sharp insists he must have:

Tommy: You're not having it.
Customer: I want the manager.
Tommy: Oh well – that's different.

On the page the joke is as flat as a flounder, but somehow Cooper's delivery lifts it out of the mire of limp Seventies sitcom. There is no pause to telegraph what he is going to say. Once the line is uttered – with the merest flicker of a smile – he moves speedily on. It is not a major laugh, but within the Milligan terminology the proportionate reaction it triggered in the studio unquestionably qualified it as 'a bull's-eye'.

If he skilfully downplayed this line, what arguably remained the most obvious tag in his repertoire was pushed fearlessly to the limit as he returned on stage in defiance of the audience pre-empting him. I refer once more to that moment when having attempted to shoot himself for failing to land the third card in the hat he declares for a third time, 'Missed!' The joke is obvious, but however many times one saw it performed, however transparent it appears in retrospect, one never heard the word without feeling a twitch of surprise. Like the master magician he was at heart, Cooper never let go the gift of surprise, even if, as his daughter says, he hated being surprised himself. Whatever the definition of timing in the comic's handbook, it is difficult to imagine him as anything but a blue riband exponent of it at times like these.

Comedy has its own unfathomable secret workings, professing rules that are incapable of rational explanation. As Walter Matthau's character, Willy Clark explained in Neil Simon's *The Sunshine Boys*, 'Words with a *k* are funny. *Chicken* is funny. *Pickle* is funny. *Kleenex* is funny. *Tomato* is not funny.' A great deal of what made Cooper so enduringly funny is inexplicable too. If it is true that the brains of a Beckham are in his boots, it may be equally true that Cooper's were locked away somewhere within the innermost, imponderable reaches of his physiology. It would help to explain the most astonishing aspect of his technique whereby physical business cultivated in the earliest years of his career remained constant until the end. His pace slowed down through the years, as did that of Pelé and of Best, but something stayed amazingly constant in his combined physical and mental make-up that many a soccer player would have killed for.

Study the earliest and latest recordings of a set piece from his act and very little discrepancy will be found between them. A film or video editor could cut back and forth haphazardly from one to the other and still arrive at a continuous whole. Whatever Tommy's physical condition, albeit compromised by age, health or merely the weather, the performance remained sharp and precise. As Bob Monkhouse said, 'Once he'd got the piece of business correct, it remained perfectly that way always. He never altered it. The precision gave the lie to the apparent clumsiness that he produced. The only time I ever saw him in any way being clumsy with his clumsiness was when he was doing something for the first time in rehearsal. And he wouldn't do it on stage until he got it right.' In this approach he was as painstaking as the greatest practitioners of serious stage conjuring. There is no better example than his cabinet routine.

In its pacing and dramatic structure the sequence is a short one-act play of its own. At Tommy's silent beckoning two stagehands wheel on the wardrobe-size piece of furniture with red curtain in lieu of door. It comes on faster than expected. At the split second it reaches centre-stage, Cooper, clearing the decks for its arrival, just so happens to be standing in its path. The abrupt force of the collision leaves him dazed and disoriented until, pulling himself together for the miracle ahead, he draws our attention to the pitch black interior. As he adjusts the prop first to right and then to left before returning it to central position, no one in the audience can have a single doubt about its innocence: 'Empty! Empty! Empty!' Reaching over the threshold he knocks against the three interior walls with his clenched right fist to prove the point further. Genuine hurt steals over the Cooper countenance as he hits too hard, but the show must go on. With all the bravura of Dante or Jasper Maskelyne he steps inside, draws the curtain across and almost instantly whips it back again. There has been no time for anything to have happened, but he looks as if he has seen the ghost of Rasputin, or maybe – in this retro sentry box – that of his old commanding officer: 'Ooh! It's dark in there!' Back on *terra firma* he pulls the curtain across once more and almost fussily proceeds to make a series of mystical passes towards it, each pointedly from a different direction and loudly accompanied by a tymp roll. Then with anticipation and precision he jerks the curtain back sharply. There is no one there. Nothing has happened.

Nothing will happen. For a nanosecond expectancy hangs in the air, before Cooper succumbs to disdain and dismissal. For one incredible moment the audience ceases to exist. He shrugs, almost subliminally, to the stagehands to take the cabinet back whence it came, slapping the side nearest him as he does so: 'Right!' The bathos of his delivery tells us all we need to know. In that one word is wrapped up more than the secret admission of his own failure, but the guilt and frustration of every one of us who sets out high-handedly to achieve a personal goal we know we can never attain. The underplaying of the end says a thousand words, while the routine is studded with detail that could take up many more. The sound of the metallic swish of the curtain on its rail is as correct as a musical note needs to be. The danger that he will be carried away with those mystical passes shows a mind spiralling out of control.

The basic emotions of pain, fear and, come the end, guilt are enacted with his whole body at a level with which the audience for all its laughter truly empathizes.

His interaction with long established props testified to the same exactness throughout his career. The supposed muddle with the box of hats, the catalogue of errors with top hat and cane in the Frankie Vaughan send-up, the confusion with the bottle and the glass, the demonstration of the 'very famous' vanishing wand, all provide evidence of the process. If one wanted proof that it is more difficult to burlesque straight magic well than to accomplish what one purportedly sets out to do, the latter serves as a prime example. Picking up the wand he went into traditional screech mode: 'Look. A solid wand . . .' The words are timed to coincide with the moment he brings the wand down against the plate in his other hand. The plate shatters. He is not deterred: '. . . will vanish in front of your very eyes.' He grabs a sheet of newspaper from a small table to his left, wraps the wand inside and as if he were tussling with some unknown force attempts to make the rod disintegrate within. He fails and tries again. On the third and final attempt the wand makes contact with the table, which collapses into a heap. The fancy footwork he shows as he attempts to sweep away the evidence under a magic carpet of his own imagining takes us back to football pitch and ballet stage. His legs are their own expression of embarrassment as, above the waist, he attempts to retain dignity and composure. Tommy said it himself: 'Straight magic and funny magic are almost equally difficult. If it's straight, it's hard and takes a lot of practice, you see. But to send it up is still hard, so it's more or less on the same level, although the magic has to go wrong at precisely the right time, so I suppose it's harder.' The paradox was that within his own twisted parameters he set himself higher standards of personal perfection than anybody.

In my opinion, he could have added that his own choreography was more impressive than that ever accorded the occasional dancers on his television shows.

Tommy once surprised Bob Monkhouse by claiming that when it came to physical comedy and magic he had learned not to practise in front of a mirror. He maintained that by so doing you became so engrossed in yourself that you lost sight of the audience, whereas by working to an imaginary crowd, albeit a blank wall, you were constantly aware of the fact that ultimately you had to deliver across the footlights. Bob said, 'I believe that was one of his secrets. I never saw him perform or do any kind of business where he wasn't totally involved with reaching out to people. It was never a case of "Look at me. Look at me." It was always "Here, this is for you."' His skill in handling an audience was never seen to greater effect than in his presentation of the evergreen juggling stunt with the eggs and the glasses. This had long been a standard item in conventional juggling acts, the cue for well deserved applause before the performer moved onto his next feat. Cooper enlarged the whole concept. It was no longer about a mere display of skill, everything about the interplay he could establish through that fourth wall that exists between performer and spectators. The climax to the routine when he knocks the tray from between four tumblers of water and four eggs precariously balanced on tubes set on the tray in such a way that the eggs fall into the glasses was always impressive, but in Cooper's hands the destination was never as important as the teasing detours he took *en route* with those seated in the auditorium.

First the four eggs were 'selected' from a box of six: 'Now, I'd like someone here at random – oh, Mr Random, would you point to any egg you like, sir. This one? Why this one? Why not that one? Alright.' This is the one he breaks to show that they are all genuine – 'so fresh that the hens haven't missed them yet' – before setting up the intricate structure that he will soon capsize with one blow of his hand. Gradually he leads the audience into a state of comic apprehension, to which at this stage, trapped in their seats as they are, laughter can provide the only antidote: 'What I do is go like that see and the idea of the trick is this – the tray goes over there (he points decisively) – and the eggs – huh, huh – they're supposed to go into the glasses. I want to know why it hasn't worked – just like that – boom – like that! And I'd like to point out that you are in direct line of fire!' The way he plays on his own nervousness brilliantly increases the laughter as he approaches the resolution. However, he does have one word of advice: 'I'll give you a little tip. If they fly out, just catch them like that (he cups his hands together carefully), not like that (he claps his hands together), else it will go all over you like that (he uses his hands to mime the mess dribbling down his shirt front).' The audience is encouraged to join in the count, not least so that he can catch them out at the last moment: 'One – two – two and a half . . .' When the climax arrived, he seldom failed, but when an egg did miss he always claimed, 'That's three more than normal!' However many eggs ended up in the glasses, the routine always scored as a piece of audience involvement on a grand scale.

Whatever was going on within Cooper's physiological make-up when it came to the playing of physical comedy, the fact that he could replicate complex physical business over a chasm of many years was only half of the achievement. It is equally extraordinary that as he did so he never left you in any doubt that what you were seeing performed was taking place for the very first time. One soon realizes that one is talking of something more than comedy, namely comic acting of a very high order. He might be older, droopier, even sadder

– possibly as a result of having done it a thousand times – but the immediacy somehow remained, in a way that Frankie Howerd never achieved in his struggle with the lady pianist who was hard of hearing – 'Poor soul. Don't mock!' – or Tony Hancock with his intentionally hackneyed display of Hollywood idols of yesteryear: 'And now here's one for the teenagers. George Arliss!'

Hancock was too young to attempt an impersonation of William Gillette, the celebrated American actor–playwright of the late nineteenth and early twentieth century. Gillette helped to define the image of Sherlock Holmes with his portrayal of Conan Doyle's character in the play he based on the stories, but arguably his greatest contribution to the theatre was the concept that he articulated concerning performance: 'The Illusion of the First Time in Acting'. He wrote that each successive audience before which a scene is played 'must feel – not think or reason about, but feel – that it is witnessing, not one of a thousand weary repetitions, but a life episode that is being lived just across the magic barrier of the footlights. That is to say, the whole must have that indescribable life-spirit or effect which produces the Illusion of the First Time.' Directors struggle and strain to achieve this mystical quality from their casts. If it may be accepted as a criterion for success as an actor, then Cooper in his restricted way must be considered an accomplished actor indeed.

Many British variety comedians matured into successful straight actors, not least Max Wall, Jimmy Jewel and Nat Jackley. All had reached the Indian summer of their careers by the time they did so and were less compromised by the spontaneous connection that an earlier audience would have made with their comic achievements. Leaving aside for the moment whether Cooper might at a later age have been able to submerge himself into a straight part, the superficial idea of our comic hero in a serious role is quite impracticable. However hard Cooper might have tried to tame his comic gestures and keep a straight face, distraction would have won the day. A routine that occasionally found its way into his act was a card trick that required him to play the part of a cockney spiv to justify the aces changing into pictures of ice-creams: in the cockney patter 'Aces' became 'Ices'. For this he donned cap, scarf, clip-on walrus moustache, and an attempt at an accent: 'All right, me old cock sparrer!' The funniest line in the whole piece was his admission 'You'd never know it was me.' With Cooper the combined resources of every theatrical costumier in London could not have prevented such knowledge. He was beyond disguise.

A television sketch from 1975 in which he played all the parts in a one-man identity parade in an old-fashioned police station was built around this very premise. Cooper not surprisingly has the time of his life amid a flurry of false moustaches, giant sunglasses, and assorted headgear. Of course, the concept of confused identity underpinned his cod impressions, the *Hamlet* sketch, the famous 'Hats' routine, and not least the World War Two duologue where his costume is split between the German Kommandant on the one side and the British officer on the other. As the two soldiers wrestled with the uncertainties of monocle and clip-on half-moustache and the constant turning from one profile to the other, the two parts became hilariously out of sync until it slowly dawned upon the brigadier that he was speaking the part of the Nazi. They had been discussing escaped prisoners:

Kommandant: When zey are caught zey vill be shot.
Brigadier: Oh, no, they won't.
Kommandant: Oh, yes zey vill.
Brigadier: Oh, no, they won't

Kommandant: Oh, yes, zey vill.

Brigadier: And ven zey are caught everyone vill be shot because . . .

(Cooper thinks quickly and turns again)

Kommandant: Vy are you imitating me?

The real joke, of course, was that he could play neither, remaining unmistakably Tommy Cooper whatever the costume, the accent, or the facial appendage. And yet at another level, in order to make this very point, he was resorting to comic acting of considerable skill.

In real life Cooper was obsessed with identity. Bob Monkhouse claimed that at the height of the poll tax demonstrations when West End streets were at a standstill he was cajoled by Cooper into travelling with him on the underground and no one appeared to take a bit of notice. But such occasions were the exception. He envied his friend and hero Arthur Askey who could whip off his spectacles, put on his hat and coat, and walk out of the theatre with the audience, disappearing into the crowd. For Tommy anonymity was usually a challenge of Sisyphean proportions. While there were times when he liked to be the centre of attention – he once expressed concern to magician, Ian Adair that he had been ignored at the hotel where he was staying in Blackpool because a wedding had taken centre stage that day – he also valued his privacy. Mary Kay recalls the summer season in Skegness where in order to walk around unnoticed he went to a wig-maker. Tommy imagined he was leaving the consultation a new man, complete with spectacles, a false moustache and his new hair. He had scarcely walked a few steps when a woman came up to him and asked, 'Excuse me, Mr Cooper, may I have your autograph?' The wig was never worn again. Dennis Kirkland would tell of bumping into him once on the concourse at Kings

Cross Station. Tommy was wearing a psychedelic Hawaiian shirt, shorts, white socks, pumps, sunglasses, and clutching a brown paper carrier bag. 'What are you dressed like that for?' asked the producer. He took off the glasses and said, 'Oh, I didn't want anyone to recognize me.' Dennis swore he was being serious. As if the spectacles made a difference!

As an actor there was no way Cooper was born to be the next Alec Guinness, but, as Anthony Sher has pointed out, acting is less about disguise, more about revealing your soul. In this chapter alone we have observed his ability to portray pain, fear and guilt in the cause of laughter. The way in which he projected these emotions was no cardboard pretence. Drama teachers could have done worse than point their pupils in the direction of Cooper nursing the pain of his rapped knuckles in the cabinet routine. It was the simple detail rather than the obvious burlesque – like trapping a finger or thumb in a wayward prop, even clapping his hands too hard in a gesture of showmanship – that revealed the act as the minefield of disaster it was and neither Peter Sellers nor Alastair Sim, let alone Guinness, could have registered the emotion more tellingly. The reaction was often delayed – as when he smashed the jug stuck on his hand with a rolling pin – only to make the grimace all the more authentic. His wide-eyed stare with hand on heart acknowledged fear even when – as with his roar as Frankenstein – it was of his own making. 'Frightened the life out of me!' he'd say, stepping out of character, and he meant it. After he had finished pretending to strangle himself with one hand round the side of a flat or the edge of a curtain – an impressive optical illusion of its own – he didn't have to say a word as giddy-eyed he regained his balance: it could have been the hand of the Boston Strangler. When his magical prowess let him down, the subtle insinuation of self-reproach as he ignored the world and took refuge in the nearest table top said it all, as if the President of The Magic Circle was about to tap him on the shoulder and ask for his medal back.

Equally impressive was his ability to summon up real tears. Although he abjured sentiment and self-pity in his performance, he traded on the genuine emotion to send up pathos. Barry Cryer remembers there was no need for a make-up girl's glycerine: 'He could genuinely cry to order.' A television sketch designed to make capital of the trait had Cooper bemoaning the fate of his lost budgerigar. It happens to be perched on his fez in full view of the audience throughout, but their laughter does not deter him from weeping buckets: 'He was in that little cage – (sob) – and now he's gone – (sob) – I bought him a little ladder so that he could go up and down like that – (sob) – and now he's gone.' It all gets too much and he pulls out a handkerchief to mop up the tears: 'I'll be alright. I'll get over it.' But still they come, until Cooper absentmindedly takes off the fez and discovers the object of his affection, which in an instant switch of feeling he proceeds to hit repeatedly. In another sketch he emerged tight-lipped and resolute from a casino having lost a million francs: no sooner was he outside than the water gates opened and he was bawling like a baby. Had they been anything less than realistic, none of these reactions would have been half as funny, bearing out the old adage about truth in comedy. Because none of it was happening to us, it was funny, but only because we believed implicitly that the pain, the fear, the guilt, the sadness *was* happening to him.

His television sketches are full of brilliant moments when he brings such skills into play: the registering of pain as he brings his hand down on the pile of bricks in the karate sketch; the conviction with which, in the restaurant sketch, he handles the wet rubber fish as if it were alive; the agony with which in another casino scene he eats the chips from the newspaper, too hot to hold and to eat. But if there were any doubt of his skill in this area of expression one has only to look at the way in which he would physically embellish an otherwise straightforward monologue. Consider one of his favourite routines, the one centred upon the seaside town of Margate:

I was in Margate last summer for the summer season. A friend of mine said, 'You wanna go to Margate. It's good for rheumatism.' So I went and I got it. And I tried to get into a hotel. It was packed. So I went to this *big* boarding house and I knocked at the door *and the landlady put her head out of the window and said, 'What d'you want?' I said, 'I wanna stay here.' She said, 'Well stay there' and shut the window.* And while I was there I bought one of these skin diving outfits. Have you seen them? Like a frogman's suit. I bought *the whole thing. Goggles – flippers – tank on the back.* And I had a photograph taken *like that – and like that.* You never know, do you? You never know. And I went to the bay and I jumped in – *cos you're not supposed to dive in – it's dangerous.* And I jumped in *like that* and I think *I turned a little bit on the way down* and I went down about a hundred and fifty-five feet. It was lovely. Very quiet. *And I'm going along like that. I've got the instructions here. And I get rid of them and start doing out like that. And the feet are going like that. Not in the front – in the back – d'you know what I mean? And I don't care now – d'you know what I mean? I'm all over the place – the goggles getting all misty – and I'm humming to myself – hmmm hmmm, hmmm hmmm – not loud – just hmmm hmmm –* and all of a sudden I saw a man walking towards me in a sports jacket and grey flannels. I thought, 'That's unusual for a Thursday.' *So I went towards him, moving like this,* and I got right up to him *and I took this pad out and wrote on it, 'What are you doing down here walking about in a*

*sports jacket and grey flannels?' and he took this pad from
me and wrote on it 'I'm drowning!'*

The whole sequence was a physical powerhouse, the words in
italics spelling out where his body went into overdrive in
the cause of expression. The arms flung wide to denote size;
the dialogue directed at the landlady on the upper floor; the
ludicrous representation of Cooper the frogman; the prim
half-profile turns to accommodate the catchphrases; the
finger-pointing admonition on deep-sea safety; the boisterous
threshing against the sea with the right hand while the left
holds the instruction manual; the hands flip-flopping nineteen
to the dozen to illustrate the feet – in the front and in the back;
the growing sense of disorientation; the mime of the pad and
pencil; not to mention a myriad of casual winks and looks
to acknowledge the audience in best Max Miller fashion; all
contributed to a bravura performance that, with the exception
of Ken Dodd, no contemporary stand-up comedian was – or
is – capable of delivering.

Equally impressive was the energy he threw into the telling
of his quaint repertoire of shaggy animal stories, of which the
most notable was that concerning the king of the jungle:

You know – the king of the jungle – the lion. And one day
he woke up – he had a very bad temper – and he said to
himself, 'I'm just going outside now and teach them all
who's king of the jungle: Just to teach them. So he gets up
and he goes, 'Grrrrr'. He was really mad, you know what
I mean? 'Grrrrr'. And he saw a little chimp and he said,
'You! Who's the king of the jungle?' And he said, 'You.
You're the king of the jungle.' 'Well that's alright then.
Alright.' And he walked along a bit more and he came
across a laughing hyena and he said, 'Hey you, laughing

boy.' And he went, 'Hah hah, hah hah hah. Hah hah, hah hah hah!' He said, 'Who's the king of the jungle?' (He mimes the lion clawing at the hyena's nose) 'Ooh, aah aah hah, ooh ooh aah, you are, you are.' So he walked on a little bit further and right at the very end was an elephant and a gorilla talking. And this gorilla looked at the elephant and he said, 'Here he comes, Jumbo. He's gonna do that "king of the jungle" bit again. He always does it.' He said, 'I'm not gonna stand it any more. I'm gonna leave you.' And he went up a tree. He said, 'I'll give you a trunk call later.' Hah hah hah! So he went up to this elephant and he said, 'Hey you. I'm talking to you, Big Ears.' He said, 'Who's the king of the jungle?' And this elephant got his trunk and wrapped it right round him and threw him up in the air and as he was up in the air coming down he was going, 'Who's the king of the jungle? Who's the king of the jungle?' And he hit the ground hard. And he picked him up again and he threw him against the tree and he threw him against the other tree. Then the other one. Then the other one. Then the other one. And he sank to the ground like that. It may have been like that. No. It was like that. And the lion said to the elephant, 'Look, there's no good getting mad just because you don't know the answer!'

In his telling one feels the apprehensiveness of the chimp, the stupidity of the hyena, the sharp clawed anger of the lion. The final encounter is a visual triumph as Cooper takes upon himself the part of the pachyderm as it subjects the lion to the indignities it has been holding in reserve for the beast. This climax magnificently embraces mime, burlesque, audience acknowledgement and sheer physical effort. When added together they must come close to something called 'acting'. According to Val Andrews, Tommy had immense respect for members of the acting profession. Val states that he would come away from performing on television shows with the likes of Deryck Guyler complaining of his poor performance: 'You've no idea how terrible I was, but Deryck couldn't put a foot wrong.' Within his own charted territory, neither could Cooper.

The acting profession has always doffed a cap in his direction. Sometime in the early Eighties Trevor Howard begged Michael Parkinson to arrange a meeting between himself and Cooper, so strong was his admiration for the acting ability he saw at the core of the comedian's act. More recently Anthony Hopkins has revealed himself as the foremost Cooper fan, identifying with the apparent anarchy within the performance and using his own vibrant impersonation to break the tension on many an uptight film set. It is difficult to give any credence to his repeated chat show claim that he based aspects of Hannibal Lecter, his Oscar-winning role from *Silence of the Lambs*, on the great clown. More relevant is his less publicized admission that in *August*, the version of Chekhov's *Uncle Vanya* by Julian Mitchell that Hopkins directed for Theatre Clwyd in Wales in 1994, he played the leading role with a touch of Tommy: 'I started putting these laughs in – in the middle of this scene describing the professor's pomposity. It just happened one night by accident and I think the audience picked up on it because I started laughing like Tommy Cooper and I thought I'd better not go too far because I'll step outside the play and make the other actors start laughing too much. But I was tempted to. I wish I had actually.' Another knight, Michael Gambon, capable of no mean Cooper impression himself, succumbed to a similar tendency at the National Theatre in 1995, where, according to supporting actor, Martin Freeman – later to achieve prominence in television's *The Office* – he proved 'an absolute joy, somehow weaving Tommy Cooper into the ad-libbing.'

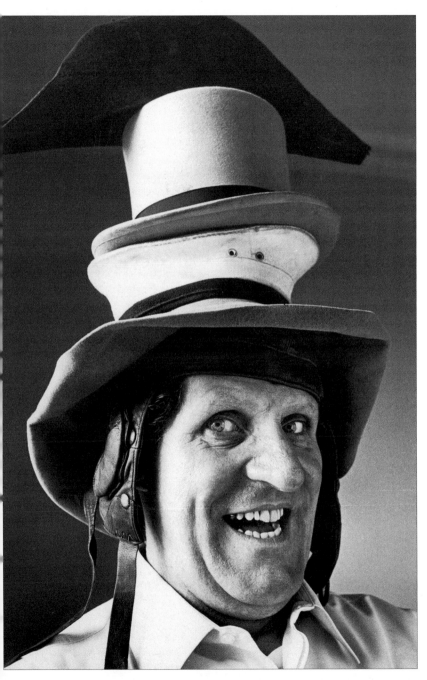

A modern Mad Hatter.

The caricature by Bill Hall.

'Where's Jerry Lewis when I need him?': Dean Martin at the Variety Club Lunch held in his honour, with Tommy and Morecambe and Wise.

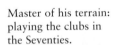

Master of his terrain: playing the clubs in the Seventies.

With Mary Kay during the latter years.

'Look into my eyes': the New London Theatre television series, 1978.

A modern Punch and Judy: 'That's the way to do it!'

'On a clear day...'

'Look at the buffalo and speak into the tennis racquet': with his son, Thomas Henty.

'You've done some terrible, terrible things in your life!': with Frank Thornton.

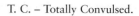
T. C. – Totally Convulsed.

With staunch straight man,
Allan Cuthbertson.

'And do have a
piece of my
homemade cake':
with Betty Cooper
and Robert
Dorning.

Tommy as the public seldom saw him: at rehearsals during the late Seventies.

Our hero sleepwalks for his hero, Arthur Askey.

With Eric Sykes, special champion and dear friend.

Image taken from the final television show, 15 April 1984.

The last photograph, Las Palmas, 1984.

Tommy's 'Dove' amongst her souvenirs.

When Tommy was playing a club in the Birmingham area in 1976 Trevor Nunn took a party of actors from the Royal Shakespeare Company at Stratford to see the master performer at work. In return for the hospitality extended by Cooper after the show, Nunn invited Tommy and Mary Kay to a matinée of *A Winter's Tale* the following day. When Michael Williams as Autolycus arrived on stage wearing a fez – part of his basic costume – Tommy interpreted this as a gesture to himself. To Mary's embarrassment, the actor's opening lines were punctuated by the comedian's trademark laugh and the audience roared out of all proportion to the comedic weight the words carried. Nunn had arranged an informal get-together for after the performance, at which Williams's wife, Judi Dench was likely to be present. It later transpired she did not appear, being too much in awe of meeting the comedian. Happily Williams himself, a frustrated vaudevillian whose impersonation of the much imitated music hall veteran Robb Wilton was considered the best, had not been in the least perturbed. It is significant that in the last years of his life Cooper's own performance assumed aspects of the quiet, puzzled thoughtfulness that had once characterized the mood of Wilton's act.

It is a pity that for all his strength as a live performer on stage and on television, Cooper never managed fully to flex his muscles in the cinema, if only to leave behind one film that would properly epitomize his talent long after the vagaries of television scheduling and the video industry have ceased to have any need for him. Nothing could do justice to his live talent, but the clues to the magic of Sid Field and Max Miller that remain captured on celluloid do more than justify the inferior quality of the films that purvey them. As his career gathered momentum in the Fifties, Cooper was not considered an obvious cinematic option. No one was rushing to make him the new Norman Wisdom. The little man was a stand-alone phenomenon whose success would help to sustain the British film industry for the better part of fifteen years. There was no possibility that the likes of Harry Secombe, Benny Hill, Dave King, Charlie Drake – all given a fleeting moment of film fame in the hope of providing competition for Wisdom – would ever draw level with his amazing national eminence in the medium. The enquiries for Cooper that came the way of Miff Ferrie were for a ragbag of character roles rather than the long-term prospect of a movie star future, not surprisingly perhaps given the lower level of his theatrical billing in those early days.

At the end of 1954 the invitation to play a schoolmaster in support of overgrown schoolboy comic, Cardew 'the Cad' Robinson in his 1956 vehicle, *Fun at St. Fanny's* was mercifully turned down. Three months later a more prestigious offer came with the opportunity to play the Danny Green role of the punch-drunk boxer, 'One-round Lawson' as one of the team alongside Alec Guinness, Peter Sellers, Cecil Parker, and Herbert Lom in Sandy Mackendrick's *The Ladykillers*. His commitment to *Paris by Night* at the Prince of Wales Theatre stood in the way – or so Miff said – of a film role that could have made a significant impact on his career. The following year he was given a screen test at Elstree by MGM for a part in *The Little Hut*, that of the native chief who arrives on the desert island to upset the eternal triangle of its stars, Ava Gardner, Stewart Granger, and David Niven. The role would have given Cooper fourth billing to the big names, but nothing came of the test and it was eventually taken by Italian screen comedian and, coincidentally, former boxing champion, Walter Chiari.

There were the inevitable queries for movies that never got made or were dangled in front of him with illustrious stars attached and materialized later with lesser names as standard

B-movie fodder. It is ironic that when he did accept an invitation to go before the cameras it was as another punch-drunk boxer in a desultory affair called *And the Same To You*. The film, best described genre-wise as sub-Ealing comedy, was released in January 1960 and featured Brian Rix and William Hartnell billed above Cooper in the cast. So insignificant was he to the plot that its précis in the *Monthly Film Bulletin* makes no mention of his character. Tommy played Horace Hawkins, a dim-witted pugilist of the kind that Bernard Bresslaw would soon make his own in the short-lived BBC sitcom, *Meet the Champ*. Cooper passed in and out of the action – some nonsense about a vicar hiring out a church hall for illegal fights to raise money for the roof of the hall – wearing an air of bewildered innocence that veered between fear and geniality. He later admitted he was awful in the role, laying back in his chair and rolling his eyes around like blue glass marbles to prove the point. The movie epitomized the poor record of the British cinema in transposing vibrant variety talent to the screen. It was slow, unsubtle and old-fashioned and made no attempt to capitalize on his presence, in spite of the promise of his first shot on camera, registering pain – as only he could – as he punches his own left fist in the excitement of cheering on a colleague in the ring.

His next excursion into a film studio was prompted by Michael Winner's decision in 1962 to direct a 'modern musical' version of *The Mikado*. It was only the second feature to be made by the colourful director and was rushed into production by producer, Harold Baim in an attempt to be the first to put Gilbert and Sullivan on the big screen once the pair came out of copyright. Tommy was appearing in Blackpool at the time and fitted in his entire scene on a Monday morning before being flown back to the seaside for his evening shows by fellow comic, Stan Stennett in his private plane. Winner remains in awe of Cooper's professionalism under such pressure. Whereas he found Frankie Howerd, who played the gangster Ko-Ko, surly and uncooperative, Cooper breezed in, did not – as was feared – turn the whole enterprise into an excuse to keep the crew in stitches, and got on with his role as the Detective in a pleasant and efficient manner. He was script-perfect, having added, with the blessing of Winner and co-writer Lew Schwartz, one or two pieces of business to make the part his own. Tommy shared the four minute scene with Hank Mikado, an ex-GI played by Kevin Scott, who consults the detective on how to get rid of Ko-Ko in his attempt to win the unfettered attention of his girl friend, Yum-Yum. It was not the intention that Cooper should be of any great help in this matter.

The Cool Mikado resembles one of those Hollywood ensemble movies where too many entertainers are pulled together in one studio at one time for their own good. Howerd had top billing over Cooper. Other television names of the day like Stubby Kaye, Mike and Bernie Winters, Lionel Blair, and Pete Murray give the movie the air of an overblown television special rather than that of a feature film. It was not a success, one critic making the surprising judgement that 'this shoddy film contains some enjoyable dancing by Lionel Blair, but little else,' but today its curiosity value as quintessential Sixties kitsch outweighs any worth, or lack of it, that it might have shown at the time. To Gilbert and Sullivan purists the whole enterprise inevitably showed a severe lapse in creative judgement, but it was never Winner's intention to cling to the original story. Any pretence at production values was compromised when the budget ran out and the director found himself unable by using chroma-key to overlay shots he had envisaged shooting in Japan against the blue walls of the Shepperton sound stage. The lack of time Cooper had in studio gives itself away.

He gallops through his lines, like a poor man's Groucho on speed, and is at times difficult to comprehend. Tommy interpolates some classic Cooper moments, as when he picks up a briefcase and strikes it with a mallet: 'I've been working very hard on a new case,' but there is no space left within the dialogue for the audience to laugh.

The next decade would see enquiries by Ken Annakin for a cameo in the Stanley Baxter/Leslie Phillips/James Robertson Justice vehicle, *The Fast Lady*; by Stanley Baker for a part in his film on the life of the highwayman Jack Sheppard, *Where's Jack?*; by Richard Lester for the film of *The Bed Sitting Room*, the nuclear war fantasy by Spike Milligan and John Antrobus; and again by Lester to play the part of a Gothic villain in *Royal Flash* based on the *Flashman* books of George Mac-Donald Fraser. The requests always seemed to come through relatively late in the day and Cooper's television and cabaret commitments always seemed to stand in the way. Another possibility of becoming associated with Ray Galton and Alan Simpson presented itself with the starring role in a proposed film version of *The Wind in the Sassafras Trees*, the play they had written for Frankie Howerd. For no apparent reason the project appears to have gone away almost as soon as it was mooted and was never made. One heaves a genuine sigh of disappointment that several requests for him to feature in an episode of the comic adventure series, *The Avengers* were all frustrated. Happily a move by Peter Rogers to recruit him to the *Carry On* team with a cameo in *Carry On . . . Up the Khyber* went no further than a lunch between Cooper, Ferrie, the producer and his associates. Miff wrote to Tommy after the meal: 'I have now been advised that they do not think it would be practical to continue this matter, so, with all the goodwill in the world, they suggest that we disengage from this project and trust that we may be able to get together in the future.' One heaves another genuine sigh – this time of relief – that they never did.

It was left to a fellow comedian to sense the true potential for Tommy in the cinema when in 1967 Eric Sykes, wearing his director's hat, featured him in *The Plank*. This was the nearest he came to appearing in a masterpiece and was the better for avoiding feature length. Its fifty-four minutes chronicled the misadventures of two inept builders, played by Cooper and Sykes, who go in search of one last plank to complete the flooring of the house they are working on. Their attempts to transport the plank from the timber yard on the roof of a cantankerous small car set in motion a chain of minor accidents among other road-users. The piece of wood creates even further chaos when it becomes detached from the vehicle and is finally retrieved by the workmen who throughout have been oblivious of the mayhem caused. Eventually the last nail is hammered in, only for Sykes to start ripping the floorboards apart when he suspects mistakenly that his pet kitten is trapped beneath.

The rapport between the two men had long been cemented in an ongoing friendship of mutual respect. Sykes as a scriptwriter had been one of the prime movers of British comedy from the time he established himself as scriptwriter for Frankie Howerd on radio's *Variety Bandbox* in the late Forties, sweeping up additional credits for *Educating Archie* before emerging as a performer in his own right by the end of the Fifties. He could best be described as a star in a minor key, one who put up with the bother of the spotlight to get his project off the ground, but happier at the creative drawing board, resulting not least in the long running series, *Sykes And A . . .*, in which he co-starred with his fictional sister, played by Hattie Jacques, and took the staid form of the domestic sitcom into surreal territory it has seldom entered since. His knowledge of

332

comedy, however much founded upon watching Laurel and Hardy and their peers in his youth, is instinctive. Himself a physical clown of brilliance, he remains the nearest Britain has to a Jacques Tati figure – how strange that name is so evocative of Hattie Jacques – and as such arguably never needed Cooper. But he corresponded to Laurel and Hardy producer, Hal Roach as much as to Stan Laurel and his shrewd comic eye had long recognized that his friend had qualities worthy of cinematic attention. The fact that in *Busy Bodies* and *The Finishing Touch* Stan and Ollie had already worked and reworked every carpentry and construction gag known to history makes the freshness of *The Plank* all the more amazing. Eric later admitted, 'There was no script, just a concoction of ideas. Nobody knew what I was doing, neither did I.' In fact he knew perfectly well what he was doing in casting Tommy alongside himself.

Originally Eric had Peter Sellers in mind for the part, but the total budget of £26,000.00 targeted for *The Plank* was less than what the ex-Goon could command for a major feature. When Hollywood beckoned, Tommy proved the ideal replacement. Eric was totally sincere when he later admitted, 'It turned out to be one of those lucky choices because, as much as I admired Peter, I don't think he would have been, for my money, in the same class as Tom.' Although not technically a silent movie, it had minimal dialogue with imaginative use of sound effects, musical and otherwise. Tommy loved the surreal naturalism of Tati too and fitted the genre effortlessly. Beyond the outer carapace of the crazy conjuring Sykes had discerned his friend's physical knack of sidestepping life for comic effect: 'He had that wonderful expression that he could look at things like an idiot – and the people I love are the people who know they're idiots. It's the people who don't know they're idiots that I'm frightened of. But, you see, if you look at an object, like say I'm looking at you. Now Tom would go – (Eric edgily shifts his gaze several degrees out of kilter) – now that is just that much that differentiates the people who have control of everything. They just say like, "When did you last see your father?" But that's the quality of Tom.' The masterclass needs to be seen, but it perfectly conjured up the look that defined the vulnerability of the clown.

It is futile on the basis of the success of *The Plank* to claim, as several have done, that Cooper was born out of his time. Not even Sykes could dispute that his true métier was in command of a theatre stage or cabaret floor, where one could hear the laughter, listen to the jokes and marvel at his physical dexterity in all its forms. By contrast neither Chaplin nor Keaton had had the opportunity to project themselves properly as individual star talents before the cinema intervened. On the other hand Cooper never came to develop a relationship with the camera as they did. Unlike Charlie (the pioneer of the look to camera), Buster, Stan and Ollie, Morecambe, Howerd, Hancock, Hope, Benny Hill and Jack Benny, he never forged a link through the lens between himself and the home or cinema audience. Even in television the camera reported on what he was doing as if it were a football match. But then no one expected Best or Pelé actually to shoot at the camera.

Had Cooper flourished during the golden era of silent film comedy he would have missed out on something that Eric understood intuitively, namely that only with the coming of sound was film comedy able to deal effectively with silence itself. As film critic, David Thomson, has pointed out, until that time the technical limitations of the medium forbade this: films were never busier in their efforts to communicate words than they were in their early days. *Vide* the many captions or 'titles' that impeded the action. One of the things that is funny about *The Plank* is that so little is said. Sykes, following the guiding light of Jacques Tati himself, devised for Cooper the perfect sound space in which the characteristic noises – the laugh, the cough, the muttering – that issued from his throat underscored the soundtrack. With an occasional word here or there it was, given the plot, all we needed to hear. The movie would not have been as effective, would have been positively frustrating, had an aural iron curtain shut us off from this aspect of both men. But this did not take anything away from the visual quality they brought to the screen.

Eric's stated premise of comedy is to lead an audience to expect one thing and then to deliver the reverse, namely to plant the banana skin on the path and then to have the person walk into a lamppost as, to our surprise, he steps to avoid it. The tone is set when Tommy enters the half-finished room of the house to see Eric kneeling with head bowed in front of the silhouette of a cross depicted on the wall. He gets down on his knees to join in the prayers. The reality is that Sykes is bent over because he has trapped his tie beneath a floorboard, while the religious motif is no more than the shadow of two boards stacked diagonally outside the window. One plot detail involves red paint applied to the plank. This gets transposed to Tommy's ear. Walking along by himself he trips and falls. Passers-by mistake this as blood and come to the rescue. The soundtrack allows us to hear his protestation, 'I'm all right. Let me get up. I'm all right. Oh dear!' Regardless, a crowd quickly gathers. One lady arrives with a bowl of water to bathe his face, another with a cup of tea to revive him – 'Thank you very much' – a third person offers a cigarette – 'Thank you' – while a fourth cushions his head with his folded coat. When the blood fails to shift, they soon realize what it is. All amenities are swiftly withdrawn and Tommy's head crunches against the pavement. At another point he sits happily eating a banana. A plank is swung forward horizontally from behind, but swings back before hitting him. It swings forward again, this time making contact, but the payoff is not the blow itself, rather the banana that gets stuck on his nose under the force of the impact as the plank pushes him forward. Befuddled he walks out of screen, bleary-eyed and banana-nosed.

Sykes described the three weeks of working with Cooper on the film as 'more beneficial than a health farm'. His friend was always there to surprise and entertain in the lulls between shooting, and not always with magic tricks extracted from the pockets of the capacious blue overalls he wore throughout. On one occasion cast and crew were having lunch in a pub when Tommy for no reason whatsoever got up from the table and lay down on the floor. After a short while he returned and continued with his meal. 'What did you do that for?' asked Eric. 'I just wanted to do something visual,' replied Cooper. If he presented the director with a problem it was in being too self-conscious at times in front of the film camera. In one scene all Tommy had to do was walk down the street looking for the plank. Having pretended to shoot a version with Cooper over-reacting, for which the cameras were not rolling, he told him he wanted one last take for insurance, 'but this time I don't want you to act. I just want you to look gently and carefully, but I don't want all the big stuff. So he said, "Just walk down?" I said, "Just walk down, Tom. That's all I want." So Tom walked down towards the camera and I said, "Cut and print." Now Tom said to me, "D'you think I was funny?" I said, "That was very funny, Tom." He said, "I didn't do anything." I said, "Tom, you're Tommy Cooper. When you walk down a street, you walk down it different to what anybody else does."' Cooper couldn't understand that he was getting paid for just walking down the street. In post-production Sykes dubbed the beat of a snare drum onto one section of the walk to create the effect of a funny little dance. Only when Tommy saw the finished result did he fully comprehend. But it did not really need the accompaniment. Generalizing on great comic originals, Sykes has said, 'They don't realize that it is the fact that they are what they are that makes them special.' Of course, he is too modest a man to include himself in that company, but in that regard – as an inspired performer in his own right – he remains as guilty as Cooper.

It seemed a foregone conclusion that the success of the project would bring them together again professionally, but Eric would have to wait fifteen years until 1982 before they could reprise the roles of the accident-prone working men. In the summer of 1969 Sykes and Jon Penington, the producer of *The Plank*, attempted to get a sequel off the ground. The idea was to shoot during the day in Scarborough to take advantage of free time during Tommy's summer season at the Floral Hall. Both found themselves at loggerheads with Ferrie who declined the offer, citing Tommy's health – his leg problems were a constant strain – and the fact that he was under exclusive contract, thus precluding him from accepting any other engagements. Tommy, anxious not to have his friendship with Sykes compromised, was caught in the crossfire. On 30 July Eric wrote to Miff, claiming that Cooper wanted to make the movie and making a persuasive argument that the shooting schedule would be its own holiday for the comedian. The action was to take place largely on a golf course, which, as Sykes argued, 'would be more beneficial than his present situation, i.e. staying in his hotel room all day'. He reasoned that the exclusive contract held by impresario, Richard Stone for the summer season had never been a viable excuse since the film did not compete with the live theatre show and claimed that what was a fairly stock clause could easily be surmounted in the circumstances. Moreover, the publicity attracted by the shoot in the resort would provide valuable coverage for the Floral Hall season. However, Penington had committed the cardinal sin of going behind Miff's back to clear the matter with Stone himself. Stone was more than happy to support the venture, provided that his production was sufficiently covered with insurance, but irreparable damage had been done as far as Ferrie's dignity was concerned.

Eric was also humiliated into having to explain his supposedly 'unethical' behaviour in even mentioning the project to Cooper before bringing it to the attention of his manager. To save time he had wanted his pal's reaction before they even approached Ferrie. This was the way projects came together among friends. He conceded that had his agent approached Tommy direct, then that would have constituted unprofessional conduct, but not a sufficient reason for refusing to allow a picture to be made. On that point he had Miff cornered, since he went on to make the point in his letter that in the past Miff had approached him to ask if he would be prepared to write television scripts for Tommy without approaching *his* agent first! He summed up the situation: 'All problems can be overcome, whatever arguments, reasons, or excuses put forward. It boils down to one simple fact – if you say *"yes"* we go ahead – if you say *"no"* we don't.' The decision rested entirely with Miff, who remained true to his inflexible self. The film was not made with Cooper. Nor did Tommy protest. Whatever he might have said to Sykes face to face, he does not appear to have been over-enthusiastic about the project. With Jimmy Edwards and Harry Secombe in the cast, it reached cinema screens as *Rhubarb* in 1970. It never came close to making the impact of *The Plank*.

Sykes would stay in the background of Cooper's career until June 1977 when Philip Jones raised the matter of a remake of *The Plank* for Thames Television. One is puzzled by what could have been gained from the process. The original was already regarded as a minor classic. It had been made in colour, and there were no obvious technical advantages that suggested themselves. Supposedly Cooper had again expressed to Sykes that he wished to cooperate. When money was discussed, an offer of £1,750.00 was dismissed by Miff as derisory. Ten years earlier he had received £1,000.00 from Associated London Films alongside a small percentage of the profits. Now, as Miff emphasized, he could earn £8,000.00 for a mere week in cabaret. He was doing just that in Dublin at the time of the phone call. Ferrie suggested £7,000.00. Thames came back with a best offer of £2,500.00. Miff declined. This time, whatever he said to Eric, Cooper agreed unreservedly, as he made clear in a phone conversation with his manager on 12 July. To his credit Sykes did not give in, trying hard, but unsuccessfully, to make Thames meet Ferrie's demands. And there the project was left until November of the following year when Cooper, doubtless under prompting from Eric, appears to have suggested the possibility of a new percentage deal. Miff explained that it was a television project as distinct from cinema venture, the finances of which would not be structured in this way. To compensate, he held out with Iris Frederick in the Thames booking office for £14,000.00 for two weeks filming. This was way beyond their budget. After an attempt at gentle persuasion by Philip Jones, arguing what he perceived as the benefit to Tommy's overall career of such a venture, the project, a lacklustre affair, went ahead without him. This time Arthur Lowe played Sykes's principal sidekick. Brilliant an actor as Lowe was, Eric could not claim he was in the same league as Cooper for the style of comedy in question.

The Plank in its revised form was transmitted in the run-up to Christmas 1979, marking the first of a short run of occasional specials by Sykes within the semi-silent genre. The following year *Rhubarb* was submitted for a makeover. In spite of the risk of incurring the wrath of Miff, Sykes had exerted pressure on his chum to take part. Again Tommy appeared compliant. In February 1980 Thames offered £5,000.00 for the new project. Miff said 'No' and Tommy concurred with the words he usually used when he agreed the deal was not up to scratch: 'You do the business!' Not until 1982 did the pair work together again, first in a Sykes television special, and then in the fourth of the semi-silent shows, *It's Your Move*, for which he was paid £5,000.00 and £6,000.00 respectively. *The Eric Sykes 1990 Show*, in which Tommy appeared in a guest line-up alongside Chic Murray, Dandy Nichols, guitarist John Williams and veteran announcer, Leslie Mitchell, was an uneasy attempt to guy the television of the future, where programmes are the items squeezed in between the commercials and those same programmes have to be paid for by the people who star in them. It did not do Cooper justice.

It's Your Move was more rewarding, with Tommy and Eric reprising their workmen roles, now recast as removal men, with Richard Briers and Sylvia Syms as a newly married couple moving into their first home. Although only half the length of *The Plank*, it achieved something like the same rate of visual gags as the intrepid pair and their colleagues brought chaos to the entire street. The soundtrack is sadly plastered with unsubtle and raucous audience laughter, the curse of its television origins. Nevertheless, the pleasure of watching Cooper advance towards camera holding a giant Oriental urn in front of himself, suggestive of some bizarre fugitive from the Arabian Nights, is matched by the joy of seeing him use a bed as a trampoline. To the strains of 'Pop Goes the Weasel' he becomes for a fleeting moment a child again, jumping up and down until he is spotted by Eric, at which point he steps off the bed and walks into the house a much older man. Throughout the film the walk that Sykes strained so hard to capture in

The Plank is more tentative, more spasmodic, and – at the cost of greater pain – even funnier. It is also rewarding to see Sykes exploring the reaches of white magic, Stan Laurel style, on Tommy's behalf. As Bob Todd amuses himself playing a grand piano, Cooper comes along and takes the strut supporting the lid to use as a snooker cue: the lid of the piano stays suspended in the air. In another sequence a scantily clad Sylvia Syms pushes a wardrobe in front of the bedroom door in her desperation to get some privacy to change. No sooner has she done so than the film cuts to Cooper opening the same door from the landing. He steps through the door and emerges from the wardrobe on the other side with a pile of blankets. He puts the blankets down, acknowledges his embarrassment by doffing his bowler to Syms, and then walks back through the wardrobe, the doors of which close behind him. Syms wastes no time in inspecting the cupboard, but there is no one inside and no sign of any exit by which he could have left. It is seldom that a camera trick offers genuine mystery, so skilfully is the gag executed.

Today, Sykes looks back on the working partnership with his friend with great frustration, blaming Miff for coming between himself and Cooper by asking for amounts that Thames couldn't afford. However, in fairness, Tommy was, in Eric's own words, 'the biggest thing in the country', capable of commanding vast sums for his appearances. It would have been totally remiss of Ferrie to have debased the coinage of his client's value and it may sadden Sykes to learn that this was the line often endorsed by his client. He also overlooks how the harsh working hours of filming cut against the grain of Cooper's lifestyle. Tommy never relished getting up at six o'clock in the morning to be at location and then, in his own words, 'having to be funny in cold blood'. Appealing as *The Plank* and *It's Your Move* are, they in no way represent the best archival evidence of Cooper's true talent. Nevertheless, as bonus diversions within a major career they are to be cherished. Sykes has the great gift of inspiring trust within his profession and it is to his credit that a colleague of Cooper's stature and individuality was prepared to place himself so unequivocally in his hands. No sooner had the saga of the removal men been completed than both men were talking of another film in which they played two plumbers tackling a big freeze. It would not be the only project with Sykes's name attached to it to be thwarted by Tommy's death.

Few careers progress without opportunities falling by the wayside, whether by luck or judgement. Fortunately for Cooper those that were missed would not have made too much difference in the final reckoning of his achievement. However, if it were possible to wind back the clock and magic one into reality, I personally would have no hesitation in bypassing the prospect of *Educating Archie*, the important interest shown by Galton and Simpson, or a further minor masterpiece by Eric Sykes in favour of the film opportunity that presented itself in July 1966. The request came from Hollywood producer, Arthur Jacobs, for Tommy to play the part of 'a seedy circus proprietor' in the film version of *Doctor Dolittle* starring Rex Harrison in the title role. It would have entailed four weeks shooting in California from the end of September in lieu of a week in Dunstable and a few scattered cabaret bookings prior to recording the first of the *Cooperama* shows for ABC Television at the end of October. It is impossible to imagine the situation was not flexible. Maybe Miff would have looked more favourably on the vehicle if the character had not been described as 'seedy'. The extended cameo of Albert Blossom, the boisterous circus showman went instead to Richard Attenborough, who turned in a convincing enough interpretation of the vaudeville spirit to win a best supporting actor Golden Globe award. And so Cooper lost out on immortalizing himself as a latter day Stanley Holloway or even Harry Champion, bouncing along with the song Attenborough made famous: 'I've never seen anything like it in my life!' Tommy could have brought the song back home to England as an alternative signature tune. Had screenwriter and lyricist, Leslie Bricusse agreed, the circus attraction to end them all – the two-headed llama known as the pushmi-pullyu – might well have attracted a demonstrative 'Not like that, like that' from the master. In retrospect it is all supposition, but it feels so right. One can even see the magnificent Rex for once in his career conceding his picture to a lowlier cast member.

Outside of the Dolittle context, Rex Harrison may seem an unlikely performer to call to the witness stand in evidence of Cooper's potential acting prowess. In his book, *The Incomparable Rex*, his brilliant evocation of the star whom he describes as 'the last of the high comedians,' writer and director Patrick Garland allowed his subject to reminisce on the great matinée idols of the first half of the twentieth century. While Cooper could never pretend to the suavity and elegance of Hawtrey, du Maurier, and Hicks, he did share what Harrison described as 'their extraordinary *concealment* of art'. In other words, they didn't look as if they were acting: 'They played their comedy on the balls of their feet. I remember to this day, their alert posture, well-balanced, but pitched slightly forward, attentive and yet relaxed. Producing gold cigarette cases out of inside pockets, with a kind of magician's sleight of hand, removing, opening, closing, concealing the case again, and then flicking up the cigarette from finger into mouth with the same effortless dexterity.' The magician analogy is an amazing red herring of a coincidence, but the description of these great light comedians corresponds eerily with the sloping grace, the unexpected poise and delicacy, not to mention the dexterity of Cooper in action. According to Harrison they shared a special inner energy that allowed them to stand on a stage and do nothing: 'By definition, an actor can't get up on the stage and do nothing. That isn't acting. But equally he shouldn't be *seen* to be acting . . . The true comedian, like the true bullfighter, should *affect* to do nothing.' The italics in *affect* are mine.

Comparing videotapes of Cooper from the beginning and the end of his career, it occurs that he was almost alone among comedians of his generation in being allowed to grow old by his public. Others achieve longevity and stay in the public favour purely because they retain the illusion, whether physical or mental, of youth. Ken Dodd's energy as he approaches his eightieth year would defeat many a young pretender on the alternative comedy circuit. Max Bygraves looks amazing for his age and may yet prove to be the British George Burns in this regard. Norman Wisdom still has an impish quality and he has passed ninety. Their popularity was and is dependent in no small part on the age-defeating process. Milligan, although physically frail, remained as bright as a button to the end of his days. Cooper, however, was not so blessed. As ill health took its toll, the timbre of the manic laugh became gruffer and more resonant. His features became fuller, his shoulders slumped, his pace decelerated, his outward energy waned, the mood of his act became even melancholic at times, but the public continued to give of their laughter and affection. It was as if something remarkable was happening to the comedy process. While the individual personas of those mentioned have remained constant throughout their careers, Cooper's noticeably changed with age and the wear and tear that went with it. With maturity he developed an attitude – or, more accurately, a shift in attitude – and audiences, aware of the ravages health had played on him, were more than happy to subscribe to the revised version of their favourite buffoon.

In this way he forestalled the potential disappointment of audiences as it became impossible for him to keep up with the frenetic nature of his earlier style. The look that had once been a darting glance of comic acknowledgement as a trick misfired now took on a more searching, more contemplative aspect. His habit of dispensing with one prop and then meandering apparently aimlessly, even illogically to the other table to find the next became funny in itself. Peter Hudson recalls the occasion he genuinely lost a prop on stage and spent a minute searching from table to table, in his quest shifting things from one place to another amid the debris that had piled up through the act. By now, audiences assumed it was part *of* the act. As with W. C. Fields, they were able to read into his behaviour a comic statement about life in all its frustration and futility, straight man, in Tynan's phrase, 'to a malevolent universe which had singled him out for siege and destruction'. Like Jack Benny and Tony Hancock at the height of his powers Cooper had caught up with Rex Harrison's criterion of *affecting* to do nothing. It is a quality that, had his health allowed, may – with the blessing of the same audience – have given him the ability to have progressed to the type of dramatic role that writers like Beckett and Pinter spun out of the cadences of banal commonplace speech and the hidden meanings implied between their lines.

Significantly Max Wall, Cooper's near-contemporary, who became the prime exponent of such parts within the so-called 'theatre of the absurd', is the only other top British comedian I can call to mind who sustained a similar shift in audience tolerance, the much publicized problems within his private life providing the catalyst in this instance. His transition from tap-dancing novelty act and grotesque piano-master to bearer of seemingly all the woes inflicted upon man in the cause of laughter underlined the skill with which he, like Cooper, brilliantly subverted the art of comedy in his later years. His reaction to tripping over some invisible obstacle – 'A little hole sticking up! (Pause) How desperate can a comedian be?' – is the visual equivalent of every 'bad' joke Cooper ever told, making comic capital out of the sheer desperation that so often accompanies their profession. Tommy's typical look – the one that said, 'What am I doing here in the first place?' – corresponded so aptly with Wall's general demeanour and with Beckett's most famous opening line: 'Nothing to be done'. It may not be so difficult to imagine him as Estragon in *Waiting for Godot*. Interestingly, among all his papers – the gag sheets and American joke bulletins, the magic trick instructions and dog-eared television scripts – was a stray sheet from a more serious source. How it arrived there, no one knows. One would like to think that in Tommy's closing years an enterprising Peter Hall or Trevor Nunn sent the fuller version to him. I refer to a single page of dialogue from Harold Pinter's *The Dumb Waiter*, the part where the two gunmen, Ben and Gus, discourse on road accidents and the crockery at their disposal as they play their own waiting game. It doesn't take too much imagination to hear Cooper saying: 'Listen to this! A man of eighty-seven wanted to cross the road. But there was a lot of traffic, see? He couldn't see how he was going to squeeze through. So he crawled under a lorry.' It is a temptation not to resist adding, 'Just like that!'

ELEVEN

Health and Home Affairs

The Coopers were never ostentatious in displaying the fruits of their success. The solid red-brick suburban house in Chiswick, to which they moved towards the end of 1955, remained the principal family home until Gwen's own death in 2002. It was the residence of a successful professional couple, but not the lavish abode of a major star on a locked estate with exclusive private access to the golf course at the bottom of the garden. At the end of the Sixties they acquired a second home in the old quarter of Eastbourne. A pair of modest labourer's cottages converted into one, this was little more than a bolt hole where no one paid them attention, Gwen could feel close to her roots and Tommy could learn his lines, rather than an elaborate coastal mansion in stunning grounds. Its garden, in perpetual shade, was hardly larger than the Chiswick kitchen.

The Coopers were decent, unpretentious people with their feet on the ground and no delusions of social status, never appearing to need the reassurance that materialism brings. Those who enjoyed their hospitality will testify to the complete lack of side displayed by the couple. As Gwen admitted to Janet and Jimmy Farrow, who became two of their closest friends after Jimmy, a delivery driver, knocked apprehensively on the door asking for an autograph, 'If it wasn't for the likes of you, we wouldn't be where we are now.' Tommy's philosophy of success was quite simple. As he said in one newspaper interview, 'I live quite well now, but not expensively. The idea of making money is only to make your life a bit easier, isn't it?' Fortunately Gwen, nothing if not down-to-earth where her husband was fanciful, took care of all financial matters. It never occurred to Tommy to open bills, let alone to pay them. As his wife said, 'He had no idea about money. If I'd let him have his way, he'd have spent every penny he earned.' The live-in presence of their dedicated maid, Sheila was the only tell-tale clue to the fact that they could have afforded a more lavish life style once Tommy's career consolidated itself in the Sixties.

The mock-baronial interior of the converted hall and dining area was a shrine to domesticity with few clues to the show business connections of its inhabitants. A motley collection of antique prints and paintings and a dresser groaning with antique blue Staffordshire china were more dominant than the few pictures of show business colleagues scattered among the predominantly family portraits displayed on the baby grand piano. Unless you include the period coaching scene entitled *Laying the Dust* on the wall in the tiny next room – depicting, as it does, an array of ladies peeing under their fulsome skirts during a comfort break on their arduous journey from one side of the country to the other – a mirror with the smiling faces of Laurel and Hardy silhouetted into the glazing and framed signed photographs of Max Miller and Bob Hope were the only indication that comedy might be of more than passing interest to the people who lived there. However, there were times, of course, when the space became transformed into a laboratory of comic research, scattered with the tricks of the magician's trade like a cartoon version of an alchemist's eyrie. Once the curtains were drawn, the large oak dining table would become transformed into a vast experimental bench as Gwen with stop watch at the ready timed her husband's rehearsals to the last second. Each gag, each trick was subjected to her own shrewd appraisal. The length of time she suggested they allow for laughs and applause was uncannily accurate. Tommy always set store by her opinion: 'I don't know how I'd manage without her. She says, "Do that gag there. Move that trick somewhere else. And then finish your act with such and such." And she's never wrong. She's always right.'

The address at Chiswick also provided the background to another kind of comedy, an unintentional domestic sitcom that might have been scripted by the legendary cartoonist, Giles, had he been persuaded to swap drawing board for typewriter and the camera's lens. Giles was, in fact, a friend of the family and Tommy did one year provide the foreword to his cartoon annual, joining a distinguished roll call that included Sir John Betjeman, Denis Norden, Dave Allen, and Frank Sinatra, no less. His knack for depicting the most intricate comic detail within the wider domestic scene would have brilliantly captured the surreal obstacle course Tommy set around the house for Gwen and their children, Vicky and Thomas. If he brought his wife breakfast in bed it was to take advantage of the trick rubber spiders he had concealed on the tray. His penchant for practical jokes extended to imitation beetles left in the bath, snakes that sprung out of cocoa tins, books that burst into flames or gave out an electric shock when opened. On one occasion he installed a full-size ventriloquist's dummy in the downstairs cloakroom and gave his daughter the fright of her life. One journalist recalls interviewing Tommy at home when a chilling scream reverberated down the stairs: Sheila had just discovered a 'severed hand' in the laundry basket. Tommy would quite lose control of himself when the jokes worked. Gwen described the aftermath of the occasion he placed a wind-up jumping spider under her make-up bag: 'The damn thing leapt across the room when I moved the bag and I nearly died of a heart attack. He just fell about. He laughed and laughed and laughed, lying on the bed with his feet in the air. You have to laugh at him.' Towards the end of his life Tommy had a simple explanation of just what he was up to when he involved her in his shenanigans: 'She hates it. But it's the way she knows I love her, because I'm still thinking about her – searching the world for any trick to frighten her – after all these years.' Gwen reciprocated: 'I wouldn't swap him for anything. Not even for a few hours' peace, although I'd be sorely tempted.'

Another domestic hazard was the likelihood of household objects – even their children's toys – being spirited away into some mysterious black hole in the service of magic. The kitchen clock was a prime target in this regard, conscripted for the 'Watch, Watch, Watch' gag as it was whisked out of the folds of a voluminous silk scarf. Gwen recalled the procedure: 'I had a lovely old wooden spoon vanish. I was using it to make a cake in the morning and in the afternoon it had gone. The next time I saw it, it was on television!' This was not her only cause for complaint: 'Wherever he goes he's got to have a whole lot of bags with him. We haven't got a suitcase left in the house that'll fasten, so he goes out with half a dozen carrier bags and even parcels tied up with string.'

A telling detail of the way in which Cooper's working methods invaded the day to day running of the house is recalled by scriptwriter and producer, Neil Shand. In the very early days of Cooper's association with David Frost, Tommy did appear twice on his New York based talk show. He was on holiday at the time and had few props with him. It was suggested by Shand that he feature his comedy juggling sequence, but he explained that to do the routine justice he would need the clubs he was used to handling and the downside was that they were in Chiswick. Neil insisted this was no problem as they could be flown over in time by Concorde, the least the airline could do for Frost, their most frequent celebrity passenger. Cooper visibly relaxed when it became apparent he would not have to pay for the phone call home. 'We'll phone Sheila and get her to wrap them up,' explained Shand, adding as an afterthought, 'Just tell us where she can find them.' 'In the kitchen in a plastic bag under the sink,' was the reply. Both maid and airline came up trumps. Tommy was able to dazzle America with his *bona fide* juggling skills and for a short while Sheila had a little more space in which to store the Brillo Pads, Vim, and Fairy Liquid that used to keep the clubs company.

When it came to the practicalities of house maintenance Cooper was nowhere to be seen. 'Useless!' was Gwen's instant response to what he was like around the house. There was the night he came home late from a cabaret engagement. When he switched on the lights they fused: 'He hadn't the foggiest idea what to do. I had to get out of bed and fix the fuse while he stood there clutching a candle like Wee Willie Winkie.' One summer the whole family decamped to a rented house in Blackpool for the summer season. Vicky remembers Sheila becoming agitated when she discovered a leak in the roof. Most people would have been spurred to immediate action, calling the builders in as soon as they could. When the maid pointed it out to Tommy, he reacted, 'You can have a shower under there!' He couldn't care less, shrugged his shoulders, gave out the famous laugh and left the room leaving the poor girl upset, confused, and quite unable to see the funny side of the situation. Apparently he loved watching westerns and horror movies on television, but as Gwen said, 'You have to put up with him going round the house being Dracula or somebody for hours afterwards.' You sense that mother, daughter, even maid would not have had it any other way. You also sense that the likes of Eric Morecambe, Frankie Howerd, and Benny Hill hung up their public personas once they locked the front door at night. With Cooper you could never be sure.

Pictures of Tommy taken with his two children when they were growing up reveal a third kid at heart, but the evidence shows that he was an excellent and caring father. To both their parents' credit Vicky and Thomas appear to have enjoyed a relatively ordinary upbringing, protected from the excesses of media attention. This involved Tommy having to absent himself from school speech days and sports days: the time he did attend, the event turned into an autograph-grabbing fiasco. And while it was easier for him than most parents to connect with them at a child's level, there were moments when he revealed a more astute side to the parental role. On one occasion Thomas, who had been born on 19 January 1956, became involved with what his mother described as a 'bad lot' and found himself pilfering a pen knife and a ball of string from the local Woolworth's. Gwen went hysterical, but Tommy said not a word, prolonging the agony until the time of reckoning that his son knew must come. That evening he took him aside and laid into him in the most fearsome tones he could muster: 'If you ever, ever steal again . . . get me a packet of my favourite cigars.' Of course, he never did.

His daughter Vicky recalls that he never helped her with her homework, built her sand castles at the seaside, or drove her to her first party, but claims she always knew that in his eccentric way he loved her. Especially important were those moments on a Sunday evening when she too would be drawn into the assessment of her father's new tricks. 'That was only amber, was it?' he'd enquire if she wasn't impressed. He'd laugh if there was one she didn't like. But always she felt special in his company, finding him to be an excellent listener who never appeared bored with the mundane problems she would force him to hear: 'After sitting quietly for a few moments, he'd give me some absolutely sound advice. He was wise and kind and a great person to have on your side.' But there were inconsistencies. Vicky still finds it hard to reconcile the man who would lay down the law like a strict Victorian paterfamilias one moment with the one who would keep her up in a restaurant until four o'clock in the morning the next. Thomas recalled the occasion his decision to become a skinhead caused domestic upheaval: 'When I was a teenager I had my hair cropped to about a quarter of an inch all over because it was fashionable. Mum went berserk. She sent me to my room saying, "Just wait till your father sees that." But when dad came up he opened the door and then fell about laughing.'

Many are the tales told by Tommy's contemporaries of visits to the household that fit so perfectly with the Giles cartoon view of the world. Eric Sykes remembers the time Tommy unexpectedly invited him back to lunch after a morning's golf: 'So there's only the two of us sitting there and Dove came in from the kitchen with the biggest joint of beef you've ever seen. I've never seen one so big. She put it on the table and she looked at me and she said to Tom, "Why didn't you tell me you were bringing company?"' During a Blackpool summer season Jimmy Tarbuck received a more formal invitation to lunch after a morning on the links at Lytham St Anne's. 'She's making a roast,' said Tommy to the young comedian and two of the King Brothers who were playing with them. At the time the brash young comic was subsisting on a diet of junk food and the invitation to a meal like mum used to make was irresistible. As they came through the porch Tommy told his guests to wait and went in to see Gwen. The words needed no deciphering: 'He said, "They're not coming. They decided to play another nine holes." She said, "They're not coming? They're not so-and-so coming?" And all the magic words were coming out. And she went, "They're not coming? Well, I'll tell you what . . ." and she came out and we were in the corridor. And she went, "Oh, hello boys! Isn't he naughty?"'

Roy Hudd tells of the occasion a group arrived back at the house after a Water Rats meeting. It was very late and Gwen was roused from her slumbers to come down to attend to their guests. Half awake in dressing gown, slippers and curlers she slumped in her chair as Tommy went into his goose-stepping Erich von Stroheim mode, circling round and round the room as he made the pronouncement, 'Vhere are ze plans of ze Blenheim Bomber?' 'What about Dove?' nudged one of them. 'She'll be fine,' said Tommy. He would rib his wife mercilessly and not merely as the butt of all those gags bequeathed by Max Miller. One day the Farrows arrived early for a meal and Gwen was still in the bedroom changing. Tommy bellowed upstairs, 'Dove, come down and meet your guests.' She came down all apologies: 'I didn't mean to keep them waiting.' 'Well, put your wig on straight.' Doubtless again it was Tommy's way of telling her that he loved her.

One memorable visit to Chiswick was made by Gene Detroy, the vaudeville animal trainer who brought his chimpanzees with him. Tommy couldn't resist popping down the road to a home for unmarried mothers with a chimp wrapped up in a shawl. The matron opened the door and immediately went on the defensive: 'Please, no more children! No more children!' Tommy pushed the bundle into her arms. Gwen thought the woman was going to faint as the head of the chimpanzee popped out. Tommy's laugh was heard all the way back down the street. Detroy's expertize was not confined to the simian breed. Tommy and Gwen wanted a dovecote to add a touch of gentility to the garden. Most probably Gwen also saw it as a gesture of recognition of Tommy's pet name for herself. Their friend agreed to install a pair of doves. Dove was over the moon until it was discovered they were not a pair, but two females which proceeded to mate with all the pigeons in the neighbourhood. For weeks they were overrun with mangy birds.

Throughout Gwen was happy to assume the role of long suffering spouse, her stoic attitude founded upon a love for her husband that entailed him coming home every Sunday wherever he might be appearing in the land. As long as she served him his favourite meals, kept his bed warm and ensured that his soup and tea were piping hot, all would be well with the world. Once when Freddie Starr observed, 'She's an angel,' Cooper retorted, 'She's fucking gonna be, if this soup's cold!' When she was at a loose end there was the charity work for her Masonic lodge and for the Grand Order of Lady Ratlings to keep her occupied. For a short period she involved herself in the running of the magic and joke shop in Shaftesbury Avenue and in the late Fifties became responsible for displaying a most unusual exhibit at venues like the Festival Gardens at Battersea and the Schoolboys' Own Exhibition at Olympia. This was a Victorian living room in which the furniture was entirely decorated with stamps, the pictures on the wall were made completely from stamps and all other ornaments and fittings were covered with them. It had been the life's work of the musical clown, Albert Schaffer, for the benefit of whose widow the Coopers hoped to raise money. Gwen told the press, 'The paintings look like oil paintings, they're so lifelike. In one picture Mr Schaffer sent all over the world for a stamp to cast a shadow on a flower in a wood.' Cooper had started out wanting to buy some musical instruments that Schaffer had used in his act. His own schoolboy enthusiasm was carried away when he discovered what else was on offer. Pathé Pictorial had a field day: 'Imagine having to lick all those stamps – you'd want a constant water supply.' Cut to shot of comedian with tap stuck to his forehead! As the Coopers lined up together to publicize the eccentric venture for the press, all seemed right with the world.

However, there is always a price to pay for success and Tommy was eventually seduced by the affluence it brought him. Friends and relatives concede that Gwen always enjoyed her tipple. The same was not always true of her husband. His pals from the early days playing the nightclubs and variety houses in and around London testify that it was difficult to get him to succumb to half a pint of light ale between performances on a Friday night. However, he did once confide to Edwin Hooper, the boss of Supreme Magic, that his big ambition when he started in show business had always been to reach that stage where he could afford to sit back and relax after a show with a glass of champagne in one hand and a good cigar in the other. One wishes the money had been invested elsewhere. Eventually Cooper's drinking habits would have devastating effects on his home life and came close at times to ruining his career and his sublime comical skills.

The comedian who takes refuge in drink to allay the pressures of his work has become a biographical cliché, with Tony Hancock, Marty Feldman, and Peter Cook providing cautionary tales among recent British comic heroes. No one can deny that Cooper himself did not face similar pressures. The uncertainty that an audience may or may not find you funny on any one night, in any one town is an occupational hazard for the stand up comedian. No one summed it up better than veteran comic, Ted Ray when he explained to magician, Patrick Page what it meant to sign a contract as a comedian: 'What you are doing, in effect, is saying to a future employer, that sometime next year, at a given date, time and place, *you will be funny*. It doesn't matter what happens between now and then. You can be ill, broke, lose everything you have ever held dear. On that night you *have* to make them laugh, because you have signed a contract that says so.'

Tommy knew within his bones that no one ever forgave mediocrity in a comedian and faced up to the challenge of his own particular situation. He once confided to Eric Sykes, 'People say I've only got to walk out on stage and they laugh. If only they knew what it takes to walk out on stage in the first place. One of these days I'll just walk out and do nothing. Then they'll know the difference.' His daughter vouches for the fact that he was a nervous performer, becoming more and more hyper as the curtain call approached, terrified he wasn't good enough, his stomach all knotted up inside. He once told her, 'People don't know real fear until they've stood in the wings night after night.' Hard as it is to believe, there was one occasion towards the end of his career when he went five minutes before raising a decent laugh. The venue was the Walthamstow Assembly Hall. Peter Hudson had done a warm-up spot ahead of him and died the death. As he came off, Tommy asked what they were like. 'A bit sticky', Peter replied. As the silence persisted in Cooper's own act, he walked towards Hudson in the wings and whispered, 'Is it time to come off yet?' He then ambled back to the centre and for Peter's benefit muttered – with the trademark shrug that did service for a thousand words – 'Sticky?' He brought them round in the end. He never took any audience for granted.

As Eric Sykes has said, 'Comedy is a thing that everybody thinks they can do, but they can't – any more than they can balance those twelve teacups on a cane.' However, I refuse to believe that in the beginning Cooper resorted to alcohol as Dutch courage to get him 'onto that stage'. He drank because he was successful. He had not done so in the earlier years of his career simply because he could not afford to do so. Now – beyond his wildest expectations – he could. Sadly in due course what began as a well-earned luxury with which to wind down after a show became the crutch that helped him through the challenge not only of pitting his wits against the world but of reproducing the highs he knew he was capable of. Michael Parkinson recalls working with Tommy on board a dry ship where the strongest drink served was Coca-Cola. There was much agitation among the crew when Cooper requested a bottle of brandy. They asked Parkinson for his advice. He replied, 'It's not a problem. You give him the bottle or he doesn't go on. It's as simple as that. That's how he works.' It had come to that.

Aspects of his eventual dependency have farcical overtones. Vicky recalls his habit for hiding things: a general tendency to secrecy is a recognized trait of the alcoholic. After his death they found money and pills in the most unlikely places: 'My mother once found a cheese sandwich under his pillow.' According to Barry Cryer, there was the breakfast-time at a Bournemouth hotel when he demanded a large gin and tonic with his cornflakes. Television had produced a culture shock to his system with its early starts and this was the only way Tommy could face the day of location filming that loomed ahead of him. The poor waitress remonstrated, but Tommy pulled rank claiming the manager was a friend. He then poured the booze all over the cereal with the comment that it was far better for him: 'Milk is full of cholesterol!' One day Royston Mayoh had his film cameraman, Teddy Adcock, who was passing through Chiswick, deliver a script by hand to the house. Gwen answered the door and immediately went into overdrive: 'Right – bring him in, throw him on the couch and fuck off!' She thought Adcock was a hire car driver deputed to bring home her husband the worse for wear. Thankfully, in view of his problem, Cooper was himself a reluctant driver, travelling by train whenever he could, occasionally with a chauffeur bringing up the rear with his props by road. A favourite joke went, 'I was driving home the other week and a policeman stopped me. He said, "Is this car licensed?" I said, "Yes, constable. What would you like? A gin and tonic?" The gag concealed a daunting reality. Brandishing a bottle of brandy he was once overheard asking a Chatham taxi-driver, 'Have I got enough to get me to Chiswick?'

And yet in the world of television I have yet to meet anyone who saw him drunk. Peter Reeves recalls that when making the series for Paradine at the beginning of 1970 he did manage to forego drinking on the day of the show. This had something of an adverse effect. As Peter perceived things, 'He was starting to dry out during this time. He would sweat profusely and energy would be diverted from the performance itself.' The only time Cooper fell out with Peter Hudson was on the matter. During one of their many seasons together the comedy impressionist tried desperately to lure Tommy onto lager. He thought he had succeeded, until he noticed that no sooner was his glass half empty than he was topping it up with gin. When he begged him to stop, he flew back at Peter with an uncharacteristic 'I'm the star of this show. I'll drink if I want.' The eyes would be glazed, the energy lowered, but he never appeared inebriated as such.

I shall never forget the occasion one afternoon at Ken Brooke's magic studio in Soho in the mid-Seventies when Tommy strolled in carrying a sturdy black leather pilot's bag. He lowered himself into an armchair, opened the case and began to extract several small tot glasses followed by a series of bottles of fascinatingly different colours. I recall green chartreuse, yellow advocaat, in addition to gin, scotch, brandy, and other liqueurs and spirits. Then with concentration and precision, for all the world as if he were performing a magic trick, he began to pour small measures into the glasses, mixing two at a time, then three, sipping them all the while. Several minutes went by before he volunteered any sort of explanation to those present: 'You have to keep experimenting to get any sort of taste.' One drew the conclusion that his taste buds had burst like bubbles long ago. He kept up the ritual, sipping first this concoction and then that, all afternoon. No one needed telling that the 'taste' was immaterial. The liquid had the same effect regardless. Even in the last years of his life, when he did try considerably to limit his alcohol intake – and with some success as his later television performances reveal – you always knew that the black coffee was likely to be laced with whisky and that the principal purpose of the bottle of milk in the dressing room was to line the stomach in preparation for the bottle of brandy lurking not far away in the recesses of yet another plastic career bag.

Tommy's general health did not improve the situation. In many respects he was a hypochondriac, although Eric Sykes makes the fair point that had he been one he would have taken better care of himself. Nevertheless the fascination with doctor jokes might suggest otherwise and there wasn't a patent medicine that he didn't buy at some time or another. Gwen would joke that if she gave one of their dogs a worming tablet, Tommy would want one too. He did for a while become fixated about his weight and would leave home sheepishly clutching a carrier bag, according to his daughter the sign that he was on his way to Cass's, the chemist's shop in Brewer Street where in those days slimming pills could be acquired only under the counter. When he began mixing them with the tablets he took for his insomnia – never mind the drink – you had a fairly lethal cocktail.

In reality most of his ailments were far from imaginary and at all levels where health was concerned he was his own worst enemy. He could never be persuaded to adjust the erratic demands of his working schedule to the need for eating and sleeping properly, staying up into the early hours practising his magic tricks even when he was not engaged in theatrical work. His daughter recalls how he would make a joke of his chronic indigestion, jumping up and down after a dose of milk of magnesia because he forgot to shake the bottle. His general sense of wellbeing was also clouded from the early Fifties by recurring bouts of lumbago and sciatica, a situation only relieved by acupuncture – a cure he kept from his doctor like a guilty secret – in the early Seventies. Bronchitis and a constantly recurring bad throat did not help matters. At the beginning of 1965 there was a minor heart scare, but Tommy insisted upon continuing with his pantomime at Golders Green, in spite of medical advice that intimated otherwise. It was a mark of his professionalism, though not necessarily his common sense, that he would always go on stage when he could. A short while later, his mother wrote to him from Southampton: 'I hope this will find you much better. You are like me, Tommy. You haven't time to be ill, but sometimes we have to find time.'

In 1968 surgery for his varicose veins, a problem left painfully dormant from his army days, was postponed from before his Blackpool season until afterwards, The reason for the delay was summed up by Gwen in a telephone call to Miff: 'He's a coward.' Ferrie, who had to disentangle the arrangements and put them back together again, was not best pleased, although he always conceded the benefit of the doubt to Tommy on all health issues. 'Your health is always the most important thing,' was the constant mantra throughout the calls and letters that passed between them. When the matter of the veins was at last attended to, a period of convalescence was called for. Las Vegas beckoned; it was not the destination most conducive to a speedy recovery from such a procedure. The following year phlebitis set in and continued to cause him problems until the end of his days. When in 1970 a broken toe briefly incapacitated him while appearing in a summer show at Torquay, he did not endear himself to impresario Bernard Delfont by spending the evenings when he should have been resting attending the show at a rival theatre in Babbacombe, where he was mobbed by autograph hunters. Towards the end of his life he was visited in hospital by his friend, Peter Hudson. 'What's wrong?' asked Peter. 'My blood pressure. It's a little on the high side.' It was actually a hundred and seventy-five degrees. Patient kept visitor entertained with magic tricks for two hours and had him crying with laughter throughout. As he departed, Tommy called after him, 'You won't forget my Guinness, will you?' He discharged himself within a couple of days.

When it comes to lifting the spirit and alleviating pain, alcohol may be said to have its own medicinal properties. Cooper subscribed to the view and Mary Kay has admitted as such: 'I did feel drink helped him to forget his physical problems and to sustain him.' He used to joke in his act: 'I drink only for medicinal purposes. I'm sick of being sober. Look – bottle, glass – glass, bottle!' But it was a vicious spiral. The big tragedy of the latter half of his working career is that all his other ailments provided the misdirection for his alcoholism, the one predicament that was never properly diagnosed in isolation and therefore never treated. His doctor first explained to Miff that something might be amiss on 7 May 1969: 'Dr Jacobs examined T.C. Sunday, but he still has to take urine test. Says he thinks he is drinking too much.' Gwen, for all her hysteria and the calls to Miff that he was unwell – often contradicted by Tommy who turned up for the show regardless – never received, and would never have recognized, a formal diagnosis of his actual condition. Miff, perhaps understandably in light of the fragile nature of his business relationship with the Coopers, never showed the insight, the courage or the sympathy to grasp the nettle of a cure. Barry Humphries towers above the international comedy scene today only because at a similar stage in his life he was told by the medical profession that if he continued drinking he had only six weeks to live.

The telephone journals maintained by Ferrie throughout his long association with Tommy provide a painful glimpse of a marriage at times seemingly near to breaking point as a result of Cooper's capacity for liquor. There was always something about his profile that recalled Mr Punch, but while in the context of the rambunctious anti-hero of the puppet world we expect belligerence and jocosity to go hand in hand, in reality it is a disappointment to discover the darker side obtruding into the make-up of the flesh and blood icon. It resonates with what for myself has always been the most disquieting moment in the whole Cooper canon. On the occasion of the Variety Club luncheon to celebrate his thirty years in show business in March 1977, he had hardly begun his speech when Gwen, pre-rehearsed, tugged at his side. 'What?' asked Cooper. 'You've got to put your fez on,' said his wife. 'Not yet. Not yet.' He then delivered the line I have always found disconcerting: 'I told you to wait in the truck, didn't I?' It is said without a smile, almost with vindictiveness. Of course, the situation, the attitude made it funny. Gwen smiled demurely and everyone present was helpless with laughter. However, in retrospect it is hard not to see – just once – a fleeting glimmer of a bully behind the jutting chin and sombre eyes, the nastiness of the true Punchinello coming to the surface. He could have been beating Judy with a stick. For a fleeting moment we had come light years from the performer who was best advised not to punch a teddy bear in his act because it rang untrue with what was perceived as his basic nature. Two and a half years earlier on an episode of *The Tommy Cooper Hour* for Thames he had prefaced his one-man version of Dr Jekyll and Mr Hyde with the following words, taking a mickey-taking sideswipe at his scriptwriter in the process: 'Now you know it's the story of a man who takes to drink and he turns ugly and nasty – (and then as an aside) you know what I mean, Dick?' To the best of my knowledge Dick Hills never had an alcohol problem. Cooper was well in the throes of his at the time.

In April 1969 Gwen made the first of several calls of desperation to Miff, telling him he was the first to know she was leaving her husband because he had 'struck her in front of the children'. It marked the beginning of a decade of domestic rows that coincided with the period of his acknowledged success as a public figure. In fairness to Cooper we have only his wife's account of the situation. Alan Alan has observed that they could *both* become very aggressive in their cups, to which son, Thomas added, 'He hated any trouble with mum. She was more than a match for him. They had some colossal fights and dad would spend all his time ducking.' Notwithstanding, a second plea came in March 1973, again telling Ferrie he was the first to know. Miff chronicled the call: 'She is divorcing Tommy. Can't stand it any more. He keeps beating her up. Last time was on their anniversary. He drinks all the time. Buys bottles of spirits like anyone else buys beer. Would I have a word with him? I spoke to T.C. who said she must be drunk!' It would be farcical if it weren't so tragic. Within forty minutes she has rung Miff back: 'When she said T.C. buys bottles of spirits like another buys beer, did I not say that that was his problem? Would I tell this to T.C?'

Three years later on 28 March the same pattern was repeated. The phrase used this time around was 'legal separation'. She stressed she could not stand being knocked about any more and added, rather optimistically, 'There will be no publicity – just a legal separation – I do not wish to harm his career.' A longer exchange took place six months later on 28 November 1976, when Miff wrote: 'I had better speak to Tommy. She has had enough. Can't get any sleep. He drinks all the time. He sits at dressing room table drinking whisky all night. He gets violent when drunk. Just a pissing bastard. Goes to bed at 5.00 a.m. then goes downstairs to kitchen and starts drinking again. She smashed a chair at him. She has had more than enough. Is going to phone all the national papers tomorrow and tell them. She sounded quite hysterical. Then T.C. came on the other extension. I suggested he phoned me later. He said there was a bit of exaggeration on her part, but would phone me later.' He does not appear to have done so. Miff speaks to Gwen again first: 'Has had a word with Tommy and has come to an understanding. If he gets to bed in good time instead of staying up all night she will give him one more chance. But if not, she will throw the book at him.'

It would not come to that. Within a few months he would receive his biggest health scare yet and the domestic violence would not obviously occur again. When he suffered a heart attack prior to a show for business executives in Rome in April 1977, Gwen immediately flew to Italy to be beside her husband. There were no further pleas of help to disturb Miff's Sundays, but the basic problem did not go away. The Rome episode served only to cloud the issue of the drink dependency, with Gwen in total denial about this aspect of her husband's predicament. The Italian hospital report had specified chronic alcoholism as a contributing cause. Almost a year later on 15 March 1978 Miff called her with a doctor's report following another examination: 'She didn't believe me at first. Said there was nothing wrong with his liver.' Another significant phone call came on 1 December. Tommy had collapsed the night before after a show and could not work that evening. Since Rome ill health had already triggered a spate of cancelled bookings: 'Going to sue every one who says her husband is faking illness. Could not understand what was wrong with T.C. It could be the effect of giving up smoking!'

Interestingly, throughout the decade – that of her husband's greatest success – Gwen loved giving interviews to the press and made no secret of the fact that they both had flaming tempers and that when they rowed you could expect to see sparks emerging from the chimney: 'We fight. I throw things and he throws them back. But we often end up laughing.' She was too down-to-earth a person to draw a veil over the situation, but it always emerged as so much water under the domestic bridge, with never a hint of the uglier side attached. It might have been so much domestic slapstick. On one occasion she was not above a joke: 'When we wake up, no matter what – even if we've had a row and had our backs together not speaking for the night – we always have a cuddle. So that's the way we are. Tommy might smash the furniture around a bit – that's why we haven't got any matching chairs – but it's all forgotten the next day.' At another time she explained, 'I threaten to leave him but he's like an old pair of slippers. I've got used to him. We've had a marvellous life and we still kill ourselves laughing.'

For a while Sunday lunch at a favourite restaurant in Brighton was a popular ritual. There was the occasion the day began with a blazing row and Gwen jumped in the car and drove down to the coast by herself. She was halfway through her meal when a taxi arrived outside. Tommy emerged and walked in wearing only his trousers. He went up to his wife and asked, 'Where's my shirt?' Both enjoyed telling of an incident that occurred a short while after they were given a most unusual present, a painting of Big Ben with a music box mechanism attached. Tommy arrived home late from playing golf, ruining another meal in the process. Who threw what at whom is unimportant. The missile ricocheted off its target and landed on the picture, which promptly crashed to the floor and started to play the tune of 'Home Sweet Home'. In time, from one interview to another, the story became a talisman with which to shield the unhappier aspects of their marriage.

Couples make up. Tommy bought his wife flowers and, acknowledging her birthstone, opal rings and brooches galore and from the levity of her tone in the press, it is not difficult to see why Miff might not have taken matters more seriously. Besides, surely no one knew her husband better than Gwen. He was a great big bruin of a man – a cuddlesome bundle of talent and fun for whom no one had a bad word. As she said, 'he was the nicest, kindest – and most awkward man in the world.' Their friends of many years, Janet and Jimmy Farrow, stress that there wasn't an aggressive bone in his body. He was not intrinsically a wife-beater or a negligent husband. A publicity still to publicize the 1974 Christmas television show depicts a picture of seeming domestic bliss with an all-smiling Tommy, his fez replaced by chef's hat, having commandeered the stirring of the pudding and a bespectacled Gwen giggling close to her husband's side with cookbook in hand. It is the cheery stuff of festive celebration, but nevertheless we are back in the world of Punch and Judy. The wooden spoon is the largest you have seen. It is not too much to imagine the mood shifting and Punch using it to clout Judy over the head with a cry of 'That's the way to do it!' which, when all is said and done, is only a scarier variant of 'Just like that!'

The fact remains that had his problem been treated, he would have lived longer. In spite of the long telephone chats discussing his client with Gwen when she was in a less hysterical mood, Miff failed to interpret the more erratic extremes of Tommy's behaviour towards him as a cry for help. At times they bordered on the unlawful. A typical episode occurred in the early hours of 19 February 1970 when a series of four 'drunk and abusive' calls from Cooper to the Ferrie household was stopped when Miff's wife switched over to their answering service. The following morning Miff recorded the outcome: 'The operator, who was most tactful, said T.C. phoned about a dozen times during the night using different names, e.g. Police Sergeant Grey.' If ever evidence was needed of the strain he was under as a result of the Paradine fiasco, here it was.

On 20 November 1974 – around the time of the pudding stirring – a series of 'rude and abrupt' messages purporting to be by an Inspector John Smith [*sic*] from Scotland Yard with news that Miff's London flat had been burgled came through in the early hours and might suggest a mind even more seriously deranged. The calls were a hoax and there is nothing on record to say that Tommy was responsible for them, but the conclusions are obvious. Miff decided against the police following through with the matter. Only a few days before Ferrie had written to Cooper to complain of his telephone manner in recent weeks: 'I must advise you that such foul-mouthed abusive language cannot be tolerated any further . . . because of your insulting behaviour conduct of our business is becoming increasingly more difficult . . . I am prepared to meet you either here or at your own home, providing you will agree to conduct yourself in a civil and rational manner.' The person who came closest to the nub of the situation was Miff's wife,

Beatrice, who found herself contending with him on the telephone around the time of the hoax. Her husband recorded the conversation: 'T.C. came on line and sounded drunk. He asked, "Is that you, Beatrice? Are you still sick? You've been sick for thirty years!" Beatrice said, "I think you need treatment.' He said, "Where is your stupid idiot of a husband?" Beatrice said, "My husband is here in the house, but does not wish to speak to you." He said, "Tell him I never want to speak to him again." Beatrice said, "Well, why keep calling him?" T.C. put phone down.'

The whole situation had been complicated in January 1967 by the arrival on the scene of Mary Kay. They first met in a church hall used by Thames as a rehearsal space somewhere beneath the Hammersmith flyover. As the structure of British show business changed with the club boom, Tommy found himself travelling more and more. Never did he have a greater need for Gwen by his side, but she decided not to accompany him, torn between her husband and the attention parental duty demanded she pay their two teenage children at home. Vicky recalls the tears and distress this caused her father in the private moments they shared together. With all thoughts of romance aside, Mary, a divorcée with a respected background in stage management for both theatre and television, was an obvious candidate to step into the breach of a travelling factotum. Before long, however, Tommy found himself in the not unprecedented position of loving two women. Those who saw him together with Mary will testify to the fact that they were a devoted couple. As Royston Mayoh has said, 'They loved each other. Mary provided something that Gwen didn't.' His words carry far more than a sexual connotation: 'She fell flatly in love with him in the same way that you and I had. She knew that if ever a human being required someone to bring order into his life, he did. She didn't "Svengali" him. She made it easy for him.' I am certain that he lived longer because of her presence and attention, but it is also conceivable that had she not figured in his life he would – in time – not have subjected himself to the ordeal of touring so much. He quite obviously relished the excuse his work gave him to be with her.

Even Mary failed when it came to pulling him back from the abyss of alcohol. Her argument in response has a chilling truth: 'Anyone who knew Tommy well would agree that I had very little chance of changing his habits.' Sadly she too failed to interpret the signs of his schizoid rages, like the time in a Derby restaurant he flung her to the floor when she laughed at his complaint that the crackling with his roast pork was soggy; the time when in some kerfuffle about luggage he ripped apart the seam of an expensive new dress that he had just bought her; the time she was anxious about keeping an appointment and he tore another gift, an expensive watch, off her wrist and threw it across the room. The ogre soon mollified, but always lurked in the distance. The most telling line is Kay's memoir reads, 'Brandy, I noticed, didn't bring out the best in people.'

When Gwen found out about the affair, supposedly after his death, she dismissed it as a mere slip on her husband's part, a casual one-night-stand and nothing more. One will never know whether she did know beforehand. There had been a loud tabloid whisper in 1975 when the *Daily Express* ran a story about Tommy Cooper having a mistress. It was categorically denied. Mary was his 'assistant' and no more. But there must have been times when his wife suspected that her husband's attentions might have strayed elsewhere. One Monday in March 1973 she made an anguished call to Miff at one o'clock in the morning to advise that he had not been home that Sunday, the 'first time in twenty-six years'. It is a fact that the more he travelled with Mary in tow, the more he came to appreciate the home away from home she provided for him on the road. The lifestyle came with a freedom attached, even if at times the caravan did resemble a small circus. His son Thomas, well within the secret in later years as his father's occasional stage manager, confided to her two years before his death, 'Mary, if you ever leave Dad, it will be the death of him.'

Reading between the lines of a newspaper interview Gwen gave at the time of the *Express* story, one has difficulty differentiating between suspicion and gross naivety: 'Even now Tommy books a double room when he's on tour just in case I turn up. We love each other so much. Mind you, I'm fifty-five and I know I couldn't compete with beautiful twenty-year-old showgirls. Some are so star-struck they would do anything to get at men like Tommy. So what can I do? I've got to be wise. I'd realize he'd rather come home for a good steak anyway!' What she did not realize is that her husband had fallen for a lady who was much closer to her own age and was prepared to travel around with a camping stove and kitchen utensils to cook him that steak at three o'clock in the morning in hotel suites and dressing rooms wherever they might be on the road. Mary was never an ego-boost. She was a pillar of support during some of the emptiest times of his life. Vicky has said, 'The thing is my dad hated his own company and he was an insomniac. My mother simply got fed up with the hours he kept and eventually stopped going on tour with him. But he desperately needed someone to look after him.' Following the emotional neglect of his mother at an early age, he had always needed love and attention. Mary now provided that all over again, as Dove had once done.

As seems inevitable when Cooper is concerned, farce intrudes. According to Peter Hudson, one morning Tommy was sitting up in bed when Gwen entered the room angrily brandishing a hotel invoice just delivered by the postman. It was made out to Mr and Mrs Cooper. 'What's this? What's this?' she demanded. 'What's what?' asked Tommy. 'This bill.' 'I was on my own.' 'You bastard!' 'I was on my own. They've got it wrong.' Gwen slammed the door and Tommy thought quickly. He pulled on his street clothes over his pyjamas and leaving the house by the side door made a dash to the nearest phone box. He called the manager of the hotel and asked him to resend the bill, even better to phone his home in half an hour and apologize for the mistake they had made. Nobody denied Tommy Cooper a favour. He rushed back home and back to bed. A short while later the phone rang. Dove answered. A few minutes later she came back upstairs all smiles. They had sent Tommy the wrong bill. There had been a Mr and Mrs Cooper staying at the hotel at the same time and there had been a mix-up in accounts. She told Tommy she had explained to the manager on the phone, 'That's just like him not to pay it!'

He would never have dreamed of trading the one woman in his life for the other. His constant love for Gwen and the need to protect his public image as a family entertainer at a time when such things mattered – witness the pudding stirring again – drew him into a nightmare of deceit of which the hotel bill incident was a petty detail. If you worked with Cooper, the paranoia was obvious. Everyone was taken into his confidence as added security: 'Promise you'll never mention Mary when Dove's around.' In his daughter's opinion the pressure of hiding the relationship must have been relentless: 'He was a traditional man and didn't want to hurt Dove. Personally I thought it fairly harmless, although keeping it a secret was a strain.' Drink was one way of dealing with the guilt of the situation.

Although his performances on screen offered no clue of a

tortured soul, it is not difficult to imagine the maelstrom stirring within Cooper's mind as the affair accelerated. Apart from the pressures of having to shield his infidelity, there was the accumulated stress caused by the spate of impersonators threatening to devalue the impact of his act, the uncertainty of the new direction in which British show business was heading for an entertainer of his kind, the constant emotional tug-of-war that constituted his relationship with his agent and manager, the encroachment of advancing years – on his fiftieth birthday he bemoaned to Mary Kay, 'I'm dying slowly now. It's all downhill from here' – the strain of stardom on a man who genuinely did not appreciate how big a star he was and the perplexity of why people found him funny at times when he had no intention of being so. Jimmy Tarbuck tells of the occasion they were at the nineteenth hole at Sudbury: 'He said, "I'll have a gin and tonic," and the fellow behind the bar started to laugh. Tommy went, "What are you laughing at? Don't you laugh at me!" I said, "Tom, he loves you." "I'll bloody love him, laughing at me." He was genuinely upset.' The lack of sympathy that came his way when he broke a toe or an ankle – as happened when he fell *upstairs* on a visit to a submarine on holiday in Gibraltar in 1976 – did not help matters: whenever he had to hobble about it looked like part of the act and people laughed even more. Of the latter incident he did have the caution to comment: 'And that was before I even got to the bar.' In fact, drink was the inevitable escape from a ghost train ride along which all these pressures constituted individual horrors.

When his daughter discovered her father was having an affair, she confronted him with it. After a first denial, his subsequent admission put into perspective much that she would otherwise have found strange about his subsequent lifestyle under the influence of Mary Kay. He became more and more depressed at home, distracted by things like biorhythms. Vicky explains that 'he bought this compass and I would read it for him. "This week you are feeling good," I would say. "Oh, am I? That's good," he'd reply.' There was a spell when he would pay her five pounds a month to chart out his moods. Like golf and the idea of installing a sauna at home – to save on slimming tablets – it appears to have been a passing phase. She still finds it hard to accept that he believed in fairies and goblins 'for heaven's sake!' but it was always difficult to know when he was being serious or not. In a radio interview in Bahrain the year before he died he professed to a conviction in astrology: 'I read the horoscopes and I pick the best one – always my own – from different papers.' In the same interview he even professed to a ghost in the house: 'Sometimes when I look through the hatch I can see a shadow go past and many times when I'm sitting in the lounge I hear someone coming down the stairs in one of those dresses that ruffle. Chiffon?' 'Taffeta.' 'Yes – and I can hear it coming down the stairs right to the last door and sometimes I say, "Come in," and there's no one there.' 'Are you frightened?' 'No, not at all.' None of this behaviour is too far removed from the irrational super-stition of a man who always made sure he put his fez down with the open side upwards – 'to let the bad air out' – and demanded that anyone who whistled in his dressing room leave, turn round three times in the corridor and then knock three times before coming back in. In fairness it was done only to protect the performance and ensure the working of a magic that not even he could understand.

Tommy used to joke of his wife that she always stood by his side: 'Well, we have only one chair in the house!' The unassailable fact of his life is that he needed her. In domestic violence the perpetrator is as much the victim as the one who suffers physically, the casualty not least of the resulting loss of self-esteem. Perhaps Gwen sensed this intuitively. Dove was both suburban housewife and Mother Courage. Bob Monkhouse knew them both well: 'I think Dove was probably a lady who had to endure much. Tommy was a child with an infant's rage, as many waiters will tell you. But he was fundamentally a lovely man. And he just adored tricks and jokes. He never tired of being funny, though I think he never understood why he was funny.' Had he done so, life might have been easier and eventually less reliant on alcohol. There can be no doubt that she responded to the child as much as to the adult in him. Nor can there be any doubt that he cared for her. Anyone who witnessed, as I did, his tearful anguish and concern at the time when Dove herself was critically ill, would have recognized that love, although it would come as no surprise to learn that the flowers he sent her on that occasion squirted water in her face when she went to take in their perfume.

TWELVE

The Days Dwindle Down

Professionally Cooper embarked on the Seventies with every
assurance in the world. Give or take the odd royal and the
occasional politician he was arguably the most recognizable
figure in the land. The London Palladium beckoned, the clubs
promised a cornucopia of riches that had been unimagi-
nable a few years before and he was the comedian who most
readily found himself on the tips of people's tongues when
jokes and catchphrases entered the conversation. In September
1975 the *Sunday Mirror* received ten thousand entries for its
Tommy Cooper joke competition. Peter Black wrote in the
Daily Mail: 'If you conducted a really thorough nationwide
enquiry you might find somebody who doesn't like him. I
never have and would be interested to hear from one. It must
be pleasant to be the best-liked man in Britain.' The word
'pleasant' strikes a discordant note. Such a reputation presented its own additional strain on top of those already catalogued. In reality the ill-discipline that became a by-product
of his health problems as the Seventies progressed gave more
than a handful of people cause not to like him at all, his
manner and conduct making life more than a little difficult

for those who tended the golden goose that was the club circuit.

From February 1974 drinking began sadly to make occasional inroads on his professionalism. Cooper's only defence was out-and-out denial, spinning a web of distrust between him and Miff Ferrie that only exacerbated the strained relations between them. One club-owner complained of his behaviour backstage: 'He is not the easiest fellow in the world to get along with. He was complaining about the heater in his dressing room, but he would not let the electrician into the room to switch it on. He stayed at the club till 7.00 a.m. drinking, and it's been like that most nights of the week.' Cooper put the flu that kept him from working the following evening down to the lack of heating; the doctor claimed he'd be able to go on the night after that if only he'd get some rest. Tommy reported the situation to Gwen and used her as the messenger to Ferrie: 'Tommy denies he was up till seven o'clock. He thinks it is a diabolical lie and she is going to sue them.' Solicitors representing the club – Allinson's in Litherland on Merseyside – pre-empted her, complaining of Cooper's inability to appear on time in addition to the night he did not appear at all. Eventually the matter was resolved without matters reaching the courts, Cooper foregoing a quarter of his £5,000.00 fee for the full week. He would not play Allinson's again.

He did no more to endear himself to the management at his next engagement, the Talk of the South in Southend. The report to Ferrie by telephone wasted no words. Miff recorded, 'Drunk, etc. One night did only five minutes and walked off.' Three hours later the performer came on the line himself in an attempt to explain. Miff recalls that he was clearly intoxicated: 'Could hardly speak. Wanted to tell me there was a bit of trouble at the Talk of the South and that I may be hearing from the manager. I asked him which night and he said he was not sure whether it was Thursday, Friday, or Saturday. He did not remember. I said, "You know where you are tomorrow?" He said, "Birmingham". I said, "No. It's Sheffield Fiesta."'

The following October, the day after his opening at the Cavendish Club, Blackburn, Tommy beat the management to the phone. The tone of the message hints at the tail he was hiding between his legs: 'Bit of a mishap – lack of props – cabaret at 10.30 – he was ready to go on – they said 11.00 – went on at 11.30. Manager came round and said there had been complaints that he didn't do long enough.' Less than an hour later his dresser rang Miff, presumably on Cooper's instructions, to stress that he had gone on at 11.30 and did not come off until 12.15. Before the afternoon was out, Eve Colling, the booking agent for the Cavendish had followed through with the official line, so surreal it has to be true: 'T.C. arrived at 10.20 and was not ready to go on because of some lack of props. Eventually went on at 11.30 for 10 minutes – came off – then on again for five minutes – then off for five more minutes – then on and finished his act – in all a total of approximately thirty-five minutes.' She added that some people had complained and were given free tickets for the next show.

Miff wasted little time in dashing off an admonitory note to his client: 'I should just like to reiterate here that it is most important that you adhere strictly to the times of performance as per contract so as not to give any would-be "knockers" the slightest opportunity to open their mouths.' He would never cure Cooper's latterly unpunctual ways and it is fortunate that more than a few managements were prepared to be tolerant, ready to take the unpredictability in their stride. Bob Potter of Lakeside Country Club remembers Tommy as the hardest of all performers to get on stage, recalling how he would lock himself into the dressing room before a show and not come out until he was ready, sometimes leaving the band to fill in for three quarters of an hour before he appeared. When he did emerge he'd say, 'What are we waiting for? Let's get on with it!' as if they had been holding *him* up. As Potter said, 'He gets away with it – just because he's so popular.' Years before Al Jolson had toyed with his audience's patience in a similar way, sometimes deliberately leaving them waiting for an hour before he arrived on stage, often giving an unfinished meal as his excuse. But in his case the ploy was a calculated sounding board for his own ego; he would proceed to make-up on stage and invariably had them shouting for more two hours later. At an earlier stage of his career Cooper would have applauded the entertainer's bravado while decrying his lack of profession- alism. Had he been able to see himself objectively at these times when he let down so many people – himself included – he would have been appalled that in his own case bravado, a quality that he had in greater abundance than any British comic, had no part in the equation.

It is hard to reconcile such behaviour on Cooper's part with this period of his greatest prestige and visibility in television terms, given the high profile that accompanied his return to Thames only the previous year after the prolonged absence following the Paradine episode. Mercifully, the club circuit was a provincial phenomenon that did not attract attention in the national press and Fleet Street failed to pick up on local copy that could have made headlines for them had it been so disposed. Occasional mention was made of audiences chant- ing 'Why are we waiting?', their slow hand clap to usher him on stage and his loss of timing once he arrived there. The reporter for the *Blackburn Times* in October 1974 expressed what unfortunately was fast becoming a consensus on the live circuit: 'One felt that for many people some of the glitter surrounding their idol had disappeared.' The most hurtful review of them all appeared in the *Thurrock Gazette* in July 1975: 'Virtually every impressionist in the country "does" Tommy Cooper and after seeing Cooper at the Circus Tavern last week it's my bet that nine out of ten of them do a better job . . . I for one wish I hadn't seen him, for the same reasons that I would avoid seeing Jimmy Greaves play football now. I would rather remember the greats how they really were – and Tommy Cooper on this showing is great no longer.' There can hardly be a more judicious argument for staying away. None of the reports that I have read mentioned, even hinted, why things were as they were. In that one regard they kept faith with the man. In fairness, he was still capable of turning on the magic, as his television shows proved. In truth, the lethal combination of failing health and excessive alcohol was writing the bad reviews for him.

Ferrie's patience was continually strained to the limit. For example, on 11 May 1975, Cooper called the office. Miff reported the exchange: 'T.C. rather drunk sounding – rude – re next week's change of venue, why don't I call him to remind him of dates? More rudeness till I said he should hang up and speak to me again when he was more rational.' The following day Ferrie put pen to paper in a letter to clarify matters: 'Further to the flap on the telephone yesterday, I must place on record the facts re the switch of venue from Slough to Ilford. You were first advised of the switch in my letter of 27 March, which contained a copy of the letter from the Management for your signature, and which you duly signed and returned here. I also reminded you personally on the telephone on 22 April, whilst a letter was sent to you on 7 May further reminding you. What more can one do???' Those last five words with their hat trick of question marks express the impossibility of Ferrie's position, underlined by the revelation spelled out in the subsequent paragraph that a year had passed since performer and manager had been in each other's company, a quite remarkable state of affairs. Miff adds, with what seems like diplomatic understatement in the circumstances, 'This is far too long.' There is nothing to indicate that they came face to face with each other again until the Coopers entertained him to lunch at Chiswick in January 1976.

Cooper always complained that Ferrie treated him like an errant schoolboy. At times he certainly lived up to the part in the way he retaliated. His late appearance on stage on the opening night of his season at Manchester's Golden Garter club in December 1976 brought his unpunctuality back to the top of Ferrie's agenda, when the management threatened to withhold Tommy's first night fee. For a while he entered into a silly game whereby he would get his dresser, his driver, even a friend in the audience to telephone Miff with the time he did go on stage, as if he were expecting to receive coloured stars for good behaviour. It was only ever Tommy's word against that of the managements and when he did concede going on late it was always the fault of the club, which had kept *him* waiting. Inevitably, the versions did not always tally.

Around this time I experienced at first hand the extraordinary hold Ferrie exerted over his client. Towards the end of 1975 the publication by Jupiter Books of a comic autobiography ghosted for Cooper presented an opportunity to feature him on the BBC's *Parkinson* show. Until that point all requests to Miff for his services had fallen on deaf ears, his frequent exclusivity to Thames being the principal objection to his appearing on a BBC programme. However, at the time in question Tommy was between Thames' contracts. He desperately wanted to do the show for Christmas Day transmission, but Miff's response remained categorically, 'No'. It then occurred to Tommy that Miff was going to be out of the country for a cruise for one month, not returning until shortly after Christmas. For Cooper that clinched matters. He was determined to appear on the programme regardless. He would do it while Miff was away. We waited until Ferrie set sail and then held a comprehensive research and production meeting at which the shape of an interview was constructed, special props ordered and every last detail arranged. I then pointed out to Tommy that there was one final outstanding matter, namely that it would be essential for him to sign a contract prior to the appearance.

A further meeting with the magician and his friend and publisher, John Maxwell was arranged. I went along with the official document. I laid it out before Cooper. He took the pen I offered and his hand began to shake. The pen hovered over the page. He could not bring himself to sign. He confessed he could not work like this behind Miff's back. He apologized profusely, almost on the verge of tears. One could not express anger, only disappointment. He did not appear on the show. The man's vulnerability made a lasting impression on me. To experience the Svengali-like hold Ferrie exerted over his client many hundreds of miles away on the high seas was a disconcerting experience. What made the situation even more uncomfortable was the subsequent missive from Ferrie's solicitors received by Bill Cotton, by now the BBC's Head of Light Entertainment, bearing the complaint that the BBC had been 'importuning' his artist in his absence. Cooper's contrition had extended to confessing to Ferrie upon his return. Four years later, with his manager's blessing, Tommy would make an amazingly successful appearance on the same show.

Mary Kay insists that Ferrie had no understanding of the extreme conditions in which Tommy found himself performing as they crisscrossed the length and breadth of the country, intimating that he often went on stage against what would have constituted sound medical advice, however hard she might try to stop him. The telephone conversations between Miff and Mary were never recorded in his journal, but in a letter to the author she has provided an insight from Cooper's point of view: 'Why could I never convince Miff that my interests were with Tommy . . . I would listen to the audience whenever I had the chance to mingle, which wasn't for more than ten minutes in an evening because Tommy wanted me there every time he came off, even for a second to collect a prop or drink some water. I heard lots of remarks, but the ones that worried me most were when they'd say something like, "He's not as good as last time" – when he had a ghastly throat and spent most of the evening trying to clear it – or "Oh! Look he's drunk" – when he did that marvellous trip across the stage. I hated that and eventually he cut it out to prevent comments. I rang the Management several times to cancel a performance. It was not always possible and he has even worked with one leg in plaster . . . we had a great idea of borrowing a big white djellabah for the show. It was a great success and he only made fun of his leg. What the audience didn't know was that he was in such pain – we had to get a taxi to the hospital at three o'clock in the morning to have the plaster changed. We got back to the hotel at 5.30 a.m., had bacon and eggs and a glass of whisky and went to bed. Then people say, "What do you do all day, Tommy?" They always imagined him having a gloriously easy time! It was never as straightforward as that. I sometimes wished dear Miff had understood all this.'

In another letter at the time of Cooper's death she wrote, 'You just don't know the number of times before a show I've said "Please, Tommy, don't drink. I'll be able to see it in your eyes." I have watched him for years and years and sometimes I've had to push him to bed to sleep for an hour before a show wherever we've been.' There can be no doubt of her sincerity or of Cooper's discomfort, even if hers would be a losing struggle come the end. But she was fully aware she was nursing, in her own words, 'a child amongst children,' to whom the best medicine – sufficient sleep and not drinking to excess, if at all – came with a bitter taste and a cataclysmic effect on his eccentric body clock. Miff, who had been a performer on the club and dance band scene of the Thirties and Forties, had fully experienced the lifestyle at first hand and, I am sure, always had Tommy's interests at heart, not least because – cynically speaking – they were his own. But, as has been indicated, when it came to facing up to his alcohol dependency, all three of the adult pillars in his life must be accounted partly responsible, however valiant Mary's own efforts in this regard might have been while they were on the road together.

In retrospect the rumours of Cooper's unreliability that spread through Clubland in the mid Seventies stand as their own metaphor for the decline that had beset the club industry. Before it went into almost total meltdown, it would establish a new more economically viable level on a reduced scale, but for a while agents like Ferrie, who had come to rely on the medium as the chief source of income for their clients, were deeply worried men. During the first few months of 1976 Cooper lost engagements scheduled for the Showboat Club in Cardiff, the Fiesta in Sheffield, the Talk of the Midlands in Derby, as one by one they were declared bankrupt. As the year progressed contracts for Skegness and Chester would be similarly affected. The clubs that did stay in business were becoming slower in paying up, with the result that agents insisted more and more that fees should be paid in advance of the engagement. The precarious spiral this created was not helped by the principal cause of the recession outside of general economic factors, namely the unrealistically high fees being demanded by performers, in some cases out of all proportion to their drawing power. In many ways the clubs had only themselves to blame, having dangled what were tantamount to open cheques to enlist the services of several international headliners in the early days.

Iris Mitchell, the respected booking agent for the Circus Tavern at Purfleet, set forth what amounted to a plea for reality on behalf of the entire industry in a letter to Miff on 3 September 1976: 'May I take this opportunity of saying that I find it impossible to understand the reason artistes put up their fees by such considerable amounts from one engagement to the next when the economic situation in our business is so precarious. Even at existing fees clubs are unable to make a profit. No doubt artistes think when they see clubs reasonably full, they are responsible for attracting in paying customers. I wish that this was the case, but in actual fact yet another amount of money has to be spent on promotions to encourage patrons to visit our clubs on a complimentary ticket basis. Therefore with the high fees some of the artistes, including Tommy Cooper, are demanding, it is no wonder clubs are losing two thousand pounds plus a week. I feel that if all clubs gave stars a true picture of their actual value and drawing capacity, they would hesitate and think again before putting up their fees.' Cooper was not exactly blameless as far as this situation was concerned. But there was always the matter of supply and demand. In June 1976 Tommy received £6,000.00 for his week's engagement at the Tavern. When he next appeared there – one year and one major health scare later – in September 1977, his contract was for £7,000.00. There were hundreds of mohair-suited, joke-telling stand-up comedians, but there was only one Cooper.

It was not all gloom. In June 1976 the London Palladium expressed interest in Cooper's services for an eight week variety season during July and August of the following year. Looking even further ahead, in March 1977 impresario Harold Davidson enquired about the possibility of Tommy opening for Frank Sinatra at the Royal Festival Hall in September 1978. Eventually this fell through, almost certainly when Sinatra came to realize that even he would have a hard job to follow the great comedian on his home ground. The excuse was fudged. Davidson had originally asked for thirty minutes. Sinatra's people then explained that they wanted a shorter act. When Miff pointed out that Cooper was more than amenable to doing less time, the official line came back: 'They do not want anything as elaborate as Tommy Cooper.' A starring season at the Palladium, the natural home of a performer of his kind, would have been more than consolation, but by then other events had, tragically, intervened.

Whatever the excesses of his behaviour on the road, Cooper was well aware that his body was slowing down. In March 1976 he volunteered to Miff that their existing arrangement whereby he worked for two weeks and then had a third in which to recharge his batteries should be commuted to one week on and two weeks out. Eventually a compromise was reached and the pattern established whereby Miff would endeavour to book him for two weeks on and two weeks out, with an added provision for two holiday periods of three weeks during any one year. With such an arrangement no one could genuinely complain that Miff was the hard taskmaster many – Tommy's wife included – have made him out to be. Unfortunately the new pattern had little chance to establish itself before in August a cardiograph revealed a further blip in Cooper's health. Dismissed by Gwen as 'nothing to worry about,' nevertheless it was serious enough for the doctors to stipulate that he had to take things easy and 'should only work 3 nights a week.' The medical report came through in the same week that an embarrassed Iris Mitchell rang Miff to find out what she should do about Tommy's outstanding bar bill from his recent engagement at the Circus Tavern. It amounted to £250.00.

Miff began to listen more carefully to lucrative one-night offers for his client. One such was an invitation to perform in Rome for booking agent Michael Black before a gathering of 950 delegates at an IBM conference at the Rome Hilton on 22 April 1977. Almost twenty years later Michael still agonizes whether – in defiance of the look that said, 'You're not serious, are you?' – he did the right thing by keeping the booze at arm's length from the star before the performance, promise as he did that once the show was over they would go and get pissed on behalf of all the gladiators who had ever stared a lion in the face in the Coliseum. Tommy had complained of feeling unwell earlier in the day and as they stood in the wings the typical agent's humour asserted itself: 'Tommy, you're on in a minute. All you have to do is to walk out there to constitute a contract.' Just as he was about to go on stage, he collapsed in the arms of a stagehand. Michael recalls the scene: 'Suddenly his right leg started to shake and a tremor ran up his body. At first I thought he was doing one of his funny acts and actually laughed, but not for long. He collapsed and began rolling over in agony, fighting for breath. His dentures fell out and he was bleeding from the mouth.' Within ten minutes an Italian doctor arrived who saved his life with a cardiac injection. He was admitted to a private clinic and IBM rushed Gwen to his side by special plane.

The press reported that he had suffered a heart attack. Gwen protested that he had been working far too hard lately, implying that Ferrie had a responsibility in the matter. This became a constant refrain on her part when she was under stress due to her husband's ill health. In actuality, as a result of doctors' advice and the new working pattern, before

departing for Italy he had given a mere thirty-one performances in the 110 days that had passed since the beginning of
the year. No sooner was she installed in the nursing home than
she rang Miff in the early hours to assure him: 'Everyone was
telling her T.C. was dying. Well he is *not*!' Michael Black
reported to the agent more realistically: 'T.C. nearly died. The
doctor said he must not smoke or drink or even smell it.' In
due course the doctor attending him wrote to Ferrie, diagnos-
ing 'a cardio-circulatory attack due to overwork.' Almost certainly – and not unreasonably – he had been listening to Gwen.
The fuller thirty-three page medical report that Cooper forbade Miff to see specifies chronic alcoholism and bronchitis
as attendant causes. He was discharged from the clinic on
4 May, when he returned to London with Gwen half a stone
lighter and with strict instructions not to resume work for a
month.

The special material he had prepared for the delegates was
never delivered: 'They say all roads lead to Rome. I think with
all the traffic you've got here, they must do! I've had a quick
tour – saw the Coliseum – it will be nice when it's finished.'
However, no sooner had he recovered than Tommy had the
heart attack routine all ready for any member of the press who
wanted to use it: 'When I came round the doctor was slapping
my wrists, which isn't easy when they're in the praying position. Anyway, they pumped me full of drugs. I said, "Do I
really have to have all this lot?" "You should be so lucky," he
said. "Those drugs will make you the most popular man in
Rome. Every time you sneeze you'll cure someone."'

The reality was beyond levity. For a considerable time
Cooper had become increasingly difficult to insure. When he
was up and about again, Tommy went out of his way to deny
that he had suffered anything as serious as a heart attack.
Dennis Kirkland admitted, 'He had his own interpretation of

what happened and blamed it on blood pressure. He denied the heart attack strenuously and had a piece of paper to that effect which he waved around. I think it cost him a thousand pounds.' Kirkland must have been referring to a letter from the Cardiac Department of the Charing Cross Hospital dated as late as 30 December, in which the consultant cardiologist informed the interested parties that in his opinion 'it was unlikely that Mr Cooper had had a heart attack when he was in Rome. He certainly had a mild abnormality of his electrocardiogram which is of no special significance and I believe a presumptive diagnosis was made of a heart attack on the basis of a transient loss of consciousness and the finding of a minor abnormality on the electrocardiogram.' To a layman it reads like a medical version of 'Now, you see it – now you don't!' In the absence of 'any evidence of myocardial damage,' it concludes, 'he should not be rated for insurance purposes on the grounds that he has had a past history of myocardial infarction since I think there is considerable doubt that this ever occurred.' Mr Cooper got his insurance.

In the wake of Rome he promised his doctor to give up smoking and to compromise on drinking, later admitting with poignancy bordering on the macabre, 'I never did drink for drinking's sake. It's just to give my hands something to do – like shake!' The trade-off had entailed the abandonment of all spirits in favour of white wine, implying a dereliction of duty by members of the medical profession or the admission that his condition had already teetered over the precipice of non-recovery. A short while after his return he met up with Kirkland in a bar on the King's Road to discuss an appearance on the Thames television show, *London Night Out*. He explained to his friend that he was now allowed a glass of Dubonnet. Three bottles later Dennis commented, 'I thought you were only allowed one glass?' He replied, 'I've only used one glass!'

Kirkland may have been the first person to be given an intimation that something ominous was looming when he called Miff's office a few days before the Rome incident to convey a message from Mary Kay: 'T.C. cannot remember 'Hats' routine.' With grotesque irony on the day of the attack Miff was posting a copy of the original script to Chiswick. It is hard not to see this as a warning sign that something was amiss.

Within a few weeks it was apparently back to business as usual. Cooper recorded the *London Night Out* show for Kirkland on 19 June without incident and the new more lenient working pattern continued. Soon, however, the old drinking habits reasserted themselves, alongside the fractiousness that invariably accompanied them. At the beginning of July Miff took the blame when the transportation of Cooper's props to Ireland for a week's cabaret in Dublin appeared to hit a bureaucratic snag. Ultimately his manager's understanding of procedure proved to be correct, while the hearsay version picked up by Tommy and Gwen in a local pub turned out to be a total fiction. In September Ferrie must have felt a sense of *déjà vu* when he found himself recording a conversation: 'T.C. sounded drunk. Heard his wife say, "Must you always have a glass in your hand?"'

Fortunately, his appearance in the special Royal Variety Gala Performance in honour of the Queen's Silver Jubilee in November was, as we have witnessed, a personal triumph. Maybe this instilled a new sense of confidence and self-respect, enough for Gwen to inform Miff on 23 January 1978 that he had not had a drink since New Year. She may have been correct. In that period Tommy had been resting at home, but for a single cabaret at the London Hilton and another in Leeds. He might have been shocked into abstinence – however temporary – by the clause in his new Non-Appearance Insurance cover that came through in early January, carrying as it did an exclusion clause relating to his being 'in a state of intoxication or whilst suffering from alcoholism directly or indirectly attributable thereto.'

Any attempt at a revised lifestyle did nothing to keep at bay the old spectre of unreliability. According to the management, he kept the audience at the London Hilton waiting for forty minutes, prompting solicitors for the organizers to demand compensation for the loss of 'the pace and atmosphere of a very successful evening to that point,' adding that 'we had the impression, with great regret, that Mr Cooper did not approach the preparation for his performance with sufficient care both as regards his props and, more importantly, timeliness.' Similar complaints followed an engagement at the Holiday Inn, Heathrow a month later. After that Cooper appears to have made an extra effort as far as punctuality was concerned, taking wicked delight in calling Miff late in the evening on arrival at a venue, but more often than not sounding drunk when he did so. By the end of the year his health had suffered further setbacks. In an absurd twist of *volte-face* on behalf of his client, Ferrie found himself writing to all the managements for whom Tommy was booked into the foreseeable future, requesting that his performance time actually be brought forward to 10 o'clock 'on medical grounds'.

An all time professional low was reached during the late summer months of 1978 with the recording for Thames of the television series, *Cooper – Just Like That* from the New London Theatre. As we have seen, the performer transmitted into people's homes was a sad, sluggish shadow of his former self. Kenneth Tynan observed that towards the end of his life the once dynamic Phil Silvers had been so 'slowed down by infirmity that he might have been performing underwater'. At times one longed for Cooper to emerge with snorkel and flippers to make the analogy, which now applied equally to the man in the fez, funny rather than sad. Any viewer would have been surprised at the suggestion that he would ever be offered a series again, let alone bounce back on television with something approaching a new spring in his step. However, there was a moment between the nadir of the New London fiasco and his last series for Thames in 1980, *Cooper's Half Hour*, when he genuinely did start to pull himself together, even if the long-term damage to his health was now done. The tolerance and affection extended to him by the public – give or take those let down at a few of his live shows – were far stronger than the damage one sub-standard series could inflict.

Notwithstanding, the recriminations from managements regarding lateness and sobriety persisted into 1979. What may have been a defining moment in helping to change his ways occurred in March when Miff was telephoned by the representative of Geers Gross Advertising Ltd, for whom Tommy had spent three days making a television commercial for Sodastream immediately after recording the New London series. His performance had been mediocre and inadequate, leading to an almost impossible technical challenge in the editing and a damaging impact on the whole campaign. To bolster the latter, the advertising agency was suggesting a series of local radio advertisements for which they would need the approval of Cooper and Ferrie. It was proposed that they would use 'someone impersonating Tommy Cooper's voice'. Both artist and manager went along with the plan, but, to Cooper, it must have represented the ultimate indignity. In view of Tommy's love–hate feeling on the whole impersonator issue the proposal must have stung like iodine on an open wound, even more so than the episode of the television show, *Who Do You Do?* that, as he used to complain, 'ended with everyone doing an impression of me – including a bleeding emu!', a reference to the aggravating arm-extension of puppeteer, Rod Hull that seemed to crop up everywhere during the Seventies. In the end Russ Abbot did the radio honours for Sodastream.

It is significant that Ferrie should have even contemplated a television commercial for Cooper, having given them a wide berth for the greater part of his career. One important aspect of the wavering pattern of his client's health was the impact it had on his earnings. With the events in Rome and the change in his working pattern the steady climb to the £169,589.00 that he earned in the financial year ending in April 1977 fell away sharply. From that point his earnings became unpredictable and it is to Miff's credit that at a time when the club industry was in recession he maintained for his artist the relatively high levels he did. As Tommy grew older, medical certificates to excuse engagements unfulfilled became almost as natural a part of Ferrie's working routine as contracts and commission notes. For the record, the following are the amounts Cooper earned annually to the end of his life. It is not possible to tell how much he was reimbursed by insurance companies for engagements lost to illness. The sums in brackets represent fees – where available – that he would have received from managements had he appeared: the amounts may still have accrued to him – minus any excess – if the policies were in his favour. There were, of course, many enquiries that had to be declined, interest that in happier times would have evolved into profitable bookings.

1977–8 £116,158 (£23,416)
1978–9 £181,464 (£17,500)
1979–80 £156,500 (£15,500)
1980–1 £159,792 (£6,500)
1981–2 £108,097 (£12,500)
1982–3 £129,306 (£12,000)
1983–4 £117,150 (£31,250)

Throughout his long career there had scarcely been a product in the British shopping basket that had not tried to pin its price tag to the Cooper image and since the time of the Cape Fruit campaign Miff had refused them all. Before that campaign Tommy had featured in a little seen television ad for Gibbs toothpaste and in what was described as a Pearl and Dean 'filmlet' promoting Currys Stores for showing in the cinema. In the interim Kellogg's, Nestlé, Cadbury, Mars, Bird's Eye, Heinz, Kleenex, Tesco, the British Egg Marketing Board – who subsequently got lucky with Tony Hancock – and many more all tugged at the tassel on the fez, only to be politely shown away. With his penchant for poultry jokes, Tommy would have had a field day with the latter, as he would have done with a similar approach made by Kentucky Fried Chicken. At one stage Bisto even wanted to portray Tommy and his wife as a couple of Bisto kids. It would have been neat casting. The exception was a photo campaign for Horne Bros tailoring stores at Christmas 1967. The seasonal catalogue is today a collectors' item. The photo-session netted Cooper £1,000.00 at the time.

Now the floodgates were opened and the basket showed an eccentric mix. It is as if Miff had been reserving the commercial advantage as security for a rainy day. As occasional split weeks and one night stands became the pattern in a schedule dominated by periods of ill health and recovery, Miff now had another money machine to milk. It is staggering that 1978–9 should represent Tommy's best year in financial terms in view of the dip of the previous twelve months. Some of the more affluent clubs were still prepared to pay top dollar, for which he remained happy to play an occasional week, and as we know Thames television was a continuing benefactor. However, for the likes of Cooper live show business generally was not as profitable an area as it had once been. His biggest single fee of the year was £15,000.00 for the Sodastream campaign. In the last six years of his life he lent his name to lucrative marketing campaigns for KP Nuts, McVitie's Biscuits, Family Hampers, Farfisa Electronic Organs, as well as commercials for Cream Cakes (Milk Marketing Board), Reckitt and Coleman's Nurture Plant Food, Crackerbread, Yellow Pages, and Co-op's Christmas gift range. The latter generated even more publicity for the retail group when in December 1980 the Independent Broadcasting Authority, failing to see the schoolboy nature of Cooper's humour, banned one of the commercials that showed Tommy stealing a present from Santa Claus's grotto.

In this six year period his earnings from product endorsement totalled £177,000.00, approximately a fifth of his income and a fair return given that he was often required to do little more than attend a photographic or voice-recording session. In the final year alone he recorded commercials for Batchelors' Saucy Noodles, Dexion Shelving, British Telecom and a voiceover campaign for the *Daily Express*: these four brands accounted for no less than £45,000.00. Ironically the most poignant commercial to feature Cooper did not involve him at all and dated back to 1972. The vignette, for a short-lived charitable scheme named 'Bottle Losses', featured two old ladies chatting happily to each other about the Tommy Cooper show they had seen on television the night before. A third old lady hovers in the background. It transpires that she does not have a set. The voiceover explains to the viewers that by returning their empty milk bottles they could help her to acquire one. It is ironic that in part Cooper owed his career to an empty bottle of milk.

In spite of the bonus income from the commercial sector, the individual salaries earned in each successive year during this period provide a fitting barometer of his general physical condition. Although he was far from a well man, he had at last been forced to accept a more realistic position of self-awareness as far as his health was concerned. In the aftermath of Rome, phlebitis, bronchitis, asthma, pyrexia, chronic sore throat, exhaustion, even suspected mild thrombosis of the leg that required anti-coagulant treatment would all continue to lead to the cancellation of bookings and even the occasional short hospital stay, but on 22 June 1979 Miff was at least able to write to him that the medical report recently submitted for insurance purposes was 'most encouraging, so keep up the good work'. In Tommy's rest weeks the Coopers would make ever more frequent visits to Forest Mere, the health resort in Hampshire they had frequented since the early Sixties, principally for his recurring back trouble. Gwen made sure she always had a bottle of gin in her handbag.

It is quite clear from the files that in the past 'exhaustion' had frequently been used by doctors as a euphemism for the side effects of 'excessive drinking'. However, in October George Savva, the boss of Blazer's at Windsor, took the trouble to call Miff to tell him not only that Tommy 'did very well last week', but to add that there had been a 'minimum of drinking'. A month later a red letter day was achieved as far as Miff was concerned when Tommy found himself siding with him and not Gwen over making an exception to his regular working routine and performing a run of twelve consecutive shows without a break at the London Room in Drury Lane. Miff annotates the journal entry: 'Quite pleasant!!!'

When at last he appeared with Miff's full approval on the Christmas edition of *Parkinson* in 1979, his first television appearance since the desultory New London series, he was on the top of his form. For the studio audience his entrance down the famous stairs was tantamount to a real live Santa Claus coming down the chimney, even if the fez was missing:

Parkinson: What's that you've got on your head?
Cooper: A bucket.
Parkinson: That's not a bucket. It's a saucepan.
Cooper: Is it? I've got the wrong hat!

During the course of the interview he shed genuine tears at the thought that he had 'backed a horse at twenty to one – it came in twenty past four'; frightened Michael out of his skin as he let loose a 'dangerous man-eating mongoose' (*generis* joke-shop) from its cage; and gave all his fans the worry of a lifetime as he explained that new Common Market regulations forbade the wearing of the fez – little more than an excuse to try on an exotic assortment of headgear before cocking a snook at the authorities and persisting with the fez regardless. Crazy inventions and short mime vignettes were interwoven into the interview, which also gave Cooper the opportunity to show off his *bona fide* sleight of hand skills from the same chair where a few years earlier Fred Kaps, the world's foremost prestidigitator had enthralled a similar yuletide audience.

The only false note went undetected by the home audience after Tommy overlooked to set the safety catch on the guillotine illusion into which he cajoled Michael at the end of the show. Cooper's technical consultant, John Palfreyman spotted the inconsistency only a few gags away from the moment when the blade would have fallen and seriously injured, if not worse, the talk show host. Tommy in the exhilaration of the moment, performing an item that was not a part of his standard nightclub repertoire, had disregarded the detail. As the producer involved, I quickly relayed instructions from the studio floor to the director to cut to a close-up of Cooper while Palfreyman dived in, put the catch in proper position and saved Parky's life and several professional reputations – my own and Tommy's included – in the process. It all took a matter of seconds. What the three hundred members of the studio audience thought of the strange man darting on and off the set at lightning speed to tamper with the props remains unrecorded. It did not stop every single one of them, given fezzes for the occasion without Tommy's knowledge, rising at the end to salute their hero in unison with a communal 'Just like that'. In a single appearance he had atoned for the mass disappointment of his poor series the year before. Cooper regained his dignity and, happily, Parkinson kept his head.

After an extended seven week rest period over Christmas and the New Year it was business as usual. As a result of his *Parkinson* success and in the face of genuine BBC interest to build a series around him, Thames played their own hand and commissioned what would be his last series, six shows to be recorded fortnightly between May and July. Tommy was not overstretched with greater emphasis being placed on the tried and tested routines of the great solo performer of old, any sketches being nostalgic playbacks to his early revue repertoire. Television aside, 1980 would see him perform no more than sixty-two other shows, principally on the pattern of split weeks or one-night stands. However, the enhanced performance and the semi-abstinence could not alter the fact that beneath the surface all was not well.

On 25 May, with one show of the new series recorded, Gwen phoned Miff to announce that her husband was not well and that the doctor had given him antibiotics. She takes great pains to stress 'He is not drinking.' Her calls to Miff became more frequent over the summer, in which the series was his only work commitment. Within three weeks of its completion on 18 August he was admitted to the Royal Masonic Hospital according to his wife, looking 'like a skeleton'. On 4 September 1980 the medical report diagnosed 'acute chest infection which has been slow to resolve, complicated by rapid heart rate which has delayed his recovery'. On the same day Gwen wrote to Miff after her visit to the hospital, 'In himself Tommy looks wonderful and is not smoking.' He was home within a couple of days. While he was sleeping, she called Ferrie: 'He is booked into the Royal Masonic Hospital 29 September (but he doesn't know) for electrical treatment to be carried out under anaesthetic on his heart.' She added, as if to remind us amid all the seriousness that we were back in Cooperland, 'He says he wants to go to Las Vegas!' On 16 September he was well enough to ring Miff himself. All that is reported of the call is: 'He ended up putting phone down on me, so I called him back and told him!' Tommy must have been feeling better. Eventually the electrical treatment was not deemed necessary and Manhattan was added to the itinerary of the crazy transatlantic rest-cure Cooper was determined to take. When one reflects on Cooper's life up to this point, the truly amazing thing is that he still had three and a half more years in which to live, in retrospect a surreal extension to a life that might already appear to have been strained to total exhaustion.

At great cost, the October holiday was curtailed. The Coopers were summoned back home when their daughter, Vicky was involved in a serious car accident that required a three day stay in Charing Cross Hospital. Tommy lost out on the Nevada climate and his occasional fix of neon lights and state-of-the-art magic, but there was some cheer to welcome him home in the form of a letter from George Savva to Miff to announce that his forthcoming week at Blazer's in the approach to Christmas was already sold out: 'Tommy, as you know, opened Cesar's Palace for me in 1966 and has worked a total of fourteen weeks cabaret for me over the past fourteen years. I can honestly say that each and every one of the weeks have been winners and I offer this letter as my tribute to a great artiste who has continued to "pull them in" for me for almost a decade and a half. Long may he continue to do so.' It is an important letter, reminding us that for all the aggravation and upset his health problems had caused in recent years the man remained box office and, as the *Parkinson* appearance proved, was still capable of warming the hearts of the nation as an entertainer. He would play the Windsor club three more times before he died. A further note of optimism was spelt on 3 November with a message from the management of Jollees Club in Stoke-on-Trent attached to their payment for Tommy's recent appearance: 'No problems. Pleased to see that he is drinking more moderately and is also getting off to bed at a reasonable hour.' Later in the month, with Miff about to go on holiday, Cooper's own hand-written message from Norwich, where he was playing a few nights at the Theatre Royal, was positively cheery: 'The doctor says that I'm resting very well indeed and if I keep it up he says you will be able to go away for at least another ten holidays. I'm now so relaxed last night I nodded off in the middle of the act. Have a nice time and stay as long as you like.'

As far as health and career were concerned, the mood surrounding Cooper was more buoyant than it had been for a long time. Before the year ended, the only false note came with the acceptance of possibly the most misguided booking he – or Miff, on his behalf – ever accepted. On 21 and 22 December he was subjected to the challenge of opening for the rock group, Police in a concert staged in a tent on the muddy outer reaches of Tooting Bec Common. Maybe Miff had been misled by the earlier success of comedy veteran Max Wall, who during that lull in his career when he passed out of media recognition had gone on tour with the band, Mott the Hoople. Wall, however, was always allowed to parade a more virulent streak within his public persona. When the raucous mob that often passed for an audience threw beer cans at him, he just slung them back. Four letter words were flung about in the same way. Invariably Max won over the crowd and walked off in triumph. But this was not Cooper's style. He fitted into the South London extravaganza as comfortably as Harry Corbett's Sooty at a stag night. Moreover, for all its emotional ups and downs, his career had not really dipped in public perception. Wall had nothing to lose in such circumstances; Cooper's situation was the reverse. In 1975 Ferrie had already rejected a similar enquiry for Tommy to appear alongside The Who. He should have abided by his original instinct.

Tommy was clearly out of his element, even though for a fleeting moment the audience was enthusiastic. According to the reviewer in the music newspaper, *Sounds*, 'He's so popular that you could sense a thrill going through the crowd when his name was mentioned, even though they were literally aching to see Police. Tommy took about five minutes to translate his initial welcome into booing, catcalls, and a minor bombardment of plastic cups. For one thing he seemed terrified of the fine mess he'd got himself into and for another he'd forgotten how to project himself beyond the living-room close-up of television. In sum he died the death.' He had not been helped by the totalitarian efforts at crowd control that were taking place while he was on stage. The audience, pushed and shoved this way and that, turned tense and irritable. The Red Cross received a seemingly unending chain of casualties while the familiar strains of the Cooper repertoire sounded in the background. Tommy never minced words about the disaster: 'Police were great – they were sensational – I wasn't, but they were great.' It may have been the most embarrassing engagement of his career. In his own words, 'It was the most terrifying night of my life.' The experience does not appear to have had any specific side-effects on his health. No sooner was Christmas Day over than he was heading south for the comparative comfort and safety of a short festive season at the Winter Gardens, Bournemouth. If ever an auditorium had been devised to test his ability to project himself beyond the more intimate dimensions of the television screen, this was the one. He had conquered there many times in the past and would now do so again. Psychologically it was the ideal venue for him to play to regain any confidence he may have lost in the South London debacle.

As 1981 began his health continued to hold steady. In July the doctor who now regularly examined him for appearance insurance purposes was pleased to write: 'Mr Cooper told me that his alcohol consumption had diminished considerably. He admitted to drinking about four glasses of wine a day . . . He is obviously more of a risk than average for his appearance in view of his past history. However, I found him to be in a better state of health than when I last saw him a year ago.' If one aspect of his physical condition did now begin to cause even greater concern it was his legs. For a while bookings were accepted with a view to as little travelling as possible. This inevitably had an effect on his income. During the last six months of 1981 he managed to fulfil forty-two appearances in cabaret and theatre; between the beginning of the New Year and a guest appearance for Eric Sykes at Thames at the end of March 1982 he made only six, a single week at Blazer's for Savva at Windsor.

Things were noticeably winding down, although he still found the stamina to work with Sykes again in his latest semi-silent film, *It's Your Move* in June 1982 and to travel to the Netherlands to appear on the *Willem Ruis Lotto Show* the following month. His mobility was not helped when on the latter trip he was rammed in the shin by a luggage trolley at Heathrow. In great pain he went straight to a two week theatre season at Sandown in the Isle of Wight. The engagement had to be curtailed after a week. Tommy would walk out onto a stage or cabaret floor no more than seven more times before the year closed. The irony is that as other aspects of his general health appeared to improve – or at least hold steady – his mobility let him down.

Whatever he might achieve in the remaining two years of his life was a bonus. The indomitability of his spirit was shown by the decision – one Miff allowed him to veto had he so chosen – to tour the Middle East the following year. A reasonably lucrative contract for £17,000.00 saw him playing exotic locations like Abu Dhabi, Dubai, and Bahrain over a three week period in February 1983. During this time he had to work for only nine days, although considerable travelling was involved. Doubtless the appeal of the dry desert heat exerted its pull. He returned to something resembling a normal routine, although soon a recurring cough, the result of his chronic bronchitis, developed into pleurisy, which kept him out of action for most of May and June. In July he recorded a successful special for the BBC within the Saturday evening series strand, *The Main Attraction*, but the resumption of his standard touring pattern was disrupted again, by 'post-pleuritic complications', for most of August and September. He ventured back into a television studio for what would be the last time when he recorded, again for the BBC, his appearance on *The Bob Monkhouse Show* on 4 October 1983. He had been discharged from the Esperance Private Hospital in Eastbourne only three days before, having had no less than seven pints of fluid drained from his lungs, ultimately the result not merely of smoking what George Brightwell had once referred to as 'his wretched cigars', but chain-smoking them at the rate, according to his son, of forty a day. 'His breathing got so bad,' said Gwen, 'he sounded like a train.' His friends were becoming increasingly anxious. Eric Morecambe bumped into Peter Hudson at Thames around this time and asked, 'How's the big fellow doing?' Peter explained about the fluid. Eric replied, 'I've heard of people trying to smuggle spirits through customs, but this is ridiculous.'

In spite of his frailty, his entrance on the Monkhouse talk show may have been the most memorable he ever made. From the moment he spotted an absurd chicken costume left over from another production on a wardrobe rail in another part of the rehearsal rooms he was determined that he would make his entrance wearing those grotesque feathered legs with their ungainly claws, however painful it might be to thrust his own legs, ulcerated and permanently swathed in surgical bandages by this time, into them. Again I was the producer involved and he swore me to secrecy as far as Bob and the crew were concerned. Indeed only the wardrobe supervisor, director Geoff Miles, Mary Kay and I were alert to his plans, which once he arrived on set were not surprisingly accompanied by an avalanche of chicken jokes: 'What have I done? I've fouled it all up. That's what I've done ... I've been silly haven't I? I've gone off half-cocked ... I've spoiled a big entrance, I have really. I mean was it something big I did or was it something paltry?' I doubt if there was a chicken joke from all the American gag sheets he had filed away in Chiswick that wasn't buzzing through his brain that evening.

Monkhouse was on the floor, bent up with laughter at the entrance of this strange hybrid, a man from the waist up, a chicken from the waist down, not content merely to walk on, but strutting like the genuine article as he pecked his passage this way and that towards the host to the uproar of the house. No one could have written the idea into a script for him, let alone for anybody else. Only Cooper could have grasped the initiative of such a mad device and carried it off for all the physical discomfort it entailed, as if he were a kid again revelling in riding his bumpy bicycle down the lane while reading a newspaper at the same time. The appearance also showed that he had lost none of his boyish enthusiasm for the latest joke shop gizmos, as he used a suction pad to plug an electric razor to his forehead for a shave and revealed his prized family heirloom of a genuine milking stool. As Tommy exerted pressure on one of the traditional three legs, milk squirted from the end. Again he was on such good form that even Miff was encouraged to write: 'Your stint on *The Bob Monkhouse Show* was excellent. Even made me laugh. How about that?'

Away from his form on camera, the reality was less encouraging. Within six days of the Monkhouse taping Tommy was back in hospital. He appears to have recovered sufficiently to perform for four nights at the Circus Tavern in Purfleet at the end of October, but had scarcely completed that engagement when he was back in hospital with severe chest pains. Tests indicated the possibility of a heart attack. That the diagnosis was not conclusive appears to have been because of a veritable cocktail of complications relating to all his past frailties. He resumed his theatrical routine in February, but would fulfil only three engagements before embarking with Gwen on a ten day holiday to Las Palmas on 21 March. Common sense had prevailed when his favoured location of Las Vegas was embargoed by his wife. Photographs from the spell in the sun show Tommy beaming with happiness and ostensibly at peace with the world. He returned to fulfil a four night engagement at the Circus Tavern. It brought him back to performance pitch for his commitment to appear on the television show *Live from Her Majesty's* on 15 April. A few days before going to Spain he had spent some time taping tracks for a possible commercial recording. The title had a prophetic irony all of its own. It was the cover of an old Cliff Richard single, 'Just Enough to Keep Me Hanging On'. Sadly fate decreed he was unable to hang on much longer.

Surveying the last few years of his life, his family could take comfort from the fact that the cliché of the clown who in a trough of despair seeks alcoholic refuge from which he will never return did not apply to him. Although far too late, he did rally to the cause of his general well being. In this regard he represented a total contrast with Tony Hancock, perhaps not surprisingly given the drift of their respective comic personas, the one morose and lugubrious, the other a jester to the twinkling tips of his magical fingers. I am convinced that Cooper never really understood the problem that drink posed, namely that constant treatment and total abstinence were a *sine qua non* of recovery. To Tommy there was no such thing as total abstinence. When he came to rehearsals for his appearance on *The Bob Monkhouse Show*, he explained he *had* given up alcohol and tobacco. He then wasted no time in popping open a can of lager and lighting up a Panatella. Bob said, 'I thought you'd given up smoking and given up drinking?' He replied, 'I have – but you can't call this smoking and you can't call this drinking, can you?' The response was serious. The man was unstoppable. It never occurred to any of those present that the end was not far away. The paradox is that Hancock, a more intellectual man, probably did realize only too well what was happening to him. Ultimately his own hand signed the end of his life. Cooper had no idea he was on course so soon for an exit of a different kind. The very contrast in setting is chilling and characteristic at the same time, the one demise consigned to the privacy of a seedy Sydney apartment on the other side of the world, the other paraded sixteen years later under the happy gaze of millions of admirers. That is where we must join him now.

THIRTEEN

Death and Resurrection

The convoluted way in which the tragedy of Tommy's death interacted with the routine of my own life on the evening of 15 April 1984 will remain stamped on my mind forever. The recent possessor of a video-recording machine, I decided not to watch his scheduled appearance on the LWT show, *Live from Her Majesty's* when it aired at 7.45 p.m., preferring to tape it for enjoyment later in the evening when the chores of the day had been set aside. However, as the clock indicated that the programme must be coming to a close, I could not resist the temptation of switching on to sneak a preview of the finale for the sheer pleasure of savouring at first hand the accolade he was bound to achieve. A star studded cast including Howard Keel, Donny Osmond, Les Dennis and Dustin Gee, Adrian Walsh, The Flying Pickets, and the Brian Rogers Dancers joined host Jimmy Tarbuck for a final goodbye, but Tommy was nowhere to be seen. As I switched off the set, various explanations began to bombard my brain – the listings magazines had the week of his appearance wrong; the producer, David Bell had jumped the gun in including his name in a billing required by the press two or three weeks previously;

there had been some disagreement at Miff's end that scuppered the contract at the last minute; he had even imbibed a little too freely after performing his act earlier in the show. Denial kept at bay the possibility that his health might have been somehow responsible for the puzzling turn of events. And then, before I even began to think about playing back the tape to check on his presence, the telephone went berserk, a succession of calls releasing within me a capacity for tears I never knew I possessed: 'Had I heard the news? Tommy Cooper was dead.' Within minutes of the end of the show, Trevor MacDonald had resolved the mystery on the ITV mid-evening news bulletin.

At the end of the day I braced myself to watch the act that had been witnessed by twelve and a half million viewers a few hours before. He appeared to be as much on form as he had been on the Monkhouse show six months earlier, his complexion healthier, his smile as relaxed as at any time in his career, even if his legs betrayed the real truth of his condition. According to Tarbuck a special room with all creature comforts was improvised for him at the side of the stage so that he would not have to negotiate the tortuous backstage staircases that led to the dressing rooms proper. Jimmy's introduction was loving and auspicious: 'If you asked one hundred comedians who their favourite comic is, they would all say – the one and only – Tommy Cooper!' The last person to speak to him was choreographer Brian Rogers, who remembers wishing him well in the wings as he got off the stool on which he was perched in the prompt corner to walk on stage. Brian remembers him handing a long clear glass to someone at his side. He assumed it contained vodka, but cannot be sure.

In the eight minutes that followed viewers were treated to a whistle stop tour of many of the gambits that had stood this favourite funny man in good stead for almost forty years. Here were wife jokes – 'My wife's just phoned me. She said, "I've got water in the carburettor." I said, "Where's the car?" She said, "In the river."' And conceptual jokes, "My memory's going. I cut myself shaving this morning and forgot to bleed.' Here was the furtive preparation of a magic prop that the audience wasn't supposed to see, but could not possibly avoid – as he secreted coins in a tin can from which he was going to produce them – and the surreal use of a prop that bordered on lunacy – as he aimlessly guided a pair of bicycle handlebars around the stage: 'I can't ride it. I've got a flat tyre.' Here were the casual asides – as he addressed the orchestra, 'I want you to play tonight like you've never played before. Together!' – and the familiar props – the table that developed female legs, the three metal rings that refused to unlink and his ever-present tribute to Gwen, the dove that turned out to be made of rubber.

He was in complete control of the theatre as dancer, Sandy Lawrence came forward to help him into a voluminous scarlet cloak. The last words he spoke as she fastened it down the front were an affectionate 'Thanks, love.' He then clutched his chest – something he had done in mock panic for comic effect thousands of times before – and without any ceremony or histrionics appeared to crumple to the ground, slowly sinking into himself as if the air was being sucked out of him. As the dancer departed, his body rolled gently back against the curtains. The fez stayed on his head, if slightly askew. People had always said he'd die with his fez on, but, as he used to joke, 'I never took it literally. I mean the doctor said it would be the last thing I'd do.' It all now happened so quickly. Freddie Starr, who was watching at home and is not an obviously sentimental person, wrote in his autobiography, 'It probably doesn't mean a lot to most people, but I've never forgotten that Tommy Cooper's last word was "love".' At the same time Tarbuck, another comic from a younger generation who loved him quite as much as Starr, was watching the tragedy unfold on the monitor in the wings.

The theatre audience could not stop laughing, believing it to be part of the act. Meanwhile the radio microphone he was wearing only enhanced the sound of the death rattle, interpreted by the audience as a bizarre extension of the distinctive rasping cough-cum-guffaw that hallmarked every Cooper performance they had ever seen. For David Bell and director, Alasdair Macmillan time was standing still. Les Dennis recalls being in the wings with Bell and Tommy's son: 'When Tommy collapsed, David said, "Is that a joke?" His son said, "No, my dad has a bad back and wouldn't be able to do that."' All Mary Kay remembers are four other words from Thomas: 'This is for real.' Macmillan cued the orchestra to play the music for the commercial break, the first of two in the three-part show. At that point on playback I stopped the machine, took out the video cassette, placed it in its box, wrote 'Tommy RIP' on the spine and consciously placed it not among the fast growing mound of cassettes a television producer and comedy aficionado automatically acquires in the combined line of duty and pleasure, but separately in a filing cabinet reserved for personal documents and papers of importance. It stayed there, not to be watched again, until circumstances of an exceptional kind prompted its playback almost twenty years later.

Those familiar with his repertoire – and of course the whole production team – knew from rehearsals that putting on the cloak was merely the prelude to a sequence that had constituted one of his funniest routines since the early Seventies. Stamping the floor with great self-importance to emphasize that there were no trap doors, he would stand with his back against the join in the curtains and proceed to extract from the garment a ludicrous assortment of objects that included a bucket, a long pole, a nylon stocking display leg, a beer crate, and a ten foot ladder. The comedy derived as much from the semi-silent asides between Cooper and the obvious back stage confederate who was feeding the things between his legs – 'Hold it! Put it down a bit!' – as from the incongruity of the items produced. On this occasion viewers were deprived the bonus of Jimmy Tarbuck as the accomplice, invisible to the end until he appeared in the gap to protest he couldn't pass anything more through.

For legal and medical reasons Cooper's body could be removed only by paramedics or the police, leaving Les Dennis and Dustin Gee, as well as Howard Keel to present their acts in the middle section of the show in the limited space before the front cloth, made even more restricted by the bulge in the curtain caused by Tommy's body in the centre of the stage. For a long time a rumour circulated that his outsize feet protruded in vision from beneath the tabs. If at any stage this was the case, it was not observed by the home audience: so sensitive was the direction that it kept any such moments in a mid-shot on the two young comedians or the veteran Hollywood singing star. According to Peter Prichard, Tarbuck's manager and coincidentally a fully qualified Officer of the Order of St John ambulance brigade, he managed with the help of others to ease him back some way through the curtains: 'We couldn't pull his whole body, as he was too heavy. I started to hit his chest and give him the kiss of life, but got no response.' Meanwhile his client was inches away the other side of the curtain, summoning up every ounce of his professionalism to keep the live television show rolling.

Joe Kerr, a painter attached to the production and a recently qualified first-aider, grasped the initiative and took over the resuscitation attempt. Matters were not made easier by the darkness backstage. With the help of one of the stage riggers, another first-aider, he applied the bag mask technique, desperately anxious against all the odds to pump the air around inside his lungs: 'Tommy was not breathing and we commenced CPR, taking turns on the chest compressions. After a delay the company nurse arrived from the front of the house and we all worked together. The scene backstage was a nightmare.' It was not until the second commercial break that Tommy could be moved by ambulance men and transported in the company of Mary Kay and his son, Thomas to Westminster Hospital. Kerr valiantly kept up the compressions as they moved him out of the theatre and into the ambulance, until the paramedics had sorted out their equipment. He was pronounced dead on arrival at the hospital. One of the ambulance men is said to have remarked that they knew he was dead as soon as they set eyes upon him. A short while before the performance Tommy had asked Prichard to look after a carrier bag holding several cans of lager. When Peter returned to the bag he saw the cans contained Kaliber, the alcohol-free lager. Maybe Brian Rogers' earlier assumption had been wrong. It provided an ironic footnote to a life of excess.

A few days later Kerr received a formal letter from the LWT management thanking him for his 'initiative and efforts in trying to revive Tommy Cooper after his collapse on stage'. It added, 'The nurse has also asked to pass on her admiration and sincere thanks for your assistance and support.' For Tarbuck, to see the life wrenched from the man he loved and admired so much was a traumatic experience. In 1964 on the occasion of the Royal Variety Performance the upstart young comic from Liverpool had been encouraged by the support he had received from the older performer. How he survived the ordeal on camera without betraying emotion as the show continued was remarkable and part of the legacy people like Cooper and Eric Morecambe, another mentor, had entrusted to him. On the following week's show Jimmy waited until the finale to acknowledge the tragedy and in the process revealed a dignity that surprised many. As he later recalled, 'At the end of the show I said on behalf of Mrs Cooper and all the family, thank you all very much. Because the response to his death had been like Churchill or royalty – a truly great person dying – and she thanked me for that, did Dove.'

The consensus was that this was the way he would have wanted to have died, surfing the void of life's emptiness with the sound of laughter in his ears. It was as if he had willed his destiny to follow this course ever since witnessing the death of Bert Lahr's character in *Always Leave Them Laughing* thirty-five years before. The view was endorsed by his son, Thomas, who two days after his death said, 'If I had said to him, "You are going to drop dead on stage tonight in front of millions of people," he would have replied, "I'll settle for that." I always knew he would drop dead on stage. I had a premonition of me pulling off his bow tie and ripping open his shirt . . . and that's exactly what happened.' The day had been uneventful, although a doctor was called to tend to Tommy's voice in the afternoon – a not uncommon occurrence with performers, especially opera stars and song stylists, so there was little cause for alarm. Thomas had been tending to his father throughout the day, helping to set his props and keeping him from the cigars that were a constant temptation. His hardest job came much later when he had to call his mother from the hospital. She had been watching at home, having last been with her husband when she sent him on his way that morning with his flask of coffee and his packet of lamb and egg mayonnaise sandwiches: 'I didn't go because I wanted to see how it looked on the box, but when he didn't go into the cloak routine, I knew . . . I knew . . .' Besides, only a few days before she had timed the act for him at their dining room table as she had always done. Thomas later revealed the joke that his father had intended to use between the cloak routine and the commercial break: 'Is there a Mr Smith in the house? Could you please remove your Jaguar from the car park? It's already bitten a policeman and we're a bit worried what it's going to do next.'

Tommy was not the first funny man to suffer such a visible death. Doyen of comedy actors, Sidney James had collapsed on stage while appearing in a farce called *The Mating Game* in Sunderland eight years previously and died *en route* to hospital. Kenneth Horne, radio stalwart of *Much Binding in the Marsh* and *Round the Horne* had died soon after keeling over while hosting a television awards ceremony at the Dorchester Hotel in 1969: the BBC transmitted the programme later that evening with the tragedy edited out. The press went to town in using Cooper's death to highlight the precariousness of his profession, oblivious of the fact that before the year was over both Eric Morecambe and Leonard Rossiter would also have succumbed to heart attacks. People close to Morecambe have surmised that Eric's own demise was accelerated by the shock of the departure of his longtime friend. In fact, he died only six weeks later, having collapsed on stage at the end of an evening being interviewed at a theatre in Tewkesbury by another Welsh wizard of laughter, his – and Tommy's – friend, Stan Stennett.

The funeral of Tommy Cooper took place at Mortlake Crematorium the following Friday, 20 April. At times it appeared as if the entire British comedy establishment was in attendance. Crowds lined the route and a two feet high model of a fez found itself among the floral tributes. The cause of death on his death certificate was given as 'coronary occlusion due to atheroma'. This time there could be no hiding the fact that he had a coronary condition, but, as his daughter has admitted, 'It was the booze, cigars and the late nights that killed him.' Although he was far too young to die at the age of sixty-two, in retrospect his death could not have been far away; his body, if not his spirit, devastated by the frailties and excesses of the preceding years. However, David Ball, a close friend of the family as well as Tommy's bank manager, has provided an insight into the specific circumstances of his exit. After the death Gwen admitted to him how especially anxious Tommy had been in advance of this particular transmission, constantly agitated throughout their stay in Las Palmas by the fact that it was a live show. By a strange paradox a live broadcast appears to exert an additional strain on performers whose core role is the entertainment of live audiences in nightclubs and theatres. The pre-recorded programme with its potential for editing and sound dubbing has about it a sense of security that is bound to appeal to intrinsically nervous performers like Cooper. Nothing could alter the fact that on that April evening at Her Majesty's Theatre in London's Haymarket the vulnerability of the performer – not for the first or the last time in history – turned pallbearer.

After the funeral Thomas sprinkled his father's ashes among the daffodils – Tommy's favourite flower – in the garden at Chiswick. According to his will he left an estate of £327,272.00 gross, £326,686.00 net. This was a surprise to many of those close to him who thought he had spent most of the money he made. As is so often the case, his true wealth was partly assigned to his widow through assets they shared and which passed to her sole ownership on his death. The larger part of his magical and stage properties were sorted and put into auction at Christie's where they raised £7,500.00 later in the year. Gwen stayed away from the sale. For her time had no meaning. Before long she found herself writing a note of apology to Miff and Beatrice: 'I am not sending Christmas cards this year. Tommy always ticked the bird catalogue and I'm sure you understand. We all wish you a happy Christmas and good health in 1985.' The card was dated 17 August.

Few people were drawn closer to the tragedy than Eric Sykes, who recalls receiving a telephone call from Tommy on the morning of the show, begging him to watch later in the day to check out a new gag he thought he would like. As Eric explains, in all their long association Cooper had not alerted him to an upcoming appearance in that way before. It was not something pros did. You took your work in its stride and moved from one job to the next without fuss, not least because you had no idea how good you were going to be. If the gesture could be interpreted as a presentiment of death, maybe another harbinger of something untoward could be discerned in the behaviour – or lack of it – of Miff Ferrie. It is significant that the preceding October Miff, foregoing the habit of a career, did not go through the usual rigid routine of submitting to Tommy the formal notice extending the Sole Agency Agreement that had existed between them for so long.

Technically speaking in those last few months of his life Tommy could have been out of contract with Miff without realizing it. But if Miff did reveal his value and astuteness as an agent and manager, he did so now. I have always found it disconcerting that on that final television show he had not taken a stand for Tommy on the matter of billing: once Cooper had established himself in the medium, whenever he appeared on a show other than his own, top billing among the guests had always been a *sine qua non*. Perhaps this was another sign that something was amiss in the Cooper world order. Nevertheless, the fee negotiated by Miff was outstanding for an eight minute spot, namely £6,000.00. More remarkably, as Tommy embarked on a new financial year, Miff, without compromising the pattern that favoured rest days over working ones, had already negotiated contracts signed by his client that amounted to an income of £99,000.00 in the first six months through to mid-October, including an advertising campaign for Bassett's Wine Gums for Saatchi and Saatchi in Holland and a new high of £8,500.00 a week for a couple of return visits to Bailey's in Watford and the Night Out in Birmingham.

Not included in the reckoning of potential earnings were the fees he would have achieved for a BBC situation comedy that showed every possibility of becoming a reality in the months ahead. Co-starring Tommy and Eric Sykes, it was to be written by Johnny Speight, who knew both men well. True to type, Cooper was to play the owner of a joke shop who rents the room above to Eric, cast against type as an Arthur Daley-style wheeler-dealer whose talent agency acts as the front for an assortment of crooked business opportunities, from which the show derived its working title, *Harry Moon Conglomerates*. Eric described the intended relationship between the two men: 'I'm a schemer and Tommy is the innocent. But it turns out that I'm really an idiot and Tommy is an even bigger one.' The pilot episode had been scheduled for recording on 24 March, but industrial action intervened. The holiday in the Canaries filled the gap nicely. With Tommy's death, the project stood no chance of revival. Only one person could have played the joke shop owner, although Miff in an echo of times past had always been against the idea.

Whatever their artistic differences and the legal formalities that tied them together, it is debatable whether any other representative in British show business could have achieved as much for Tommy over such an extended period. For all the rows and insults and rudely aborted telephones calls, the emotional wear and tear experienced by both parties, the business arrangement could only have survived based on an undertow of respect and – dare one say – affection. When Miff himself was hospitalized for a short while at the beginning of 1979, the Coopers individually and together were more than solicitous in enquiring after his health. Equally concerned was the last letter the agent wrote to the comedian on 14 March 1984. In it he educated Tommy to the work plan for the half year ahead: 'Bearing in mind the health situation I do not think much more should be negotiated during this period, with the possible exception of any suitable commercials which would only mean a minimum amount of time in a studio. I hope you both have an enjoyable time in Las Palmas, but it can be windy there!' It is good that it ended on a smile. They could not have prospered without each other. Tommy's death meant semi-retirement for Ferrie. Tommy had been his sole client for several years. He continued to look after residuals for the estate on behalf of Gwen until his own death from bronchopneumonia in 1994.

Relations between Tommy's widow and the Ferries would remain cordial, in spite of an initial upset when Miff with his trademark lack of tact instructed Gwen that for business and legal documentation she was no longer technically-speaking Mrs Tommy Cooper. He was punctiliously correct, as usual, although he could have tackled the procedure in a gentler way. Dove was devastated, admitting, 'I am nothing without Tommy. I don't know what my life will be now. He was my life. I've never wanted a Rolls Royce or a yacht. I only ever wanted him.' No writer of melodrama could have prepared her for the series of ordeals that this large-hearted lady still had to face. The public humiliation when her husband's affair with Mary Kay became tabloid fodder paled into insignificance when on 13 August 1988 her son, Thomas died of haemophilia following complications caused by liver failure. After he collapsed at home, doctors pumped seventy pints of new blood into him. He was kept alive on a life-support machine for three days, but when the new blood failed to clot, Gwen had to make the decision to turn off the machine. He was thirty-two years old and left a son, Tam, of six years; his 1981 marriage had fallen apart only six weeks beforehand.

Having experienced the living death that is watching your own child die, this bounteous, big-bosomed soul never fully regained her former resilience. But the second tragedy did provide the one moment she was glad Tommy was no longer around: 'He could not have coped. He'd have fallen to pieces. You can never, ever recover from the death of a child.' She was stating the obvious, but melancholy invested her words with dignity, although as she progressed through her seventies there was one thing she could never understand, 'Why didn't they take me instead?' Nor were things destined to get better the following year when on 19 October her brother-in-law, David, a successful businessman in the area of magic and party supplies also died, a victim of cancer of the bronchial tubes. He was fifty-nine, ironically three years younger than his brother at the time of his death.

I came to know Gwen properly only in the years after Tommy died, united as we were in wishing to preserve his reputation for future generations. It was gratifying when two series packaged under my remit at Thames Television, *The Best of Tommy Cooper* and *Classic Cooper* attracted audiences in the Nineties commensurate with those he had secured twenty years previously. On the back of a further television project – a profile of Tommy within my documentary strand, *Heroes of Comedy*, for which Dove graciously agreed to be interviewed for the first and only time before the cameras – I received a call from the actor and theatre producer, Patrick Ryecart. Within days I had accepted his challenge to revive

419

the magic of Tommy Cooper as a stage project. The thought had long simmered in my mind whether Tommy, had he lived longer and had his health allowed, would have taken to the stage like Frankie Howerd and Max Wall in a swan song evening of combined reminiscence and performance. The two other great comedy veterans had crowned their careers with such presentations. I wasted no time in putting pen to paper and with Gwen's encouragement produced an imaginary transcript of what such an evening might have entailed.

Lee Menzies was invited to participate as co-producer and when Alan Ayckbourn, so keen to direct, had to back down through the pressure of his other commitments, Simon Callow – in direct line of descent from memorable names like Emlyn Williams and Michael MacLiammoir – brought his vast personal experience of the one-man theatre show to the task. His passion and commitment to the ethos of the vaudevillian was all consuming and energized the project from the moment he came on board. Magician and erstwhile actor Geoffrey Durham had always been my first choice as the person to mastermind the technical side of the magic, not least the conjuring tuition of whoever found himself playing the legendary performer. That casting presented the greatest challenge of the whole enterprise.

An uneasy shadow had always lurked at the back of my mind. Who could possibly play this most singular of clowns? Encouraged by Maureen Lipman's spellbinding interpretation of unique comedienne Joyce Grenfell, we began the quest to find the actor to play Tommy. But we were not looking for yet another Tommy Cooper impersonator. We were searching for more than that, for an actor who could interpret the essential spirit of his comedy in a personalized way. If anyone at the time had asked us what we meant by this we would not have been able to answer satisfactorily. We would only recognise what we were looking for when we saw it. We turned a corner when we heard that Jerome Flynn, in spite of his standing on television, wanted to audition. At an obviously emotional time in his life, his father – the actor Eric Flynn – having died a few days before, Jerome was the first to step onto the audition stage. We sensed we had found our Tommy the moment he produced in one hand a small black bag that a friend had hurriedly sewn for him and in the other an egg. He had no inkling of how the classic trick worked, but set about putting the familiar words to the actions, in the course of which the egg – he had not thought of using a prop one – was smashed unintentionally in the pocket of his extremely expensive velvet jacket. The audition process henceforth became a courtesy exercise for those queuing to follow him.

Sadly Gwen did not live to see the production. Throughout the Nineties with support from her daughter and her close friends within the Grand Order of Lady Ratlings she had enjoyed some consolation in being able to relive the memories of happier times. On 27 August 1986, she wrote to Miff when he was unwell, revealing her intrinsically cheery and caring self and, between the lines, appearing to atone for so much of the unpleasantness over the years:

Dear Miff
    We are all very sorry indeed that you are under the weather. One thing, you look after your self and are pretty fit. On the other hand, you've always been a 'worry guts' and you've got to pack it in. If you do what Terence, the Latin dramatist says, I know you are going to be fine: "If you cannot do what you wish, wish what you can do."
    We all send our very, very sincere best wishes to you.
    As ever,
    Gwen

She too died from bronchopneumonia on 27 October 2002, six months before *Jus' Like That!* opened at London's Garrick Theatre. Her will revealed the true extent of the estate she had built up with her husband over the years, namely £1,845,328.00 gross, £1,839,660.00 net. In an ironic footnote to all their lives, two years earlier Miff's widow, Beatrice, had passed away leaving £330,384.00 gross, £315,803.00 net, close enough to fifteen per cent of their clients' wealth for one to reflect, 'In death, as in life.'

Fortuitously Gwen was able to meet Jerome just two weeks before she passed away. Late and harassed from being a witness to a motor accident between his own home and Chiswick, Jerome came into her presence, imposing but shy, just a little distraught from the journey, just a trifle detached from the world. As he walked across the space where Tommy had rehearsed a thousand shows, she gave him the once–over, cast a glance at me, and then passed judgement, 'He'll do!' To know Tommy's Dove is to realize that no actor could have received a stronger endorsement.

From the first morning of rehearsal we were fully conscious we were engaged in an act of resurrection, entrusted with the task of protecting the flame of the comic spirit held most dear in recent British memory. Every available archive tape of Cooper was perused and analysed. Slowly Jerome absorbed the man. And then I was able to play my trump card. I had never forgotten the video-cassette of his final appearance that I still had locked away at home among my personal papers. I suggested that Simon and Jerome and I should allow ourselves a single viewing. The experience proved to be as emotional as watching the programme the very first time around nineteen years before. Memory is selective. I certainly recalled the business with the bicycle handlebars and the shaving joke. I cannot pretend that I remembered the bit with the coins in the can. I had totally forgotten his hilarious use of a dummy hand attached to a black banner which he held in front of a bell on a table to make it supposedly ring by itself, while all the while his free hand was blatantly doing the job for him. His entrance with a giant tube of Tunes cough sweets stuck on his head carried a certain resonance. The memories, however, were as nothing compared with what we now heard. His exact opening words sent a respectful shiver down our spines: 'Do you believe in reincarnation? Sometimes I think I'm Beethoven come back. I do really, because I've had tunes through my head all day.' But that was not all. The giant packet of Tunes said so much more. There, spelt out for all to read, was the line, 'Helps you breathe more easily.' The unintentional black humour, not to mention the acknowledgement of the process of reincarnation we were undergoing on his behalf, left us speechless, suspended in a curious fez-coloured limbo between black sadness and rosy elation. It was as if Tommy was speaking to us across the years. The end of his act, because it was the end of his life, had been disturbing. Everyone had overlooked the fact that the beginning – in the way it addressed matters of life and death – had been quite as upsetting. It was hard to watch the sequence again without feeling that a chilling intimation of his own mortality must have lingered in the air that day.

It came as a surprise to learn from his daughter that Tommy had a spiritual dimension that expressed itself in an actual belief in reincarnation. According to Vicky, her mother was more pragmatic, avowing that when you die you die, while her father pondered with considerable depth whether upon his death his soul would pass into somebody else: 'He would say, "What happens to our minds when we die? What do we do with all that we've learnt on this earth? Where does the mind go?" He came to the conclusion that reincarnation was the answer. He believed in the magical things that the naked eye can't see.' He had once said to Mary Kay, 'Just think of being burned. Ashes to ashes. Suppose you're not quite gone. Not quite dead.' It reads like a joke, but was contemplated with a profound seriousness that Mary feels played its own part in undermining his health. Perhaps surprisingly for a practising magician whose tricks were grounded in the pedestrian methods of the hocus pocus craft his personal position along the sliding scale between secular practicability and spiritual awareness was much closer to the latter.

I would position myself towards the other end of that scale, but the experience of the production on its out-of-town tryout tour was overloaded with moments that challenged one's intellectual, emotional and spiritual equilibrium. How else to account for the occasion when I drew to Simon's attention that it was Tommy's birthday, only to hear a few minutes later the strains of 'Happy Birthday' accompanying a cake on stage for Jerome, whose birthday had been a few days before while the production was in transit? There was the unsettling frequency with which I was besieged by fez imagery – in the lampshades that adorn the choir stalls in Malvern Priory; the single tarboosh discovered on the luggage rack on the train home from the West Country with not a member of the company in sight; the name and logo of the restaurant in Oxford where at total random my wife and I found ourselves taking Vicky for a meal before the show, 'Tarbouch', a variant spelling from the original Arabic. A substantial part of the first half of *Jus' Like That!* takes place in Tommy's dressing room. With this in mind, the weekend between Malvern and Oxford I took from my shelves the text of Ronald Harwood's dressing room drama, *The Dresser* to check out somebody else's take on presenting backstage onstage. The part of the veteran barnstorming actor in that play, supposedly based on Donald

Wolfit, had been originated by the magnificent Freddie Jones. On Monday night in Oxford, who should appear in the auditorium but Jones himself? I have no explanation for these strange coincidences, other than to add that when Vicky after watching the show observed, 'It is almost as if Jerome is reincarnating my father,' she struck a chord that no open-minded soul could dismiss out of hand.

Barry Cryer put it another way and, in the process, provided the answer to that unanswerable question we had set ourselves at the audition stage: 'The point is that Jerome Flynn didn't become Tommy Cooper – Tommy Cooper became Jerome Flynn. There was no sense of someone doing an impression. And at the end they were cheering for both of them.' Jerome's admiration for Cooper had been fired by that of his father, whose funeral took place the day after his audition. Jerome and his friends had held Tommy evenings, where you paid a forfeit if you lapsed out of the Cooper voice. He and television co-star, Robson Green had often conversed with each other on the telephone as Tommy. But stand-up comedy had at no point played a part in his career, making it all the more surprising that when he went on stage he found himself ad-libbing as Cooper would have done, as with this response to a heckler Vicky noted at Eastbourne: 'I remember having my first drink too.' You can learn the lines, practice the magic, enact the mannerisms, but how do you acquire a comic mind-set that has played no part in your life before? Jerome has no idea where lines like this came from. However mystical the process, he was able to recreate far more than the man. As Simon Callow pointed out, 'If the play were just an impersonation there would be little point to it. The interplay between an audience and Tommy could be a really wonderful thing . . . we're recreating the impact that person had.' Ultimately, I think we all felt that somehow Tommy was behind us all, up there pulling the strings like George Bernard Shaw on the *My Fair Lady* poster.

Even Tommy would be impressed by the way his legend endures as part of the fabric of British cultural life. There can be no dispute that his reputation has survived his death more potently than that of any of his comedy contemporaries, and in a way unconnected with television re-runs, which have in fact been comparatively sparse when set against the saturation repeats of the *Dad's Army* school of sitcom and the overblown promotion by the BBC of Morecambe and Wise after Eric's death, oblivious of the fact that their freshest and greatest personal comedic hour had arguably been working for Lew Grade at ATV in the Sixties. Meanwhile Tommy Cooper has quietly entered the folklore of the country. His jokes and mannerisms and catchphrases will live on in the manner of nursery rhymes and playground chants, a vibrant part of the heritage of a nation at play. This is a far greater testimony to his greatness than the fact that on those interminable polls of 'all time greatest comics' that newspapers and television channels fling in our faces in the sad name of celebrity culture he invariably comes near the top of British funny men, if not – as with the case of the *Readers' Digest* poll in 2004 and that conducted by the sponsors of Comic Relief in 2005 – at number one. Such surveys are necessarily driven by the memory span of those who participate in them. It is impressive that Cooper still holds his own today among fly-by-night names that will be forgotten in another twenty-five years. In truth, behind the wacky props and traditional theatrical setting, he was always more alternative – in the true subversive sense of the word – than any of the parvenu younger performers depressingly cultivated by the television production machine to fit a limited, laddish eighteen to thirty-two year old demographic.

426

The world of stage magic that Cooper loved so much may be seen as a metaphor for the whole death and resurrection motif, as people are transported inexplicably through time and space and in the cause of entertainment brought back to existence from sawing, decapitation, dismemberment, and other fates beyond man's worst imagining. Tommy would probably see it as his greatest achievement that his continuing fame is its own form of resurrection, even if he could never have envisaged that the first part of the big trick – one minute he was there, the next he was gone – would be paraded on live television in front of so many. But perhaps he did. I often wonder if the ghost of Bert Lahr's *alter ego* flitted through his consciousness that sad April day. But I take heart from a comment overheard from a couple on the opening night on tour at the Malvern Festival Theatre: 'He'll never go away now.' Freddie Jones at Oxford added, 'It's as if he's never been away.' In London one reviewer said all we wanted to hear, 'I laughed to the bottom of my soul.' The resurrection was complete.

FOURTEEN

The Real Me

There was a routine in which Tommy used to joke about his visit to the psychiatrist: 'He said I wasn't the real me. Or you. D'you know what I'm talking about? I don't.' All of us are far more complex creatures than we care to admit and there was no reason why Tommy Cooper should prove to be a special case, however uncomplicated his exterior might appear. In the growing area of comedy biography it has become a cliché to tender obeisance to the tortured soul that supposedly lurks beneath the comic persona. As we have seen, Tommy certainly had his demons, but I question whether he was more troubled than the rest of us. Always first in line to be amazed by the latest miracle to arrive on the magic scene, he maintained a child's wonder to the end of his life. Like many a child he had an impulsive temper and a love of the spotlight. His main reason for living was making people laugh and sharing that wonder. In many ways he would have ceased to be the moment that gift was taken from him. But it is a fact of life that there is no such person as the great comedian who does not carry a cross for the responsibility that commits him to conjure laughter out of the crowd. The catalyst is fear and this can manifest

428

itself in a number of ways – meanness, lateness, vagueness, quirkiness, rudeness, anger, sheer bloody mindedness. Cooper was no exception, but not content with a single failing would work his way through them all, much in the way he would obsessively try every patent medicine on the shelf.

There can be no question that his whole career was pervaded by the insecurity of whether he deserved the accolades that the spotlight accorded him. This may provide a psychological clue to his increasing lack of punctuality in later years. Few entertainers have been guaranteed the waves of public affection that washed over him the moment he set foot on stage, and yet he would do everything – fixing his buttonhole, tweaking his hair, adjusting a prop for the umpteenth time – to prolong the moment when he had to step out of the dressing room door. That he should contrive a sequence, however expedient it might at times have been, where he appeared to be locked in the same room carries its own message. When he walked out on stage he was always genuinely taken aback by the reception he received, however many times it occurred during his career. This was the mark of a genuinely modest and humble man to whom the self-regarding swagger of the traditional star was alien, although he was the first to be impressed by the panache of others. When Liberace and Jerry Lewis – with both of whom he had established a dialogue in the past – gave his telephone calls the cold shoulder on a visit to America in the mid Seventies he was genuinely, if naively shocked, unable to come to terms with the more shallow side of show business, 'hail-fellow-well-met' one day and forgotten the next.

The general consensus of those who knew him is that he was the most popular, most unassuming guy in the business. To be in his company in a crowd for just five minutes was to have this confirmed, not least because to be in his company was to laugh. Eric Morecambe said of him, 'I never met any-body who disliked him as a man,' adding, 'if you didn't like Tommy Cooper, you didn't like comedy.' As has been said, there was no side to him. For a comic whose act was for all its simplicity rooted in the fantastical, he was nothing if not down to earth, according to his son always happiest when treated like one of the lads in the local who stood his round and joined in a game of darts with the rest. With Gwen to help him keep those outsize feet on the ground, he was, in the words of his friend, Peter Hudson, a genuine case of 'what you see is what you get'. David Hemingway, who built many of Tommy's props in later years, recalls the impression he made on his family when he would drop by their stand at a magic convention to say 'Hello': 'He was the most polite man of all the show people we met, with no "ego" whatsoever.'

That modesty extended to the praise he would bestow on others at his own expense. As producer Royston Mayoh observed, 'If you took him into a corner and told him he was the greatest comedian in the world – which he is – or that millions of people fell about laughing every time he walked on, he'd never believe you. He is totally unaware of the impact he has.' According to Gwen, he contrived never to miss people like Morecambe and Wise or Frankie Howerd on television and wandered around the house, lost in praise, laughing for hours afterwards, unable to accept that he was up there in their class. Milligan was another personal hero. When Norma Farnes, Spike's manager, rang to tell him that her client had included a short poem celebrating Cooper in a collection entitled 'Goblins' he was over the moon: 'That's one of the nicest things that's happened to me,' adding with humility, 'You know, among all of us Spike's the one with the original talent.' Not surprisingly he had no time for ceremony of any kind. Jimmy Tarbuck recalls the Foyle's literary lunch he attended with Tommy. Christina Foyle was addressing the assembled crowd. Halfway through her speech Tommy leaned over to Jimmy and *sotto voce* asked, 'Could you pass the salt? This is boring the arse off me.' At which point the *grande dame* of the book world turned to the younger comedian and enquired, 'And what did Mr Cooper say?' 'I'm sorry, ma'am, I didn't really hear,' at which the incorrigible pair became creased up with laughter like a couple of schoolboys.

He might have refused to be the subject of *This Is Your Life*, but at Thames he received the far greater honour of having the chef make his favourite rice pudding whenever he was recording his show. Johnny Speight recalled him as the only star he ever knew who walked around with a carrier bag containing his own sandwiches and half a dozen cans of beer. On one occasion when they were at the BBC together there was a fire alarm. Tommy sensing – perhaps knowing – that it was not the real thing stayed inside eating his sandwiches and drinking his beer until bureaucracy finished playing its games and everyone returned. It would have been quite out of character to have played along with the exercise. Once Speight accompanied Cooper, television producer Dennis Main Wilson and their wives on a train journey to have lunch with Carl Giles, the cartoonist at his Essex home. He met up with the Coopers in the buffet at Liverpool Street Station, where he found them eating their sandwiches on British Rail plates and drinking their flask of coffee out of British Rail cups. When Johnny went to get his own cup, Tommy shouted out, 'Don't have one of theirs. It's rubbish!' and turned to the girl behind the counter and asked, 'Have you got a cup and saucer for Mr Speight, please?' Not for the only time, the laughter excused the impertinence. On the return trip Dennis was holding forth in his usual garrulous fashion, when Tommy excused himself to go the lavatory. After a while Gwen became worried that he had been away for so long and asked Johnny to investigate. Cooper was nowhere to be seen. Eventually he discovered a cubicle showing the engaged sign. He shouted out to Tommy or whoever was inside, but gained no response. He banged on the door and there was still no answer. Fearing the worse, he summoned the guard and prevailed upon him to break the door down. As the man put all his weight against the lock, the familiar head came round the door. Speight remembered, 'There was Tommy sitting on the toilet with his big feet stretched out – he's a big man and he filled it – and he said, "Has he stopped talking yet?"'

Many people might be surprised to learn that a character like this could ever be depressed. He was specific to journalist Alan Kennaugh, 'Never associate with miserable people. They'll drag you down to their own depression.' Lynda Lee Potter once recalled the impact he made upon her and her father a few weeks after her mother died: 'We laughed until our laughter turned to tears and we couldn't stop crying. It was a tremendous release of grief . . . the truly great comics help people through despair in a way they probably never know.' And yet Cooper was shrewd enough to recognize the responsibility on his shoulders: 'For most people life is a bloody awful grind. They do jobs they hate, if they are lucky enough to have a job. So when someone comes along who makes them forget their troubles, it's a relief for them.' He meant the remark as a measure of his own relative happiness, but there can be no denying the burden he carried, constantly worried whether he was funny enough.

Both Barry Cryer and I have shared the company of a more solemn Cooper, a quieter man searching for a private space, staring into the distance with nothing to say, in total contrast with the idea that he was 'always on'. To his credit, Miff was always sensitive to these pressures. As he was quoted earlier,

'I know only too well how you have to put the act "on and off", and I fully realise that it is sometimes just not humanly possible for this effort to be maintained.' Everyone deserves a chance to step back from the parade, not only to recharge one's energy but to realign one's emotional equilibrium. The requisite silence, loneliness even, is not only compensation for the giddy sociability that comes with success, but a condition of the closeness that friendship brings. At moments like these he surely reflected upon the tug of war between his private self and the public image. He never fully came to terms with the physical advantages in the name of comedy that birth had given him. This not only caused him distress when people laughed at him in unexpected, non-theatrical situations when he wasn't supposed to be funny, but caused him to be more anxious about whether they would respond when a contract made their laughter binding. He never took the latter for granted. In time he came to an extent to deal with the former situation by giving in to it. Mary Kay is perceptive on this aspect of Cooper: 'If the world was going to say that he was in any way grotesque, he would answer by saying the same before they could. He would act the part out in public – the awkward, bumbling, unhinged giant that the public seemed to expect.' In this way he compensated by pre-empting the situation, but it undoubtedly imposed a strain. Here too she found some basis for his drinking: 'It helped to dissolve the barrier that he felt between the real man and the stage figure.'

David Hemingway was also allowed access to the doubts and deeper mental recesses of the man. On the occasion Tommy had his leg in plaster in Manchester, he reasoned quite seriously to his friend, 'If I worked in an office, I wouldn't have to work this week, would I? I'd be at home lying down and I'd be paid. But if I don't go on stage, they won't pay me. It's the only way I can get the money. It's not right.' Those last three words became a private mantra with him. For all his star status he could not accept that the rules that applied to the less-advantaged man in the street did not apply to him. He then added, 'Do you know what the worst thing about it is? When I walk out tonight they'll laugh. They'll laugh at my leg. It's not right.' On another occasion, in what amounted almost to a mirror image of the situation, David was waiting for him backstage at the Palladium during rehearsals that were placing him under considerable stress. He came in and said, 'I wish I could go out in the street and fall down and break my leg.' Naively Hemingway asked 'Why?' 'I wouldn't have to go on, would I? I could go to hospital instead.' Peter Hudson recalls the occasion Tommy suffered a car accident on the way to the show. It was a matter of deadly seriousness, one of the few occasions when lateness was justified. No sooner had he arrived at the theatre than he launched into an explanation for cast and crew: 'I was on the M2 and I accelerated a bit quickly and my head hit like this and I slid on the hard shoulder like that . . .' By now everyone was in stitches, but the reality was that he could have killed himself. It hurt him that they should find it so funny.

His frustration was palpable in another area. For all the success comedy brought him, he would almost certainly have swapped everything for the opportunity to step into the shoes of his idol, the suave American prestidigitator Channing Pollock, who in the Fifties redefined the image of the stage magician as he stood with aristocratic aloofness in the centre of the stage and sculpted doves out of the air with his sinuous fingers. Immaculate in white tie and tails, he was often referred to as 'the most beautiful man in the world' and was arguably the first magician to bring genuine sex appeal to the trade of the tricks. He epitomized both elegance and technical perfection in a magic act and went on to enjoy a successful career as a movie star in European cinema. Tommy was as jealous as the next humble hocus pocus worker. Henry Lewis, the Vice-President of The Magic Circle, who advised Tommy on many matters in a professional business capacity, is convinced that as long as the example of Pollock confused his ambition he never considered himself truly fulfilled. He saw himself as a magician by trade and, as long as Pollock was there, he felt he could never claim to have truly succeeded, even feeling guilty that through comedy he had taken what some might have perceived – misguidedly – as the easier route. Channing, who died in March 2006 as this book was nearing completion, became a friend of Cooper as they competed for attention in West End production shows in the Fifties. A deep, meditative man, he always acknowledged his admiration for the fellow in the fez for providing a platform for the popularization of magic that capitalized on his unique style. In that respect alone they had far more in common than their contrasting personas suggested.

If Tommy fancied himself as Channing Pollock on stage, he did so again as Cary Grant off. Grant, himself a product of the music hall circuits of Great Britain, never lost his love of the variety scene and went out of his way to catch Cooper on his visits to Britain. The actor's own passion for magic helped to cement a friendship: from its earliest days until his death he was a member of the board of Hollywood's famous club, The Magic Castle and in his youth had worked with the legendary conjuror, David Devant. Grant and to a lesser extent another friend, Roger Moore provided the fashion plate image to which Tommy misguidedly aspired. Savile Row suits and handmade shoes were an indulgence that ran counter to the man of the people whose pockets were destined to bulge with tricks. His son once explained how all his life Tommy searched for a hat that would complement the image he craved, but the more they cost him, the more ridiculous he looked in them. Gwen recalled how in the mornings the taxi would be kept waiting as he tried on half a dozen ties only to revert to the one he had put on in the first place. Meanwhile the suits had a habit of hanging on him in mournful fashion, longing for Pollock, Grant or '007' himself to come to their rescue and promote them to the style pages of *Esquire* where they belonged. The choice of wardrobe admits he expected to be on view all the time: he knew he was anything but unmissable.

His daughter acknowledges that he had no wish to be performing all the time, but concedes that his best way of dealing with most social situations was by doing just that. It helped that he had discovered at an early age that laughter was a means of deflecting disapproval and unpleasantness as well as being the easiest way of relating to people. According to Vicky he was not a great fan of parties, preferring the quieter company of friends in small groups or on a one-to-one basis, but this did not deter him from being the life and soul of every social gathering he ever attended, not merely conjuring little miracles out of his pockets but revelling in stunts like the one where he picked up a foaming pint of beer, stuck his chin in the froth and declared, 'You wouldn't hit an old man like me, would you?' or doing his celebrated impression of 'an Eskimo taking a leak' with a handful of ice cubes, a stunt that went round the business in no time. Backstage at any Royal Variety Show in which he took part the tension among the other comics would be magicked away by his spontaneous dressing room performances, the likes of Bruce Forsyth, Dickie Henderson, Rolf Harris, and Tarby reduced to hysterics by the great man holding forth in his long baggy underpants, short socks, and suspenders.

The roll call of the japes and jests he played in public places is celebrated. There were the teabags deposited in the top pockets of unsuspecting London cabbies with a reassuring, 'Have a drink on me!'; the pens he gave away with 'Stolen from Tommy Cooper' engraved along the side; the occasions the table cloth trick went wrong in sedate restaurants, resulting in broken crockery everywhere: 'I could never get that trick right!'; the short phase of wearing shoes with toecaps resembling pork pies, exact to the detail of the crusty indentations around the edges; the period when he went around with a roll of treasury notes stuck together with sellotape – whenever he went into a shop he would take delight in unrolling the requisite amount and cutting off what he owed with a pair of scissors. When he wanted it to be, all of life was a playground, a perennial nod to the joke shop culture of his childhood years. Even a routine letter to his mum was not exempt:

Dear Mum
How nice to hear you are getting on so well. Looking forward to seeing you in January. All day yesterday I heard a ringing in my ears. Then I picked up the phone and it stopped. I was going to see the doctor, but he's not a very good doctor. All his patients are sick. Dove and I are on a new diet. We eat breakfast in the raw. Then we eat our lunch raw. For dinner we put on clothes. See you soon.
All my love
Tommy

But for the marriage reference it is the letter of a child writing home from boarding school rather than that of a man in his forties.

His sense of humour could be perverse in the extreme, displaying a childlike flair for mischievousness that was sometimes innocent, sometime irksome, sometimes cruel. According to agent Kenneth Earle, his colleague Peter Prichard was the proud if politically incorrect owner of a magnificent tiger skin rug. A few weeks after Prichard had shown this off to Tommy, he invited Peter over for a meal. Aside from casual social courtesy there appeared to be no agenda attached to the invitation. As the meal progressed, Peter could see that Tommy was becoming agitated. 'Well, what do you think about it?' asked the host. 'About what?' asked Peter. 'Over there. On the floor. I so admired your tiger.' Peter looked and there was a mangy cat skin spread out on the carpet. Paul Daniels recalls how he was notorious for phoning friends and acquaintances in the middle of the night after he returned from a show: 'Hello, Paul. It's Tommy here. I just thought you'd like to know I got back home okay.' He would then hang up. It was four o'clock in the morning and he hadn't even thought of going to bed. You didn't even know he'd been away.

His capacity for winding people up was infamous. Freddie Starr recalls the time he took him back home from a club where he had been working. As he drove into the road, Tommy asked Freddie to stop a few doors away from where he lived, explaining that he did not want to wake up Dove and that it was a very sedate neighbourhood where you never heard any noise after eleven o'clock. He then asked Freddie in for a nightcap, but begged him to tread quietly lest he wake any of the neighbours. The walk on tiptoe to the house, the opening of the gate, the turning of the key were all carried out with the meticulous hush of burglars on the prowl. Once inside the house Tommy offered his guest soup. That he had to rouse Dove from her slumbers rather than face the challenge of tin opener and gas stove in order to act upon the suggestion is an incidental footnote to the domestic sitcom husband and wife enacted between them. Ten minutes later, after much clattering of pots and pans in the direction of the kitchen, she brought in a tray with two bowls. With a face like thunder she banged it down without saying a word and retreated to bed. 'If I were you,' said Tommy, 'I'd hurry up eating your soup!' Freddie did not need the advice. Within a couple of minutes the two bowls were empty and Tommy saw his guest on his way, beseeching him in a whisper to remember what he had said about noise before they came in. Gingerly Freddie made his way down the neat, quiet suburban street and was about to get into his car when he looked back to see Tommy still standing at his front gate. At the top of his voice he shouted, 'Now fuck off – and don't fucking come back!' He then slammed the front door with a resounding crash and disappeared inside. It could have been heard in Hammersmith a couple of miles away. Once, when waiting for Dove at Ken Brooke's Magic Place, he had everyone promise that when she appeared there would be no swearing. When she came through the door, ostensibly late, he took one look at her and said, 'Where the fuck have you been?' Gwen gave one of her prim, 'Isn't he awful?' looks and the room reverberated with laughter. It was a ploy she obviously became used to over the years.

His school friend, Peter North recalls the time he saw Tommy after a long separation towards the end of the Second World War. He was on leave in Guards uniform waiting to catch the Hythe ferry to Southampton one Saturday morning. Peter approached his friend full of bonhomie, but Cooper feigned not to recognize the man whose answers he once cribbed in school. The pretence was kept up all the way across Southampton Water, while North used every endeavour to jog the other's memory. They disembarked and walked up the High Street together. When they came to Bernard Street, one of their old haunts, Tommy sprinted away and jumped onto a passing tram. In Peter's words, 'He dashed up the stairs and sat in a back seat on the side, leaned against the window and thumbed his nose at me with a great big grin on his face. That was the last time I ever saw him.' One presumes that Tommy set little store by the friendship.

These stories show the deadpan skill with which he would ensnare an unsuspecting victim. As Norman Wisdom has said, 'some days he could be so incredibly dry that you really thought he was being serious – that is, until he had suckered you in long enough for the pay-off line.' Sometimes there was no pay-off line at all. Back when they shared a dressing room at the Cambridge Theatre for *Sauce Piquante*, they also shared a dresser, an old pro whose opinion of himself tended at times to go a little over the top for the two young comics. One day when they were all together Tommy asked Norman, 'Who does Charlie remind you of?' 'I'm not sure.' 'I know it's a film star, but I can't quite place it.' The dresser beamed with curiosity at the teasing compliment. To his continuing frustration the guessing game continued all evening, the name of many a Hollywood movie star brought up for consideration only to be discarded as they scrutinized Charlie even more closely. 'I'll think of it,' insisted Cooper. 'Don't you worry. It will come to me.' But as Norman says, 'It never did.'

There were times when it was difficult to know whether he was having you on or not. Comedian Jim Davidson once overheard him quizzing the barman while on the telephone in the pub next to the Thames studios at Teddington: 'Can you tell me whether this pub is called *The Anglers*, or is it *The Anglers*?' 'It's *The Anglers*, Mr Cooper.' 'Oh, thank you very much.' Once he came out of the Palladium with Roy Castle at four o'clock in the morning. There was one lone fan waiting in the cold for his autograph. As he signed the album, Tommy looked up and down Great Marlborough Street and commented, 'Bit of a slight, isn't it? Only one!' The way he said it, he could have meant it. There was the occasion he was sitting with Bob Potter in the office at Lakeside and asked for fish and chips. They duly arrived and Tommy carried on talking. Eventually they got cold and he asked if they could be sent back to the kitchen to be warmed up. This went on three or four times until it was time to depart and he asked for them to be wrapped up to take back to the hotel. When he had a gathering of people in his dressing room, if somebody put their head round the door or got up to leave, he invariably followed through with, 'Who's that?' The bewildered look gave little clue whether he meant it or not.

Waiters were easy prey. Having tasted the wine, he would contort his face into an expression of absolute loathing and disgust, before relaxing into a beaming smile and a softly spoken 'Very nice. Thank you.' Once he was with Mike Yarwood in a restaurant after the show in Blackpool. It was very late, most of the kitchen staff had gone home and they were lucky to be served. Mike ordered chips with his meal, but was served boiled potatoes. Yarwood did not want to make a fuss, but Tommy insisted on calling the waiter: 'We'll get them changed. We'll get them changed. It shouldn't be allowed.' Eventually the waiter came over. When the situation was explained he was full of apologies, but there was nothing he could do as the chef had left for the evening. Tommy looked at Yarwood and said, 'He's quite right, you know, Mike. He's quite right.' It only then dawned that he had been set up by his friend, the man who had saved his impressionist act on so many occasions: 'If ever I was struggling, all I had to do was put on the fez, go into his laugh and the audience was back with me.'

There were moments when *schadenfreude* might have seemed to be his middle name, in a curious manner befitting someone who made comic capital out of the hilarious portrayal of a soldier half-English, half-German. Barry Cryer observed the cruel streak that ran counter to his image on more than one occasion. Once on location they were in a pub together in Hammersmith. He remembers it well because on this occasion Tommy bought *him* a drink. A man came up to Cooper and punched him in the arm: 'Hello, Tom. I don't suppose I can tell you a joke you don't know?' To begin with he played along, all ears and seriousness as the guy launched into the tale. No sooner had he started than Tommy asked for a piece of paper. The man went back to the beginning and Tommy asked for a pen. He started again, 'There were these two men in a pub . . .' 'Is this pub important, or is it any old pub,' interrupted Cooper. 'Any old pub.' Back to the beginning, only for another interruption: 'Excuse me, who are these two men? What do they do?' 'No, just two men in a pub.' By now the man was really embarrassed. To Barry it was obvious that Tommy knew the joke, but was not letting on. As the fellow approached the tag, the film crew filtered in. Tommy couldn't resist it: 'Harry, Pete, Joe, you've all got to hear this.' Then turning to the man he said, 'Do you mind?' He made him start all over again and – the sting in the tail – made sure he had left before the guy even reached the punch line. People cornering you to share a joke is an occupational hazard for any star comedian, but on this occasion the man had taken advantage and crossed a barrier of propriety. He had punched Cooper in the arm in an unwanted display of over-familiarity and Tommy was getting back at him for that. There was another time when he was buttonholed in a similar situation by an amateur gagster standing round the corner of the bar: as he began to tell the joke, Tommy, only visible to the other fellow above the waist, let drop his trousers. Cryer will never forget the spectacle of the most famous man in Britain standing with his trousers round his ankles with everyone on his side of the bar weeping with mirth while the poor unsuspecting joker ploughed on regardless, confident that the laughter was for him.

On stage he never took the rise out of anybody, always turning the comedy on himself. It is therefore not difficult to understand the therapy incidents like these provided, not least because his privacy was so important to him. While he always had time for his public – he once said to his daughter, 'The time to worry is when they stop coming up to you' – it had to be at the right time and in the right place. On one occasion he was enjoying a meal with the comedian Bobby Knoxall when a woman in her eighties approached him with a request for him to sign her book. 'Of course, but after my meal,' Tommy said politely, but firmly. 'But, Mr Cooper, my coach is waiting for me outside.' Not best pleased, he slammed down his knife and fork, took the book and signed it. He later confided to Bobby what he had written. It must have caused quite a shock when she returned to the coach and shared the inscription with the other old dears. At times like these he stands revealed as the British equivalent of W.C. Fields, although had the behaviour been broadcast it would not have enhanced his public image; in the case of the sometime juggler with the chip on his shoulder, it would only have boosted his popularity rating. Michael Black once spent a couple of anxious hours stuck in a lift with the magician. When the fire brigade arrived to release them, it wasn't long before one of them saw who they were rescuing: 'Here, Bert, I don't believe it. It's Tommy Cooper.' As he walked away, Tommy responded with an abruptness that those close to him would recognize as a sign he was under pressure: 'I know who I am. Who the hell are you?' Fortunately there were times when laughter had a way of excusing what would have been construed as rudeness in others.

Mary Kay was a constant witness to his strange behaviour

patterns, not least the temper tantrums with waiters and officials who failed to pass his personal efficiency standard, outbursts that quickly gave way to laughter in the way that sun follows the passing cloud. Bob Monkhouse, we know, dismissed his petulance as that of a child, never better displayed than in the episode recounted by Mary in which they needed to borrow a tin jug from a hotel kitchen in which to heat milk. They were requested to leave it outside the bedroom door each evening, since it appeared to be the only utensil of its kind in the establishment, in spite of the fact that the hotel, near Manchester, had over three hundred bedrooms. One night they forgot, with the result that early next morning they were woken by a knock on the door from a member of staff requesting its return. To Tommy this represented the proverbial red rag. Simmering with rage, he stomped down the corridor in his pyjamas, clinging to the cord with one hand to stop them falling down and clutching the jug in the other. ' "Here's the damn thing!" he roared to the receptionist, banging it down so that the remaining contents splashed all over the desk. He then made a dignified exit, cord still intact, face livid with displeasure.' On that occasion the sun did not come round so quickly. It took him three hours to recover.

During the times I shared his company I observed his bad temper on only one occasion. We had agreed to meet at the Corn Exchange in Brighton one afternoon during the mid Seventies at the magical trade fair staged under the auspices of the annual magic convention held every September by the British branch – or Ring, as it is known – of the International Brotherhood of Magicians. He had asked me to accompany him around the stands and point him in the direction of any new tricks that I felt might be suitable for his act. I was half way through a preliminary recce when I heard the raised angry tones of his famous voice in the distance. Upon investigation it transpired that Tommy was expecting to enter the proceedings *gratis*, while the official on the door was adamant that Tommy should pay like everybody else. They were both out of order. Tommy, arguably the wealthiest magician in the land as well as the most famous, should never have made the assumption that he should be so privileged, while the official should never have allowed small-mindedness to cross the path of the public relations potential that the star's presence would have bestowed on the event. Besides, as Tommy explained, he only wanted to go round the dealers' stalls, having no time to attend any of the lectures and shows that justified the high registration fee. In the end common sense prevailed and he was admitted without harm to his bank balance. But the incident had proved to be a waste of energy on his part and a cause of unnecessary unpleasantness for those caught up in the swell. He went and sat on a chair at the stand of his friends, Edwin and Ian from the Supreme Magic Company, where he semi-sulked the rest of the afternoon away, leaving Mary and myself to go the rounds for him, picking out what I thought would fit his style. I remember one prop especially, a colourful item involving cut-outs of various animals that gave him ample scope for characteristic confusion en route to the climax, but after the earlier kerfuffle he was by now unreceptive to any ideas and I don't think he ever performed the item. However, I do remember that he paid me what he owed me – or maybe Mary did.

He had a pathological dread of reaching into his pocket if it could at all be avoided. Peter Hudson recalls the many afternoons on tour when the pair of them would present themselves at a cinema box office, ask for the manager and then without so much as a flash of their Equity card be waived inside on the back of Tommy's fame: 'Oh, that's very nice of you.' They hadn't reckoned with the Classic, Coventry. The manager wasn't in and the ferocious old biddy behind the glass was having no truck with free admission, at which Cooper turned to Peter and said, 'You've got to pay this time, Peter.' Almost as frequent were the occasions at motorway service stations when the old Fifties ploy of 'You get the teas – I'll get the chairs' was given a different twist. Invariably it was half past two in the morning and there was a line that seemed half a mile long. Tommy walked to the head of the queue and announced 'We've got a plane to catch in Luton,' before turning to Hudson to add, 'You pay, Peter. I'm just going to the toilet.'

The number of people in magic who have said he went to his grave owing them this sum or that for some prop or other would probably extend beyond the length of any cafeteria queue. People like David Hemingway who claimed Cooper always paid him 'promptly on the nail' are the exception. When he was appearing in Blackpool he spent much of his spare time in the shabby magic shop run by Murray, the old-time variety magician who had once enjoyed top of the bill status but to whom life had been more of a struggle in recent years. Tommy spent nothing there all season. The nearest he came to a transaction was when he picked up a handful of second-hand magazines and asked if he could borrow them. There was no way Murray could refuse. It never occurred to Cooper that for a pittance, a sum he would never have missed in a thousand years, he would have been doing the old man a favour.

It became something of a joke how he would lock his liquor away under padlock and chain in dressing rooms across the land, even his telephone the time all the Royal Variety comics had to share his room at the Palladium. As he explained to Tarbuck, 'You've got to watch these people. I'll be out there and they'll be phoning New York.' Barry Cryer remembers that when he walked into a pub he would never go straight to the bar, holding back as if in suspended animation, always long enough for someone to volunteer, 'What you gonna have?' 'Oh, that's very kind,' became a private catchphrase. Writer John Muir remembers another refrain, 'I'm just looking for my cigars,' as the excuse to keep his distance until rescued by the generosity of others. More subtle, if more distasteful was the ruse, again remembered by John, whereby he would ask the barmaid to keep back for him an unfinished glass of wine until later in the afternoon. This meant one of two things. Either the girl would throw it away and pour him a new one when the time came, or she would keep it and run the risk of his anger when he complained he had left a full glass.

Royston Mayoh also recalls the way his drinking would interact both with his thriftiness and his magician's cunning, marvelling at his capacity for looking a complete stranger in the eye and almost hypnotising him into offering to buy him a drink. It was all done by little nods and eye gestures, in total silence until the fall guy walked over. The dialogue that followed was invariably the same. Tommy would say, 'Yes?' 'Well, can I get you a drink?' 'What are *you* drinking?' replied Cooper. Thinking Tommy had taken the initiative, the guy visibly relaxed: 'A gin and tonic'. In an instant Cooper turned the tables, 'I'll have one as well then!' It was a routine Mayoh saw him perform time and again, executed with all the psychological skills of a great magician. By the end of the evening the table in front of him was littered with drinks of every description that he had cadged in this way.

At the end of a season he has been known to confront stage doormen and stage managers with a word of thanks and the offer of an envelope. Instead of handing over a conventional tip, he had three envelopes, one of which contained the money. 'Pick an envelope' became a familiar phrase backstage on closing night. No one knew that this was an old magician's ploy known variously as 'Just Chance' or 'Bank Night,' and that they had absolutely no chance of choosing the money for themselves. As he opened the envelope with the ten bob inside, he'd exercise his nervous laugh, give an apology of sorts, 'Oh well! Bad luck. Better luck next time,' and ride off into the sunset. Of course the teabag stunt was a much better ploy, as there was no hiatus for excuses and he left people with something tangible to keep. In that one magnificent joke the spendthrift, the child, and the jester all came together as one.

Quite simply he was acknowledged as the tightest man in the business, with little of the secret kindness and philanthropy at work behind the scenes to belie that reputation in later years, as in the case of his heroes, Max Miller and Jack Benny. It might be possible to devise a graph that showed how a comic's stinginess in later life equated with his poverty at the beginning, but as his magician colleague, Patrick Page tried to reason with me, 'Nobody was poorer than my family. All of us lived in a Scottish tenement, my father was disabled from the First World War and there were only two men employed in the whole community. And none of us turned out like that. But it didn't alter the fact that he was the funniest man in the country.' Pat, Bobby Bernard, and Val Andrews knew him well enough to be able to joke with him about not buying his round. He stood up for himself: 'Hold on. It's all very well, but one day I might walk out on stage and no one will laugh. Who'll buy the drinks then?' Harry Secombe, whose bounteous generosity was his own way of dealing unwittingly with the basic insecurity of being a comic, once summed it up for them all: 'You live in constant fear that one morning the phone will ring and a voice at the other end will say, "Mr Secombe, we'd like it all back now please."'

I can personally understand the meanness, even if I cannot

condone it. Aside from the reasons discussed, it is feasible that at one stage it might have been calculated as a deliberate comic ploy. Maybe he was taking the personas of Benny and Miller too literally. The trait never obtruded into his stage act, but it is interesting that among his early papers was a parody of 'The Sheik of Araby' that he – or someone for him – had written for stage use:

> I'm the Freak of Araby
> As crazy as can be
> *Maybe you think I'm tight*
> Or say I'm not quite right

As things turned out he had no need to go beyond the character assessment of the second line to become a success.

Cooper's attitude to money was curious. In many ways it was unimportant, a barometer of his success, capable of funding holidays, private education for his kids, copious presents for Dove and a cornucopia of magic tricks for his own pleasure that he would never use professionally. It certainly never changed the size of his head. David Ball, his friend and bank manager for the last five years of his life, admits that Gwen essentially controlled the Cooper exchequer, although beyond the fact of its existence she knew little about the safe deposit box that Tommy kept in the branch of the National Westminster Bank in Eastbourne. Upon his death, Gwen asked for it to be transferred to the Chiswick branch that came under David's remit. No one knew what was inside. One Monday morning they gathered in his office and opened it with no little anticipation. It contained £36,000.00 in readies. If people had wondered what he did with his spare cash, now they knew. One is tempted to say that it represented all the money he had saved from all the drinks he never bought.

It always puzzled me how Mary was paid. Nothing appears to have gone through the Ferrie office and this was of course one aspect of the finances that could not be processed by Gwen. In a press interview in 1986 she admitted, 'Apart from the odd one hundred pound cheque to cover the rent, all I lived on for those seventeen years was the loose change out of Tommy's pocket. He'd give me some money to go out and buy food and even if it was two items I'd have to come back with a bill for Tommy to check. "Tommy," I'd say, "what am I supposed to live on?" "Don't you worry, Mary," he'd reply, "when I'm dead you won't have to worry about money ever again."' Of course, it seldom works out that way, although thankfully Gwen herself was well-provided for.

The one area of Cooper's behaviour with which I have the greatest problem is not his meanness, but his ingratitude. Gratitude costs not a penny, making those moments marked by the lack of it in someone as generally charming and friendly as Tommy all the more disconcerting. Val Andrews will never forget the occasion in their early days when he went out of his way to repaint a prop that Cooper needed urgently for a show. A distinctive brand of quick drying enamel was the answer and the item made the curtain in time. When he met up with his friend the following Saturday, he flung a parcel down in front of Val with the complaint, 'Call that a paint job!' Andrews remembers, 'He was really nasty – arguing that the smell had given him a headache. I had done the best I could for him in the circumstances and all he could do was complain.' Alan Alan can recite a litany of tried and tested Cooper classics that found their way into his act through his initial recommendation – not least the signature trick with the goldfish bowl that proved too big to go back into the tube from which it emerged until he squeezed it smaller – with no acknowledgement whatsoever. It was not that Alan was seeking open recognition. His own reputation in magical circles as an escapologist was almost as high as Cooper's. But it amazes him, as it does me, that even at the incidental level of passing the time of day thanks were *verboten*.

The recollections of Andrews and Alan pale into insignificance besides the experience of Billy Mayo, an old time variety pro who had seen better days and was living in retirement in a flat above an Italian restaurant in Soho. He was a Saturday afternoon regular at the magic studio run by Harry Stanley in Brewer Street in the Sixties. This particular Saturday afternoon in 1964 was an especially anxious one for Tommy. He had given in to pressure from impresario Bernard Delfont and producer Robert Nesbitt to open the Royal Variety Performance at the Palladium in a week's time. The first act after the dancers was the worst possible spot. Moreover, he had nothing with which he could confidently begin the act that the audience hadn't already seen many times before. Billy said he would put on his thinking cap and contact Tommy if anything came to mind. It did. A couple of days later a memory from the Forties comedy movie, *Hellzapoppin'*, sent him scurrying to the nearest hardware store where he purchased a paraffin oil heater. He then made his way by public transport to Chiswick and explained to Tommy what he had to do: 'Just walk on at the beginning with this, put it down beside you and explain, "They told me to go out there and warm them all up." It cannot fail.' Cooper took both the advice and the prop to heart. On the big night everything Mayo had said came true. From that opening gag Cooper could do no wrong. He stole the show. The following Saturday the gang were together again at Brewer Street. Compliments were thrown in Tommy's direction from left, right and centre, but not a word of thanks or acknowledgement did he offer Billy. It then came time to go. Mayo stood up and asked the younger pro a favour: 'My legs are not so good at the moment. Would it be possible for your driver to drop me off at the flat?' Tommy surveyed his benefactor with querulousness, pronounced, 'I'm not a fucking taxi service. You can make your own way home,' and walked out. Feasibly it might have been said as a joke. Bobby Bernard, who told me the story, insists not. We shall never know. Max Miller once put his car and chauffeur at the full disposal of a similarly straitened old-timer to visit his ailing wife in a hospital two hundred miles away.

The novelist, John Le Carré was once described by film critic, Anthony Lane as inventing the idea that any person will on closer inspection turn out to be 'not so much a solid body as a dance of seven veils'. The image is especially apt for Cooper. With a teasing nod to Marqueez, his old nightclub co-star, one imagines the bizarre spectacle of Cooper peeling away gauze after gauze to divulge one layer after another of character evidence that cut against the grain of his popular image. And yet at the final reckoning nobody – certainly none of those who have shared their memories with me – disliked him, his quirks, moods and foibles feeding the general picture of his eccentricity rather than detracting from the warmth generated by him. Murray recalled the cheer he brought into his dingy emporium, Andrews loved his company and Alan found him nothing if not 'an approachable sort of guy'. As for Bobby Bernard, he expressed surprise that I should question his attendance at Tommy's funeral in view of the rancour with which he described the anti-social tendencies he witnessed on occasion. The justification was simple: 'He was a terrible sod, but he was my friend.'

Tommy's strengths outweighed any character defects. The simplistic approach is to say he was tolerated as a child or a fool, in the Shakespearean sense. Those who are more honest would concede that he was tolerated as a human being, one whose inner psychic drama was not much more, not much less complicated than that of the next man. Possibly comedians are weighted in the former direction, but when it comes to basics we all reflect one another. Without wishing to delve into the inner reaches of Kleinian philosophy, Tommy Cooper – to paraphrase the moral philosopher, Alexander McCall Smith – was not a nice person, *because nobody's nice*. Allowing for that view, he might in the scale of things have rated closer to Mother Theresa then to Margaret Thatcher than one might imagine.

For most of the time to be in his company was to bask in the sun. To walk through the street with him on the cloudiest day was to experience the glow manifested towards him by passers-by, as if a hurdy gurdy were playing and a fun fair lurked around the corner. It should be stressed that charity was not alien to him. His son recalled how they would be walking along together and he'd disappear: 'I'd look round and he'd be tucking a fiver into some tramp's hand.' Every Christmas a large sackful of toys was delivered to Variety Club headquarters from the Cooper household: it is not difficult to imagine the fun he had going round Hamley's and selecting them himself, under the pretence, of course, that he was 'just looking for something for the act'. He was a major contributor to the Club's funds as well as to the Grand Order of Water Rats and only time, health and modesty prevented him from aspiring to high office in both organizations. But his greatest generosity was reserved for the stage where he gave everything, his capacity for comedy welling from deep within him in an unstoppable flood. After a show he would be drained, empty, a spent force. In that sense he proved a colossus with a heart and spirit to match. To public and friends alike he was irresistible. He was also incorrigible. Once he arrived late for a cabaret date to be greeted by the distraught organizer, Michael

Black. 'You were on half an hour ago,' said Michael. Without batting an eyelid he replied, 'Was I? How did I do?' Who could resist a man like that?

His friends still debate how high his IQ was. As Michael Parkinson has said, 'I could never work out whether he was the dimmest man I ever met – or the brightest.' David Hemingway once overheard him in a hotel foyer: 'My wife is coming later today. You will look after her until I get back, won't you? Her name is Mrs Cooper.' According to David, he was totally serious. Veteran comic, Jimmy Jewel recounted the occasion he gave Tommy a lift home from Blackpool one weekend during the summer season. Jewel was in considerable pain at the time, forced to wear a neck brace for a week after an accident on stage: 'Tommy was the type of man who had to try everything – if you had a sandwich, he'd want a bite – and he said, "Can I try your neck brace?" I said, "Don't be daft. I need it."' Nevertheless Jimmy gave in and for the entire journey Cooper sat there smiling happily while Jewel drove on in agony. He never decided whether the behaviour was that of an innocent kid or an inconsiderate adult.

When Tommy returned from his first trip to America he brought a miniature tape recorder that he soon discovered wouldn't work in this country. He moaned to Val Andrews about the shop that sold it to him, quizzing him on how he might dispose of it here. Three days later Val was back in the dressing room, being plied with sales talk for a wonderful recording machine he'd picked up in the States and spinning the line that what he really needed was a movie camera. Val thought, 'You lying bastard!' He had voiced the original complaint to so many he'd forgotten the conversation with the writer three days before. The naivety outweighed the deceit. On the other hand, magician John Derris remembers accompanying Tommy and a plane load of journalists to Gibraltar for a British Airways function. Cooper played 'Spoof' all the way with members of the British press and deductive reasoning became the order of the day. He never lost. He was an unlikely chess player, but picked up the game quickly with quite some success after Peter Hudson educated him to it during the lulls of a lethargic summer season.

In over thirty documentary programmes produced on the lives and reputations of great comedians I have scrupulously avoided the 'g' word. The jury will remain out on whether Cooper was a 'genius' or not. Loftier minds have applied themselves to the precise definition of the word, the coinage of which has become debased by celebrity culture and the attempts of unthinking people to slap the label on anyone who achieves an above-average degree of success in virtually any activity from bee-keeping to napkin-folding. If the word implies a prodigiously skilled intellectual machinery linked to a thoroughgoing alertness and understanding of one's ability, he was not. Tommy's was an intuitive talent. If the similar gift of a painter or an inventor can command the tag, he almost certainly was. But, to say so categorically would be to sub-scribe, to what Alistair Cooke once described as that 'method of bullying the reader into sharing a prejudice'. Genius, simple-ton, or just plain lucky, no one could dispute that he was among the most original comedians of the last one hundred years, the century in which funny men and women were pro-moted out of the crowd and accorded a prestige and a platform that had not existed before. More importantly he maintained an innocence in an increasingly cynical age. At the risk of sounding propagandist, he emanated the most expansive comic aura of any comedian of his generation. He was also a magician without subterfuge, a clown without ego. It is no surprise that his memory touches depths in those to whom laughter and wonder are sacrosanct.

Today his legacy is kept alive less in the reconstituted British comedy scene, where the performer and writer must come together as one, than in the heightened awareness on a global scale of comedy magic as purveyed by great clowns and skilled magicians both, like The Great Tomsoni and Teller, of Penn and Teller, in America, and Norbert Ferré and Gaëtan Bloom in France. Meanwhile it would be comforting to think that in the fertile comic realm that exists between lofty aspiration and pratfall reality, he might today be surveying his subjects. Stan and Ollie, Bob Hope, Jack Benny, Hancock, Frasier, Captain Mainwaring, Basil Fawlty, and David Brent must all be there, different icons for different times, but timeless in attitude if not in cultural reference. As reputations in comedy are eclipsed with even greater rapidity, the fez will remain a constant emblem of a remarkable man who drew upon an endless capacity for fun and captivated all who came within his orbit. At a combined level of skill and technique, innocence and cunning, wisdom and wonder, eccentricity and human fallibility there has been nobody in British show business quite like him. He was his own invention and as vulnerable as the next man. At one point in his act he used to tell the audience, 'When I do this trick, I don't want you to clap. I want you all to sing, "For He's a Jolly Good Fellow".' More often than not they did.

He used to take pride in being impersonated away from the theatrical arena: 'Women come up to me dragging little kids who can't be a day over three. They nudge the kid and say, "Do it. Do it," and then the kiddie says, "Just like that!" in exactly my tone of voice. It's incredible and it kills me – I think people are marvellous. I'm a great observer of the human race and if I could, I'd sit on a bench and watch the world go by. We've never cottoned on to the fact that we're so hilarious.' He certainly never fully realized just how funny *he* was. I wish

I could be back in his dressing room now to provide one last word of reassurance. Whatever his flaws and venialities, as his guardian angel, Max Miller would have said, 'There'll never be another!'

Index

TC denotes Tommy Cooper.

459

Index

Index